Queer Natures, Queer Mythologies

Queer Natures, Queer Mythologies

Sam See

Edited by

Christopher Looby and Michael North

With essays by Scott Herring,
Heather Love, and Wendy Moffat

FORDHAM UNIVERSITY PRESS

New York 2020

Fordham University Press gratefully acknowledges
financial assistance and support provided for the
publication of this book by the University of
California–Los Angeles and Yale University.

This book was published with the assistance of the
Frederick W. Hilles Publication Fund of Yale University.

Fordham University Press has no responsibility for the
persistence or accuracy of URLs for external or third-party
Internet websites referred to in this publication and does not
guarantee that any content on such websites is, or will
remain, accurate or appropriate.

Fordham University Press also publishes its books in a
variety of electronic formats. Some content that appears in
print may not be available in electronic books.

Visit us online at www.fordhampress.com.

Library of Congress Cataloging-in-Publication Data
available online at https://catalog.loc.gov.

Printed in the United States of America
22 21 20   5 4 3 2 1
First edition

CONTENTS

Introduction   I

Part I   QUEER NATURES

Charles Darwin, Queer Theorist   11
The Comedy of Nature: Darwinian Feminism
    in Virginia Woolf's *Between the Acts*   50
Art for Science's Sake: Wilde in Whitman's Wilderness   90
Exfoliating Modernist Realism: Carpenter,
    Darwin, and Forster   97
"Spectacles in Color": The Primitive Drag
    of Langston Hughes   106
Epilogue: The Myth of Nature   134

Part II   QUEER MYTHOLOGIES

Fast Books Read Slow: The Shapes of Speed
    in *Manhattan Transfer* and *The Sun Also Rises*   159
Making Modernism New: Queer Mythology in
    The Young and Evil   194
American Failurism: Hart Crane's *The Bridge* and Kenneth
    Burke's Paradox of Purity   229
The Cruelty of Breeding: Queer Time in *The Waste Land*   258

ESSAYS

The Ancients and the Queer Moderns
    SCOTT HERRING   271
Contrary / Sexual / Feeling
    HEATHER LOVE   288
Late Sam See
    WENDY MOFFAT   300

Acknowledgments   309
List of Contributors   311
Index   313

Queer Natures, Queer Mythologies

Introduction

The purpose of this book is to present, in as robust a fashion as possible, the scholarly work that Sam See had completed at the time of his death in 2013. The strong ongoing interest taken in See's work may be measured, in one way, by the panel devoted to his scholarship at the annual conference of the Modernist Studies Association in 2015, where a discussion was convened under the title "The Futures of Queer Modernist Studies: Reading Sam See's Writings," organized by Scott Herring and Wendy Moffat, chaired by Heather Love, and featuring as speakers Benjamin Kahan, Kate Marshall, and Michael Snediker, along with Herring and Moffat. Many others in modernist studies and queer studies have wondered since then if See's scholarly writings might be gathered and made more widely available. To that end, we have organized the present volume, featuring a rich selection of See's writings, some previously published and some unpublished, organized in such a way as to represent as fully as possible the two book projects he had underway.

To guide our organization of this collection, we are fortunate to have a number of explanatory documents See had prepared for his third-year faculty review in 2012, including a cover letter and a "Statement of Scholarly

Interests and Plans," as well as the "Morse Fellowship Proposal," which earned him a yearlong faculty leave in 2011–12. It is evident from these documents that neither of his book manuscripts was yet in a finished form at the time of his death. But they were fully conceived and their shapes can be seen from the completed parts of them—published and unpublished essays along with a few carefully crafted conference papers—that we have gathered here in the two main sections of this volume, "Queer Natures" and "Queer Mythologies." And by way of attesting to the value and ongoing importance of See's work, we have solicited responses to it from Herring, Love, and Moffat, who speak to the intellectual inspiration See's scholarship and critical thinking have provided them. It is our hope that this volume will initiate and propel further study of See's writings and further inquiry along the original and compelling lines he set out so strikingly.

The first of the two book projects represented here is a revision of the dissertation See filed at UCLA in 2009, which he hoped to publish under its original title, *Queer Natures: Feeling Degenerate in Literary Modernism.* In its revised form, this project would have been considerably shorter and quite different from the dissertation as filed, which is available from UMI/ Proquest. Though he hoped to cut the dissertation manuscript by almost half, See also intended to add an introductory chapter on Darwin, as well as a chapter to be called "Exfoliating Modernist Realism," on Whitman, Wilde, Edward Carpenter, and Forster. That book project is represented here by the chapters in Part I: "Charles Darwin: Queer Theorist," a finished, but unpublished version of the projected introductory chapter; two published essays, one on Langston Hughes and one on Virginia Woolf, originally taken from the dissertation; two unpublished talks, one on Whitman and Wilde, the other on Forster, representing material developed for "Exfoliating Modernist Realism"; and the Epilogue to the dissertation, which represents See's effort to sum up the first project and declare its relation to the second on myth.

The central concept of the first project is obviously that of "queer nature," a term that is meant to provoke a certain stereotypical response. As long ago as Roland Barthes's *Mythologies*, first published in 1957, astute readers were taught to resist the efforts of culture to masquerade as nature, which is to represent what is temporary as if it were unchangeable, what is the result of certain political choices as if it were the spontaneous result of impersonal forces. The classic expression of this resistance is perhaps the 1971 debate between Michel Foucault and Noam Chomsky, in the course of which Chomsky insisted that "there is something biologically given, unchangeable, a foundation for whatever it is that we do with our mental capacities."[1] To which Foucault replied, "doesn't one risk defining this human nature . . . in terms borrowed from our society, from our civilization, from our culture?"[2] In the following decades, in the humanities at least, Foucault's position came to dominate, to such an extent that "nature" came to be a radioactive term. This was especially true in studies of sexuality, given that the argument from nature was used so extensively in coercive heteronormative propaganda. Thus, the notion that sexuality is not "by nature" but rather by culture or by discourse came to be seen as the basis of an enlightened understanding of sexual identity.

Of course, by 2009 this bias against nature had itself started to look like a particular cultural phenomenon and not an inevitable intellectual principle, in part because of arguments against heteronormativity that were biologically and genetically based. Non-normative sexuality might be defended against prejudice on the grounds that it is genetically determined and therefore inevitable. But this is not what See means by "queer nature." Reaching back past genetics altogether, See appeals to Darwin to argue that nature actually has most of the qualities that humanists had been associating with culture. Because variation in nature, though it is limited by natural selection, is not driven to any particular end, it is not teleological and therefore cannot be used to justify any particular norm. More particularly, See reminds us that even natural selection does not necessarily select "for" anything particular in the course of selecting against certain traits. Traits may persist simply because they are not negative in respect to the survival of the species. In other words, everything in nature need not advance the cause of reproduction. Thus freed of teleological norms and of ties to reproductive necessity, nature can be considered queer.

In his theory of sexual selection, Darwin also implies that evolution can be diverted by purely aesthetic considerations. Of course, his own notions about this run along strictly heteronormative lines, but the important fact for See's argument is that sexual selection brings into the evolutionary scheme a principle that is free of reproductive necessity and also independent of natural selection in general. Sexual desire, in other words, can be shaped by purely aesthetic considerations, which also means for See that aesthetic considerations are often tied to desire. This is where he situates the principle he calls *feeling*, which is an aesthetic state and a biological reaction at once. Feeling, therefore, is the link between nature and art, grounding the latter in the real world, but in a real world that has to be understood as constantly changing in shape and direction. See's argument from evolution thus shifts dramatically away from the more common one based on survival value. For him, art persists not because it conduces somehow to the reproductive success of the species but rather because nature perpetuates a kind of feeling that is independent of any concrete purpose.

See's approach to literary modernism is strongly conditioned by this evolutionary model. The modernism he concentrates on is the one that begins in the fin-de-siècle, in intimate tension with the degeneration theory of Social Darwinists like Max Nordau. For Nordau, many of the aesthetic trends we now think of as progressive and forward-looking were atavistic and regressive. Though See disputes with Nordau in many ways, he also intends to adapt and reorient the charge of degeneration, so as to understand how there might be a modernism that, instead of always looking forward, might also look back. This kind of modernism follows the model of nature in generating constant variation without any teleological purpose or direction, either social or personal. In form, it is militantly non-narrative because narratives always bend their episodes to some particular end. Above all, it emphasizes the uselessness of the aesthetic, but only in a context in which that uselessness is also natural. One of the most recognizable versions of this modernism is to be found in Wilde and the decadence, but it is also visible, See shows, in the apparently more committed and progressive work of Whitman, Hughes, and Woolf.

In particular ways, this project addresses the sexuality of these modern writers. In a more significant way, though, it helps to separate modernism in principle from heteronormative temporality. The notion that modernists must by definition always look toward the future has been hard to sustain in face of the obvious fact that so many drew deeply from art and literature of the past. See's work thus helps to support a new account of modernism, as offered by Vincent Sherry, in which it is situated not at the beginning of a new time but rather at the end of an old one.[3] But this also helps to disentangle modernism from its notorious association with traditional sexuality, by disengaging it from the time scheme of reproductive necessity. In large part, then, this project extrapolates Heather Love's statement that "backwardness is a feature of even the most forward-looking modernist literature,"[4] where the term *backwardness* means not just reference to the past but also opposition to the normative force of traditional time. Modernism separates itself from tradition, in other words, not by leaping forward but rather by resisting the pull of conventional chronology.

Part II of this volume represents work toward a second book that See projected under the title *Queer Mythologies: Community and Memory in*

Modern Literature. See's two book projects might seem, at first glance, potentially antithetical. Nature is real, material, an ontological ground, however unstable and essentially changeable in See's considered Darwinian view. Myth, on the contrary, is unreal, immaterial, invented, however deeply it is believed in. See referred to myth repeatedly as "a foundational story and a falsehood," taking this definition from Michael Bell's *Literature, Modernism and Myth* (see, for example, the chapter "Making Modernism New: Queer Mythology in *The Young and Evil*" in this part). But the two book projects formed, in See's view, different aspects of the same capacious intellectual project, the alpha and omega of a singular inquiry. The hinge between them, represented by the Epilogue to See's dissertation, "The Myth of Nature," is that the idea of queer nature came to be embraced in the twentieth century as a foundational myth for the building of queer communities.

Of course, this second book project was less fully executed than *Queer Natures* at the time of See's death, and the materials gathered here—two published articles, "Fast Books Read Slow: The Shapes of Speed in *Manhattan Transfer* and *The Sun Also Rises*" and "Making Modernism New: Queer Mythology in *The Young and Evil*," along with a finished but unpublished essay on Hart Crane's *The Bridge* and a conference paper on Eliot's *The Waste Land*—would doubtless have undergone transformation if they had been integrated into the second book. Still, their common threads are certainly evident—among them a persistent interest in modernist formal techniques of fracture, elision, and recursion; also the refusal or derangement of teleological narrative structure; and spatial form à la Joseph Frank as offering a literary version of a place for queer dwelling, a place apart from the normative coercions of conventional temporality; and thus a paradoxical way of telling the queer "tale of the tribe," another important concept for See, borrowed from Ezra Pound (see the final chapter in Part I of this book: "The Myth of Nature").

The fundamental question for See in this second book is whether there can, in fact, be something like "queer community," or whether that is in truth an impossibility. A community ordinarily depends upon—is defined by—its norms and identities, its inclusions and exclusions. If queers are (or ought to be) constitutionally antinormative, as some queer thinkers claim, and if they also refuse to assume a stable identity, then wouldn't that forestall the creation of community, or at least a community on any familiar model? For See, queer community very well might be a "fantastical endeavor" (see "Making Modernism New" in Part II of this book), a project inevitably headed for failure—and for that reason only susceptible of achievement in art, in the imagination, in literature, and particularly in modernist works of art that staged their own failure to achieve wholeness.

It is perhaps best to quote here at some length from the document See prepared for his third-year review at Yale, the capacious "Statement of Scholarly Interests and Plans" in which he described his accomplishments to date and laid out his research and writing plans for the future, including the second book on *Queer Mythologies*.

> My second book project, "Queer Mythologies," analyz[es] the domi-
> nant mythologies through which queer communities and literature
> emerged in the Anglophone 20th century. Queer writers have ap-
> pealed to mythological forms throughout literary history, most
> notably in ancient Greece and Rome, Renaissance England, and
> Victorian England. But the Western (including French, German, and
> Italian) 20th century witnessed the unprecedented creation of self-
> identifying queer communities and literatures whose appeal to
> mythology as a foundational falsehood tells a forgotten story about the
> relationship among sexuality, secularism, spirituality, and politics in
> the 20th century. Scholars from Max Weber to Gayle Rubin have
> recorded how sexuality became a criterion of ethnic group identifica-
> tion in the 20th century, but their records rely upon Weber's more
> famous claim that scientific rationalism disenchanted the secular world
> of that century. Ranging from H. D. to Gil Cuadros to Angela Carter,
> the writers that I analyze in this project don't use or create mytholo-
> gies with religious devotion, nor do they disenchant those mytholo-
> gies, nor do they replace them with the myth of reason. What these
> writers show is that the myth of secularism—which is the title and
> subject of the book's first chapter—that aligns non-normative sexual-
> ity with a disenchanted secularity suppresses the historical fact that
> queerness became secular in the 20th century through its appeal to
> the spiritual. It's only when queerness made mythologies that it was
> able to make a politics.
>
> "Queer Mythologies" remembers this history by analyzing six
> different myths that structured queer community and literary forma-
> tion in the last century: the myths of secularism, history, desire,
> whiteness, AIDS, and queer theory. Paradoxically, each of these
> concepts subtends and subverts the formation of queer communities
> and literatures. This tension results from the fact that "queer commu-
> nity" and "queer mythology" are oxymorons that attempt to contain
> the unity that queerness intrinsically fractures. Community and

mythology both rely upon normative principles of inclusion and exclusion that, as with the "house of difference" that Audre Lorde describes in *Zami*, queerness fractures so wide that it falls into its own fissures. So while queer mythologies produced remarkable literary and political activity in the 20th century, "Queer Mythologies" follows the desirous logic of queerness to its unloving limit. Queers have wanted us to know nothing about sexuality so that the epistemology of the closet might at last become historical. But the full achievement of that effort would threaten the most nihilistic version of knowing nothing: when everything is queer, after all, nothing is. And when nothing is queer or can be queered, queer mythology forgets its politics.

One reads that list of six queer myths—"the myths of secularism, history, desire, whiteness, AIDS, and queer theory"—and wonders what See would have said about each of them. We have hints in the essays assembled here about a few of them, to be sure. Others seem susceptible of inference, at least to some degree. But what of the cited myth of AIDS? Certainly the ongoing crisis of HIV infection has been a vastly important impetus for queer political organizing and empowerment; but how would *myth* have entered into See's analysis of it? And what of the myth of queer theory itself? To be sure, the emergence and charismatic intellectual power of queer theory in the late twentieth century has been the foundation of an important academic field and its attendant intellectual and social communities. But was See ready to claim that queer theory was in some sense imbued with myth, that it derived its glamor from its own foundational falsehoods, whatever they might be?

Wendy Moffat in her essay in the present collection, in speaking of See's late turn to his project on "Queer Mythologies," calls him "recklessly brave." Heather Love similarly writes of See's "mettle," his "courage," and his "willingness to break with norms of academic argument and value" as he prosecuted his frequently surprising and sometimes contrarian arguments. See had already anticipated (and joined) Sedgwick's turn, in collaboration with Adam Frank, against a strain of "reflexive antibiologism" in queer theory that automatically responded "it's not natural" in response to any claims to locate sexual norms in a fixed natural order.[5] But would See have argued, in concert, or by extension, against the reflexive antinormativity of much of current queer inquiry?[6] That is one of many unanswerable questions with which See's death leaves us. One thing seems certain, however: He would have been an astute and engaged participant in the futures of modernism and sexuality studies.

NOTES

1. *The Chomsky-Foucault Debate: On Human Nature* (New York: New Press, 2006), 7.

2. Ibid., 43.

3. Vincent Sherry, *Modernism and the Reinvention of Decadence* (Cambridge: Cambridge University Press, 2015).

4. Heather Love, *Feeling Backward: Loss and the Politics of Queer History* (Cambridge: Harvard University Press, 2007), 6.

5. Eve Kosofsky Sedgwick, *Touching Feeling: Affect, Pedagogy, Performativity* (Durham, N.C.: Duke University Press, 2003), 109.

6. See Robyn Wiegman and Elizabeth A. Wilson, eds., *Queer Theory Without Antinormativity*, a special issue of *differences: A Journal of Feminist Cultural Studies* 26, no. 1 (May 2015).

PART I

Queer Natures

Charles Darwin, Queer Theorist

Doing It Naturally

And when night falls without apology
You can give me a lesson in biology.
For I so want to go when you do,
Back to nature with you.

—COLE PORTER, "Back to Nature with You"[1]

One of the most popular modernist lyricists, and often regarded as one of the queerest, Cole Porter was a naturalist. Yes, his songs are indisputably clever and urbane, but they are not for those qualities uninterested in the material objects and processes that constitute the natural world. Songs like the simple "Moon, Moon" (1913), the elaborate "The Sponge" (1922), the boisterous "Find Me a Primitive Man" (1929), and the wryly sentimental "Back to Nature with You" (1933), quoted in the epigraph, all demonstrate Porter's career-long interest in writing about nature, especially in relation to sexuality. Nothing could seem less unusual for a writer in the lyric tradition than to use images of nature, of course, but Porter's mention of "biology" in "Back to Nature" indicates that nature, for writers composing in the wake of late nineteenth-century evolutionary theory, is inextricably linked with the natural sciences. And what could seem more unlyrical than science?

Perhaps more than any other, Porter's 1928 song "Let's Do It" takes this question as its subject and reveals a critically neglected relationship among nature, literature, science, and sexuality in the modernist era. The lyrics' description of nature's injunctions to sexual humans also exemplifies why this relationship has been tempting to disregard in studies of modernist sexuality. The piece opens with its speaker claiming that, "when the little bluebird" sings, "when the little bluebell" rings, when even "the little blue clerk" croons to the moon, "It is nature, that's all / Simply telling us to fall / In love." After this opening verse, the song proceeds into five stanzas that catalog, in Whitmanic fashion, how nature's injunction to "do it" explains "why" a host of different species "do it." Those species include the human—which Porter taxonomizes by nationality—but *homo sapiens* gets short shrift in the song compared to non-human animals ranging from nightingales to jellyfish to dragonflies to hippopotami. These species span the range of what naturalist scientists at the time deemed higher and lower organisms: Owls do it, even though "they're supposed to be wise"; "sentimental centipedes" and "the most refined lady bugs do it"; "giraffes, on the sly, do it"; "even pekineses in the Ritz, do it."[2]

Juxtaposing creatures of the highest and lowest structural complexity, these five stanzas of thirteen lines each catalogue no less than forty species (a count that includes the referenced Boston beans but not each human nationality) whose example impels the speaker to request his/her addressee, "Let's do it, let's fall in love" in each stanza's refrain. When preceded by "do it," the phrase "fall in love" must be read at least in part as a euphemism for sex. Porter writes, after all, "Why ask if shad do it? / Waiter, bring me shad roe," where the eggs serve as a symbol not of love but of sexual reproduction and therefore negate the question of whether shad "do it" genitally.[3] Nonetheless, Porter's linking of the two clauses with the pronoun "it" also suggests that he might be referencing not just sexual contact nor only chaste romantic feeling but some combination of sexual "doing it" and affective "love": what one might call sexual feeling. Playing coyly with the possibility of seeming either sentimental or outrageously bawdy, "Let's Do It" takes and engenders pleasure in its refusal to distinguish between genital sex and erotic feeling.[4]

If he is focused on sexual feeling, however, why does Porter fill his lyrics with so many examples of neither feelings nor sex but various species?

Like Whitman often can, Porter sounds less like a lyricist here than a scientific naturalist: He documents evidence of sexual feeling in animals and relates that evidence to human behavior. Biologists have long made such associations to justify or condemn particular human sexual behaviors on scientific grounds: Bruce Bagemihl's *Biological Exuberance* (1998) and Joan Roughgarden's *Evolution's Rainbow* (2004), for example, align same-sex behavior in animals with human homosexuality to provide scientific bases upon which to make moral judgments about non-normative sexual behavior.[5] But why would sex ever need justification on behalf of nature, especially in the potentially insulting forms of sponges and centipedes? And why would Porter write that justification—if it is one—in a song? What aesthetic value, in other words, did Porter find in using scientific evidence of sexual feeling in both humans and animals?

Considering that special pleading for heterosexuality alone is unnecessary on the basis of "nature" and that recourse to lower life forms would constitute, at best, a tenuous defense of non-normative sexual behaviors, "Let's Do It" seems to be after something much more ambiguous— something queerer—than a defense of any particular sexual identity or act.[6] The ambiguity of the lyrics' titular "it" refers, after all, to sexual feelings, not the genders of the bodies that possess them or the acts they commit.[7] Even more like Charles Darwin than like Whitman, Porter uses scientific discourse here to suggest dispassionately that all sexual feeling has a place in nature, for nature itself creates sexual feeling. Rather than to justify sexual behavior on a moral basis, this song implies, the task of post-Darwinian literary art is actually quite scientific: to express nature's call as objectively as possible. As a campy expression of that call, "Let's Do It" certainly earns its place in the canon of queer literature, but it does so for more than its affiliation with Porter's biography. "Let's Do It" is a testament to modernist art's queer natures, for it is an artifact of queer feeling and post-Darwinian nature at once.

Judging by his claims in the first volume of *The History of Sexuality* (1978), Michel Foucault would likely bristle not only at this interpretation but at the last three lines of the song's first verse alone: "It is nature, that's all, / Simply telling us to fall / In love." These lines would appear to exemplify what Foucault calls the repressive hypothesis, for they enjoin a human addressee through language to embrace sexuality, to do it, including the doing it of simply listening to nature. Speaking of nature, Foucault might say, Porter is only speaking of speaking, not of nature itself, least of all not of the "bodies and pleasures" on which Foucault asks sexual historians to train their attention.[8]

While I will explore at greater length the difficulties that Foucault's influential text poses for the literary historian of sexuality—modernist or not—it is worth noting that, throughout "Let's Do It," Porter focuses on symbols of the non-discursive and non-linguistic: that is, non-human animals. Exemplifying what Theodore Däubler's *A New Point of View* (1919) identified as the widespread "return of man to animal as exemplified through art" during the modernist era, the animals in Porter's song are so hyperbolically anthropomorphized that phrases like "educated fleas" expose rather than conceal (as many efforts at anthropomorphism do) their ascription of human attributes to animals.[9] What nature is "simply telling us" in this song is actually not told at all: Sexual feeling is everywhere implied in the lyrics, but Porter's coy techniques of indirection require that we interpret what "doing it" means. If Porter were making a discursive argument on behalf of sexological beliefs in the nature of sexuality, he would not need to use animals as symbols of sexual feeling, nor would he need to "do it" in literary art.[10]

Falling outside the purview of Foucault's influential history of logical discourses, Porter's work exemplifies an overlooked strain of modernist aesthetics that views nature itself as an aesthetic object, a source of aesthetic and sexual feeling, and literature not just as a representation of nature but as itself a part of nature. As a reflection and generator of the aesthetic and sexual feelings evident in the natural world, literature becomes for the modernists an artifact of nature itself: It is a repository of feeling as mutable and material as the natural world that Charles Darwin describes in his theory of evolution. That theory develops at the turn of the century into a strain of aesthetic theory called "evolutionary aesthetics" that consistently conflates sexual and aesthetic feeling. It thus entwines concepts that, since Immanuel Kant's *Critique of Judgment* (1790), were long separated in Western aesthetic philosophy, and thereby offers modernist artists scientific grounds for creating historically experimental aesthetic forms and sexual themes.

As I will argue in the following pages, Charles Darwin is a queer theorist of the material world who conceptualizes nature as a non-normative, infinitely heterogeneous composite of mutating laws and principles. Contextualizing queer literature within a Darwinian framework presents opportunities to reassess contemporary literary histories of modernism that oppose modernist aesthetics and positivist science and theoretical orthodoxies about the conceptual dangers of nature.[11] Such well-intentioned rejections of nature have pervaded poststructuralist critical theory, especially queer theory, which on the models of Foucault and Freud especially has repudiated nature as an ideological construction meant to oppress the unnatural (a constructed concept itself) or viewed sexuality's location in nature within the immutable system of physical drives.[12] While such scholarship—including *American Literature*'s March 1997 volume *Unnatural Formations*—has told us much about cultural ideology and the sexual identities propounded therein, it has told us little about the materiality of sexual feeling or the relevance of material forms to one of the most frequently plumbed archives of evidence for scholars of sexuality: literature.

In concert with Timothy Morton's recent claim that "queer theory has a strange friend in nonessentialist biology" (275) because the latter shows how "queerness, in its variegated forms, is installed in biological substance as such and is not simply a blip in cultural history" (273–4), I examine in this essay how Darwin's queer theory of nature, specifically his theories of sexual and aesthetic feeling, provide overlooked interpretive tools for scholars of both the sciences and humanities.[13] Rather than to Foucault or Freud, I propose that queer theory—and critical theory more broadly— turn to Darwin for a theoretical model with which to interpret the complexity of biological feeling, whether sexual, aesthetic, or otherwise. Darwin's model offers particularly relevant interpretive tools for scholars of the arts, for his work presents opportunities to elucidate the variety of sensational responses that distinguish the arts as objects of humanistic experience and inquiry in the first place.

The Sexes of Art

Sexuality is something that we ourselves create—it is our own creation, and much more than the discovery of a secret side of our desire.
MICHEL FOUCAULT, *"Sex, Power, and the Politics of Identity"*[14]

Before delving into Darwin's theories and their relation to sexual and aesthetic theory, it is worthwhile to review the challenges that Foucauldian historiography—perhaps the primary model for both literary and sexual historiography in the past three decades—has established for a Darwinian analysis of sexual aesthetics. Foucault's legacy in sexuality studies has, for better or worse, been predicated almost wholly on the first volume of the *History of Sexuality*. Whereas he would later argue that "sexuality is something we ourselves create," Foucault argues in the *History of Sexuality* that sexuality is something created for us. Sexuality, he avers, is "the set of effects produced in bodies, behaviors, and social relations by a certain

deployment deriving from a complex political technology," where individual "bodies, behaviors, and social relations" are syntactically subordinated to the "set of effects" produced by public discourses (127). Modern
science is, for Foucault, one of the primary instruments of this "political
technology." Consequently, even when proposing that "we ourselves create" sexuality, Foucault opposes such creation to science: "what the gay
movement needs now is much more the art of life than a science or scientific knowledge (or pseudoscientific knowledge) of what sexuality is."[15]

Positioning science as the enemy of both art and sex, Foucault would
likely regard evolutionary art like Porter's "Let's Do It" as exemplifying
"the over-all 'discursive fact,' the way in which sex is 'put into discourse'"
at the turn of the century, especially within sexological science (11). Sex
entered discourse through, Foucault says, the following injunction: "Not
only will you confess your acts contravening the law, but you will seek to
transform your desire, your every desire, into discourse" (21). Foucault
traces how this disciplinary injunction itself transformed in the regimes
of "economy, pedagogy, medicine, and justice" (33), yet he bypasses the
fields of literature and evolutionary science throughout the *History of Sexuality*, omitting the latter entirely and attending with limited consideration
to the former.[16] Around these lacunae, Foucault condemns "science" primarily through the example of *fin-de-siècle* sexology.

In that critique of sexology, Foucault argues that "the medicine of per-
versions and the programs of eugenics" that arose in the nineteenth century
marked an unprecedented development in the history of Western sexuality (118).[17] Committing what contemporary scientists call the naturalistic
fallacy—the association of nature with normativity—*fin-de-siècle* sexology
and eugenics both exemplify Foucault's concept of "*bio-power*," an institutional formation that "brought life and its mechanisms into the realm of
explicit calculations and made knowledge-power an agent of transformation of human life" (143). Sexology and eugenics worked within ideological frameworks, in other words, to create a bestiary of sexual
identities—ranging from the sadist to the masochist to the urophilist—
and to offer somatic therapies meant to cure deviant sexual behaviors.[18] As
a result of such science, Foucault famously claims, "the homosexual was
now a species," one that many sexologists were keen to extinguish (43).

For these reasons and more, Foucault is right to claim that sexological
writings' "feeble content from the standpoint of elementary rationality, not
to mention scientificity, earns them a place apart in the history of knowledge. They form a strangely muddled zone" (54). Because sexology focused
on "moral obstacles, economic or political options, and traditional fears"

rather than bodies and their pleasures—because, that is, this science re-garded nature as a moral rather than empirical category—Foucault claims that sexology "was imbued with age-old delusions, but also with system-atic blindness [. . .] a refusal concerning the very thing that was brought to light" (55). Sexology was not actually that interested in sex, in other words, especially not sexual feeling: It was more interested in identifying particular persons within taxonomic language and offering eugenic means to modify and/or eradicate those persons.[19]

Useful though these insights are and have been as applied in queer the-ory and elsewhere, sexology and eugenics represent only a portion of the biological sciences, yet scholars have used the *History of Sexuality* as a jus-tification for being suspicious of biological science's inquiries into nature *tout court*. As David Halperin influentially writes, Foucault "divorced 'sex-uality' from 'nature' and interpreted it, instead, as a cultural production. He thereby made possible an extremely profitable alliance between certain radical elements in philosophy and anthropology."[20] From Judith Butler's focus on the discursive effects of naturalization rather than nature in *Bod-ies that Matter* (1992) to Ann Cvetkovich's claim in *Mixed Feelings* (1992) that "affect is not a pre-discursive identity," sexuality studies has so ritually de-naturalized the sexual body that it has naturalized nature itself as the to-temic enemy of liberal philosophical inquiry.[21]

Such scholarship necessarily protests the oppressive naturalization of nature in evolutionary psychology and eugenics; what has been lost in such protest, however, is the fact that Darwin himself did not naturalize nature and that sexual theory's "radical elements" therefore need not derive from an artificial rupture between nature and sexuality. As we will see, by the terms of Darwin's science of feeling, Foucault's claim that a homosexual could constitute a species is unscientific (as Foucault surely knew), for both sexual feelings and species are in Darwin's nature subject to change. We have cause, then, to reassess Foucault's complaint that "sexuality was de-fined as being 'by nature'" (68) at the turn of the century from a broader historical perspective that acknowledges how queer the concept of nature was in its Darwinian conception.[22]

For understanding the relation between nature and sex in the modern-ist period, Foucault's neglect of literature in the *History of Sexuality* is as unfortunate as his neglect of Darwinian theory. As the elusive "it" in "Let's Do It" exemplifies, literature is a discursive genre that resists definitions of *discourse* as a transparent window onto what Foucault calls the "learn-ing" and "truth" (61) that create the biopolitical sphere's "ordered system of knowledge" (69). The genre of literature is distinguished, after all, by its creation of information and experience through implication and suggestion, not transparency. Moreover, whereas other discursive forms such as expository prose generically attempt to communicate dispassionately, literature embodies and creates feelings not unlike those experienced somatically outside of discourse. Literature is a discursive medium, then, but one whose non-discursive feelings fall outside the scope of Foucault's repressive hypothesis.

Constitutively grounded in somatic affect, literature thus offers one site for consulting what Foucault calls the "rallying point for the counterattack against the deployment of sexuality"—that is, "bodies and pleasures" (157), the bodies and pleasures through which we might view sexuality as our own creation. While Foucault demands that "the history of sexuality— that is, the history of what functioned in the nineteenth century as a specific field of truth—must first be written from the viewpoint of a history of discourses" (69), if we are to write the history of sexuality from the locus of "bodies" and "pleasures," we must discuss aesthetic discourse: how and why objects please and displease sensationally. When the aesthetic field of literature enters into the "history of discourses," therefore, what counts as "truth" holds quite different value than in less aesthetic fields. If "power's hold on sex is maintained through language" (83), what happens when such language is itself full of sexual feelings?

Whereas aesthetic feeling has received a great deal of attention in recent studies of literature, sexual feeling has been largely neglected in favor, again, of historical alterist and psychoanalytical examinations of sexual identity.[23] But as Eve Sedgwick writes in *Tendencies* (1993), sexual taxonomy is a "modern invention [that] embodies less a set of subjective desires than a particular, historically contingent process of labeling applied in the first place from without."[24] To analyze sexual identity is therefore not to analyze sexual feeling but logical discourse. While the (sometimes) admittedly speculative theories of Freudian psychoanalysis might seem more amenable to an analysis of aesthetics, an evolutionary account of somatic feeling discounts that theory's premise that sexuality is a drive. Working persuasively from Silvan Tomkins' biologistic studies of affect, Sedgwick writes in *Touching Feeling* that "sexuality is clearly the least constrained (most affectlike) of the drives" because it is "much more malleable in its aims and objects than are the other drives."[25] Whereas hunger and excretion are drives that have single aims and limited objects of satisfaction, sexual feeling can be satisfied and produced in many different ways. Demanding attention to aesthetic rather than logical or psychoanalytic discourse, literature thus offers an opportunity to historicize and theorize sexual feeling, which is, like aesthetic feeling, rooted in questions of sensational taste and pleasure: what does and does not turn one on.

By attending to feeling as a locus of literary sexuality, I concur with Jane Thrailkill that "attentiveness to the experience of a literary work need not eradicate meaning (or its concomitant, civilized society) if we come to accept that feeling is not opposed to interpretation but is part of it."[26] Like the people who write and read it, literature itself has feelings—what Theodor Adorno calls art's "inner life"—and interpretation is a process of making those feelings available to logical discourse.[27] While it is true that, as Donna Haraway writes, "nature cannot pre-exist its construction" because the category of nature is itself a discursive construct, it does not follow that the discourses of cultural construction are therefore immaterial or removed from the feeling body.[28] On the contrary, aesthetic artifacts of the feeling body are primary sites for examining what Elizabeth Grosz, in her recent reclamation of Darwin for feminist theory, describes as the process through which "biological complexity impels the complications and variability of culture itself."[29]

In this view, art's status as natural object is the precondition for its status as cultural object. What Darwin reminds us is that, if the aesthetic object is defined by its representation and creation of feeling, and if the non-aesthetic object is distinguished by its dispassionate attempt to convey information, all aesthetics may be said to have their place in nature.[30] This reminder may have led George Santayana to write in 1922, a landmark year for modernist aesthetics, that "some philosophers seem to be angry with images for not being things, and with words for not being feelings. Words and images are like shells, no less integral parts of nature than are the substances they cover."[31] Recovering art's location in nature, we may reconsider Foucauldian maxims such as Jeffrey Weeks's claim that "even when we feel we are most overwhelmed by our instinctual urgings, what we are usually doing is reworking the scripts which tell us about our 'needs' and 'desires.'"[32] As Grosz writes, a Darwinian perspective reminds us that "nature is open to any kind of culture [. . .] Culture produces the nature it needs to justify itself, but nature is also that which resists by operating according to its own logic or procedures."[33] Embodying this resistance to the cultured "scripts" that Weeks describes, literature and even the scholarship about it can represent post-Darwinian nature while offering sites from which to reevaluate cultural constructions of nature that have, throughout Western history, naturalized it for the purposes of social domination.

The modernists' theory and praxis of sexual aesthetics should therefore not be likened to Foucault's formulation of the reverse discourse, wherein

"homosexuality began to speak in its own behalf, to demand that its le-
gitimacy or 'naturality' be acknowledged" (101). As expressed in art, sexual feelings are not discursive claims but aesthetic feelings represented and
engendered by the particular formal qualities of art. While Foucault maintains that the reverse discourse historically failed because "it always un-
folded within the deployment of sexuality, and not outside or against it"
(131), literature's opposition to rational discourse must unfold outside
discourse because the feelings that such work elicits are not encoded
within its discursive properties alone. Created through implication and
suggestion—as with the characteristic modernist technique of parataxis,
for instance—feeling can also, and perhaps primarily, well up in discourse's gaps. An analysis of feeling as it emerges in this period's literature
and science thus offers an opportunity to analyze material experience that
occurs not only "within" discourse but very much "outside" and "against"
it as well.[34] It is in the archives of such experience that we can find expressions of not only the art of life, in Foucault's phrase, but the sex of art: art's
own sexual feelings.

A Nature without End

Axiom 1: People are different from each other.
EVE KOSOFSKY SEDGWICK, *Epistemology of the Closet*[35]

Darwin's theories of nature and sexual aesthetics elucidate the claims I have
been making thus far and their relevance to scholars of sexuality and art.
For Darwin, nature is not an essentialist category. As expressed most famously in his challenge to teleological evolutionary theories with the claim
that "species are not immutable," Darwin maintained that biological forms
undergo an unpredictable, perpetual process of change.[36] Even as natural
selection temporarily stabilizes some species' physical traits, Darwin avers,
those traits are subject to change over time, depending on environmental
conditions, reproductive behaviors, and spontaneous variation, such that
"no character appears to be absolutely fixed."[37] In his earliest inquiries into
the natural world, recorded in *The Voyage of the Beagle* (1845), Darwin, in
fact, asks "what is an individual?" and then recounts a story of a animal
that can be "'transformed into different natures.'"[38] Offering nearly the
same axiom for *fin-de-siècle* evolutionary biology that Eve Sedgwick would
offer queer theory a century later, Darwin concludes that "no two individuals, and still less no two varieties, are absolutely alike in constitution
and structure."[39] Opposed to sexology's predilection for identity, then,

Darwin begins and concludes his interrogations into evolutionary theory by observing and theorizing that nature is non-identical with itself. Nature, for Darwin, is always "transform[ing] into different natures."

Although the field of evolutionary theory had been a coherent system of inquiry since the eighteenth century, and although theories of nature's mutability existed since at least Longinus, Darwin's unprecedented theories of natural selection, variation, and descent made his name essentially synonymous with evolutionary theory soon after *The Origin of the Species* was first published in 1859.[40] This association is somewhat ironic because, as established in his four primary works—*Origin, The Variation of Animals and Plants under Domestication* (1868), *The Descent of Man, and Selection in Relation to Sex* (1871), and *The Expression of the Emotions in Man and Animals* (1872)—Darwin's evolutionary theory is remarkably provisional. He does not claim a teleological principle for nature, nor does he offer an etiological account of biological origins. Darwin, in fact, admits that what would come to be his three claims to fame—the principles of descent, natural selection and variation, and sexual selection—are all incomplete theories about partially unrecordable phenomena.

Despite the title of his most enduring work, for instance, Darwin introduces *Origin* by modestly offering "to throw some light on the origin of species—that mystery of mysteries" (25). A "mystery" that will only gain "some light" from his theory, the origin of the species remains, throughout *Origin*, a cipher, as it does in *The Descent of Man*, wherein he labels inquiry into "how life first originated" "hopeless."[41] In the case of natural selection, Darwin admits that the laws of that process will also remain ciphers: "The laws governing inheritance are for the most part unknown. No one can say why the same peculiarity in different individuals of the same species, or in different species, is sometimes inherited and sometimes not so" (*Origin* 34–5). Similarly, in the case of sexual selection, Darwin writes that "from our ignorance on several points, the precise manner in which sexual selection acts is to a certain extent uncertain" (*Descent* 1:259) and that "these laws, from unknown causes, are very liable to change" (1:296).

This liability arguably constitutes Darwin's most coherent principle of evolution, for nature's vulnerability to change generates the material world's seemingly infinite array of biological species. In his contemplation of "the endless points of structure and constitution in which the varieties and subvarieties differ slightly from each other," Darwin can conclude only that "the results of the various, unknown, or but dimly understood laws of variation are infinitely complex and diversified" (*Origin* 34). The principles of natural selection and variation are, for Darwin, the driving engines of nature's diversity (57). While his theory of "the survival of the fittest" was applied in Social Darwinism and eugenics to pathologize racial and sexual minorities—to pathologize those deemed morally unfit as biologically unfit—Darwin himself makes no such claims on scientific grounds. On the contrary, he writes that "natural selection, or the survival of the fittest, does not necessarily include progressive development—it only takes advantage of such variations as arise and are beneficial to each creature under its complex relations to life" (130). Natural selection can thus account for "the continued existence of lowly organisms" (130), those with whom Porter associates humans and their sexual feelings in "Let's Do It," and even forms that are not particularly useful, for "all organic beings, including man, present many modifications of structure which are of no service to them at present" (*Descent* 1:153). Rather than be selected out of any given species' evolution, "variations neither useful nor injurious would not be affected by natural selection, and would be left either a fluctuating element, as perhaps we see in certain polymorphic species, or would ultimately become fixed" (*Origin* 91).[42]

Transforming endlessly or ultimately stabilizing within the species, useless features exemplify the pluralistic nature of Darwin's theories of natural selection and variation. They also exemplify his theory of aesthetics, for Darwin writes that, more than those that are obviously beneficial, useless traits such as atavism and analogous variation (a term denoting similar variation within creatures of different species) undergird nature's aesthetic diversity: "although new and important modifications may not arise from reversion and analogous variation, such modifications will add to the beautiful and harmonious diversity of nature" (*Origin* 166). Aesthetics thus explains the enduring life of the apparently useless, features that will proliferate at least as much as the useful, for "the number and diversity of inheritable deviations of structure, both those of slight and those of considerable physiological importance, are endless" (34). Contrary to both teleological and adaptationist conceptions of evolution, then, Darwin's nature comprises both the useless and the useful, neither of which will result in purity of form, for "natural selection will not produce absolute perfection" (199).

The aesthetics of Darwin's infinitely proliferating material world are the subject of Sean Carroll's *Endless Forms Most Beautiful* (2005), which examines how, until recently, evolutionary biology's neglect of embryology left open the question of how the formal qualities of any given object in nature evolve. Explaining the genetic foundations of nature's aesthetic forms—foundations that are, Carroll maintains, grounds of possibility rather than destiny—evolutionary developmental biology ("evo devo") confirms Darwin's basic principle that, in terms of aesthetics' adaptational qualities, "we just do not know what purpose they serve."[43] Despite such research, most scholarship about the relationship between evolutionary theory and art (particularly literature) attempts to prove that art is evolutionarily adaptive: that is, useful. Written from sociobiological and evolutionary psychological perspectives especially, texts ranging from E. O Wilson's foundational *Consilience* (1999) to Joseph Carroll's *Literary Darwinism* (2004) and Brian Boyd's *On the Origin of Stories* (2009) chart how the plots of fictional narratives accord with received views of Darwin's theory of natural selection (though often not variation). Under the mistaken assumption that, as Dennis Dutton writes, "a Darwinian explanation of the arts" must "somehow be connected with survival and reproduction," such accounts focus upon heterosexual struggles to survive and procreate, leaving queerness to be accommodated as an exception to the heterosexual rule, whether as a maladaptation, an "evolutionary byproduct," or an inexplicable "mystery" and "conundrum."[44]

Through their attention to adaptation, such studies misrepresent Darwin's theories of natural selection and variation and their relevance to the studies of art and sexuality alike. In the first volume of *Descent*, Darwin himself notes that "in the earlier editions of my 'Origin of Species' I probably attributed too much to the action of natural selection or the survival of the fittest [. . .] I had not formerly sufficiently considered the existence of many structures that appear to be, as far as we can judge, neither beneficial nor injurious; and this I believe to be one of the greatest oversights detected in my work" (152). Stephen Jay Gould and Richard Lewontin have provocatively explored such traits as evolutionary "byproducts" (famously likening them to architectural spandrels) in their adroitly "pluralistic view" of evolutionary biology, yet such a view still unnecessarily prioritizes certain structures as secondary to a primary reproductive engine, whereas Darwin tells us that the useless is as central to biological life as the useful.[45] Critical attention to narrative fiction's evolutionary plots makes a similar misstep, prioritizing pedagogy as nature's ultimate aim and regarding aesthetic feeling itself as an evolutionary byproduct. Such conflations of evolution with pedagogy commit the naturalistic fallacy that has misrepresented nature in critical theory: they posit nature as the arbiter of normativity, as though survival were the ultimate biological norm.

Notwithstanding this faulty logic, such accounts tell us little about unplotted art, including not only poetry like Porter's lyrics but modernist narrative fiction, which characteristically abandons plot. If art is about feeling, but not all art is plotted, even if we grant that plot is pedagogical, it does not follow that aesthetic feeling is primarily pedagogical. Since Aristotle's *Poetics*, the aesthetic has been defined primarily for its ability to elicit and depict feeling, not only its ability to teach (though Aristotle and, of course, the Kantian tradition made such associations as well).[46] Whereas David Wilson proposes that all "emotions are evolved mechanisms for motivating adaptive behavior" and Ellen Dissanayake suggests that art's pleasures "contribute positively to biological survival," Darwin proposes that the reverse might also be the case: Some emotions might be adaptationally useless traits that contribute to nature's aesthetic diversity.[47] While it is therefore true that, as Gillian Beer writes in *Darwin's Plots* (1983), "evolutionary theory has inherent affinities with the problems and processes of narrative" because they share a "preoccupation with time and with change," scholars' conflation of evolution and narrative has neglected Darwin's overarching theory of aesthetic feeling's mutability and adaptive uselessness and offered the kind of heteronormative views of nature and art against which queer theorists have argued for decades.

As a corrective to the heteronormative bias undergirding adaptationist approaches to evolution, some evolutionary biologists have attempted, at least since E. O. Wilson's famous altruism theory, to adapt queerness itself to Darwin's theory of natural selection by claiming that it is adaptationally beneficial. Such positions reinforce heteronormative views of evolution by mistaking reproduction as the sole engine of selection and variation, and they neglect the fact that Darwin already includes queerness within nature by claiming that, although natural selection may not select for the adaptationally useless, it also does not select against it.[48] Heterosexual copulation is clearly a "beneficial" trait for the species insofar as it can perpetuate the species. However, contrary to Roughgarden's claim that, "according to Darwin, homosexuality is impossible because the purpose of mating is to transfer sperm with the intention of producing offspring, and a homosexual mating can't produce offspring," Darwin also maintains that it is "certainly an error" to suppose "that all variations are connected with the act of sexual reproduction" (*Origin* 32).[49] Darwin argues repeatedly that many variations occur without reproduction, including spontaneous budding in plants (*Variation* 1:411) and "spontaneous variations of instincts" (245), which would include sexual instincts.[50] While Darwin is shy to broach the subjects of non-reproductive sexual feelings and behaviors, then, his theories of non-reproductive production (especially aesthetic production) are not only queer but account for traits like queerness that are of no exigent use to the species and therefore either exist in perpetual flux or become permanently useless features.[51]

Such queer features surprisingly undergird some of the most far-reaching claims that Darwin makes about biological life. In keeping with his ambiguity about the precise origin of any species, for example, Darwin maintains that "some extremely remote progenitor of the whole vertebrate kingdom appears to have been hermaphrodite or androgynous" (*Descent* 1:207). The most precise—yet still tentative ("appears")—origin of not only the human species but the "whole vertebrate kingdom" is thus a queer body that defies naturalized definitions of sex. Ironically, and remarkably, Darwin claims that such defiance of taxonomy is what distinguishes the human species, for he claims in *Descent* that innocuous racial differences—notably aesthetic features of the species—prove how "man resembles those forms, called by naturalists protean or polymorphic, which have remained extremely variable, owing, as it seems, to their variations being of an indifferent nature, and consequently to their having escaped the action of natural selection" (1:249). Contrary to the teleological aims of Social Darwinist and eugenic naturalizations of the species, Darwin observes here that *homo sapiens* is a species whose aesthetic diversity exemplifies how it is always in flux. Darwin posits, in other words, that humans comprise a queer species whose ostensibly nonadaptational traits exemplify rather than are exempt from the species' rule.[52]

In *Evolution's Rainbow*, Roughgarden confirms these views from an early twenty-first-century perspective by documenting a compendious array of sexual variations that demonstrate "the evolutionary stability and biological importance of expressions of gender and sexuality that go far beyond the traditional male/female or Mars/Venus binary."[53] Reproduction contributes to the production of material variation, but it is the diversity rather than identity of the materials produced that, Darwin believes, allows biological forms to survive (*Variation* 2:247, 245). For this reason, Roughgarden accepts the idea that "the purpose of sex is to maintain the rainbow's diversity, resynthesizing that diversity each generation in order to continually rebalance the genetic portfolio of the species."[54] Heterosexual reproduction, in other words, works in the favor of sexual variation: It selects in part for queerness.[55]

Roughgarden rightly points out, however, that "the facts of nature falsify Darwin's sexual selection theory" as established in the second volume of *The Descent of Man and Selection in Relation to Sex*, wherein Darwin famously propounds a theory of sexual selection that holds "that males and females obey certain universal templates—the passionate male and the coy female—and that deviations from these templates are anomalies" (2:3).[56] Considering the array of evidence that she assembles to prove, among other things, that females do not always aim to choose dominant males, Roughgarden destabilizes Darwin's theory of sexual dimorphism on empirical grounds, especially Darwin's theory that females are unable to attain the "higher eminence" (327) of males' universally more powerful bodies, minds, and creative faculties (316). But even this evidence is not required to disprove Darwin's central conclusion that "man has ultimately become superior to woman" (328).

Darwin's gendering of nature needs no more condemnation than Roughgarden has given it and, indeed, than it gives itself. As we will see, his theory of sexual selection betrays (even as it unintentionally manifests) his theory of aesthetic feeling, and he seems throughout *Descent*'s second volume to be aware of his theory's troublingly normative Victorian gender standards. Darwin introduces that binaristic theory, after all, by acknowledging that some species do not have separate sexes (1:253), and he explores throughout the volume how "the two sexes of many animals have probably come to resemble each other" (363). Darwin had been amassing such evidence for some time: In an 1862 paper, for example, he documents how the *Primula* flower species divides "into two bodies of hermaphrodites with different sexual powers, instead of by the more common method of the separation of the sexes" and nonetheless "absolutely require for their sexual union the presence of another hermaphrodite." Darwin concludes from his research into this species that "we do not even in the least know the final cause of sexuality; why new beings should be produced by the union of the two sexual elements, instead of by a process of parthenogenesis [. . .] The whole subject is shrouded in darkness."[57]

Roughgarden's and Darwin's own evidence of sexual variations disproves his binary theory of sexual selection, then, as do his broader claims about aesthetic feeling. While it is true, as George Levine writes, that, "through sexual selection, Darwin introduces aesthetic taste and female intention as driving forces in the evolutionary process," Darwin betrays with that introduction his principles of natural selection and variation through which, in all of his major writings, he depicts aesthetic feeling as mutable.[58] In *Origin*, for example, he posits that not all ostensibly useless traits were "created for the sake of beauty, to delight man or the Creator" (196) and that "the sense of beauty obviously depends on the nature of the mind, irrespective of any real quality in the admired object; and that the idea of what is beautiful, is not innate or unalterable" (*Origin* 197).[59] Darwin extends such ideas throughout his career, claiming in *Variation* that "secondary sexual characters are apt to differ much in the species of the same genus, and to be unusually variable in the individuals of the same species" (1:253) and even in *Descent*'s second volume that "it is certainly not true that there is in the mind of man any universal standard of beauty with respect to the human body" (2:353). In *Expression*, Darwin clarifies that one such aesthetic feeling—sexual feeling, specifically love—is the only emotion that "has not habitually led to any special line of action."[60]

Such principles contradict Darwin's postulate in *Descent* that the only form that has "been rendered beautiful for beauty's sake" is the form that "has been effected through sexual selection, that is, by the more beautiful males having been continually preferred by the females, and not for the delight of man" (2:198). Here Darwin evinces the kind of anthropomorphism that Porter parodies and celebrates in "Let's Do It," for he can only ascertain what is universally beautiful to, say, the female peacock by (rather queerly) deciding for himself that male peacocks are beautiful (151–3). Offering what, we will see, Kant would call a subjective universal claim about beauty in the natural world, Darwin's taxonomy of animal beauty contradicts his theory that aesthetics are as mutable as the materials that comprise aesthetic objects. Yet this contradiction also confirms that general theory: In his theory of sexual selection, Darwin offers his own subjective aesthetic reactions to the material world's useless forms.

To revise Levine's claim, then, what Darwin introduces with his theory of sexual selection is the idea that sexual feeling is always aesthetic feeling. As we will see by comparing Darwin with Kant, Darwin also reintroduces into aesthetic theory the idea that aesthetic feeling is grounded in desire, if not always sexual desire, for the aesthetic reaction is a subjective response about pleasure and displeasure. As Grosz writes, "sexual selection adds more aesthetic and immediately or directly individually motivating factors to the operations of natural selection; it deviates natural selection through the expression of the will, or desire, or pleasure of individuals."[61] It is his own desirous reaction to sex, rather than "the truth of sex" in a Foucauldian sense, that Darwin records in his uncharacteristically unqualified theory of sexual selection.[62]

Darwin's theories of aesthetics and his personal evaluations of natural beauty thus unsettle the heteronormative implications of his claims that "sexual selection implies that the more attractive individuals are preferred by the opposite sex" (*Descent* 1:421).[63] If aesthetic feeling is mutable, and if sexual feeling is aesthetic, then sexual feeling itself must be mutable—unable to be codified within heteronormative binaries. Moreover, if useless features of biological forms are aesthetic, and if aesthetics can be disentangled from sexual reproduction alone, then the aesthetics of the material world are a primary locus for inquiry into its queerness. I consequently argue that what Darwin's theories of aesthetic and sexual feeling ultimately present is a theory of queer feeling: erotic sensation that defies categorization within any sexual or affective taxonomy.[64] Manifest in literary works such as "Let's Do It," queer feeling is like an *Ur*-feeling in that it resists identification within logical discourse but finds expression through the aesthetic features of nature, in which I would include the feature of literature.

Such mutable feeling bears comparison with what we have seen to be Darwin's speculative (and, when more precise, queer) theory of the species' origins. Discussing aesthetic feeling, Darwin writes, "How it comes that certain colours, sounds, and forms should give pleasure to man and the lower animals,—that is, how the sense of beauty in its simplest form was first acquired,—we do not know any more than how certain odours and flavours were first rendered agreeable" (*Origin* 469). Insofar as they are unidentified, mutable, but nonetheless material phenomena, the origins of the species and of aesthetic feeling are for Darwin homologously queer. If it is true, as Ann Cvetkovich writes, that "the value of a theory, like the value of historical analysis, resides in its ability to challenge assumptions about 'nature,'" Darwin's challenge to the supposed ends of nature has value for queer and aesthetic theorists alike.[65]

Evolutionary Aesthetics

Straight lines are almost, if not quite, unknown in nature.
GRANT ALLEN, *Physiological Æsthetics*[66]

Considering the centrality of aesthetics to Darwin's theory of evolution, it is no surprise that a branch of aesthetic theory called evolutionary aesthetics—what Herbert Spencer in his *Principles of Psychology* (1870–2) called "Æstho-Physiology"—arose just after Darwin's theories were publicized. Although writers in this field often pathologized non-normative sexual behavior, they propounded a theory of sexual aesthetics that revolutionized aesthetic theory in ways amenable to modernist writers such as Porter and that warrant further attention from contemporary scholars of art and sexuality. Theorists of evolutionary aesthetics liberate nature from the Enlightenment ethical values in which Kant encased both nature and the aesthetic in the *Critique of Judgment*. For them, sexual and aesthetic feeling are so entwined that even the neo-Platonist Stuart McDowall would write in 1920s *Beauty and the Beast: An Essay in Evolutionary Aesthetic* that, "brought up against the fact of sexual selection," aesthetic theorists must admit that "beauty is most probably associated initially with sex."[67] Kant's time-honored proposal that the aesthetic object is purposive without purpose—that it has a sense of meaning without any single teleological end—also elucidates how Darwin makes nature itself aesthetic and how contemporary theorists of both the aesthetic and the sexual might disentangle sensational feeling from the naturalistic fallacy through which Kant naturalizes it.[68]

Kant extends Aristotle's introduction of feeling into aesthetic theory by claiming that the aesthetic judgment rests on "a feeling, which makes us judge the object."[69] Kant locates the feelings of pleasure and displeasure somewhere "between the faculties of knowledge and desire" (11). In his lexicon, these faculties are legislated by three higher cognitive faculties: Judgment (pleasure); Understanding (knowledge); and Reason (desire as well as freedom). Kant claims that "as pleasure or pain is necessarily combined with the faculty of desire (either preceding this principle as in the lower desires, or following it as in the higher, when desire is determined by the moral law), we may also suppose that the Judgment will bring about a transition from the pure faculty of knowledge, the realm of natural concepts, to the realm of the concept of freedom" (11). Judgment thus mediates between Understanding and Reason, knowledge and desire, yet it relies for its own process neither upon concepts of knowledge nor upon desire: "aesthetical Judgment contributes nothing toward the knowledge of its objects" (24), Kant claims, and it disregards pure desire because, "for the *feeling of pleasure and pain* there is the Judgment, independently of concepts and sensations which relate to the determination of the faculty of desire and can thus be immediately practical" (25).

Kant's disarticulation of impractical feeling and practical desire is central to his principle of aesthetic disinterest. He writes that "the satisfaction which we combine with the representation of the existence of an object is called interest. Such satisfaction always has reference to the faculty of desire, either as its determining ground or as necessarily connected with its determining ground" (28). The interestedness of desire, Kant claims, makes it anathema to judgment, because "when the question is if a thing is beautiful, we do not want to know whether anything depends or can depend on the existence of the thing either for myself or for anyone else." Lacking desire, the aesthetic judgment is constituted "by mere observation (intuition or reflection)," yet it is concerned "not with that in which I depend on the existence of the object, but with that which I make out of this representation in myself" (28). Desire is ostensibly teleological (and therefore practical) because those who desire "seek one goal, that is, gratification" (29); aesthetic judgment, on the other hand, has no particular, nor practical, end in mind (23).

Kant influentially writes that the aesthetic judgment's non-teleological faculty perceives in objects "purposiveness without purpose," by which he means an object's unidentified ("without purpose") comportment with human faculties ("purposiveness") (12), especially Understanding and Imagination, "the faculty of *a priori* intuitions" (20). Yet Kant's definition of purposiveness contradicts his principle that aesthetic judgment lacks desire, for desire, which he also calls "the Will," determines an object's purposiveness (41). Thus, purposiveness can only be felt if it is imagined (in the Imagination) to accord with desire, but not if it does in empirical fact: "there can be, then, purposiveness without purpose, so far as we do not place the causes of this form in a will, but yet can only make the explanation of its possibility intelligible to ourselves by deriving it from a will" (41). In order to maintain his *a priori* rule that judgment is disinterested— in order to maintain his tenuous schema of the human faculties at all— Kant must exclude desire from aesthetic judgment, even as he acknowledges that it plays an imaginary role in the process of aesthetic feeling.

Writing of desire as if it were a drive with discrete objects and aims— as if it were "practical" only and not always enmeshed with impractical pleasures—Kant presents a heteronormative theory of desire. He writes that "there is only one external purposiveness which is connected with the internal purposiveness of organisation, and yet serves in the external relation of a means to a purpose, without the question necessarily arising, as to what end this being so organised must have existed for. This is the organisation of both sexes in their mutual relation for the propagation of their kind" (205). As represented by heterosexual reproduction, desire always has a purpose in mind (in this case "the propagation of their kind"), so Kant forbids it from aesthetic judgment.

In so doing, Kant creates a theory of non-sexual aesthetic feeling that transmutes sensation into logical evaluation.[70] When aesthetic judgment is interested—when it is motivated by desire—Kant calls the result "pleasant," because it "pleases in sensation" (131), and he degrades such judgment (repeatedly with the adverb "merely") because it "belongs to mere enjoyment" (79), which even "irrational animals" pursue (32). When aesthetic judgment is disinterested, however—when (in Kant's confusing use of the term *pleasant*) what pleases is unmotivated by desire—the object of satisfaction is called "beautiful" and deserves admiration because it calls upon our "rational" capacities (32) and "cultivates us, in that it teaches us to attend to the purposiveness in the feeling of pleasure" (79).

Kant denigrates that which only provides sensational pleasure not only for its base association with the "animal" but because it gratifies heterogeneously, for *"everyone has his own taste* (the taste of Sense)." By contrast, what pleases without interest must please homogeneously: As Kant insists, it would "be laughable if a man who imagined anything to his own taste, thought to justify himself by saying: 'This object [. . .] is beautiful *for me*.' For he must not call it *beautiful* if it merely pleases himself" (34).[71] The beautiful object can impose order on the social, then, whereas the sensationally pleasing must admit that taste is relative to every sensational body. Finally likening them to a kind of science, Kant concludes that interested judgments must be called empirical—they are "judgments of Sense (material aesthetical judgments)"—whereas disinterested judgments are called pure, for they "are alone strictly judgments of Taste" (44). The pure judgment, Kant would like to believe, is "interrupted by no foreign sensation, and it belongs merely to the form" of the perceived object (44).

By the terms that Kant establishes for aesthetic philosophy, Darwin's aesthetic theory of nature—and the modernist writers who follow him—could thus be said to support "judgments of Sense (material aesthetical judgments)" rather than Taste. Like Kant, Darwin conflates the aesthetic with the useless (the purposive without purpose), even as he disproves the possibility of such a thing as a disinterested aesthetic judgment (as we have seen him do even unintentionally in *Descent*'s second volume). How can judgment of form be pure and without "foreign sensation" if someone with a sensational body is making it? While Kant would seem to be proposing the most scientific mode of aesthetic judgment possible—one entirely objective, without motivation or interest—Darwin's science shows that such judgment is always compromised (or itself made aesthetic) by the fact that there is no purely objective, stable spectatorial stance from which to perceive any object (notably a characteristic motif of modernist literature).

Anticipating some of the problems that we have seen in Darwin's reception in both evolutionary biology and contemporary aesthetic theory, Kant's quasi-scientific position commits the naturalistic fallacy because it conflates sensational feeling with ethical judgment. The ground of that judgment is what Kant calls "subjective universality." He claims that the aesthetic judgment, because it is ostensibly disinterested, posits "a ground of satisfaction for everyone" (33). The aesthetic perceiver "cannot find the ground of this satisfaction in any private conditions connected with his own subject" (33), so the Imagination's *a priori* principle that allows for purposiveness requires a claim to "subjective universality," which allows the perceiver to make a judgment "that he can presuppose in every other man" (34).

As with desire and feeling, Kant enforces with this principle a strict division between the objective, empirical world and the subjective, aesthetical subject (28). By insisting that the pure aesthetic judgment is *"no other than subjective"* (27) and that we cannot take "sensation as the material of the aesthetical judgment" (46), Kant eliminates the subject's own aesthetic feelings—the basis of judgment—from empirical scrutiny. As Kant describes it, aesthetic judgment is therefore not empirical but discursively mandated from a tendentious teleology: "Judgment in general is the faculty of thinking the particular as contained under the Universal" (11). Like Foucault's definition of sexuality in the *History*, the aesthetic object's sense of purposiveness (that is, its aesthetic quality) derives from logical discourse: from the abstract *a priori* principle, not from particular objects themselves. As Kant writes, "The Judgment then in respect of the particular can cognise no purposiveness and, consequently, can form no determinant judgments, without having a universal law under which to subsume that particular" (188). Rather than through a deductive logic, then, Kant's aesthetic theory works inductively to show how the "conformity of the contingent to law is called purposiveness" (188), which is itself the *sine qua non* of the aesthetic.

The teleological aim of Kant's *a priori* principle is to taxonomize objects according to Enlightenment values that prioritize the rationalization and moralization of human behavior (102), which notably requires distancing humans from their animal peers (quite the opposite of Darwin's scientific ambition). Perhaps because it is so reliant upon desire (as Kant is wont to admit), taste above all needs regulation by such universal claims: It "most needs examples of what has in the progress of culture received the longest approval; that it may not become again uncivilised and return to the crudeness of its first essays" (93). Proposing that taste must become cultivated through the *a priori* principle of subjective universality, Kant's aesthetic theory has only a half-life after Darwin: Its emphasis on feeling survives, but its emphasis on aesthetic ethics—the Enlightened attempt to show not "how we judge, but how we ought to judge" (14)—stalls with Darwin's theories of material sensation.

Because desire is, for Kant, rooted in the "uncivilised" world of nature, his own desire for order estranges the concepts of art and nature throughout Western aesthetic philosophy. He initially prioritizes natural beauty over artistic beauty because the beauty of nature is immediate (106), whereas the beauty of art "vanishes altogether as soon as we notice that we are deceived and that it is only Art" (108). Art therefore must, Kant maintains, do its best to resemble nature: "Nature is beautiful because it looks like Art; and Art can only be called beautiful if we are conscious of it as Art while yet it looks like Nature" (111). Whereas Darwin claims straightforwardly that natural selection "is as immeasurably superior to man's feeble efforts, as the works of Nature are to those of Art" (76), Kant attempts in this knotty chiasmus to elevate art above nature's sensational immediacy because art "furthers the culture of the mental powers in reference to social communication" (111). Such claims can make the *Critique* read like the most melancholy of love letters to the natural world, as Kant manifests great affection for nature yet attempts to convince himself that abandoning the natural world for Enlightenment ideals is worthwhile.[72]

Kant persuades himself of culture's worthiness by establishing "*a common sense*" as an ethical paradigm (55). He imputes "the impulse to society as natural to man" and therefore defines art as a social medium (104). The social nature of art, he insists, is its ability to communicate "the universal *feeling of sympathy*." This feeling distinguishes humanity "from the limitations of animal life" because it propels them "towards a *law-abiding* social life, by which a people becomes a permanent community" (151). "Common sense" is thus less a common feeling than a common *ethic* administered by Kant himself: As he ultimately declares, "the true propaedeutic for the foundation of taste is the development of moral Ideas and the culture of the moral feeling; because it is only when sensibility is brought into agreement with this that genuine taste can assume a definite invariable form" (152). While aesthetic judgment does not proceed from a moral concept, art must proceed toward one if it is to account for anything other than "mere"sensation (30).[73] Art therefore cannot itself be nature for Kant because it must ultimately serve the "moral Ideas" and the development of a civilization that "will be always farther from nature" (152), especially in its progression from variability to invariability.

Nature is only beautiful, then, when it looks like the civilization that Kant endorses through his Enlightened ethic. Nature must therefore be comprehensible by the human faculties, for "a representation of nature would altogether displease [. . .] which would make the union of its particular laws under universal empirical laws impossible for our Understanding" (18). A theory of nature that posits nature as forever mutable (and therefore unknowable) would be ugly to Kant because it would decenter the rational Enlightenment subject and preclude that subject from being able to master nature in its entirety.[74] While Darwin's theory would be ugly by such a definition—Darwin himself admitted as much of his theory of descent (*Descent* 2:404)—Kant also grants that "if we were told that a deeper or wider knowledge of nature derived from observation must lead at last to a variety of laws, which no human Understanding could reduce to a principle, we should at once acquiesce" (18).

Kant did not have the opportunity to acquiesce to Darwin's theories of nature and the aesthetic, but a range of theorists writing in the wake of Darwin's revolution did assimilate evolutionary and aesthetic theories in often overlooked ways. While a thorough examination of those writers would exceed the scope of this essay, a few examples should demonstrate Darwin's impact on and present significance for aesthetic and sexual theory. Grant Allen's *Physiological Æsthetics* (1877), for instance, maintains that "our existing likes and dislikes in æsthetic matters are the necessary result of natural selection" and that, "as nervous constitution differs infinitely with regard to minute details in different persons, and as Æsthetic Feelings are the cumulative effect of many infinitesimal physiological factors, the perceptions of beauty and ugliness would differ in various cases to an extent depending on the structural variations of the nervous system."[75] This relativity, Allen maintains, "does not detract from the objective truth of the general result" for every individual.[76] Even a writer as influenced by Kantian theory as Max Nordau claims in his aesthetic-theoretical polemic *Degeneration* (1895) that "imitation is not the source of the arts, but one of the media of art; the real source of art is emotion" and that any "confounding of aesthetic with sexual feelings is not surprising, for the spheres of these two feelings are not only contiguous, but, as has been proved elsewhere, are for the most part even coincident."[77] Even if sexuality is regarded as a drive or instinct, Nordau writes, "instinct expresses a directly felt need, the satisfaction of which procures a direct pleasure."[78]

While texts like Allen's and Nordau's are largely neglected in contemporary aesthetic philosophy, more popular works such as Henri Bergson's *Creative Evolution* (1910) and Theodor Adorno's *Aesthetic Theory* (1970) also reflect Darwinian principles, even as they mistake Darwin himself for a Spencerian mechanist. In his decrial of Herbert Spencer's mechanistic theory of Social Darwinism, for example, Bergson claims that "there is no feeling, no idea, no volition which is not undergoing change every moment."[79] Sounding like Darwin—despite his affiliations of Darwin with mechanism—Bergson avers that "a nervous system [. . .] is a veritable *reservoir of indetermination*."[80] Such indetermination, Bergson believes, grounds the incessantly creative acts that constitute biological existence itself. In other words, queer feeling creates an indissoluble link between nature and art, such that nature must be viewed as aesthetic (creative) and art as natural (grounded in feeling).

Adorno writes a similarly sensational theory of aesthetics, relocating the topic of what he calls "natural beauty" within aesthetic theory. He complains that "natural beauty vanished from aesthetics as a result of the burgeoning domination of the concept of freedom and human dignity" that, we have seen, Kant promoted (62). Rejecting such domination, Adorno writes from an evolutionary perspective that "natural beauty, purportedly ahistorical, is at its core historical" (65) and describes such mutable aesthetic experience as sensational "comportment," not judgment: "Ultimately, aesthetic comportment is to be defined as the capacity to shudder, as if goose bumps were the first aesthetic image" (331).[81] Foregrounding the feeling body, "natural beauty points to the primacy of the object in subjective experience" (71), and one of those objects is the art object itself. Calling art's feeling "semblance," Adorno claims that "the feelings are real; the semblance is a quality of aesthetic objects" (198).

Natural though the aesthetic object and response might be, Adorno also claims that "natural beauty is indefinable" (72). It "is the trace of the nonidentical in things under the spell of universal identity" (73), a trace that, like queer feeling, is nonetheless material. The redemption of nature in aesthetics thus logically constitutes for Adorno a redemption of nonnormative sexuality. The Enlightened aesthetic condemns "polymorphous sexuality" (47), he argues, for beautiful art's taboo against nature is also "a sexual one: Nothing should be moist; art becomes hygienic" (116). Such hygienic art stems from Kant's attempt to distinguish feeling and desire through the category of interest. For Adorno, however, "art does not come to rest in disinterestedness. For disinterestedness immanently reproduces—and transforms—interest. [. . .] For the sake of happiness, happiness is renounced. It is thus that desire survives in art" (13). Whereas Enlightened beauty requires a "sublimation of sexuality" (52), natural beauty unites sexual and aesthetic feeling through the conduit of desire. Yet such desire is not, finally, teleological or reproductive, for Adorno agrees with Kant that natural beauty depicts "art's renunciation of any usefulness whatever" (74). Like queerness, art's natural beauty renounces "intentional humanization," including attempts to make art serve any external purpose, for "the purposefulness of artworks requires the purposeless" (101).

Like many twentieth-century philosophical decrials of the naturalistic fallacy, *Aesthetic Theory* nonetheless throws the scientific baby out with the Enlightened bathwater and claims that "artistic production" cannot be "scientific" (231) because it is supposedly the project of the natural sciences to

deny nature's purposelessness (288). What this brief survey of evolutionary aesthetics has shown, however, is that Darwin's theory of nature proves
both that art can be scientific and that science can be aesthetic, for he theorizes that nature is as abundant with the useful as with the useless.
Whereas Sander Gilman has written that "the attempt to reverse a hundred-
year-old tradition of aesthetic relativism by making beauty a biological
mechanism leads Darwin and other thinkers down a path that is almost
racist in its implication" (70), post-Darwinian art actually finds in evolutionary aesthetics the radical possibility of representing and creating the
material mutability of the natural world itself: for recognizing, as Foucault
did after his *History*, that "sex is not a fatality: it's a possibility for creative
life."[82] Repositories of sexual creation, evolutionary art, and theory thus
offer us new models for doing not just the histories of sexuality or literature but, in Porter's queer phrase, the histories of doing it.[83]

NOTES

1. Cole Porter, *The Complete Lyrics of Cole Porter*, ed. Robert Kimball
(New York: Knopf, 1983), 115.

2. Ibid., 72–3.

3. Ibid.

4. For an examination of how this refusal creates a sense of "free-
floating desire" in Porter's lyrics, see Ronald Schleifer's "'What is this thing
called love?': Cole Porter and the Rhythms of Desire," *Criticism* 41, no. 1
(Winter 1999): 7–23.

5. Bruce Bagemihl, *Biological Exuberance: Animal Homosexuality and
Natural Diversity* (New York: St. Martin's, 1998). Joan Roughgarden,
Evolution's Rainbow: Diversity, Gender, and Sexuality in Nature and People (Los
Angeles: University of California Press, 2004). More recently, in "Same-Sex
Sexual Behavior and Evolution" (*Trends in Ecology and Evolution* 24, no. 8
[2009]: 439–46), Nathan W. Bailey and Marlene Zuk have studied animal
sexual behavior to explain "how same-sex sexual behaviors do—or perhaps
do not—contribute to social evolution and genetic and phenotypic diversifi-
cation" (445), but even their otherwise even-handed approach neglects the
lability of sexual feeling in Darwin's evolutionary theory. For a cogent
critique of animal studies' relevance to the study of sexuality, see Jennifer
Terry's "'Unnatural Acts' in Nature: The Scientific Fascination with Queer
Animals," *GLQ: A Journal of Lesbian and Gay Studies* 6, no. 2 (2000), 151–93.

6. It is nonetheless worth mentioning that Porter could be referencing
through his zoological catalogue a general logic of sexual degeneracy
popular during the modernist period, which claims that sexually non-
normative behaviors are atavistic and therefore biophysically degenerate

(enervating and destructive to the race). Degeneration theorists naturalized atavism through a moral logic, of course, for the concept actually has a neutral if not positive history in Darwin's theories: It grounds, after all, his theory of descent—the idea that "man still bears in his bodily frame the indelible stamp of his lowly origin" (*Descent* 2:405). For more on sexual degeneracy, see Sander Gilman's *Difference and Pathology: Stereotypes of Sexuality, Race, and Madness* (Ithaca: Cornell University Press, 1985) and Daniel Pick's *Faces of Degeneration: A European Disorder, c. 1848–1918* (Cambridge: Cambridge University Press, 1989).

7. For several queer readings of Porter's songs, see William McBrien's *Cole Porter: A Biography* (New York: Knopf, 1998).

8. Michel Foucault, *The History of Sexuality*, vol. I, *An Introduction*, trans. Robert Hurley (New York: Vintage, 1980), 157. Hereafter cited in the text as Foucault.

9. Theodor Däubler, *Der neue Standpunkt* (Leipzig, 1919), 99. Cole Porter, *Complete Lyrics*, 73.

10. For compelling studies of the non-human animal in modernist literature, see Dana Seitler's *Atavistic Tendencies: The Culture of Science in American Modernity* (Minneapolis: University of Minnesota Press, 2008) and Carrie Rohman's *Stalking the Subject: Modernism and the Animal* (New York: Columbia University Press, 2008).

11. For exemplary analyses that pit modernist aesthetics—including queer aesthetics—against positivist science, see Eve Kosofsky Sedgwick's *Epistemology of the Closet* (Los Angeles: University of California Press, 1990), Joseph Boone's *Libidinal Currents: Sexuality and the Shaping of Modernism* (Chicago: University of Chicago Press, 1998), Siobhan Somerville's *Queering the Color Line: Race and the Invention of Homosexuality in American Culture* (Durham, N.C.: Duke University Press, 2000), and Robin Hackett's *Sapphic Primitivism: Productions of Race, Class, and Sexuality in Key Works of Modern Fiction* (New Brunswick, N.J.: Rutgers University Press, 2004). All of these texts provide crucial insights about how modernist literature queers the sexual identities that arose in *fin-de-siècle* sexology, yet the critical narrative they establish discounts the possibility that the positivist sciences fueled modernist sexual aesthetics in less than oppositional ways. For example, Boone's landmark study—whose title indicates his method's debt to Freud— attempts to negotiate both essentialist and constructionist positions on sexual experience, but it finally, if unwittingly, prioritizes a constructionist paradigm when Boone contends that "the sexual instincts, however much they originate in bodily sensation, 'can be known only by' [. . .] the imposition of cultural scripts" (14). Though Sedgwick posits a similarly anti-essentialist position in *Epistemology*, one that served as a model for studies

like Boone's, she revises that position through a reconsideration of positivist science in *Touching Feeling: Affect, Performativity, Pedagogy* (Durham, N.C.: Duke University Press, 2003), a text whose insights about affect and sexuality I take as axiomatic for the present essay.

12. For further information about how these methodological heuristics have pervaded queer theory since its inception, see Michael Warner's Introduction to *Fear of a Queer Planet* (ed. Warner [Minneapolis: University of Minneapolis Press, 1993], vii–xxxi) and Sedgwick's *Touching Feeling.*

13. Timothy Morton, "Queer Ecology," *PMLA* 125, no. 2 (March 2010), 273–82, 275, 273–4. Morton's article exemplifies a recent swell in ecocritical work that has addressed the concept of a "queer nature," including Myra J. Hird's "Naturally Queer" (*Feminist Theory* 5, no. 1 [2004]: 85–9) and Catriona Mortimer-Sandlilands and Bruce Erickson's edited volume *Queer Ecologies: Sex, Nature, Politics, Desire* (Bloomington: Indiana University Press, 2010). While I am in sympathy with such work, I am invested less in the eco-political than the literary historical and queer theoretical implications of Darwin's theory of the material world, which makes Roughgarden, Grosz, and Sedgwick more immediately relevant for my present argument. For more information on contemporary dispositions toward the concept of nature, ranging from the theoretical to the popular, see Roger Lancaster's *The Trouble with Nature: Sex and Science in Popular Culture* (Los Angeles: University of California Press, 2003), wherein Lancaster adroitly proposes that nature "admits the most variegated of practices," such that "there is no reason to suppose that this splendid variety is not the real plotline of a plausible story about human evolution" (51), not to mention natural evolution more broadly.

14. Michel Foucault, "Sex, Power, and the Politics of Identity" (1982), in *Ethics, Subjectivity and Truth: Essential Works of Foucault 1954–1984*, ed. Paul Rabinow (New York: The New Press 1997/1984), 163.

15. Ibid.

16. The literary writers to whom Foucault devotes desultory attention are the Marquis de Sade (21), Denis Diderot (79), Georges Bataille (150), and D. H. Lawrence (157). It is worth noting that all four writers share a remarkably expository style, thus allowing Foucault to cite their texts as expository claims rather than aesthetic artifacts.

17. See Vern Bullough's *Science in the Bedroom: A History of Sex Research* (New York: Basic Books, 1994) for a more complete history of sexology, one that he extends as far back as Aristotle (10).

18. For information about eugenic measures taken against queers throughout the twentieth century, see Jennifer Terry's *An American Obsession: Science, Medicine, and Homosexuality in Modern Society* (Chicago: Univer-

sity of Chicago Press, 1999) and Simon LeVay's *Queer Science: The Use and Abuse of Research into Homosexuality* (Cambridge: MIT Press, 1996).

19. Such science was, predictably, hard for many queers to admire at the turn of the century, but this is not to say that sexology had no value for literary writers. Despite its focus on identity, some sexology did explore the category of feeling, if somewhat unintentionally, by offering what could be called a literary history of sexuality at the turn of the century. As Richard von Krafft-Ebing's and Havelock Ellis's compendious works reveal, sexology was in part a literary enterprise, for doctors and researchers asked patients to provide sexual narratives about themselves: to relate their perceptions of their own sexual feelings. Foucault called this phenomenon "confessional science, a science which relied on a many-sided-extortion" (64), and Vernon Rosario calls it "er*auto*graphy," or a literary genre in which subjects dictated and often wrote their own sexual narratives (*The Erotic Imagination: French Histories of Perversity* [Oxford: Oxford University Press, 1997], 59). Although these narratives were represented in sexological works that then analyzed those narratives and attempted to corral them within identity categories, the narratives stand for themselves as literary aberrations within otherwise scientific accounts.

20. David Halperin, *One Hundred Years of Homosexuality and Other Essays on Greek Love* (New York: Routledge, 1990), 7.

21. Ann Cvetkovich, *Mixed Feelings: Feminism, Mass Culture, and Victorian Sensationalism* (New Brunswick, N.J.: Rutgers University Press, 1992), 24.

22. Foucault exposes his own biases about the term *nature* when he refers to the lower classes as "being close to nature itself" (121). Without a hint of irony, Foucault follows stereotypical sexological accounts of the lower classes here and reveals how difficult the process of disentangling nature from its moral contexts can be.

23. For recent studies that examine affect within the framework of sexuality, see Ann Cvetkovich's *Archive of Feelings: Trauma, Sexuality, and Lesbian Public Cultures* (Durham, N.C.: Duke University Press, 2003), Heather Love's *Feeling Backward: Loss and the Politics of Queer History* (Cambridge: Harvard University Press, 2007), Michael Snediker's *Queer Optimism: Lyric Personhood and Other Felicitous Persuasions* (Minneapolis: University of Minnesota Press, 2008), and Richard Sha's *Perverse Romanticism* (Baltimore: Johns Hopkins University Press, 2009). It is not the project of these studies to analyze sexual feeling as such, however, which is a topic that may continue to be overlooked because it can appear so subjective and—ironically, considering queer theory's preference for nonidentity—so resistant to stable identification. Acts are discrete, empirical, and easily

narrated events, and identities are discursive constructs that appeal to
scholars of language. Feeling assumes a middle ground between acts and
identities, for it is both material—embodied—and made apparent through
performative utterance, which might be as explicit as "I feel like this" or as
implied, as the bulk of literary feeling is.

24. Eve Kosofsky Sedgwick, *Tendencies* (Durham, N.C.: Duke University
Press, 1993), 79.

25. Eve Kosofsky Sedgwick, *Touching Feeling*, 18, 20.

26. Jane Thrailkill, *Affecting Fictions: Mind, Body, and Emotion in American Literary Realism* (Cambridge: Harvard University Press, 2007), 4.

27. Theodor Adorno, *Aesthetic Theory*, trans. Robert Hullot-Kentor
(Minneapolis: University of Minnesota Press, 1997), 1. Hereafter cited in
text as Adorno. Even literature produced by a computer program would
support this claim, for computer programs are produced by people: However
mechanistically they may function, algorithms are created by humans. For a
persuasive analysis of the historical and material reality of aesthetic feeling,
see Sianne Ngai's *Ugly Feelings* (Cambridge: Harvard University Press,
2005), wherein Ngai argues that "the feeling calls attention to a real social
experience and a certain kind of historical truth" (5) because "feelings are as
fundamentally 'social' as the institutions and collective practices that have
been the more traditional objects of historicist criticism [. . .] and as 'material' as the linguistic signs and significations that have been the more
traditional objects of literary formalism" (25).

28. Donna Haraway, "The Promises of Monsters: A Regenerative
Politics for Inappropriate/d Others," *Cultural Studies*, ed. Lawrence Grossberg, Cary Nelson, and Paula Treichler (New York: Routledge, 1992),
295–337, 296.

29. Elizabeth Grosz, *The Nick of Time: Politics, Evolution, and the Untimely*
(Australia: Allen & Unwin, 2004), 4. See both *Nick* and *Time Travels:
Feminism, Nature, Power* (Durham, N.C.: Duke University Press, 2005) for
Grosz's persuasive reappraisals of Darwinian thought for contemporary
critical theory.

30. As I examine in the body of this essay, this definition of the aesthetic
object has existed in Western aesthetic theory since at least Aristotle's
Poetics. For distinctions between expository and literary writing, see Adorno's disarticulation of "the artwork and the document" (182) (a distinction
that derives from Walter Benjamin) and Charles Altieri's claim that "art
cannot be treated as primarily a discursive practice precisely because
questions of significance arise in relation to the constant process by which
sensation seems charged with affect" (*The Particulars of Rapture: An Aesthetics
of the Affects* [Ithaca, N.Y.: Cornell University Press, 2004], 237).

31. George Santayana, *Soliloquies in England and Later Soliloquies* (Ithaca, N.Y.: Cornell University Press, 2009), 131–2.

32. Jeffrey Weeks, *Against Nature: Essays on History, Sexuality and Identity* (London: Rivers Oram Press, 1991), 3. Foucault established this constructionist legacy for scholars of sexuality with claims like the following: "The law is what constitutes both desire and the lack on which it is predicated" (81). For further examples of what the biologist Simon LeVay calls "strong" constructionist theory that seems "to want to replace consciousness with self-consciousness, and a highly linguistic self-consciousness at that" (56), see William Gagnon and John Simon's *Sexual Deviance* (New York: Harper & Row, 1967) and David Halperin's *How to Do the History of Homosexuality* (Chicago: University of Chicago Press, 2002).

33. Elizabeth Grosz, *The Nick of Time*, 72.

34. Literature thus cannot be contained within the "two great procedures for producing the truth of sex"—*ars erotica* and *scientia sexualis*—that Foucault claims have disciplined sexuality in Western history, for its feelings are not invested in the adjudication of truth, let alone the truth of logical discourses about sex (57–9). Literature may evince feelings *about* those discourses, however, and its feelings must be regarded as truths unto themselves, as material facts, however political or morally undesirable (or desirable) they may be. Art, like literature, both represents and creates nature through feeling: When those feelings are queer, art evinces queer natures, and it is these natures that one can analyze in the process of critical interpretation.

35. Eve Kosofsky Sedgwick, *Epistemology of the Closet* (Los Angeles: University of California Press, 1990), 22.

36. Charles Darwin, *The Origin of Species*, 1872 edition (London: Collier MacMillan, 1962), 28.

37. Charles Darwin, *The Variation of Animals and Plants under Domestication*, 2 vols. (Cambridge: Cambridge University Press, 2010), 2:82. Hereafter cited in the text as *Variation*.

38. Charles Darwin, *The Voyage of the Beagle* (New York: Modern Library, 2001), 89–90.

39. Charles Darwin, *Variation*, 2:145. Throughout the second volume of *Variation*, Darwin argues that a species' equilibrium is, in fact, contingent upon its vulnerability to differentiation (2:176–7), for "the possibility of selection coming into action rests on variability" (2:247).

40. George Levine, *Darwin Loves You: Natural Selection and the Re-enchantment of the World* (Princeton, N.J.: Princeton University Press, 2006), 74, 102. Darwin himself admits his debt to other evolutionary theorists in his introduction to *Descent* (1:1–5), even as he claims that his conclusion about species' mutability was theretofore unprecedented (*Autobiography of*

Charles Darwin: 1809–1882, ed. Nora Barlow [New York: Norton, 1958], 101–2).

41. Charles Darwin, *The Descent of Man, and Selection in Relation to Sex*, 2 vols. (Princeton, N.J.: Princeton University Press, 1981), 1:36. Hereafter cited in the text as *Descent*.

42. Elsewhere, Darwin offers a remarkably Lamarckian explanation for this possibility, writing that "we may feel assured that the inherited effects of the long-continued use or disuse of parts will have done much in the same direction with natural selection. Modifications formerly of importance, though no longer of any special use, will be long inherited" (*Descent* 2:387). As early as his *Beagle* voyages, Darwin had been fascinated by such useless features, as with "animals which seem to play so insignificant a part in the greater scheme of nature," about whom "one is apt to wonder why they were created" (*Voyage* 259).

43. Sean B. Carroll, *Endless Forms Most Beautiful* (New York: Norton, 2005), 165, 246. One might also consider Steven Pinker's much-contested argument in *How the Mind Works* (New York: Norton, 1997) that art is "cheesecake" for the mind (525) as a complementary stance because he argues that art is a byproduct of adaptations yet (except in the case of narrative fiction) not adaptational itself. Pinker's cognitivist approach nevertheless diverges from the precognitive sensational aspect of aesthetic feeling that I am tracing in Darwin's evolutionary aesthetics. The category of feeling seems most appropriate for analyzing Darwin's impact on aesthetic theory, for, as Charles Altieri writes in *The Particulars of Rapture: An Aesthetics of the Affects* (Ithaca, N.Y.: Cornell University Press, 2004), "feelings seem continuous with the senses but [are] not reducible to them" (49), thus offering "a concrete grounding for acts of imagination" (49). While not purely sensational—all affects, Altieri says, "are ways of being moved that supplement sensation with at least a minimal degree of imaginative projection" (47)—feeling emphasizes the concrete body, even as art, which insists on its own "concrete particularity," offers the imaginative projection of those feelings (5). The most "fluid and less self-staging" of the affects (73), feeling reveals how "the blocking force for contemporary thinking about the affects is not positivism but cognitivism" (50), for positivism can account for the body's sensations, whereas cognitivism refers them to the mind. Based on Darwin's introduction of precognitive feeling into aesthetic theory, it is no surprise that Altieri finds modernist literature especially to be distinguished by such feeling (51).

44. Dennis Dutton, *The Art Instinct: Beauty, Pleasure, and Human Evolution* (New York: Bloomsbury Press, 2009), 87. Jim McKnight, *Straight Science?: Homosexuality, Evolution and Adaptation* (London: Routledge, 1997),

3, 187. David Buss, *The Evolution of Desire* (New York: Basic Books, 2003), 61, vi. N. J. Peters, *Conundrum: The Evolution of Homosexuality* (Blooming-ton, Ind.: AuthorHouse, 2006), 166. Dutton summarizes the adaptationist position by arguing that "works of art are skill displays, Darwinian fitness tests, and dependent on an innate information system that emerged from sexual selection" (188). For accounts of literature that follow this rubric, all of which notably rely upon heteronormative views of sexuality's role in evolution, see Dutton, Robert Storey's *Mimesis and the Human Animal: On the Biogenetic Foundations of Literary Representation* (Evanston, Ill.: North-western University Press, 1996), John Tooby and Leda Cosmides's "Does Beauty Build Adapted Minds?: Toward an Evolutionary Theory of Aesthet-ics, Fiction and the Arts" (*SubStance* 30, nos. 1–2 [2001]: 6–27), Joseph Carroll's *Literary Darwinism: Evolution, Human Nature, and Literature* (New York: Routledge, 2004), William Flesch's *Comeuppance: Costly Signaling, Altruistic Punishment, and Other Biological Components of Fiction* (Cambridge: Harvard University Press, 2007), and Brian Boyd's *On the Origin of Stories: Evolution, Cognition, and Fiction* (Cambridge: Harvard University Press, 2009).

45. Stephen Jay Gould and Richard C. Lewontin, "The Spandrels of San Marco and the Panglossian Paradigm: A Critique of the Adaptationist Programme" (*Proceedings of the Royal Society of London*, Series B, 205.1161 [1979]: 581–98), 598. For more on Darwin's pluralism, see Gould's "Darwin-ian Fundamentalism" (*New York Review of Books* 44 [June 12, 1997]: 34–7).

46. Aristotle, *Poetics* (Cambridge: Harvard University Press, 1973), 15, 23, 35.

47. David Sloan Wilson, *Darwin's Cathedral: Evolution, Religion, and the Nature of Society* (Chicago: University of Chicago Press, 2002), 42. Ellen Dissanayake, *Homo Aestheticus* (New York: Free Press, 1992), 31. I am not claiming (nor does Darwin claim) that aesthetic feeling is inherently purposeless: Aesthetic feeling may become pedagogical (it is the very ambition of aesthetic criticism to make it so), but it is not pedagogical inevitably or teleologically. Apart from examining the potential uselessness of aesthetic feeling, such studies could be expanded in scope to analyze how unpleasant feelings might provide pleasure: How, in other words, feeling might be queerer than a tendentious rendering of affect within the paradigm of survival allows. Darwin himself discusses such perversely pleasurable pains (and the potential pedagogy of emotion, if not aesthetic feeling) in his *Autobiography* (51–2).

48. E. O. Wilson, *Sociobiology* (Cambridge: Harvard University Press, 1975), 555. See LeVay, Grosz, and Peters for examinations of a range of other such hypotheses. Bert Bender's accounts of Darwin's impact on literature in

The Descent of Love: Darwin and the Theory of Sexual Selection in American Fiction, 1871–1926 (Philadelphia: University of Pennsylvania Press, 1996) and *Evolution and "the Sex Problem": American Narratives during the Eclipse of Darwinism* (Kent: Kent State University Press, 2004) rely on a similar logic, for Bender claims that evolutionary science allowed some writers to feel "liberated by being able to explore, often in a confessional mode, promiscuous, polygamous, polyandrous, or bisexual desire—and all the other aspects of human sexuality that Darwin, Ellis, and Freud helped define as being within the range of sexual normality" (*Evolution* 358–9). From a queer (and I would argue Darwinian) perspective, "liberation" and "sexual normality" are quite opposed concepts.

49. Roughgarden, *Evolution's Rainbow*, 137.

50. For more information on such non-reproductive productivities, see the second volume of Darwin's *Variation*, in which he repeatedly argues that nature produces variation through an array of non-reproductive means (2:253, 267–9, 315, 371, 381–3, 403). See also Rebecca Stott's compelling *Darwin and the Barnacle* (New York: Norton, 2003) for an account of how Darwin's research into barnacles' sexual variations—including "a pregnant hermaphrodite eunuch"—show how "sexually diverse" Darwin's nature is (109).

51. The only moments I can isolate in any of Darwin's major works in which he even glances at the subject of non-normative sexual feeling is when he describes how "two or more females lay in one nest" (*Voyage* 82) and how "birds of the same sex, although of course not truly paired, sometimes live in pairs or in small parties." Although he does not pathologize such behavior, Darwin is certain to reassure his Victorian readership that the birds are "of course not truly paired," lest his radical theory seem unnaturally radical (*Descent* 2:106).

52. Despite this evidence, one could argue that Darwin might include queerness under the category of "monstrosities," which he defines as "some considerable deviation of structure, generally injurious, or not useful to the species" (*Origin* 58). But monstrosities will only survive if "their abnormal character" becomes "lost" (59), which would preclude the possibility that queerness—perdurable as it has been throughout time—is an injurious monstrosity. More interesting is the possibility that queerness is a trait that makes, by Roughgarden's bestiary of homosexuality, many animal species, especially *homo sapiens*, "polymorphic species." Given that the category *monstrosity* is, Darwin says, relative and applied most often to traits that occur unexpectedly in domesticated species, not in nature (99), queerness could be a trait whose "variations which are of no service or disservice" to the survival of the species convert what might appear to some as a "mon-

strosity" into something beautiful. Indeed, Darwin elsewhere claims that "it is difficult to draw any distinct line between a variation and a monstrosity" (*Variation* 1:296).

53. Roughgarden, *Evolution's Rainbow*, 2.

54. Ibid., 21.

55. This argument is distinct from Jim McKnight's suggestion that homosexuality might survive in the evolutionary gene pool as a result of heterozygote advantage (187), for it does not assume that the binary gender construction undergirding the term "gay" exists in the natural world. The variations that writers like Darwin himself, Joan Roughgarden, Anne Fausto-Sterling, and Edward Stein have shown to exist within the realm of biological sex—what constitutes male, female, or intersex—already discount the possibility of a gene that could influence a binary construction of sexuality. Nature doesn't need the Cockettes: It is already more gender-fucked than most performative deconstructions of gender can imagine, with variables extending from chromosomal sex to external and internal gonads to secondary sex characteristics and beyond. For insightful summaries and examinations of such variations, see Sterling's *Sexing the Body: Gender Politics and the Construction of Sexuality* (New York: Basic Books, 2000) and Stein's *The Mismeasure of Desire: The Science, Theory, and Ethics of Sexual Orientation* (New York: Oxford University Press, 1999).

56. Roughgarden, *Evolution's Rainbow*, 3.

57. Charles Darwin, "On the Two Forms, or Dimorphic Condition, in the Species of *Primula*, and on their remarkable Sexual Relations," *Journal of the Proceedings of the Linnean Society*, vol. 6. (London: Taylor and Francis, 1862): 77–96, 94, 91, 94–5.

58. Levine, *Darwin Loves You*, 199.

59. In both *Origin* and *Descent*, Darwin's primary example of such mutable aesthetic feeling is how people of different races admire different features of the human body (*Origin* 197, *Descent* 1:64).

60. Charles Darwin, *The Expression of the Emotions in Man and Animals* (1872; Oxford: Oxford University Press, 1998), 212. One might expect my examination of Darwin's theory of feeling to draw more than it does from Darwin's most explicit discussion of that subject, *Expression*, but that book is ironically less aesthetic in its theoretical and rhetorical disposition than his other major works. *Expression* is a relatively rigid semiotics of the human and animal body, attempting to link bodily expressions to interior feelings in schematic ways. The text is worth considering within the general premises that I've established about Darwin's aesthetics, however, because its observations about human and animal expressions derive from Darwin's interpretation of literary and visual evidence. For example, Darwin cites *Romeo and*

Juliet and *Hamlet* as evidence of emotional expression, claiming that
"Shakespeare, who from his wonderful knowledge of the human mind ought
to be an excellent judge" of the emotions, is as worthy as source of scientific
evidence as anyone else (360). In its repeated use of such evidence, *Expression*
undermines its rigid conclusions about emotional expression, for such
conclusions derive from aesthetic evidence that, Darwin's own theory of
aesthetic feeling's mutability, can be interpreted in more ways than Darwin
documents in this particular text.

61. Grosz, *Nick of Time*, 75.

62. This interpretation offers a revised perspective on Morton's otherwise persuasive claim that, "because Darwin reduces sexuality to sheer
aesthetic display (sub-Kantian purposelessness), *The Descent of Man* is as
anti-homophobic as it is antiracist. It refuses to traffic in the idea that
pleasure in surfaces contrasts with 'real' activity" (278). *Descent* has the
potential for such a reading, but it must also be acknowledged that Darwin
does not foreground it in *Descent* but in his other major writings, which
actually elucidate how Darwin's aesthetic response to sex exemplifies his
broader theories about aesthetic and sexual feeling.

63. Dutton exemplifies the problematic consequences of Darwin's claims
about sexual selection—particularly when decontextualized from his claims
about aesthetic feeling—when he writes that sexual selection is "part of a
human mating system that aims not at crushing competing members of the
same sex but at *attracting and seducing members of the opposite sex*" (emphasis in
original). Such notably heterosexual selection has, Dutton claims, "affected
the evolution of the human body and, more importantly for our purposes,
done more to create the human personality as we know it today than any
other human factor" (140). For similarly troubling applications of the theory
of sexual selection in contemporary popular science and evolutionary
biology, see Nancy Etcoff's *Survival of the Prettiest: The Science of Beauty*
(New York: Doubleday, 1999) and Karl Grammer, Bernhard Fink, Anders P.
Møller, and Randy Thornhill's "Darwinian Aesthetics: Sexual Selection and
the Biology of Beauty" (*Biological Reviews* 78, no. 3 [2003]: 385–407).

64. Grounded in the erotic—a longing to possess predicated on lack—
queer feeling is related to a Freudian understanding of sexuality, yet it
diverges there from in its status as affect rather than drive. I know of no
other discussion of the term *queer feeling* than Sara Ahmed's in *The Cultural
Politics of Emotion* (New York: Routledge, 2004), wherein Ahmed declares a
"wish to explore 'queer feelings' without translating such an exploration into
a matter of 'feeling queer.' Such a translation would assume 'queerness'
involves a particular emotional life, or that there are feelings that bodies
'have' given their failure to inhabit or follow a heterosexual ideal" (146). I do

make such an assumption here while granting that queer feelings (and feeling queer) would necessitate that one's "particular emotional life" defies any *particular* particularity other than a deviation from any normative affective or sexual state.

65. Ann Cvetkovich, *Mixed Feelings*, 43–4.

66. Grant Allen, *Physiological Æsthetics* (1877; London: Elibron Classics, 2005), 169.

67. Stuart Andrew McDowall, *Beauty and the Beast: An Essay in Evolutionary Aesthetic* (Cambridge: Cambridge University Press, 1920), 54, 72. As evidenced by the collection of essays *Evolutionary Aesthetics* (ed. Eckhart Voland and Karl Grammer [New York: Springer-Verlag, 2003]), the branch of aesthetic theory represented by McDowall's work persists to this day but is dominated by the heteronormative views that, I've argued, derive from Darwin's misunderstood theory of sexual selection. In his essay "Darwinian Aesthetics Informs Traditional Aesthetics" (in Voland and Grammer, 9–35), for example, Randy Thornhill argues that "human aesthetic value is a scale of reproductive success and failure in human evolutionary history" (10). Such values translate even into Elaine Scarry's effort to revive aesthetics for contemporary humanistic inquiry, *On Beauty and Being Just* (Princeton, N.J.: Princeton University Press, 1999), for Scarry insists that beauty is inherently reproductive: "beauty brings copies of itself into being" (1). From the delicate eggs on its cover to its claim that beauty "prompts the begetting of children" (4), *On Beauty* insists that beauty must have a purpose, specifically a heteronormatively reproductive purpose. This is most regrettable given that Scarry's is one of the rare examples of an aesthetics of nature in contemporary aesthetic theory.

68. By analyzing Kant's relation to Darwin, I am expanding on Richard Sha's precedent in *Perverse Romanticism*, wherein Sha records how Romantic writers used early nineteenth-century science to conceive of sexuality as "a kind of Kantian purposiveness without purpose. That is, rather than assuming that sex was necessarily a selfish pleasure [making it interested, not disinterested], writers linked eroticism with a mutuality that had the form of a purposiveness instead of with reproductive function" (1). The Romantics, in Sha's analysis, thus anticipate modernist writers like Porter, for they return aesthetics to the realm of sensational, desirous taste and, like Darwin, suggest that "purposiveness without purpose may be acquiring a physiology" (74): that art is returning to nature.

69. Immanuel Kant, *Critique of Judgment*, trans. J. H. Bernard (Mineola, N.Y.: Dover, 2005), 96. Hereafter cited in the text by page number.

70. As Richard Sha has persuasively shown, Kant's removal of heterosexual desire from the aesthetic judgment also makes the aesthetic (that

which is purposive without purpose) inherently queer, even as such queer-ness cannot be called desirous, the aesthetic lacking for Kant any trace of sexual desire (142).

71. Kant actually says just the opposite of this, though it is clear that what he calls "heteronomy" is, in its final product, a homogeneous under-standing of the beautiful: "Taste [merely] claims autonomy. To make the judgments of others the determining grounds of his own would be heter-onomy" (93; brackets in original).

72. Kant was, of course, writing at the dawn of evolutionary theory—which was, before Darwin, teleological in disposition and focused on individuals rather than species (Kant 203)—so it is perhaps unsurprising that Kant and Darwin actually share many of the same views of nature. Kant claims, for example, that bodies are "changeable substances" (13), defines nature simply as "the complex of the objects of sense" (153), declares that there are "infinitely various empirical laws" (15) and that "different natures can be causes in an infinite variety of ways" (14), and even humbly admits that "nature has not taken him ["man"] for her special darling and favoured him with benefit above all animals" (209). Yet these empirical claims do not accord with Kant's ethical program—his desire to create order out of chaos, "to make a connected experience out of given perceptions of nature" (15)—so he must leave them to the scientists.

73. Kant can be confusing on the topic of whether judgment has a concept, but he explains aesthetic judgment's progression *toward* a concept most clearly here: "The judgment of taste must refer to some concept; otherwise it could make absolutely no claim to be necessarily valid for everyone. But it is not therefore capable of being proved *from* a concept" (138). Judgment's concept—subjective universality—is assumed *a priori* but only proven—though Kant would not use this word—after the judgment has taken place.

74. It is ultimately Kant's own desire for the beautiful—his own interest in the supposedly disinterested nature of beauty—that leads him away from the kind of aesthetic theory that Darwin propounds. Kant allows, for example, that "we may well think that the beauty of flowers, of the plumage of birds, or of shell-fish, both in shape and colour, may be ascribed to nature and its faculty of producing forms in an aesthetically purposive way, in its freedom, without particular purposes adapted thereto" (147). But Kant is not satisfied with such an empirical possibility (itself already compromised by the subjective, as he is writing of what he perceives to be "beauty"), for he wants to isolate "the principle of the *Ideality* of the purposiveness in the beauty of nature," which is grounded on the fact that "in judging beauty we invariably seek its gauge in ourselves *a priori*" (147). Dedicated to enlight-ened progress, Kant refuses to renounce his *a priori* principle and insists

upon converting nature into an ideological construct that defies its own empirical variability.

75. Grant Allen, *Physiological Æsthetics*, viii, 42.

76. Ibid., 47.

77. Max Simon Nordau, *Degeneration* (Lincoln: University of Nebraska Press, 1993), 324, 453.

78. Ibid., 313. Whereas Kant focuses primarily upon the aesthetic feeling of the subject who perceives art, Nordau attends to the feelings of both the artist and the perceiver (though, unlike Adorno, not the feeling of the work itself—Nordau refers such feeling to the artist). In the former case, Nordau maintains, "every work of art always comprises in itself truth and reality in so far as, if it does not reflect the external world, it surely reflects the mental life of the artist" (336). Art, in this view, is always the record of real historical feelings, at least of the artists who produce it. But art also elicits material feelings from those who receive it: One cannot have a response to art, Nordau claims, until the "sensory nerves and centres of perception change the modes of the external stimuli conformably with their own nature" (335). Inextricable from the material world, art is, for Nordau, not pure construction but a biophysical record of the subjects who produce and consume it.

79. Henri Bergson, *Creative Evolution*, trans. Arthur Mitchell (Mineola, N.Y.: Dover, 1998), 1.

80. Ibid., 55, 126.

81. See Adorno's discussion of the work's lack of judgment for a discussion of this concept specifically (99).

82. Michel Foucault, "Sex, Power, and the Politics of Identity," 163.

83. Like Kant, however, Allen excludes sexual feelings from the possible emotions that can count as aesthetic. For "sexual feeling [. . .] obviously falls short of aesthetic disinterestedness" (261). Revealing the contradictions that abound about sexual feeling in aesthetic theory, however, Allen then claims that "amatory emotion [. . .] is the most poetical in our whole nature, for it is the most complex and the most all-embracing: and it is a feeling of peculiar strength and vividness" (274). This apparent contradiction may be explained by the fact that Allen seems to regard "sex" here as a drive—something not complex, not disinterested—and the "amatory" (love) as an affect. As Sedgwick's discussion of Tomkins's study of the affects reveals, however, contemporary biophysical understandings of the affects helpfully revise Allen's precedent.

The Comedy of Nature:
Darwinian Feminism in
Virginia Woolf's *Between the Acts*

Woolf's Concentration

I like wine. Air raids much less.

—VIRGINIA WOOLF[1]

In a letter that scholars provisionally date to March 18, 1941, Virginia Woolf explained to her husband, Leonard, why she was "going mad again." "I begin to hear voices, and cant concentrate," Woolf records: "You see I cant even write this properly. I cant read. What I want to say is that I owe all the happiness of my life to you."[2] In the intervening days before she took her life on March 28, Woolf sent a copy of her last novel, *Between the Acts* (1941), to John Lehmann, managing director of Hogarth Press. Despite his enthusiastic praise for the text, Woolf wrote Lehmann on March 27 to declare that she would continue to revise the novel,[3] which she had earlier called "a concentration—a screw" amidst the "many air raids" of World War II and a "concentrated small book" that contained "many varieties of mood" (*DVW* 5:311, 114). The next day, Woolf wrote Leonard a note similar to her letter of March 18—omitting the sentence about her inability to "concentrate"—and drowned herself hours later in the River Ouse.

A writer who believed that "to shut out, to concentrate—that is perhaps—one of the necessary conditions [. . .] of genius," Woolf knew that retaining her concentration was also, by the time she omitted it from her final letter to Leonard, a necessary condition of survival (*DVW* 4:179). World War II escalated the struggle that Woolf had endured throughout her life to retain such focus: Numbered 115 and 116 on Hitler's secret arrest list for England, the Woolfs both planned to kill themselves should Hitler invade England, which seemed increasingly plausible during the Blitz (*DVW* 5:165). Contemplating the alternatives of "we in concentration camps, or taking sleeping draughts," Woolf avowed her intention to do the latter or gas herself in her garage rather than submit to Hitler, for "capitulation will mean all Jews to be given up. Concentration camps. So to our garage" (*DVW* 5:292–3). The Nazi concentration camps presented Woolf with two fatal options—taking her own life or having it taken from her—that would eliminate the possibility of concentration altogether.[4]

At the expense of finishing what she otherwise considered to be a "triumphant" novel, however, Woolf did retain through her final days "a concentration" in the "concentrated [. . .] variety of moods" of *Between the Acts*, a book that critiques the Nazi regime and that provided Woolf focus during the Blitz (*DVW* 5:340). As her use of the word to describe both her personal attention and her novel's aesthetic suggests, concentration was, for Woolf, not only a state of mind in this period but a medium of aesthetic, ethical, and political agency. Her March 18 letter to Leonard establishes such links as it correlates Woolf's personal facility to "concentrate" with her aesthetic abilities to "write" and "read." The goal of this correlation, she says, is to express her belief in and gratitude for intersubjective bonds: "I owe all the happiness of my life to you."

Woolf's concentration thus highlights a central aesthetic and ethical paradigm in her late work, namely the need to overcome the boundaries of the self in order to sympathize with a world of others, what Natania Rosenfeld calls Woolf's "politics of intersubjectivity."[5] While her association of the phrases "to concentrate" and "to shut out" might appear to imply just the opposite, Woolf actually concentrates by shutting out the self, specifically the self's socially constructed identity. Woolf's concentration is, as she says, "a screw," a binding agent between subject and object made acutely necessary by the war, during which she wrote that "now's the time to see if the art, or life, creed, the belief in something existing independently of myself, will [. . .] hold good" (*DVW* 5:264). As a transitive verb, "concentrate" requires such selective focus on others: It denotes the fixation of personal faculties on an object, and it can mean bringing a group of objects together.[6] For Woolf, these definitions work simultaneously, for she posits in *Between the Acts* that one must divest oneself of self-identity—threatening but never achieving biological death—in order to create a collectivity that might survive, and in fact prevent, the self-obsessed sources and goals of warfare.

As the force required to screw objects together suggests, however, this ethic troublingly posits that instances of violence by and to the ego yield communal cohesion. Especially in her late work, as Patricia Klindienst Joplin argues, Woolf explores "whether it is possible to constitute an identity, whether as an individual or group, except at the expense of an other."[7] In her memoir "A Sketch of the Past" (1941), for example, Woolf records how the Blitz reinforced her belief that "nothing is so much to be dreaded as egotism. Nothing so cruelly hurts the person himself; nothing so wounds those who are forced into contact with it."[8] Yet such violence, she had claimed of World War I, can also yield a "whole people [. . .] concentrated on a single point," a concentration that Woolf calls during WWII "the community feeling: all England thinking this same thing—this horror of war—at the same moment" (*DVW* 1:217). Horror like war is prerequisite for collective concentration, she writes, lest come "the lull & one lapses again into private separation" (*DVW* 5:215).

While scholars have examined the politics of community in Woolf's late work—most persuasively as a critique of modernist preoccupations with interiority—they have largely overlooked how Woolf's ethic of self-divestiture hinges on this principle of violence.[9] Yet this ethic inheres in another denotation of "concentrate": to strengthen through distillation, even purification.[10] Formally and thematically, Woolf's vision of concentration in *Between the Acts* enacts such violent purification on the model of atavism, or the reversion of biological forms to prior stages of development, an idea popularized in the modernist period by Charles Darwin, whose work Woolf read and wanted to write about during WWII (*DVW* 5:274, 294, 331). Darwin based his theory of descent partially on the evidence of atavistic traits in humans, which he terms "reversions" and "rudiments," the former concept referring to biological structures that reappear during a species' development, the latter referring to obsolete structures that nonetheless endure.[11] Together, Darwin writes, "reversionary, as well as the strictly rudimentary, structures reveal the descent of man from some lower form in an unmistakable manner" (*DOM* 1:130). In his documentation of "reversions to a savage state, from which we are not removed by very many generations" (*DOM* 1:173), Darwin offered one of the famous violations of anthropocentrism in modern thought. In *Between*, Woolf extends this violation to a civilization whose efforts at domination betray, and threaten to destroy, its members' collective "lower form."[12]

Thematically, Woolf creates a concentrated community in this novel by stripping individuals of the pretensions to civilization that constitute individual and national identities alike. Such pretensions structure the novel's premise about a small English village community that gathers in the summer of 1939 at a country estate named Pointz Hall to witness and participate in an annual pageant play meant to celebrate English literary and political history. Woolf stages that play outdoors, however, in a natural setting that vexes the play and causes the audience to realize, as one anonymous character says, "there's a sense in which we all, I admit, are savages still."[13] By atavistically despoiling her characters' individual identities, Woolf concentrates them into an unidentified "we."[14] As an anonymous portion of the audience muses, "'It's a good day, some say, the day we are stripped naked. Others, it's the end of the day" (*BTA* 106). "Living near to the bone" (*DVW* 5:328), as Woolf described life during the war, *Between*'s characters have no choice about whether to regress: only about whether their submission to that reversion will constitute their civilization's renewal or its death.[15]

Formally, Woolf enacts this distillation through the novel's direct discourse and objective third-person reportage. Both formal traits detach the narrator (when one appears) and the reader from characters' private lives. This narratological detachment, or stripping away of mediation, explains Woolf's preoccupation with the drama in *Between*, for the novel form is distinguished by narratological mediation, whereas drama typically forgoes mediation and relates character through dialogue and action. Stripping her novel of a mediating "I" (or any consistent narratological voice), Woolf presents a community in the process of self-divesture. Such techniques led Woolf to claim that she had "got at a more direct method of summarising relations" (*DVW* 5:200) and found "a new combination of the raw & the lyrical" while writing *Between* (*BTA* 259). Through such aesthetic concentration, the novel formalizes its atavistic thematics.[16]

Disturbing even on their own terms, Woolf's aesthetic and ethic of concentration run troublingly close to the eugenic logic practiced in the Nazi concentration camps, which Hitler's regime used in a genocidal campaign initiated before and escalated after Woolf's death.[17] The Nazis murdered homosexuals, Jews, women, and other social minorities in an effort to purify the race of degeneracy, a term that arose with evolutionary theory to denote biological forms that were atavistic and/or enervated.[18] *Between* adumbrates this genocide, as characters read about murders and imprisonment on the continent, discuss Jewish refugees, and fear invasion as they watch threatening planes fly overhead during the pageant (*BTA* 32, 84, 131, 135). Depicting her characters in a universal state of degeneration—"all savages"—but proposing that such degeneration is salvific, Woolf parodies eugenic forms of concentration that endorse material destruction, even as she supports a form of concentration that propagates material difference by distilling social identity. With such parody, as the epigraph to this essay suggests, Woolf employs a relentlessly humorous tone throughout *Between* that engenders the "variety of moods" that she claimed her "concentrated small book" contained.

A paragraph from the early typescript of *Between the Acts* exemplifies this strange concatenation of humor and horror in Woolf's principle of concentration:

> To some, a snatch of poetry, if it were only the rhyme on a tear-off calendar, was as necessary a part of the toilet as any other; they read as they brushed their teeth. But the concentration necessary was unhygienic; they could no more read poetry by the hour—unless stretched in a sand pit or under a tree with a pine needle for marker, dipping and ceasing, dipping and ceasing—than they could do dumbbell exercises or pray. It was a concentration, a pressure upon the mind—poetry— that turned it to diamond. And how could a pressure like that be maintained without injury to the delicate fibres? (*PH* 50)

Framed within a laughable scene of British gentry reading poetry while brushing their teeth, Woolf's description of concentration, with its parodic attention to hygiene, subverts the Nazis' eugenic logic of purification. For Woolf, concentration upon aesthetic matters is "unhygienic" by normative standards: It requires "dipping and ceasing" into atavistic poses "in a sand pit or under a tree"; it demands a focus that exceeds the boundaries of self-care and must incur "injury to the delicate fibres." Yet such violence to civilized identity may be constructive, Woolf implies, for this "pressure upon the mind" transforms the mind into "diamond."

Although she omits this scene from the novel's final—but for her only provisional—iteration, Woolf uses this simultaneously humorous and disturbing logic of concentration throughout *Between the Acts* to undermine the egotistical self bent on dominating others with its own sense of identity. Epitomizing one of the novel's refrains, "the laughter died away," *Between* is riddled with affectively incongruous episodes: reflections on rape inspiring reflections on the weather, a tale of suicide followed by an adult's defending her own immaturity, murder in the name of "a child's game," and a woman (indeed a whole community) who looks "nearly extinct" as she "clapped and laughed loud" (*BTA* 40, 42, 45, 16, 31, 68, 65). Such episodes themselves riddle the text's long pageant play, a pastiche of English comedies that fails so miserably that its author repeatedly likens it to death (*BTA* 96, 122).

Scholars have long debated whether such scenes position *Between the Acts* within the comedic or the tragic mode, yet I argue that Woolf's aesthetic of concentration distills the tragedy of civilization into a comedy of nature.[19] Woolf pits the historically subordinate, feminized mode of comedy against the traditionally dominant, masculinized mode of tragedy to create a formal allegory for the novel's feminist politics: as Woolf herself claimed, "when tragedy and comedy collide it is comedy that wins."[20]

Whereas tragedy classically offers a "change of fortune [that] should be not from bad to good, but, reversely, from good to bad,"[21] Woolf's comedy of nature employs the tragic structure of decline as a good: as a submission and return to a Darwinian understanding of nature as infinitely heterogeneous and transformative, one wherein "species are not immutable" but exist in "infinitely varied diversities."[22] Distilled to this state of material mutability, *homo sapiens* might renounce its civilized claim to a static identity and submit to the remarkably "protean and polymorphic" quality that, Darwin believes, characterizes the human species (*DOM* 1:249).[23] For Woolf, the transformative possibilities inherent in the atavistic human seem promising in an era tragically committed to ideological stasis.[24]

When Woolf's character Isa requests a "new plot" in *Between the Acts*, then, a "plot [that] was only there to beget emotion," Woolf provides one in the form of what Dana Seitler terms the modernist "degeneration narrative," which, "rather than resulting in the closure of the conventional heterosexual love plot or adventure novel, results in the regression of an individual to an atavistic state," such that its plot "regresses as it progresses."[25] Refusing a heterosexual telos, Woolf's degenerative comedy presents a complementary mode to what Michael North calls the twentieth century's "machine-age comedy," a historically unprecedented form inspired by that century's innovations in mechanical reproduction, for the post-Darwinian comedy of nature produces difference through a variety of reproductive and non-reproductive means.[26] On the evidence of productive forces like the "spontaneous variations of instincts," in fact, Darwin argues that it is "certainly an error" to suppose "that all variations are connected with the act of sexual reproduction" (*OS* 245, 32). Whereas the machine's comedy emerges from a confusion between the mechanical and the natural, nature's comedy emerges from their disarticulation: from the disarticulation of any identification, in fact, wherein production could be mistaken for reproduction alone.[27]

In *Between the Acts*, Woolf represents such potentially non-reproductive diversities in a queer social world that arguably realizes the "anonymous and secret Society of Outsiders" that, she envisions in *Three Guineas* (1938), might fight fascism pacifically by rejecting nationalist motivations.[28] The "many variety of moods" that permeate *Between*'s queer world may accordingly be synthesized as *camp*, an aesthetic whose resistance to definition itself exemplifies the novel's affective indeterminacy.[29] In her 1964 essay "Notes on 'Camp,'" nonetheless, Susan Sontag provides some frequent traits of the aesthetic that bear relation to *Between*: that camp "is alive to a double sense in which some things can be taken"; that camp "corrupts" and "appreciates vulgarity"; and that "camp and tragedy are antitheses," for camp "proposes a comic vision of the world" and evinces "love for human nature."[30] Reinforcing Jed Esty's assertion that *Between* "represents a group's wish to avoid collective identity as a positive feature *of* its collective identity," the novel's camp aesthetic corrupts individual and national identities to propose a communal ethic of "human sympathy," of "love for human nature."[31]

In contemporary theoretical accounts of queer experience, however, feelings like camp are characteristically set in opposition to scientific understandings of nature, as is queerness generally. Writes Sontag, "camp objects, and persons, contain a large element of artifice. Nothing in nature can be campy" ("Notes" 55). Upsetting such critical pieties, *Between* depicts queer feelings like camp as natural on the Darwinian logic that nature itself is queer, or endlessly transformative and defiant of material or conceptual normativity.[32] In contrast to the green nail polish and mangy fur coat that adorn this period's most famously campy character, Christopher Isherwood's Sally Bowles, the novel offers a distilled version of camp that, with its emphasis on forms of concentration, including biological and cultural atavism, might be called *concentrated camp*.[33] This term encapsulates how Woolf enacts in form precisely the ethic that she propounds in content: She strips an aesthetic typically laden with civilized trappings to its bare material core—the unidentified, feeling body—just as she proposes that European civilization degenerate to a social mode of material interconnection before the artifice of identity takes on such force that it eradicates materiality altogether.

As Steve Lipman and Viktor Frankl record, a related form of humor pervaded the atavistic conditions of the concentration camps themselves, where prisoners "found humor, sometimes sardonic humor, in all aspects of their disrupted existence" as a way to "embrac[e] the wider cycles of life and death" and to reject "false illusions" and "artificial optimism."[34] Woolf similarly disparaged wartime's artificial feelings: She mourned that "most people are numb & have surface optimism" derived from "the emotional falsity" of "that dreary false cheery hero-making strain" that emerged in German and British war propaganda (*DVW* 231, 292). For Woolf, such propaganda sanitized war's horror under the patronizing, and paternalistic, guise of heroism: "I dont like any of the feelings war breeds: patriotism; communal &c, all sentimental & emotional parodies of our real feelings" (*DVW* 302). With her camp aesthetic, Woolf parodies these "emotional parodies" themselves to foil the horror that Nazi propaganda rationalized under the name of health and British propaganda under the name of heroism. Such parodies might, she hoped, shock the wartime community out of its numb optimism and transform Hitler's oppressive concept of "nature as guarantor of unchanging order" on the Darwinian logic that nature is the guarantor of a changing order.[35] If camp "refashion[s] as a weapon of attack an oppressive identity inherited *as* subordination," Woolf's concentrated camp refashions nature as guarantor of the chance that queer lives might proliferate beyond eugenic concentration.[36]

Darwinian Feminism

Laughter is an indispensible tool in deconstructions of the bio-politics of being female.
Suspicion and irony are basic to feminist reinscriptions of nature's text.

DONNA HARAWAY, *Primate Visions: Gender, Race, and Nature in the World of Modern Science*[37]

As apparent in *A Room of One's Own* (1929) and *Three Guineas*, Woolf characteristically described war in gendered terms, viewing fascism as a product of European patriarchy (*TG* 12–13).[38] As we will see, Woolf also characteristically described humor as women's best weapon against such forces. With *Between*'s obscene camp, she expands this feminist politic to the realm of queer aesthetics. In the October 1938 letter in which she announces her first work on the novel, in fact, Woolf claims that she is "going to write a comedy about" the fact "that marriage [. . .] reduces one to a damnable servility."[39] By making such reduction humorous, Woolf aims, as Christine Froula argues, "to form a radical public to whom women artists,

like Joyce and Proust, can 'say everything,'" including, as Rebecca
Walkowitz aptly puts it, that "one must risk being bad—uncertain, incon-
sistent, unsuccessful—in order to keep being good."[40]

Woolf's attempt to be good with bad aesthetics—a definition of camp
itself—is cause to reassess what some have deemed her pacifism and passivity in *Between* ("Notes" 65).[41] As Pamela Robertson argues in her unprecedented analysis of female camp, "Camp offers a slightly different model
of negotiation to account for the overlap between passivity and activity in
a viewer who sees through, simultaneously perhaps, one mask of serious
femininity and another mask of laughing femininity."[42] In a position of
active passivity, Woolf's characters present a frighteningly comedic response to war: submitting to degradation, not just to martial violence but
to natural violence, including the queerly sadomasochistic pleasures of sex.
Such sexual submission, Leo Bersani writes, offers "the terrifying appeal
of a loss of the ego, of a self-debasement" that, by shattering the ego's "sac-
rosanct value of selfhood," may also prevent "sexuality [from] becoming a
struggle for power."[43]

In *Between the Acts*, this degradation emerges through evolutionary
tropes of atavism that derive from Darwin's theories of natural selection
and variation in, among other texts, *The Origin of Species* (1859; 1872), *The
Variation of Animals and Plants under Domestication* (1868), and the first volume of *The Descent of Man, and Selection in Relation to Sex* (1871). Woolf
offers these atavistic tropes in earnest; the parodic element of her evolutionary art derives from Darwin's misogynist renderings of sexual selection
in the second volume of *Descent*. Claims like the following, for example,
have long made the idea of a Darwinian feminism seem like a contradiction in terms:

> Man is more powerful in body and mind than woman, and in the
> savage state he keeps her in a far more abject state of bondage than
> does the male of any other animal; therefore it is not surprising that he
> should gain the power of selection. Women are everywhere conscious
> of the value of their beauty; and when they have the means, they take
> more delight in decorating themselves with all sorts of ornaments than
> do men. (*DOM* 2:371–2)

Whereas most of *Descent*'s second volume details how sexual selection
works on the logic that females are attracted to their more beautiful male
counterparts (*DOM* 2:78), Darwin reserves this reductive characterization
of beauty-conscious females for the human species, perhaps under the pressure of Victorian gender standards. Regardless of his motivations, Darwin

makes beauty, rather than any other aesthetic state, the paradigm of sex-ual production amongst all species, and he depicts all females in the thrall of males, whether to their beauty or their power. For *homo sapiens*, Darwin's alarming conclusion from these explorations is that "man has ul-timately become superior to woman" (*DOM* 2:328)—a conclusion upon which Hitler seizes in his eugenic practices.

In his rhetoric against degeneration, which Woolf followed assiduously on the BBC and in newspapers (*DOM* 5:245, 263), Hitler declares war against the unsanitized and degenerate on the Darwinian logic that, as he writes in *Mein Kampf* (1925–6), "every historical event in the world is noth-ing more nor less than a manifestation of the instinct of racial self-preservation."[44] Within the eugenic programs that he endorsed to eliminate degeneracy, programs including forced sterilization and state-run mar-riages, Hitler aimed to prevent women from working and to subjugate them into maternal roles, for every girl, he averred, "is one day to be a mother" (*MK* 376). Coupled with his attempt to eliminate homosexuals, whom he considered as "infectious and as dangerous as the plague," Hit-ler's campaign against non-reproductive women attempted to institution-alize reproductivity as the only natural state of sexual being.[45]

True to his pseudo-Darwinian rhetoric, Hitler calls upon "Nature" to justify his eugenic programs, citing it as a model of "selective breeding" (*MK* 39). While Darwin does flirt with eugenic ideals at the end of *De-scent*'s second volume, he more consistently holds that nature is not a se-lective breeder but a random collection of "dimly understood laws of variation [that] are infinitely complex and diversified" and whose "number and diversity of inheritable deviations of structure, both those of slight and those of considerable physiological importance, are endless" (*DOM* 2:403; *OS* 34). Natural selection cannot work in states of homogeneity, Darwin writes, for "the possibility of selection coming into action rests on vari-ability," such that "close interbreeding, by lessening [species'] vigour and fertility, aids in their final extinction."[46] Deploying Darwin's invariant theory of sexual selection to the point of obfuscating his theories of natu-ral selection and variability, Hitler perverts evolutionary theory to legis-late its laws, especially the laws of sexual nature, despite his claim that "man must not ever fall into the error of thinking that he was ever meant to be the lord and master of Nature" (*MK* 208, 223).[47]

Owing in part to such deployments of Darwin's science of gender, Woolf was generally suspicious of science, and she particularly distrusted her doc-tors, many of whom were active in the eugenics field.[48] Nonetheless, she read more sexological work in the last three years of her life than any period theretofore, including not just Darwin but "Victorian psychology" that denigrated women (*TG* 132).[49] In portions of *Between the Acts*, Woolf earnestly condemns this field's doctrine about women's "bondage" to men, to a cult of beauty, and to the preservation of hygiene. The character Mrs. Swithin, for example, reads throughout the novel a book titled "Outline of History," a fictionalized version of George Trevelyan's *History of England* (1929), a text premised on Darwinian principles. Such reading leads Swithin to wonder "'Who makes sex susceptible to beauty?'" and then skeptically to liken beauty to a boat that "sometimes leaks" (*BTA* 139). Isa, moreover, considers reading Darwin—specifically *Descent of Man* in the early typescript—but instead reads a newspaper story about a woman raped by British soldiers (*BTA* 14; *PH* 54; *BTA* 14).

Woolf's direct transition here from misogynist text to misogynist act clearly indicts Darwin. Rather than disregarding his theories altogether, however, Woolf proposes that women must redefine nature as infinitely mutable, Darwin's most consistent theorization of the concept. She records this ambition in *Three Guineas*, writing that "Nature it was claimed who is not only omniscient but unchanging, had made the brain of woman of the wrong shape or size [. . .] Science, it would seem, is not sexless; she is a man" (*TG* 39). Like Elizabeth Grosz, who has recently demonstrated Darwin's urgent relevance to contemporary feminist theory, Woolf does not repudiate nature altogether on the basis of such constructions but asks instead, "Must we not, and do we not change this unalterable nature?" (*TG* 49).[50] In *Between*, during the composition of which she claimed to "want to take naturalists notes—human naturalists notes," Woolf changes science's misogynist nature by parodying it: She depicts all of humanity under the weight of Darwin's oppressive principle of feminine submission, stripping life of constructed difference to return it to Darwin's infinitely variegated state of nature (*DVW* 5:339). Woolf camps sexual selection, in other words, to concentrate natural selection and variation.

With this parody, Woolf also attacks Hitler's deployment of Darwin's theory of sexual selection in his rhetoric of *völkisch* hierarchy and submission to the Führer. Resonant of Hitler's demand that the masses adhere to "the aristocratic principle of Nature" and "like a woman [. . .] rather bow to the strong man than dominate the weakling," Woolf forces *Between*'s female protagonists (indeed, all of its human characters) to submit to the domination of a post-Darwinian nature: As Isa muses, "'How I am burdened with what they drew from the earth [. . .] "Kneel down," said the past'" (*MK* 69, 50; *BTA* 106). Even Giles, the novel's self-declared "active" character who famously kills a toad-engorged snake in a scene of suggestive homophobia, feels "manacled to a rock" in preparation to watch the pageant, "forced passively to behold indescribable horror" (*BTA* 69, 41–2).[51] Whereas dominant modernist feminist movements attempted "to reverse the old association of woman with Nature"—the ideological fiction of nature as passive and unchanging that still permeates critical theory today—Woolf portrays women and men alike submitting to a transformative nature, such that submission to it is not a concession of but an acquisition of agency, specifically the participation in universal material differentiation.[52]

Between thus offers a queer feminist ethic of submission that parodically repudiates Darwin's, not to mention Hitler's, insistence that women embody hygienic and passive roles in socio-sexual relations mediated by the aesthetic of beauty.[53] In historical terms, this ethic represents what Theodor Adorno calls modern art's "feeling for nature," or art's ethical attempt to reveal the "wound" of what the Enlightenment aesthetics "of freedom and human dignity" ultimately "oppressed: animal, landscape, woman."[54]

This wound "is sensually displeasing and repugnant," Adorno writes, and includes feelings involved in "polymorphous sexuality," for the Enlightened aesthetic taboo against nature was in many ways "a sexual one: Nothing should be moist; art becomes hygienic" (*AT* 47, 116). Woolf requests such a feeling for nature in her essay "On Being Ill" (1930), wherein she complains that "literature does its best to maintain that its concern is with the mind" and calls for "a new language that we need, more primitive, more sensual, more obscene" that can represent states of physical degradation like illness.[55] Considering that degeneration was considered a biological ailment and that Woolf declared that "the war is like desperate illness," "On Being Ill" anticipates how Woolf deploys primitive, obscene language in *Between*, during the composition of which she was conscious of her "defiance of professional decency. About being an outsider" (*DVW* 5:285, 251).

Woolf manifests a feeling for nature in her late work by depicting women acquiring agency in unhygienic states and locales. Expanding the spatial, temporal, and sensory coordinates of the "sound-proof room" that she requested in 1929 on the feminist logic that "intellectual freedom depends upon material things," Woolf replaces the room of one's own with the prehistoric cave and the public restroom stall (*ROO* 49, 101). Sites in which the human species publicly exposes its submission to nature, these rooms are rooms of our own, rooms in which personal freedom depends upon the freedom of material things like bodies themselves.

The conclusion of *Between the Acts* features this first kind of space: the cave, an atavistic site of violent sexuality. Discussing Isa and Giles, the married couple whose strained relationship suffuses the novel's pages, the scene reads as follows:

> Left alone together for the first time that day, they were silent. Alone, enmity was bared; also love. Before they slept, they must fight; after they had fought, they would embrace. From that embrace another life might be born. But first they must fight, as the dog fox fights with the vixen, in the heart of darkness, in the fields of night.
>
> Isa let her sewing drop. The great hooded chairs had become enormous. And Giles too. And Isa too against the window. The window was all sky without colour. The house had lost its shelter. It was night before roads were made, or houses. It was the night that dwellers in caves had watched from some high place among rocks.
>
> Then the curtain rose. They spoke. (*BTA* 149)

At first glance, this scene might seem anything but queer, let alone feminist, for it resolves the novel's marriage plot between Isa and Giles, forcing them to both "fight" and "embrace" in the night to come, where the word *embrace* functions as a euphemism for sexual intercourse that "might" reproductively bear "another life." Signaled by an equivocal "might" that includes the possibility of non-reproductive sexual behavior, however, this scene is actually written by a queer character in the novel named Miss La Trobe, who writes the two plays featured in the novel: the first, the failed pageant play; and the second, the play with which the novel closes but that, unlike the pageant, is not demarcated by discourse tags. With what are ultimately stage directions for a new play, Woolf strips her novel of external mediation here and makes the novel the drama.[56]

As I will explore more fully in the next section, La Trobe's first play spoils national political and literary tradition through its ironic failure. If the camp aesthetic, construed "in terms of deficiency, decline, and the past [. . .] might be said to function as a kind of *ironic* nostalgia," the pageant camps its characters' nostalgia for an English history wherein "all the important things had stayed the same."[57] As the pageant degenerates into chaos, its audience members degenerate into an emotional collectivity stripped of claims to national identity, one resembling the Society of Outsiders that Woolf claims must reject "all such ceremonies as encourage the desire to impose 'our' civilization or 'our' dominion upon other people" (*TG* 114). Before the play, the owners of Pointz Hall admire their own genealogies and how their home was built "'obviously to escape from nature'" despite its proximity to a "cesspool" (*BTA* 4, 6, 3). Yet the owner's sister Mrs. Swithin realizes while reading her "Outline of History" that there were once "rhododendron forests in Piccadilly; when the entire continent [. . .] was all one" and contained "the iguanadon, the mammoth, and the mastodon; from whom, presumably, she thought, jerking the window open, we descend" (*BTA* 7). Allegorized in the pageant's paratactic disruption of historical continuity, history in *Between* becomes a circle rather than a line so that Swithin may wonder whether women like herself do not just "descend" from mastodons but may be, as Giles' father fears, "'ourselves, degenerate descendants'" and descend to their ancestors' level—may devolve toward nature rather than be able "'to escape from nature'" (*BTA* 34).

La Trobe's second play literalizes this descent and disrupts the heteronormative telos of Isa's and Giles's sexual behavior. In its atavistic context, this disruption also unsettles what, in *Evolution's Rainbow* (2004), Joan Roughgarden has persuasively proven to be the heteronormative implications of Darwin's theory of sexual selection. La Trobe's ironic euphemism *embrace*, for example, reads laughably high amid the harrowingly low context of dog fox and vixen fighting, which in the early typescript Woolf rendered as their murderous attempt "to tear each other asunder" (*PH* 188). These cave-dwellers' sex moreover concludes with biting irony a novel wherein characters wring their hands about what constitutes the "unhygienic" and may parody Hitler's proclamation that "he who would live must fight. He who does not wish to fight in this world, where permanent struggle is the law of life, has not the right to exist," a proclamation that could derive from Darwin's sentiment that "the season of love is that of battle" (*BTA* 109, 118; *MK* 261; *DOM* 2:48). It is doubtful that Hitler, who endorses only the most civilized, even superhuman, kinds of sexuality, would agree that animalistic sex is the kind of fighting that ensures one's "right to exist."

If, as Jane Marcus argues, Woolf suggests in this scene that "the origin of aggression, war, and oppression is in the origin of the species, in the drama of the battle of the sexes," Woolf also indicates that the comic resolution of such tragic forces may be found by descending to that origin.[58] Both possibilities inhere in Darwin's unidentified origin of the species, which he calls a "mystery of mysteries" and which is if anything a metonymy for the perpetual transformation of species' identities.[59] Framed by ironic camping, La Trobe's equivocal "might" thus responds "yes" to the audience members' collective question to her first failed play: "D'you think people change? Their clothes, of course. . . . But I mean ourselves"

(*BTA* 83). Submitting to nature, La Trobe suggests, people can and should change much more than their artificial trappings.

As the novel's queerest figure, La Trobe in fact insists that sexual feeling itself can change with atavistic devolution. Whereas Elizabeth Abel argues that "heterosexuality is repeatedly insinuated as our covert truth" in figures like Isa, Isa maintains an ironic distance from her own heterosexuality throughout the novel.[60] Although the narrator claims that, externally, Isa "never looked like Sappho, or one of the beautiful young men whose photographs adorned the weekly papers," Isa internally bucks convention: She feels "entangled, by her husband, the stockbroker," for example, and "loathed the domestic, the possessive; the maternal" (*BTA* 11–12, 5, 14). Rather than forcing Isa to capitulate to misogynist oppression, as Marcus argues, La Trobe's script for Isa proposes that she make public such private emotions by denuding herself of the civilized identity that makes her "loo[k] what she was: Sir Richard's daughter" (*BTA* 12).[61]

La Trobe strips Isa of this identity by troping her as an animal and cave-dweller. In her atavistic descent, Isa submits to the "enormous" husband of whom "she was afraid," thus literalizing "marriage" as a "damnable servility," yet she thereby grows powerfully "enormous" herself (*BTA* 35). Isa gains such agency, I would argue, because La Trobe has made her submit to her ego's shattering, a shattering that releases Isa's private non-normative feelings. As animal and cave-dweller, Isa looks nothing like "Sir Richard's daughter," and her ability to challenge Giles and the social normativity he represents grows proportionally as she allows her queer nature to violate her social identity.

Queering the novel's most seemingly heteronormative woman, La Trobe quells Isa's frustration with her own life's plot: "love and hate—how they tore her asunder! Surely it was time someone invented a new plot, or that the author came out from the bushes" (*BTA* 146). Considering that Isa's age is "the age of the century, thirty nine," her new "plot" could metonymically represent the queer plot that Woolf advises her own era to follow (*BTA* 14). Whereas the pageant play records English history, after all, La Trobe's second play records a queer sexual history wherein reproduction submits to the object world's unpredictable productions and what they "might" bear. In a scene that includes Woolf's boldest display of queer feminism, La Trobe violates to humble, not condemn, dominant social forms like heterosexuality before nature's queer transformations.

In her final completed piece of writing, a short story titled "The Watering Place" (1941)—which she typed palimpsestically on a draft of

Between—Woolf writes a similarly disturbing scene about the end of days from a perch in another obscene room of our own: a toilet in a public women's restroom. Inspired by Woolf's listening to women "powdering & painting, these common little tarts, while I sat, behind a thin door, p— ing as quietly as I could" in "the ladies lavatory at the Sussex Grill at Brighton," the story depicts the daily habits of people in a small seaside town, focally those in a women's restroom pervaded by a "fishy smell" and divided into two sections by a door: "on the one side of the door the claims of nature were gratified; and on the other, at the washing table, at the looking-glass, nature was disciplined by art" (*DVW* 5:356–7). In a scene of bathroom humor reminiscent of one that Woolf excised from *Between*'s early typescript,[62] Woolf depicts here the irony that women's restrooms are places where people go to defecate and urinate, to let nature run its course, but also to discipline nature through the self-application of cosmetics. The story then documents "three young ladies" who "were exert- ing their rights upon improving nature, subduing her, with their powder puffs and little red tablets. As they did so, they talked; but their talk was interrupted as by the surge of an indrawing tide," the sound of a toilet flush- ing. As the women gossip about a man whose amorous behavior may lead him to "'be courtmartialled,'" the narrator records the ability of the natu- ral "tide" "to uncove[r] these little fish," the artificial women, and the "queer fishy smell that seems to permeate the whole watering place."[63]

The "queer fishy smell" of the watering place, or bathroom, is evidently the natural odor of decay that cannot be concealed with "powder puffs and little red tablets." The story concludes with Woolf's dire vision of what the town becomes at night: "The town has sunk down into the water. And the skeleton only is picked out in fairy lamps."[64] When nature dominates civilization—when a town appears "sunk down into the water"—artifice, the "fairy lamps," can only illuminate the denuded core of humanity: "the skeleton." Rather than a grim portrayal of death's inevitability, these sen- tences offer this otherwise humorous story's serious theme that civiliza- tion must strip itself of its constructed identity, especially in the face of more trenchant problems than how carefully one's facial powder is applied or whether a man's sexual behavior warrants legal prosecution. To do otherwise is, as Woolf's skeletal vision evokes, to cultivate race suicide caused by artificial decadence and not, as most degeneration theorists pro- posed, biophysical degeneration.[65] From her stoop on the public toilet, Woolf's narrator encapsulates Woolf's notion in "On Being Ill" that "it is only the recumbent who know what, after all, Nature is at no pains to conceal—that she in the end will conquer [. . .] but with the hook of life in us still we must wriggle" (*CE* 4:198). For Woolf, it is not by "conceal[ing]" but by being down, "recumbent" and "ill," that allows one the chance to "wriggle" within the necessarily agonizing process of being biological that Darwin calls the "Struggle for Existence" (*OS* 77)

"The Watering Place" extends the savage indictment of the cult of beauty that Woolf began in *Between the Acts* not only with its final scene but also with the character Mrs. Manresa, who envisions herself as a "wild child of nature" but who is too preoccupied with upholding her "refeened" image to engage the world around her, which shows how her "nature was somehow 'just human nature'" (*BTA* 29, 71). During the pageant play's "present day" scene, in fact, in which La Trobe forces the audience to reflect on itself by directing her actors to hold mirrors to the spectators, Manresa uses the mirrors to apply her makeup, missing entirely La Trobe's point that, as one of the servants at Pointz Hall thinks, "if it was painful, it was essential. There must be society" (*BTA* 26). A "woman of action" alone, Manresa wants to dominate nature with artifice, which is for Woolf tantamount to murdering nature (*BTA* 76). Through the example of such characters, Woolf rejects the cult of beauty in which Darwin and Hitler alike inculcate women and proposes in "Watering" that women cultivate themselves in rooms that expose their "queer fishy smell."[66]

As she does with *Between*'s "embrace," Woolf offers with this story's titular word *watering*—not to mention her diary's redacted word "p—ing"—a euphemism about obscenity that parodies the cult of sanitization that her narrator hears in the restroom. Both texts' euphemisms exemplify what Walkowitz calls "the tension between decent feelings and dissenting thought" in Woolf's work that produce "models of social critique that would resist social codification" (*BTA* 80). Woolf uses euphemism here in part to critique wartime propaganda's own sanitary euphemisms of health and heroism. Like David Jones, who in his long poem *In Parenthesis* (1937) mocks the technology of modern warfare for producing a "perfectly sanitary war," Woolf derides civilized decency as ethically indecent: as culpable for the violence it conceals with ethical platitudes or, in the case of "Watering," cosmetics.[67] To refuse this discussion is to relegate the ineluctable conclusion of biological being, what Woolf called the "tremendous experience" of death, to fodder for either egoistic ideals or the patronizing presumption that death is the failure of life (*DVW* 5:230). If Woolf's camp renderings of a couple's violent sex or a town's mass death disturb, then, it is because she does violence to our own attempts to sanitize death, attempts that are for her a violence to death—and the life that led to it—itself.

Public Intimacy

How queer the change is from private writing to public writing.
VIRGINIA WOOLF (*DVW* 5:261)

If "p—ing" is what happens in Woolf's public restroom stall, "f—ing" is what happens not only in her atavistic cave but also throughout the degenerate, theatrical world of *Between the Acts*. Woolf uses such euphemisms at the level of diction to place into relief the obscenity she depicts through dramatic form, including the obscenity of national and literary tradition. The novel's rising curtain, after all, makes theatre of Isa and Giles' intercourse, locating laughable and terrifying private acts on the public page and stage. Woolf offers this scene of "f—ing" as her own contribution to the literary and national histories she mocks in the pageant play, using the drama to concentrate—both distill and make public—the novel of interiority. Opposed to her view in *Three Guineas* that her "Society of Outsiders," "remaining outside, will experiment not with public means in public but with private means in private," the Society of Outsiders in the book that Woolf herself called "the wild, the experimental" literally remains outside, experimenting with private means in public both to strip privacy of its location in the self and to shock the public into a concentrated collectivity (*TG* 113; *DVW* 5:228).

The very title of *Between the Acts* suggests how Woolf uses the drama to distill particularities, for she changed the title from "Pointz Hall, the Pageant: the Play—finally [to] Between the Acts" (*DVW* 5:356). Moving from a specific location steeped in national identity through particular artistic forms to an abstract concept of liminality, the title's mutation allegorizes how Woolf's aesthetic of concentration propagates variety by despoiling singularity. Such variety, she writes of *Between*, includes "all lit. discussed in connection with real little incongruous living humour; & anything that comes into my head; but 'I' rejected: 'We' substituted [. . .] perpetual variety & change from intensity to prose. & facts—& notes" (*DVW* 5:135). With the "perpetual variety & change" of the novel's form, Woolf substitutes the singular "I" of modernist interiority with a collective "we" that feels the novel's "variety of moods," including "incongruous living humor."

Between's titular transformation also highlights Woolf's career-long fascination with the tension between the novel and the drama, about which she ultimately theorized a relationship. She claimed that "it's possible that the novel to us is what the drama was to the Greeks" and Elizabethans and valued especially their comedies' "very sharp delicate laughter."[68] When she goes on to compare "the comic passages" of Elizabethan plays with contemporary novels, Woolf claims that "the emotion [is] all split up, dissipated and then woven together, slowly and gradually massed into a whole, in the novel; the emotion concentrated, generalised, heightened in the play."[69] Woolf suggests here that the novel, which distills emotion from the general ("split up") to the particular ("massed into a whole"), might learn from the drama, especially comedy, how to distill and thereby proliferate emotion from the "concentrated" particular to the "generalised" plurality.

In "The Narrow Bridge of Art" (1927), Woolf explains how this generic concentration is both aesthetically and affectively queer. She mourns the loss of poetic drama from contemporary letters because drama can encompass "monstrous, hybrid, unmanageable emotions," "this discord, this incongruity, this sneer, this contrast, this curiosity, the quick, queer emotions": in short, "that queer conglomeration of incongruous things—the modern mind."[70] Because the novel has, she writes in *Room*, been burdened by "the dominance of the letter 'I' and the aridity [. . .] it cases within its shade" (94), the novel that survives literary tradition "will be dramatic, and yet not a play. It will be read, not acted. By what name we are to call it is not a matter of very great importance."[71]

Here Woolf encompasses the formal and epistemological premises of *Between*, which shall be a "monstrous, hybrid" book that, like the collective queer feeling it examines, defies taxonomy, or "what name we are to call it." On the structural level of narrative form, Woolf's dramatic theory of fiction shapes how *Between* conveys the conflict between individual and collective experience. Woolf outlines these effects in her uncompleted essay "Anon," which she began to write just after completing *Between* and which she intended to be a history of English literature. In the text, Woolf envisions an androgynous character named Anon, similar to the writer she had envisioned in *Room*, a "sometimes man; sometimes woman" who "lives a roaming life" singing "the call to our primitive instincts" (*ROO* 91–2; *GOM* 675). A metonymy for "the theatre," Anon represents the kind of atavistic, anti-identitarian self that Woolf wants, but purposefully fails, to produce in *Between* (*GOM* 678). "Anonymity was a great possession" in the age of drama, she argues, but modern literature requires that "the individual on the stage becomes more and more differentiated," such that "the theatre must be replaced by the theatre of the brain. The playwright is replaced by the man who writes a book. The audience is replaced by the reader. Anon is dead" (*GOM* 692, 693). Resurrecting Anon in *Between*'s theatrical form, Woolf also threatens Anon's anonymity with the novel form's focus on individuality, as evidenced by the pageant's playwright, who is both sexed and named—though only, importantly, surnamed. Identity's threat to Anon thus constitutes the formal and thematic drama of Woolf's novel.

Ironically, however, Woolf maintained that this conflict was best conveyed through the mode of comedy. She believed that "you can only get comedy by using the surface layer," but such surfaces are for her detritus to be stripped away, revealing "much deeper emotion than appears upon the surface" and "the most enduring form of life [in] scenes which are outwardly trivial" (*DVW* 4:347, 197). An admirer of Jane Austen's comedies, Woolf averred that such comedic stripping was an eminently feminist mode.[72] In her 1905 essay "The Value of Laughter," for example, Woolf writes that "comedy is of the sex of the graces and the muses," whereas tragedy's "decorous [. . .] spirit of solemnity" is male (*CE* 1:58). As it has throughout literary history, "comedy has a hard fight for it," Woolf believes, because laughter is said to be "an inarticulate utterance like the bark of a dog or the bleat of sheep, and it is beneath the dignity of a race that has made itself a language to express itself thus" (*CE* 1:58–9). Co-opting such misogyny, Woolf embraces the bestial, "inarticulate utterance" as a tool with which to humble, for "laughter more than anything else preserves our sense of proportion" (*CE* 1:59). Whereas men are burdened with the "hideous excrescences that have overgrown our modern life, the pomps and conventions and dreary solemnities," women possess, Woolf says, "a knife that both prunes and trains": the "flash of laughter which, like lightning, shrivels them [the excrescences] up and leaves the bones bare" (*CE* 60).[73]

Such pruning is central to Woolf's antifascist politics. In *Three Guineas*, she claims that "laughter as an antidote to dominance is perhaps indicated," laughter that allows one "to strip each statement of its [. . .] vanity motive [. . .] before you make up your mind which fact about politics to believe" (*TG* 182, 96). Just as laughter prunes fascism's vanity, generic hybridity dismantles fascist attempts to dominate variety with purity. Woolf in fact complains in her essay "Modern Fiction" (1925) that the writer "seems constrained [. . .] by some powerful and unscrupulous tyrant who has him in thrall to provide a plot, to provide comedy, tragedy, love, interest, and an air of probability embalming the whole."[74] Rejecting that tyrant's dictates, Woolf yearns for a style about which "it is impossible to say 'this is comic,' or 'that is tragic,'"[75] a style that might take the shape of formal opacity: As she writes, "Ease and freedom, the power to change and the power to grow, can only be preserved by obscurity" (*TG* 14).

The "obscurity" of *Between*'s formal structure ironically derives from its very light pageant play, which paratactically juxtaposes scenes from English comedies resembling texts like *As You Like It* and *Love for Love*. Woolf replicates the pageant's confusing parataxis at the level of her narrative's diegesis. In the novel's first fifty-three pages, an unidentified narrator reports the actions, speech, and interior thoughts of various characters (the latter through free indirect discourse). When the play begins, however, *Between* consists primarily of staged dialogue and of dialogue between and among the audience members in response to the play, itself an obscuring narratological technique since actors' and characters' speech often blurs together such that characters wonder, "was it, or was it not, the play?" (*BTA* 53). With intermittent narrative and stream-of-consciousness paragraphs, this dialogue continues for eighty-three pages; the text then reverts to narrative mediation in the remaining nineteen pages. Altogether, then, the play and characters' dialogue about the play—Isa says, "'I wish the play didn't run in my head'"—arguably occupies more space in *Between* than does the narrative reportage (*BTA* 78).[76]

Given this proportion, why, if Woolf thought that "Pointz Hall is to become in the end a play," did she frame that play within prose narrative (*DVW* 5:139)? The answer to this question resides in the novel's title, which invokes not only the plot's temporal location between two acts of world war but its structural division between two kinds of speech act: the mediated and the unmediated. Framed between its mediated narrative acts, the characters' increasingly unmediated dramatic speech—such that even scripted theatrical speech comes to resemble spontaneous public utterance—exposes them at their most individually and collectively concentrated forms. As Froula persuasively argues, "in the acts between the acts, and in the spectators' thoughts and feelings, pageant and novel seek a 'natural law' by which to build civilization's broken 'wall.'"[77] Unable to understand the play's paratactic structure, the audience members abandon private reflection and attempt to communicate verbally about the text's meaning; in doing so, they imitate the natural world around them, "the trees tossing and the birds swirling [who] seemed called out of their private lives [. . .] and made to take part" (*BTA* 129–30; 80–1).

Woolf uses the drama to elicit public feelings from her private characters, then, going so far as to represent their private thoughts in public form. When Giles "said (without words), 'I'm damnably unhappy,'" for example,

William Dodge and Isa "echoed" and "thought" in response "'So am I'" and "'I too,'" respectively (*BTA* 119). Violating novelistic privacy by publicizing the individual's thoughts as dramatic speech, Woolf allegorizes in this passage the conflict between the novel and the drama genres. In distilled, simple sentences, the passage reports only the audience's negative feelings. In accord with Woolf's comparison of these genres, the drama concentrates the novelistic characters' emotions such that Isa later realizes the pageant "was only there to beget emotion. There were only two emotions: love; and hate. There was no need to puzzle out the plot" (*BTA* 63). If, as Darwin writes, "laughter" is "analogous with weeping" because both release "superfluous nervous energy," Woolf strips her characters of superfluous affects with a play that enjoins them to feel in concentrated form.[78]

What La Trobe repeatedly calls the play's "failure" (*BTA* 68, 142) thus produces distilled, incongruous emotions in the audience and what Sontag would call a "naïve, or pure, Camp" aesthetic in the novel, one in which "the essential element is seriousness, a seriousness that fails. Of course, not all seriousness that fails can be redeemed as Camp. Only that which has the proper mixture of the exaggerated, the fantastic, the passionate, and the naïve" ("Notes" 59). La Trobe in all earnestness aims to create "a vision imparted [that] was relief from agony," and when that vision fails, she reacts in the most "exaggerated" and "passionate" of terms: "Blood seemed to pour from her shoes. This is death, death, death, she noted in the margin of her mind; when illusion fails" (*BTA* 68, 122). Since biological death does threaten the entire community, La Trobe's "fantastic" response appears laughably naïve, as does her literalist attempt at play's end to make the community reflect upon itself with mirrors. Although La Trobe wants in this scene "to expose them, as it were, to douche them, with present-time reality," her "douche" simply confuses her audience, who wonders, "if we're left asking questions, isn't it a failure, as a play?" (135). Since the British pageant play traditionally functioned to glorify empire, yet this play ends with La Trobe lecturing her audience about how they're *"Liars most of us. Thieves too,"* one might answer "yes" to the audience's question (*BTA* 127). But as a play whose camp failure yields the audience's public intimacy, the pageant succeeds.

As a character, La Trobe embodies the very camp aesthetic that her play produces. She "had the look of a commander pacing his deck" and "the attitude proper to an Admiral," for example, yet La Trobe captains a small community play whose props consist of "cardboard crowns, swords made of silver paper, turbans that were sixpenny dish cloths"—a night at the

Hippodrome this is not (*BTA* 43). La Trobe's entire life is in fact filled with failures: "Rumour said that she had kept a tea shop at Winchester; that had failed. She had been an actress. That had failed. She had bought a four-roomed cottage and shared it with an actress. They had quarrelled" (*BTA* 40). While she actually shared a bed with that actress, La Trobe— like Dodge, the novel's would-be gay male character—is never identified as a lesbian in the novel: She fails, one could say, to achieve that identity (*BTA* 143).

La Trobe is so prone to failure that one might call her a masochist, or a Darwinian feminist, for she continually seeks ways to abuse herself. This sentiment was dear to Woolf herself: In 1934, for example, after learning of Wyndham Lewis's latest decrial of her work in *Men Without Art* (1934), Woolf writes that "I am feeling the calm that always comes to me with abuse: my back is against the wall [. . .] the queer disreputable pleasure in being abused—in being a figure, in being a martyr. & so on" (*DVW* 4:251). Feeling powerless, backed up against the wall—the same phrase she uses to describe England in wartime and to describe how she does her "best work"—Woolf claims that "the feeling of being dismissed into obscurity is also pleasant & salutary," for abuse teaches her "to be supple & naked to the truth" (*DVW* 5:297, 189, 252). In "A Sketch of the Past," Woolf summarizes this view in aesthetic terms: She converts "moments [that] brought with them a peculiar horror and a physical collapse; they seemed dominant; myself passive" into a source of aesthetic pleasure and inspiration, such that "these sudden shocks [. . .] are now always welcome [. . .] And so I go on to suppose that the shock-receiving capacity is what makes me a writer." Violence thus teaches Woolf "that we—I mean all human beings—are connected with [. . .] the work of art [. . .] we are the words; we are the music; we are the thing itself."[79]

With an acute "shock-receiving capacity" herself, La Trobe takes a "queer disreputable pleasure in being abused" and dismisses herself into obscurity for much of the pageant, central though she is to its creation. If "she was an outcast," as the narrator reports, whom "Nature had somehow set [. . .] apart from her kind," La Trobe casts herself further into nature's kind as she barks orders at actors and audience alike from behind a tree (*BTA* 143, 53). Posed in "a stooping position" for much of the play, La Trobe is a diva without an audience, an admiral of a mutinous crew, a leader with only half a name. She is a camp failure as a character who embodies the dialectic between states of particularity and generality, identity and anonymity, that she, like Woolf, attempts to communicate with art wherein "all human beings—are connected" (*BTA* 141).

The Comedy of Natures

In the earlier scene, man's impotence to contend with nature made his life brutish and brief.

To-day his very command over nature, so admirably and marvellously won, has become his greatest peril.

GEORGE TREVELYAN, *History of England*[80]

Both of the plays that La Trobe composes in *Between* could be called comedies of nature insofar as that mode's plot resembles a modernist degeneration narrative. In their own discordance—the first more humorous, the second more harrowing—the plays comprise *Between*'s own comedy of nature and proliferate the "infinitely varied diversities" and "variety of moods" that both Darwin and Woolf see in the concentrated world. Proliferating natures in nature—a material world where non-self-identity reigns supreme—Woolf parodies what Max Horkheimer and Theodor Adorno call fascism's endeavor "to place oppressed nature's rebellion against domination directly in the service of domination."[81] Bearing out Stephen Barber's claim that *Between the Acts* "vigorously confronts the homophobic impulse of modern British culture to extinguish queer existence," the more that nature dominates in this novel, the more that its queer natures rebel against social domination.[82]

In point of fact, despite their attempts to escape from nature, *Between*'s audience members watch the pageant play outdoors, which allows nature to interrupt the performance repeatedly, such that the natural and the theatrical fuse.[83] Most remarkably, just when La Trobe likens the play to death for failing, a herd of cows, as a campy *deus ex machina*, "t[akes] up the burden" and begins to bellow, for "one had lost her calf": "From cow after cow came the same yearning bellow. The whole world was filled with dumb yearning" (*BTA* 96). This "primeval voice" transitions from tragic mourning to comic perversity, however, when "the whole herd caught the infection. Lashing their tails, blobbed like pokers, they tossed their heads high, plunged and bellowed, as if Eros had planted his dart in their flanks and goaded them to fury. The cows annihilated the gap; bridged the distance; filled the emptiness and continued the emotion" (*BTA* 96). Tragic, comic, and above all theatrical, Woolf's campy cows bridge the gaps in La Trobe's paratactic play: The missing link in this literary history is nature.

Violating the play's attempt to consolidate human history, the cows are what Adorno would call the pageant play's "wound": They are the play's feeling for nature, for they show how "the reticence of nature was undone, and the barriers which should divide Man the Master from the Brute were dissolved" (*BTA* 125). The cows dissolve that barrier by spreading their affective "infection" to the audience: "suddenly the cows stopped; lowered their heads, and began browsing. Simultaneously the audience lowered their heads and read their programmes" (*BTA* 96). Ruining the play, the cows ruin the audience's grip on their anthropocentrism: The audience becomes a herd led not by a dictator but by nature, specifically its incongruous, theatrically displayed feelings. By offering such scenes in which "nature takes her part," Woolf allows nature to take back its claim to humanity: as La Trobe muses in the text's early typescript, "The great bosom of nature, she thought, takes our failures; but after all, she needs them."[84]

In contrast to Marina MacKay's claim that *Between*'s "closing emphasis on disintegration and fracture is so extreme that no centre could hold these characters together," then, the novel depicts nature as the unstable "centre" to which its failed characters concentrate.[85] Locating the drama of identity and its concentration in the dash between the repeated words "*Unity—Dispersity*," *Between* depicts a social world in constant vacillation between collectivity and individuality (*BTA* 136). When the audience begins to sing the pageant's refrain "*Dispersed are we*," then, they ultimately sing a version of Woolf's concentrated camp: they laughably and lovingly sing together about their own fracture, producing at play's end what reads like a collective stream of consciousness (*BTA* 66, 134–5). As Woolf's most innovative formal attempt to collapse the novel and the drama, this moment employs the most individually concentrated of modernist techniques to unite and disperse the text's characters. Such oscillation between civilization and nature, individuality and collectivity leads Mrs. Swithin to reflect that "sheep, cows, grass, trees, ourselves—all are one. If discordant, producing harmony [. . .] the agony of the particular sheep, cow, or human being is necessary [. . .] *all* is harmony, could we hear it," for we do not live in ourselves, she realizes: "We live in others" (*BTA* 119, 47).[86]

With her first comedy, La Trobe helps the audience to "hear" Woolf's belief that "agony [. . .] is necessary" to produce "harmony." With her second play, La Trobe helps herself to hear to it. Her humiliation after the first comedy fails leads La Trobe to degenerate emotionally: "What she wanted, like that carp [. . .] was darkness in the mud; a whisky and soda at the pub; and coarse words descending like maggots through the waters" (*BTA* 138). Absorbing the shock of her failure, La Trobe becomes enthusiastic about a new play but cannot conceive of its language: "'I should group them,' she murmured, 'here.' It would be midnight; there would be two figures, half concealed by a rock. The curtain would rise. What would the first words be? the words escaped her" (*BTA* 143). But when she looks on a picture of "a cow in a stable; also at a cock and a hen," La Trobe finds her inspiration for those words in degeneration: "Words of one syllable sank down into the mud. [. . .] The mud became fertile. Words rose above the intolerably laden dumb oxen plodding through the mud. Words without meaning—wonderful words" (*BTA* 144).

Able now to "hear it," La Trobe finds the "more primitive, more obscene" language—words fresh from the mud—with which Woolf writes *Between* and with which La Trobe composes her new play, the play that closes *Between* and that unites, by concentrating the conflict between, the novel and the drama. In accord with Horkheimer and Adorno's belief that "only when apprehended as knowledge does [nature] become the urge of the living toward peace, the consciousness which, from the beginning, has inspired unerring resistance to *Führer* and collective," La Trobe's temporary degeneration—her submission to the overpowering facts of nature—yields her regeneration, her ability to find peace within her failures.[87] *Between*'s final sentence, "They spoke," thus offers La Trobe's hopeful gesture that her comedies of nature will yield a new dialogue about our objects of concentration. Produced by her two comedies of love and hate, this dialogue might begin with the word "peace." As Isa earlier thinks, "peace was the third emotion. Love. Hate. Peace. Three emotions made the ply of human life" (*BTA* 64). It is Woolf's queer ambition with *Between the Acts* to transform Isa's thought into speech so that we might "hear it," perhaps even say it: so that peace might become the object of her public's concentration.

NOTES

My thanks to Sunder Ganglani, Laura Haupt, Margaret Homans, Kathryn Lofton, Kate Marshall, and Samantha Pinto for their invaluable suggestions about earlier drafts of this essay.

1. Virginia Woolf, *The Diary of Virginia Woolf*, 5 vols. (London: Chatto & Windus, 1984), 5:336–7; hereafter abbreviated *DVW*.

2. Virginia Woolf quoted in Hermione Lee, *Virginia Woolf* (New York: Vintage, 1999), 744.

3. Virginia Woolf, *The Letters of Virginia Woolf*, 6 vols., ed. Nigel Nicolson (London: Harcourt Brace Jovanovich, 1979), 6:486.

4. While I do not intend to postulate about the motivations for and meaning of Woolf's death, it is worth noting that, while taking one's life could be one expression of the will to overcome egotism and self-containment that, I am arguing, Woolf endorsed, it would also foreclose her ethic of active concentration. Woolf's personal records and her final novel

suggest that, whereas death marks the end of distraction and concentration both, the threat of death—the affective and psychic violation of the ego's boundaries—might motivate concentration. For a more sustained analysis of how Woolf represents in her life and writing "a division between a feeling of selfhood and a feeling of selflessness" through tropes of death and sexuality, see James Naremore's *The World without a Self: Virginia Woolf and the Novel* (New Haven: Yale University Press, 1973), 248.

5. Natania Rosenfeld, *Outsiders Together: Virginia and Leonard Woolf* (Princeton, N.J.: Princeton University Press, 2000), 9.

6. "Concentrate, *v*," *Oxford English Dictionary Online*, 2nd edition, March 18, 2010.

7. Patricia Klindienst Joplin, "The Authority of Illusion: Feminism and Fascism in Virginia Woolf's *Between the Acts*," *South Central Review* 6, no. 2 (Summer 1989): 88–104, 95.

8. Virginia Woolf, *Moments of Being*, ed. Jeanne Schulkind, 2nd edition (London: Hogarth, 1985), 147.

9. Joplin's excellent essay is an important exception to this critical trend, for Joplin argues that *Between* "legitimates the use of violence to achieve unity" (98), especially violence against "the passive, falsely neutral self" (99). Though I concur with much of Joplin's argument, I am attempting in this essay to clarify how Woolf depicts passivity not as something to be violated but as itself a form of violence against the self that might yield a concentrated unity. See Mariana MacKay's *Modernism and World War II* (Cambridge: Cambridge University Press, 2007), 18, and Jed Esty's *A Shrinking Island: Modernism and National Culture in England* (Princeton: Princeton University Press, 2004), 56, for persuasive examinations of the novel's critique of high modernist forms and themes.

10. "Concentrate, *v*," *Oxford English Dictionary Online*.

11. Charles Darwin, *The Descent of Man, and Selection in Relation to Sex*, 2 vols., 1871 edition (Princeton, N.J.: Princeton University Press, 1981), 1:113, 18. Hereafter abbreviated *DOM*. For more extended definitions and exemplifications of Darwin's theory of reversion, see *DOM* 1:122–130 and 280. See, too, the second volume of Darwin's *The Variation of Animals and Plants under Domestication*, 2 vols. (Cambridge: Cambridge University Press, 2010), in which Darwin aligns the terms "reversion" and "atavism" (27) and even claims that "the fertilised germ" subject to "the doctrine of reversion" is "perhaps the most wonderful object in nature" because it contains so many possibilities for variation that "lie ready to be evolved under certain known or unknown conditions" (61).

12. Perhaps not coincidentally, Darwin attends to the affect of sympathy more than any other emotion in *Descent*, claiming that sympathy grounds

the moral sense that distinguishes *homo sapiens* from the progenitors with whom he otherwise aims to correlate humans (*DOM* 2:394). Like Woolf, Darwin believes that sympathy "is one of the most important elements of the social instincts" (*DOM* 2:393) yet is a somewhat masochistic emotion: "the basis of sympathy lies in our strong retentiveness of former states of pain or pleasure [. . .] we are thus impelled to relieve the sufferings of another, in order that our own painful feelings may be at the same time relieved" (*DOM* 1:81).

13. Virginia Woolf, *Between the Acts* (New York: Harcourt, 2008), 135; hereafter abbreviated *BTA*.

14. My focus here on the degenerate side of modernist literature shares with Scott Herring's *Queering the Underworld* (Chicago: University of Chicago Press, 2007) an attempt to understand how modernist writers "sidestep sexual group identifications" (14). Herring examines a queer modernist literary tradition in which "queer" denotes not just the non-normative but the verbs "to puzzle" or "to spoil, put out of order," especially "to spoil (a person's) undertaking" (21). Whereas Herring proves how such spoilage undermines any attempt at community (22), however, Woolf creates a society of the spoiled: a society where feeling degenerate is a vehicle for social concentration.

15. Woolf repeatedly tropes "living near to the bone" throughout her diary entries of this period. Most notably, after the bombing of her home in Tavistock Square during the Blitz, Woolf writes that "its odd, the relief at losing possessions. I shd like to start life, in peace, almost bare" (*DVW* 5:332). One of the few possessions that Woolf recovered from this bombing was a collection of Darwin's writings (331).

16. As revealed in *Pointz Hall: The Earlier and Later Typescripts of* Between the Acts, ed. Mitchell A. Leaska (New York: University Publications, 1983), hereafter abbreviated *PH*, Woolf enacted such emotional distillation in each draft of the novel. In general, Woolf made the text more humorous and less violent. As discussed earlier in this essay, for example, the novel's conclusion first ended with Isa and Giles intending a far more violent encounter than their ultimate "fight." Moreover, the three emotions that Isa finally feels— "love, hate, peace"—were initially "four emotions [that] made the ply of man's life" in the drafts, where love and hate remained constant and were coupled alternately with "fear," "death," and "sorrow" (*PH* 105, 103–5). In the novel's final iteration, Woolf distills these negative feelings to "hate," which (like love) could but need not produce fear, death, and sorrow. Correcting her emotions' negative imbalance, Woolf focalizes how the incongruity between love and hate might produce "peace," a pacifist vision that relies not just on a concentration of emotional states but on the

simultaneously positive and negative emotions that the camp aesthetic enjoins.

17. Woolf could not have known of Hitler's Final Solution, announced in 1942, nor of the extermination camps; however, concentration camps that held political prisoners, Jews, homosexuals, and other persecuted people were beginning to be used for eugenic cleansing when Woolf finished *Between*. One might nonetheless question the ethical or, more simply, the analytical use of contemplating Woolf's relation to the concentration camps if she not only did not live to know about their ultimate horror but did not herself experience the camps. Such an objection would rely, as Amy Hungerford writes in *The Holocaust of Texts: Genocide, Literature, and Personification* (Chicago: University of Chicago Press, 2003), on the trend in Holocaust studies wherein "memory (the knowledge of what we have experienced) is privileged over learning," a position that limits imagination to identity (155). Yet "there is reason to believe that a just society requires imagination," not just memory, Hungerford writes, on the logic that "we must find not ourselves in the other (or the other in ourselves) but the other as we can know them without being them" (157). In my own imaginative endeavor to understand how Woolf aestheticizes WWII in *Between the Acts*, I am analyzing not only Woolf's experience of the concentration camps, being placed in which seemed to her an acute threat, but her imagination of them—one that breaches an ethics of memory in the name of an ethics of imagination.

18. In *Scientific and Esoteric Studies in Sexual Degeneration in Mankind and in Animals*, trans. Ulrich Van Der Horst (New York: Anthropological Press, 1932), Charles Samson Féré distinguished degeneration from atavism (29), but Cesare Lombroso—one of the first proponents of atavistic theory—held the majority view by, in texts like *Genio e follia* (Genius and Insanity) (1864) and *L'uomo delinquente* (Criminal Man) (1876), aligning degenerates with prior forms of biological development, whether in non-human animal or human stages (Daniel Pick, *Faces of Degeneration: A European Disorder, c. 1848–1918* [Cambridge: Cambridge University Press, 1989], 120). Darwin himself did not equate degeneracy and atavism: For him, reversion could be beneficial, destructive, or neutral, depending on the variation (*DOM* 1:124, 236). In his 1895 polemic *Degeneration* (Lincoln: University of Nebraska Press, 1993), Max Nordau voiced his agreement with Lombroso while expanding the definition of degeneracy so capaciously that it could include nearly anything that evoked a negative feeling (555–6). As Sander Gilman claims, "Degeneracy became as key for explaining the negative moments of human history as it was for explaining evolutionary regression in biology" (*Difference and Pathology: Stereotypes of Sexuality, Race, and Madness* [Ithaca:

Cornell University Press, 1985], 205). In its ultimate capaciousness, the term *degenerate* came to denote in the 20th century—and still denotes today—a qualitative mode of experience rather than an identity: From a scientific perspective, degeneracy can refer to a process of biophysical enervation and/ or reversion; and from an aesthetic perspective, degeneracy denotes a range of qualities associated with the negative but especially qualities (sexual license, aesthetic experimentation, racial otherness) that contradict dominant expectations for civilized culture. For more on modernist theories of degeneracy and atavism, see Seitler as well as Eugene Talbot's *Degeneracy: Its Causes, Signs and Results* (New York: Scribner's, 1898).

19. In *Comedy and the Woman Writer: Woolf, Spark, and Feminism* (London and Lincoln: University of Nebraska Press, 1983), Judy Little persuasively contends that *Between* offers a "festive comedy" that "celebrates th[e] capacity of nature, and of human nature, for regeneration" (97); in "The Politics of Comic Modes in Virginia Woolf's *Between the Acts*" (*PMLA* 105, no. 2 [March 1990]: 273–85), Melba Cuddy-Keane similarly argues that "*Between the Acts* lies primarily within the comic genre" (275). Yet Jed Esty calls the novel "a tragic document of the liberal imagination under pressure, forced to confront the political limitations of the 'English way'" (98), and Mitchell Leaska nominates it as no less than "the longest suicide note in the English language" (*PH* 451). Despite their diametrically opposing views, these scholars are not only writing about the same novel but highlighting crucial elements of this incongruous text that mutually inform Woolf's vision of a queer feminist politics. In *Fiction and Repetition: Seven English Novels* (Cambridge: Harvard University Press, 1982), J. Hillis Miller attends most faithfully to this dual sentiment when he writes that "*Between the Acts* is throughout, especially 662 in the pageant, a work of outrageous and hilarious parody [. . .] Parody is repetition as praise, but it is destruction too" (229).

20. Virginia Woolf, *The Moment and Other Essays* (London: Hogarth Press, 1952), 33.

21. Aristotle, *Poetics*, trans. S. H. Butcher (New York: Hill and Wang, 1961), 76.

22. Charles Darwin, *The Origin of Species*, 1872 edition (London: Collier MacMillan, 1962), 28, 91; hereafter abbreviated *OS*. As Michael North claims in *Machine-Age Comedy* (Oxford: Oxford University Press, 2009), any attempt at defining the comedic genre is challenging, if not impossible, because its manifestations have changed throughout literary and theatrical history—itself a subject of *Between*'s pageant play (15). For the purposes of this argument, nonetheless, it is worth noting that the mode classically features several of *Between*'s formal structures. In terms of character,

comedy typically focuses upon a society rather than individuals such that, in
narrative terms, comedy lacks a stand-out protagonist. Comedic societies
consist, Aristotle records in the *Poetics*, of base characters: "Comedy aims at
representing men as worse [. . .] Tragedy as better than in actual life" (52).
The comedy is "an imitation of characters of a lower type," then, where
"lower" is determined by "some defect or ugliness which is not painful or
destructive" (59). Because of this focus, comedy has, in the history of
Western literature and performance, assumed an inferior role to tragedy,
that "highest" of dramatic forms, ironically because tragedy charts the
degeneration of a privileged (typically male) character to ignominy (118). In
terms of plot, comedy presents a conflict that destabilizes and then restores
the status quo with which the plot opens (77). Comedy may be deemed
structurally atavistic, then, for it returns to its origin rather than develops
toward some inevitable telos, the linear goal of tragedy (77). See James
English's *Comic Transactions: Literature, Humor, and the Politics of Community
in Twentieth-Century Britain* (Ithaca, N.Y.: Cornell University Press, 1994)
for a compelling examination of comedy in British modernism, including in
Between the Acts, and Joseph Meeker's *The Comedy of Survival: Literary Ecology
and a Play Ethic* (Tucson: University of Arizona Press, 1997) for an insightful
discussion of the structural similarities between comedy and evolution.

   23. Darwin bases this claim on the evidence of innocuous racial differences, which show *homos sapiens* to "have remained extremely variable,
owing, as it seems, to their variations being of an indifferent nature, and
consequently to their having escaped the action of natural selection" (*DOM*
1:249).

   24. Following Woolf's lead, I avoid the term "tragicomedy" to describe
this novel not only because that mode has proven even more difficult to
define in literary history than tragedy and comedy but because no definition
of the mode attends to the plot reversal I am describing here, wherein
tragedy's plot is made comedic. The most standard definitions of tragicomedy are that it features tragedy's danger without its deaths (*Between* features
several reports of death and a bloody murder); that it reverses the roles of
gods and slaves (*Between* abjures the god role, or elevation, altogether to
propose total degradation); and that it envisions a yet unrealized future,
whereas Woolf gives her characters that future in the atavistic past. See
Verna Foster's *The Name and Nature of Tragicomedy* (Aldershot: Ashgate,
2004) for further discussion of the genre.

   25. *BTA* 63; Dana Seitler, *Atavistic Tendencies: The Culture of Science in
American Modernity* (Minneapolis: University of Minneapolis Press, 2008),
127.

   26. North, *Machine-Age Comedy*, 5.

27. Ibid., 22.

28. Virginia Woolf, *Three Guineas* (London: Harcourt Brace & Company, 1938), 108; hereafter abbreviated *TG*.

29. Fabio Cleto, "Introduction: Queering the Camp," in *Camp: Queer Aesthetics and the Performing Subject*, ed. Fabio Cleto (Ann Arbor: University of Michigan Press, 1999), 1–42, 4.

30. Susan Sontag, "Notes on Camp," in *Camp: Queer Aesthetics and the Performing Subject*, ed. Fabio Cleto (Ann Arbor: University of Michigan Press, 1999), 51–65, 57, 58, 63, 62, 63, 65; hereafter abbreviated "Notes."

31. *TG* 108; Esty, *Shrinking Island*, 98.

32. By describing Darwin's theory of nature as queer, I mean to highlight that Darwin theorizes the material world as endlessly mutable and non-normative (defiant of any telos or regulatory standard) and therefore inclusive of what would by any era's terms of sexual normativity be deemed non-normative sexual feeling. In the past few years, a spate of scholarship written largely from an ecocritical perspective has addressed the concept of a "queer nature," including Myra J. Hird's "Naturally Queer" (*Feminist Theory* 5, no. 1 [2004]: 85–9), Timothy Morton's "Queer Ecology" (*PMLA* 125, no. 2 [March 2010], 1–19), and Catriona Mortimer-Sandilands and Bruce Erickson's edited volume *Queer Ecologies: Sex, Nature, Politics, Desire* (Bloomington: Indiana University Press, 2010). While I am in sympathy with such work, I aim in this essay and the larger project from which it emerges to examine less the eco-political than the literary historical and queer theoretical implications of Darwin's theory of the material world.

33. As Isherwood exemplifies in his 1939 novel *Goodbye to Berlin* (in *The Berlin Stories* [New York: New Directions, 1963]), German cabaret performances featured similar blends of horror and humor to ridicule the Nazi regime, which quickly closed the cabarets upon its rise to power. Though Woolf abjures those cabarets' investment in camp's material trappings, it is worth noting that Isherwood's descriptions of Sally Bowles's nails as "hard, bright, ugly little beetles" (29) and her coat as the "skin of a mangy old dog" (44) anticipate Woolf's atavistic aesthetic. Though they lack Woolf's comedy of nature, a variety of artistic texts have used concentrated camp to examine the Holocaust. In *Laughter in Hell: The Use of Humor during the Holocaust* (London: Jason Aronson, 1991), Steve Lipman records a substantial portion of such texts, including Charlie Chaplin's *The Great Dictator* (1940)—which was itself subject to ethical scrutiny, including Chaplin's own after the war (237)—Tadeusz Borowski's short story collection *This Way for the Gas, Ladies and Gentlemen* (1948), Mel Brooks' slapstick film and Broadway musical *The Producers* (1968, 2001), Peter Barnes' play *Auschwitz* (1978), Art Spiegelman's *Maus I* (1986) and *Maus II* (1991), Robert Benigni's film *Life is Beautiful* (1997),

and Jonathan Safran Foer's *Everything Is Illuminated* (2002) and *Extremely Loud and Incredibly Close* (2005). Rodney Ackland's 1951 play *Absolute Hell* (London: Oberon Books, 1990) is of particularly relevant note, since it features a group of queer characters that gathers in a bar after WWII to talk about the relationship between the prison camps and the camp aesthetic, a relationship one character synthesizes as "horror camp" (36, 38, 56).

34. Lipman, *Laughter in Hell*, 9; Viktor Frankl, *Man's Search for Meaning: An Introduction to Logotherapy*, trans. Ilse Lasch (Boston: Beacon Press, 1962), 78. Frankl warns against pious attitudes toward camp victims "mingled with sentiment and pity" (2) and records that the camps were filled with a rigorous ethic of humor, even as (and surely because) "the average prisoner felt himself utterly degraded" (62). "Humor was another of the soul's weapons in the fight for self-preservation," he writes, as evidenced by Lipman's record of how children in the camps played games like "Gas Chamber" and "Gestapo Agent" and how prisoners formed a clandestine theatrical group in Dachau, scribing and performing plays with lines like "Everything is hell / Soon it will get well / Through this magic word: humor, humor!" (42, 14, 72). Such humor was necessary, Frankl writes, in the face of the apathy that often accrued from witnessing so much suffering. Indeed, "disgust, horror and pity are emotions that our spectator could not really feel any more" because death and decay "became such commonplace sights" (20). Humor allowed a kind of ironic shock to the apathetic system, Frankl avers, "a trick learned while mastering the art of living" (43). Frankl also records that camp life required a "retreat to a more primitive form of mental life": one stripped of civilized provisions wherein "the effort of having to concentrate on just saving one's skin led to a total disregard of anything not serving that purpose," which "explain[s] the prisoners' complete lack of sentiment" (27, 32).

35. Erin Carlston, *Thinking Fascism: Sapphic Modernism and Fascist Modernity* (Stanford, Calif.: Stanford University Press, 1998), 77.

36. Jonathan Dollimore, "Post/Modern: On the Gay Sensibility, or the Pervert's Revenge on Authenticity," in *Camp: Queer Aesthetics and the Performing Subject*, ed. Fabio Cleto (Ann Arbor: University of Michigan Press, 1999), 221–36, 224.

37. Donna Haraway, *Primate Visions: Gender, Race, and Nature in the World of Modern Science* (New York: Routledge, 1989), 280.

38. Virginia Woolf, *A Room of One's Own* (London: Hogarth Press, 1991), 31–34; hereafter abbreviated *ROO*.

39. Woolf, *Letters*, 6:294.

40. Christine Froula, *Virginia Woolf and the Bloomsbury Avant-Garde* (New York: Columbia University Press, 2005), 220; Rebecca Walkowitz,

Cosmopolitan Style: Modernism Beyond the Nation (New York: Columbia University Press, 2006), 81.

41. Walkowitz, *Cosmopolitan*, 81

42. Pamela Robertson, "What Makes the Feminist Camp?," in *Camp: Queer Aesthetics and the Performing Subject*, ed. Fabio Cleto (Ann Arbor: University of Michigan Press, 1999), 266–82, 276.

43. Leo Bersani, *Is the Rectum a Grave? and Other Essays* (Chicago: University of Chicago Press, 2010), 27, 30, 25. This understanding of art's active passivity coincides with Walkowitz's and Sianne Ngai's examinations of how, based on Adorno's postulations about aesthetic autonomy, 20th-century Anglo-American art becomes most politicized through its feelings of "limited or suspected agency" (Walkowitz, *Cosmopolitan*, 4) and a "growing awareness of its inability to significantly change that society—a powerlessness that then becomes the privileged object of the newly autonomous art's 'guilty' self-reflection" (Ngai 2). See also Jennifer Fleissner's *Women, Compulsion, Modernity* (Chicago: University of Chicago Press, 2004) for its related analysis of female agency in American naturalist fiction.

44. *DVW* 5:245, 263; Adolf Hitler, *Mein Kampf*, trans. James Murphy (Mumbai: Jaico Publishing House, 2008), 268; hereafter abbreviated *MK*. See Laura Frost's *Sex Drives: Fantasies of Fascism in Literary Modernism* (Ithaca, N.Y.: Cornell University Press, 2002) for an examination of how the rhetorics of atavism and degeneration were used by a variety of European forces in World Wars I and II (16–18).

45. Adolf Hitler quoted in Simon LeVay, *Queer Science: The Use and Abuse of Research into Homosexuality* (Cambridge: MIT Press, 1996), 38. Hitler above all proposes that miscegenation must be prevented. "Those reproductive habits which on the one hand are determined by social pressure and, on the other, by financial considerations," he says, "lea[d] to absolute degeneration" (*MK* 226). His solution for such socially based matrimonial arrangements—those that lead to cross-race and cross-class reproduction—is for the State to sanction marriage "as an institution which is called upon to produce creatures made in the likeness of the Lord and not create monsters that are a mixture of man and ape" (*MK* 365).

46. Darwin, *Variation* 2:247, 245.

47. Assuming the role of a sexologist, Hitler details the horrors of and remedies for prostitution and syphilis, which are problems "sufficient to bring about the destruction of the nation, slowly but surely" (*MK* 225). Because of this threat, Hitler writes that "the problem of fighting venereal disease should be placed before the public—not as a task for the nation but as *the* main task." To remedy venereal disease, Hitler proposes early marriages, which will allow men to settle down early; women's choices are

irrelevant, "for women are, after all, only passive subjects in this matter" (*MK* 228).

48. Donald Childs, *Modernism and Eugenics* (Cambridge: Cambridge University Press, 2001), 28–31.

49. Specifically, while composing *Between*, Woolf was not only exposed to the experience of her close friend Lytton Strachey, who was a member of the British Society for the Study of Sex and Psychology, but met with feminist and sexologist Marie Stopes; "read all Havelock Ellis," whose work she found "teased and tired" (*DVW* 5:270); and read Freud for the first time, despite having published him for years. Although scholars have focused profitably on the implications of Woolf's reading of Freud while she wrote *Between the Acts* (see Cuddy-Keane, "Politics of Comic Modes," 274), few scholars have considered her perhaps even more remarkable attention to Darwin's work while composing the novel. For analyses that begin to broach Woolf's engagement with evolutionary science in this novel, see Harriet Blodgett's "The Nature of *Between the Acts*" (*Modern Language Studies* 13, no. 3 [Summer 1983]: 27–37, 36); Gillian Beer's *Virginia Woolf: The Common Ground* (Edinburgh: Edinburgh University Press, 1996); and Elizabeth Lambert's "Evolution and Imagination in *Pointz Hall* and *Between the Acts*" (in *Virginia Woolf: Themes and Variations*, ed. Vara Neverow-Turk and Mark Hussey [New York: Pace University Press, 1993], 25–32).

50. Woolf's call for a Darwinian feminist epistemology here anticipates Grosz's contemporary intervention into feminist politics in both *The Nick of Time: Politics, Evolution and the Untimely* (Australia: Allen & Unwin, 2004) and *Time Travels: Feminism, Nature, Power* (Durham, N.C.: Duke University Press, 2005). Writes Grosz, "A reconfiguration of nature as dynamic, of matter as culturally productive, of time as a force of proliferation, is thus central to the ways feminism itself may be able to move beyond the politics of equalization to more actively embrace a politics affirmative of difference elaborated in the most dynamic forms of feminist theory today" (*Nick of Time* 72). Grosz's study insists perhaps too limitedly, however, on what she calls Darwin's being "one of the few thinkers of the nineteenth century to prefigure, not simply an egalitarian feminism, but a feminism, or perhaps more broadly, an ontology of sexual difference" wherein such binary difference is "irreducible" (10, 67). This irreducibility would appear to defy Grosz's (let alone Darwin's own) claims to nature's non-binary variability. As Joan Roughgarden has more recently and extensively in *Evolution's Rainbow: Diversity, Gender, and Sexuality in Nature and People* (Los Angeles: University of California Press, 2004), Grosz acknowledges, after all, that sexual selection "produces variations—the intersexes—that lie between bifurcated categories," such that "the posthuman future is more likely to be

sexually differentiated (in whatever form) than anything else we recognize in the present" (*Nick of Time* 67).

51. Giles kills the animals because the snake-toad looks to him like "birth the wrong way round—a monstrous inversion" (69). With his heteronormative, masculinist logic about right ways to reproduce, Giles condemns "inversion"—a *fin-de-siecle* sexological term for queerness—and thereby the novel's queer characters. Giles specifically targets William Dodge, a man whom Woolf refuses to taxonomize as homosexual but whom Giles thinks of as a "perversion" and who is elsewhere described (sometimes self-described) as a "half-breed" (34), "a toady" (42), a "half-man," and "a flickering, mind-divided little snake in the grass" (51). Woolf, in fact, denies her characters the ability to name Dodge's "perversion" by anything other than these bestial labels (42), a fact that coincides with Stephen Barber's claim that *Between* "stages a deliberate resistance to regulatory procedures of labeling homosexuality by giving the name 'Dodge' [. . .] to a gay character" ("Lip-Reading: Woolf's Secret Encounters," in *Novel Gazing: Queer Readings in Fiction*, ed. Eve Kosofsky Sedgwick [Durham, N.C.: Duke University Press, 1997], 401–3, 403). Further buttressing Barber's claim, Woolf changed a sentence about Dodge in the early typescript of *Between* from "Can you condemn people for their sexuality?" to "Can you condemn people for the way they feel?" (*PH* 81). Rejecting the identitarian terms on which sexuality has been regulated and condemned since the late nineteenth century, Woolf prefers to think of sex in terms of mutable affectional states rather than any particular taxonomic "sexuality."

52. Frost, *Sex Drives*, 130. For helpful examinations of modernist conflations of women with a passive conception of nature that resonates in contemporary critical theory, see Grosz, *Time Travels* (46) and Rita Felski's *The Gender of Modernity* (Cambridge: Harvard University Press, 1995; 38–9).

53. Although this phrase may seem to be a contradiction in anti-identitarian and identitarian terms, I mean "queer feminism" to be aligned with Woolf's own hybrid politics, that which acts on behalf of historical political outsiders, even as it anticipates a vision beyond the need for such political action. Woolf envisions, as Grosz describes, a feminist theory that engages "the struggle to render more mobile, fluid, an transformable the means by which the female subject is produced and represented" (*Time Travels*, 193).

54. Theodor Adorno, *Aesthetic Theory*, trans. Robert Hullot-Kentor (Minneapolis: University of Minnesota Press, 1997), 71, 62–3; hereafter abbreviated *AT*. Adorno claims that art that has a "feeling for nature" does not master nature rationally but temporarily suspends its inevitable loss in the polymorphous realm of historical feeling (71). Indeed, Adorno, like

Darwin, posits that that which derives from nature, "purportedly ahistorical, is at its core historical" (67). Art's feeling for nature—the suspension of loss, what Woolf might call a moment of concentration—is therefore, in Adorno's view, "all the more compelling for its ephemeralness": It is, like camp, both hopeful and sorrowful at once (71).

55. Virginia Woolf, *Collected Essays*, 5 vols. (London: Hogarth Press, 1967), 4:193, 195; hereafter abbreviated *CE*. This sentiment is not actually new to Woolf, though it might be newly expressed in her fiction of this era. In a book review as early as 1918, after all, Woolf writes, "Perhaps it is coarseness—the quality that is the most difficult of all for the educated to come by—that is lacking. By coarseness we mean something as far removed from vulgarity as can be. We mean something vehement, full-throated, carrying down in its rush sticks and stones and fragments of human nature pell-mell" (*Contemporary Writers* [New York: Mariner, 1976], 89).

56. The fact that La Trobe writes the play at novel's end is curiously overlooked in Woolf scholarship. Margaret Homans's Introduction to *Virginia Woolf: A Collection of Critical Essays* (ed. Margaret Homans [Englewood Cliffs, N.J.: Prentice Hall, 1993], 1–11) offers the most sustained examination of La Trobe's second play as a play of which I am aware (10–11).

57. Caryl Flinn, "The Deaths of Camp," in *Camp: Queer Aesthetics and the Performing Subject*, ed. Fabio Cleto (Ann Arbor: University of Michigan Press, 1999), 433–57, 436. Esty, *Shrinking Island*, 59.

58. Jane Marcus, *Virginia Woolf and the Languages of Patriarchy* (Bloomington: Indiana University Press, 1987), 77.

59. (*OS* 25); In keeping with his ambiguity about the precise origin of the species, in fact, Darwin maintains in *Descent* that, "some extremely remote progenitor of the whole vertebrate kingdom appears to have been hermaphrodite or androgynous" (*DOM* 1:207). The most precise—yet still tentative ("appears")—origin of not only the species *homo sapiens* but the "whole vertebrate kingdom" is thus a queer body, a body that vacillates between binary Victorian constructions of sex. Accordingly, Darwin claims in his theory of reversion that even gender differences bear the mark of undifferentiated similarities between gendered bodies, for all reproductive systems contain "a part which is always present and efficient in the one sex, being represented in the other by a mere rudiment," as in the case of mammary glands and homologous constructions like the uterus and vesicula prostatica (*DOM* 1:30–1). Contradicting his rigid schema of sexual selection, then, Darwin's theory of reversion posits that gender differences always bear the stamp of their undifferentiated origin.

60. Elizabeth Abel, *Virginia Woolf and the Fictions of Psychoanalysis* (Chicago: University of Chicago Press, 1989), 108.

61. Jane Marcus, *Virginia Woolf*, 15, 95.

62. In the typescript, the "wild child of nature" Mrs. Manresa has "on the tip of her tongue—an anecdote about a public lavatory, built [to celebrate] on the same occasion [. . .] but old Mrs. Swithin gazing at the swallows looked to her too refined" for such a story (*PH* 488).

63. Virginia Woolf, *The Complete Shorter Fiction of Virginia Woolf*, ed. Susan Dick (New York: Harcourt Brace Jovanovich, 1985), 285.

64. Ibid., 286.

65. Childs, *Modernism*, 8.

66. Woolf elsewhere explicitly links women's self-aestheticization with Nazi politics. In "Thoughts on Peace in an Air Raid," Woolf writes that "the subconscious Hitlerism that holds us down is the desire for aggression; the desire to dominate and enslave. Even in the darkness we can see that made visible. We can see shop windows blazing; and women gazing; painted women; dressed-up women; women with crimson lips and crimson fingernails. They are slaves who are trying to enslave" (*CE* 4:174). Although one might balk at Woolf's comparison of window-shopping to fascism here, her interest in Darwinian science and Nazi politics at this time may explain how she conceives of women's inculcation into a cult of aesthetic beauty being tantamount to the supposedly civilized endeavors of Nazi domination.

67. David Jones, *In Parenthesis* (New York: New York Review of Books, 2003), 43.

68. Bonnie Kime Scott, *The Gender of Modernism: A Critical Anthology* (Bloomington: Indiana University Press, 1990), 645; Brenda Silver, *Virginia Woolf's Reading Notebooks* (Princeton, N.J.: Princeton University Press, 1983), 20, 101. Scott's *Gender of Modernism* hereafter abbreviated as *GOM*.

69. Virginia Woolf, *The Common Reader* (New York: Harcourt, Brace and Company, 1948), 68–9, 80.

70. Virginia Woolf, *Granite and Rainbow* (New York: Harcourt Brace Jovanovich, 1958), 12, 17, 19–20.

71. Ibid., 18. This is one of Woolf's more consistent aesthetic positions. In her plans for *The Years*, for example, Woolf writes that the novel "should include satire, comedy, poetry, narrative, & what form is to hold them all together? Should I bring in a play, letters, poems?" (*DVW* 4:152). In "Modern Novels," similarly, Woolf envisions the possibility of creating "a vague general confusion in which the clear-cut features of the tragic, the comic, the passionate, and the lyrical were dissolved beyond the possibility of separate recognition" (*CE* 3:33).

72. Woolf deems Austen "the most perfect artist among women" and arguably envisions herself as Austen's torchbearer (*Common Reader* 206). In a 1918 review, after all, Woolf writes that "the capacity to criticize the other

sex had its share in deciding women to write novels, for indeed that particular vein of comedy has been but slightly worked, and promises great richness," a promise she seems to hold for herself (*Contemporary Writers* 26–7). One of the predictions she makes in *Room*, in fact, is that, should women have the resources to write, "comedy is bound to be enriched" (91). Although she rejected an invitation by the "the Women's Institute" to "write a play for the villagers to act. And to produce it myself" (*Letters* 6:391) while she was composing *Between*, the novel itself functions as a kind of play suitable, in its feminist inclinations, for that institute.

73. Woolf extends the essay's sentiments elsewhere when she claims that "humour, after all, is closely bound up with a sense of the body" (*Common Reader* 57) and that "the book has somehow to be adapted to the body, and at a venture one would say that women's books should be shorter, more concentrated, than those of men" (*ROO* 78).

74. Virginia Woolf, *The Virginia Woolf Reader*, ed. Mitchell A. Leaska (London: Harcourt Brace Jovanovich, 1984), 287.

75. Ibid., 290.

76. This accounting is only approximate but attempts to represent the remarkably large proportion of the book devoted to play dialogue and dialogue among characters; even in its approximate status, this proportion is much larger than one would find in Woolf's earlier novels.

77. Froula, *Virginia Woolf*, 291.

78. Charles Darwin, *The Expression of the Emotions in Man and Animals* (Oxford: Oxford University Press, 1998), 196–7.

79. Woolf, *Moments*, 72.

80. George Macaulay Trevelyan, *History of England* (London: Longmans, Green, 1929), 703.

81. Theodor Adorno and Max Horkheimer, *Dialectic of Enlightenment*, trans. Edmund Jephcott (Stanford, Calif.: Stanford University Press, 2002), 152.

82. Barber, "Lip-Reading," 415.

83. Apart from the various cow interruptions, one might also consider the scene in which a downpour rains upon the pageant just before its conclusion and the rain "trickled down her [Isa's] cheeks as if they were her own tears," leading La Trobe to conclude that "Nature once more had taken her part" (*BTA* 122, 123).

84. *PH* 175; While Madelyn Detloff argues in *The Persistence of Modernism: Loss and Mourning in the Twentieth Century* (Cambridge: Cambridge University Press, 2009) that the pageant's "performance, like the parodic performance of drag, makes the audience conscious of the performative construction of identities that are assumed to be 'natural'" (49), then, the

performance does not abandon the natural as an epistemological or ontological category but rather reinforces that category from a Darwinian
perspective. It is nature above all—cows, rain, sheep, and the sensational
body—that shows how performative the construction of traditional identity
has been.

85. MacKay, *Modernism*, 34.

86. For further discussion of how Woolf unites the play's audience with
tropes of abjection, see Michelle Mimlitsch's "Power of Horror and Peace:
Abjection and Community in Virginia Woolf's *Between the Acts*" in *Virginia
Woolf & Communities*, ed. Jeanette McVicker and Laura Davis (New York:
Pace University Press, 1999), 36–43.

87. Adorno and Horkheimer, *Dialectic*, 212.

Art for Science's Sake:
Wilde in Whitman's Wilderness

Judging by conventional histories of *fin-de-siècle* British and American literature, Oscar Wilde's meeting with Walt Whitman during Wilde's 1882 lecture tour of America seems like an episode out of postmodern historical fiction, not literary history. While both writers are considered to be forefathers of twentieth-century queer literature, after all, Wilde is supposed to be the poster-boy of British Aestheticism, a movement that rejected nature and science as aesthetic principles and posited that, as Wilde writes in *The Picture of Dorian Gray*, "all art is quite useless."[1] Whitman, on the other hand, unambiguously celebrates nature and science as sources of aesthetic inspiration and views art as an instrument of social change and affective cohesion.

On a stop during his lecture tour, however—a tour on which he was lecturing about Aestheticism—Wilde not only met Whitman but revealed his lifelong affection for the poet. Wilde had read *Leaves of Grass* as a child, reviewed it enthusiastically in 1871, and wrote to Whitman after their meeting that "there is no one in this wide great world of America whom I love and honour so much."[2] Whitman reciprocated such kindness, writing that Wilde "impressed [him] as a strong, able fellow,"[3] even as he told

Wilde that "the fellow who makes a dead set at beauty by itself is in a bad way."[4] Although they enjoyed one another personally, then, Whitman seems to have had no use for Wilde's aesthetic practices, even as Wilde had use for Whitman's: Indeed, Wilde admired that Whitman "carries nature always in his heart" and claimed that Whitman was "the simplest, most natural, and strongest character I have ever met in my life."[5] So what use could Oscar Wilde have had for Walt Whitman's love of nature, and how might that use help us to make our literary histories of *fin-de-siecle* literature themselves more useful?

Whereas scholars such as David Blake have argued that Wilde admired Whitman because Whitman was a celebrity and exemplified the artifice of selfhood, not to mention of nature, I will argue today that Wilde's affection for Whitman reveals an overlooked strain of nature-based queer aesthetics not only in Wilde's writing but in the literary modernist era that both Whitman and Wilde are often considered to anticipate. Such aesthetics are rooted in two evolutionary scientific principles: first, that nature is infinitely mutable; and second, that sexual feeling is aesthetic feeling grounded in the material world. For Whitman and Wilde, these principles structure a form of literary realism that George Lukács calls "socialist realism," an aesthetic that models social reality on nature. Nature, in this aesthetic, is a leveling force that aligns all forms of being, including the queer, in a variegated field, such that reality can be typified by even the individual who would, by normative social standards, be considered exceptional. While I don't have time today to explore the socialist dimension of this argument, I will demonstrate that Wilde uses Whitman's use of nature as a source of non-normative aesthetic and sexual principles to create, in his 1905 letter *De Profundis*, a nature-based revision of the realist aesthetic.

Whitman's praise of nature and of non-normative sexuality in the form of "comrade-love" is well known. Less often acknowledged is that Whitman used evolutionary science as a source of literary inspiration. In his 1888 essay "A Backward Glance O'er Travel'd Roads," for example, Whitman reflects that poetry must "conform with and build on the concrete realities and theories of the universe furnish'd by science, [which is] henceforth the only irrefragable basis for anything, verse included."[6] Lest it seem that Whitman's use for literature is to illustrate science, however, in his 1892 essay "Darwinism—(Then Furthermore)," Whitman contends that evolutionary science and literature are mutually informative practices because both create imaginative speculations from material facts. "The world of erudition," Whitman writes, will be "better'd and broaden'd in its speculations, from the advent of Darwinism. Nevertheless, the problem of origins, human and other, is not the least whit nearer its solution. [. . .] What is finally to be done by priest or poet—and by priest or poet only [. . .] remains just as indispensable. [. . .] The priests and poets of the modern [. . .] must indeed recast the old metal, the already achiev'd material, into and through new moulds, current forms" (1060–1). Offering a credo tantamount to Ezra Pound's modernist "Make It New," Whitman believes that new art forms will derive their novelty not by rejecting scientific facts but by using them to create new experiential truths. Evolutionary science and modern literature, for Whitman, thus make mutual use of each other. This stance elucidates how, in "Song of Myself," Whitman can, without contradiction, at once yawp "Hurrah for positive science! Long live exact demonstration!" and declare that "Your facts are useful, and yet they are not my dwelling, / I but enter by them to an area of my dwelling" (210). In Wilde's beloved *Leaves of Grass*, that area is a realm that, as the book's title suggests, considers art to be a part of nature as much as nature is a part of art.

In his 1882 text *Specimen Days*, Whitman reflects that he had not yet created a poem that could envision the full promise of evolutionary theory. He writes that "one of my cherished themes for a never-achiev'd poem has been the two impetuses of man and the universe—in the latter, creation's incessant unrest, exfoliation (Darwin's evolution, I suppose). Indeed, what is Nature but change, in all its visible, and still more its invisible processes?" (921) By acknowledging the incomplete nature of his own work, Whitman adheres to Darwinian logic, envisioning a homology between the endlessness of nature's self-differentiation and of literary production. In doing so, Whitman rejects the Aestheticist use of literature for its own sake and puts literature in the service of what he calls a "theory experimental": one that makes literature as much an agent of material discovery as science. Whitman offers, he writes in "Backward Glance," "nothing, as I may say, for beauty's sake," because "the true use for the imaginative faculty of modern times is to give ultimate vivification to facts, to science, and to common lives, endowing them with the glows and glories and final illustriousness which belong to every real thing, and to real things only" (659).

Rejecting Aestheticism to vivify "real things," Whitman offers a theory of realism based on natural variation that could not seem further from Oscar Wilde's aesthetic disposition, associated as it is with Paterian Aestheticism. In his 1889 essay "The Decay of Lying," for example, Wilde claims that "as a method, realism is a complete failure" because it takes nature as a model for art, whereas art, for Wilde, should be the model for nature.[7] He accordingly concludes that "The chief use" for nature "is to illustrate quotations from the poets," for "all bad art comes from returning to Life and Nature, and elevating them into ideals."[8]

While such views have been taken to represent Wilde at his Aestheticist best, he actually clarifies in essays like 1890's "The Critic as Artist" that he views nature much in the way that Whitman does: as real rather than "ideal." Wilde writes, for example, that "it is the function of Literature to create, from the rough material of actual existence, a new world that will be more marvellous, more enduring, and more true than the world that common eyes look upon, and through which common natures seek to realize their perfection."[9] Contrary to the Aestheticist hard line, Wilde argues that literature does not invent worlds *ex nihilo* or for its own sake alone but creates them out of "the rough material of actual existence" for the benefit of "common natures." The use of literature, for Wilde, is thus much like the use of science, which may explain why Wilde then names Darwin with Ernest Renan as one of "two men" who confirm that "the nineteenth century is a turning point in history," for "the author of the *Origin of Species* had [. . .] the philosophic temper."[10] For Wilde, Darwin shows how scientific principles are not opposed to aesthetic principles: Wilde writes that "aesthetics are higher than ethics [. . .] aesthetics, in fact, are to Ethics in the sphere of conscious civilisation what, in the sphere of the external world, sexual is to natural selection. Ethics, like natural selection, makes existence possible. Aesthetics, like sexual selection, make life lovely and wonderful, fill it with new forms, and give it progress, and variety and change."[11] The uses of both science and literature are therefore analogous for Wilde: to fill life "with new forms, and give it progress, and variety and change."

Wilde's association of aesthetics and sexual selection here by their similar abilities to produce material change also suggests how the queerness of Darwin's theory of nature provided Wilde with a rich source of aesthetic discovery. The scholar Lawrence Danson thus has it only half-right when he argues that, in essays such as "The Decay of Lying," Wilde "protest[s] against the realist's submission to nature and to social conditions that pose as natural."[12] Rather than protest against the kind of nature that Whitman had embraced—a theoretical, Darwinian notion of nature—Wilde protests nature as a principle of ethical, social, and aesthetic normativity, the view that nineteenth-century literary realists and social Darwinists had taken toward the concept. For Wilde, the nature of modern art should resemble the nature of modern science. An art for science's sake thus would, as he writes in "The Critic as Artist," be "the most perfect art": "that which most fully mirrors man in all his infinite variety."[13]

Such is the view that Wilde propounds in his penultimate major work, 1905's *De Profundis*. While not a literary work *per se*, *De Profundis* is highly literary in texture, and Wilde's letters to Robert Ross suggest that he intended to correct and publish it (13–14). The epistle's status as a letter, moreover, recalls the fact that the realist novel emerged as a literary form through an epistolary structure. With this letter, I argue, Wilde refashions literary realism into an aesthetic that views nature, and the social world modeled upon it, as typically queer. Composed from within the physically, financially, and socially degrading circumstances of prison life, *De Profundis* shows Wilde stripped of social pretense and humbled before the facts of his own biological existence. Wilde himself writes as much, claiming repeatedly that the letter's exhaustive history of biographical facts, especially his suffering, reveals how "the supreme vice is shallowness. Whatever is realised is right."[14] While this technique may seem to commit the error of his complaint in "The Decay of Lying" that "the modern novelist presents us with dull facts under the guise of fiction,"[15] Wilde regards his biography as the material source of imaginative change: He uses the letter, he says, to make his infamy "a wonderful beginning" rather than the "appalling ending" he had feared it would be.[16]

Wilde thus becomes in *De Profundis* the protagonist of his own realist *bildungsroman*, the goal of which is to locate queer exceptionality within nature and, therefore, within the version of typical reality envisioned in literary realist form. "We are no longer in Art concerned with the type," Wilde writes: "It is with the exception we have to do."[17] Viewing himself as such an exception, Wilde clarifies his anti-utilitarian Aestheticist doctrine—his belief that "artists, like art itself, [are] of their very essence quite useless"[18]—to create a literary epistle that views literature as useful for creating queer natures. "We call ourselves a utilitarian age," he writes, "and we do not know the uses of any single thing. We have forgotten that Water can cleanse, and Fire purify, and that the Earth is mother to us all."[19] Running directly counter to his claim in "The Decay of Lying" that "Nature is no great mother who has borne us. She is our creation,"[20] Wilde embraces nature as the last recourse for the social pariah: "Society, as we have constituted it, will have no place for me, has none to offer; but Nature, whose sweet rains fall on unjust and just alike [. . .] will cleanse me in great waters, and with bitter herbs make me whole."[21] Rejecting society as the model of realist literary form, Wilde uses nature to create a new vision of reality: one wherein the queer part represents the "whole" of reality.

De Profundis thus realizes the earnest side of Wilde's quip in "The Decay of Lying" that "we are all of us made out of the same stuff [. . .] Sooner or later one comes to that dreadful universal thing called human nature [. . .] The brotherhood of man is no mere poet's dream, it is a most depressing and humiliating reality."[22] In *De Profundis*, Wilde, like Whitman, uses scientific views of nature to create a "brotherhood of man" from the "depressing and humiliating reality" that, as he says in *An Ideal Husband*, to be natural "is such a very difficult pose to keep up."[23] It is difficult to be normatively natural, Wilde implies, because, as he writes in 1891's "The Soul of Man under Socialism," "the only thing that one really knows about human nature is that it changes. [Change] is the differentiation to which all organisms grow."[24] Using literature to create this change, Wilde also creates a brotherhood with Walt Whitman that should change our understandings of how artists writing in the wake of Darwinian science envisioned the uses of literature.

NOTES

1. *Complete Works of Oscar Wilde*, vol. 3, ed. Joseph Bristow (Oxford: Oxford University Press, 2005), 168.

2. *The Letters of Oscar Wilde*, ed. Rupert Hart-Davis (New York: Harcourt, Brace, 1962), 100.

3. *With Walt Whitman in Camden*, ed. Gertrude Traubel (Carbondale: Southern Illinois University Press, 1964), 5:284.

4. Richard Ellmann, *Oscar Wilde* (New York: Knopf, 1988), 169.

5. "Oscar Wilde," *Boston Herald* (January 29, 1882), 7.

6. Walt Whitman, *Complete Poetry and Collected Prose* (New York: Library of America, 1982), 662. Subsequent references in the text will be to this edition.

7. *Complete Works of Oscar Wilde*, vol. 4, ed. Josephine Guy (Oxford: Oxford University Press, 2007), 85.

8. Wilde, *Works*, 4:103.

9. Ibid., 4:152.

10. Ibid., 4:205.

11. Ibid., 4:204.

12. Lawrence Danson, "Wilde as Critic and Theorist," in *Cambridge Companion to Oscar Wilde*, ed. Peter Raby (Cambridge: Cambridge University Press, 1997), 86.

13. Wilde, *Works*, 4:137.

14. *Complete Works of Oscar Wilde*, vol. 2, ed. Ian Small (Oxford: Oxford University Press, 2005), 99.

15. Wilde, *Works*, 4:76.

16. Wilde, *Works*, 2:125.

17. Ibid., 2:126.

18. Ibid., 2:139.

19. Ibid., 2:152.

20. Wilde, *Works*, 4:95.

21. Wilde, *Works*, 2:152.

22. Wilde, *Works*, 4:80.

23. Oscar Wilde, *An Ideal Husband*, ed. Russell Jackson (London: Methuen, 2013), 14.

24. Wilde, *Works*, 4:263.

Exfoliating Modernist Realism:
Carpenter, Darwin, and Forster

Georg Lukács's 1957 study titled *The Meaning of Contemporary Realism* explores one of the questions implied in the title of my talk today: Is there such a thing as modernist realism? For Lukács, the answer to this question is a resounding *no*, at least when considered within the genre of narrative prose fiction. As an aesthetic period, Lukács writes, modernism revels in the socially isolated individual's subjective experience; represents and enjoins the affects of "nihilism and cynicism, despair and *angst*, suspicion and self-disgust" as conditions of such isolation; and proffers what he calls "psychopathology," including "sexual perversion," as the social norm.[1] Realism, on the other hand, especially that crafted by nineteenth-century writers such as Tolstoy and Cooper, represents the individual in relation to a social world, communicates the affect of hope for a future wherein angst and despair dissipate (72), and abjures the behaviorally pathological in favor of what he calls the socially "typical" (31). The choice between realism and modernism is, for Lukács, no less than a choice about offering a faithful representation of—and a faith in—what he repeatedly calls "human nature" (83).

In keeping with Lukács's strict binaries between angst and hope, individual and collective, modernism has come to be seen among many literary historians as a period whose artistic forms and themes reject realism on aesthetic and ideological grounds. Where, then, does such a history position the novels of E. M. Forster, which seem so social, so hopeful, so obsessed with the socially typical? Forster's status in literary history has been much contested: Virginia Woolf argued that he should be classified not as a realist Edwardian but as a modernist Georgian, a title under which she also grouped seemingly more experimental writers like Joyce and Eliot. In keeping with Randall Stevenson's confident assertion that "Forster was scarcely a modernist," however, most contemporary scholars locate Forster amongst the Edwardians.[2] To them, Forster is a realist writer who vaunts the liberal humanist ideals that the so-called "Men of 1914" dismissed.

So are Woolf and scholars such as David Medalie, author of the 2002 book *E. M. Forster's Modernism*, struggling vainly to fit a square peg in a round hole? Or could it be that Forster is a litmus test of the categories "modernism" and "realism" themselves? Might the realism that so many scholars have noted in Forster's novels actually constitute what is distinctively experimental, and therefore modernist, about his work?

In this talk, I argue that Forster's 1914 novel *Maurice* offers an exemplary instance of modernist realism, a phrase that we can consider to be an analytically productive oxymoron rather than a contradiction in terms. Completed in the year that the phrase "Men of 1914" suggests as the inauguration of modernism, *Maurice* does not endorse liberal capitalist individualism through bourgeois realist form but offers an experimental depiction of nature as the model for democratic socialism. This depiction of nature is founded on the principle of love, especially non-normative love like homosexuality that would, by Lukács's standard, be so "exceptional" as to defy the "typical" portrait of any brand of aesthetic realism; it would deviate, that is, from the "totality" that socialist realism, Lukács's preferred mode of realism, aims to represent, for socialist realism repudiates the "pathological" elements that, Lukács says, "the decadent literature of anti-realism" (102) includes to the expense of all else.

Maurice's socialist vision of a reality modeled on the natural world derives from the experimental science and politics of Forster's era, namely evolutionary theory and Marxist socialism. These experimental philosophies coalesce in the writings of Forster's friend Edward Carpenter, whose lover, George Merrill, inspired Forster to write *Maurice* when, Forster records, Merrill touched Forster's lower back.[3] By examining Forster's debt to Carpenter, and Carpenter's debt to Charles Darwin and Friedrich Engels, I argue that Forster's belief in the material world's inexorable mutability revises the tradition of nineteenth-century realism with which Forster is often associated. As scholars like Nancy Armstrong and Amy Kaplan have argued, nineteenth-century realism was a transatlantic phenomenon that endorsed capitalist, liberal individualism through the values of the heterosexual, white middle class. Forster's modernist realism, in contrast, locates reality in the very kind of "decadent" subjects with which Lukács associates modernism: the sexually non-normative, or what Lukács calls the "psychopathic"; the individual who abandons rather than enters a pre-established social world; and the affect of angst, which for Forster emerges as what Theodor Adorno calls "a feeling for nature," or a feeling of inexorable loss as modern industry eradicates the natural world.[4] For all its abandonment of nineteenth-century thematic principles, however, *Maurice* does not fetishize the sexual other's plight but depicts it as an exceptional form of social typicality: For Forster, what is typical about reality is the infinite difference represented in a Darwinian understanding of nature, the same kind of nature that grounds Engels's theory of democratic socialism and, though Lukács might balk at its association with queerness, Lukács's socialist realism. Forster's socialist realism is, in other words, perhaps more socialist than even Lukács could envision.

To think of evolutionary theory and Marxist socialism as complementary philosophies should be unsurprising because Marx and Engels themselves drew upon Darwin's thought to support their philosophy of historical materialism. Unlike Social Darwinists of the time, who contorted Darwin's theories to support eugenic programs and legally enforced social inequality (all in the name of the "fit" struggling for "survival"), Marx and Engels saw Darwin as a great leveler. Engels, for example, claims in his 1883 essay "Socialism: Utopian and Scientific" that Darwin "dealt the metaphysical conception of Nature the heaviest blow by his proof that all organic beings, plants, animals, and man himself, are the products of a process of evolution going on through millions of years."[5] This conception of nature, Engels writes, grounds on scientific bases historical materialism's Hegelian faith in dialectic philosophy, for "nature is the proof of dialectics, and it must be said for modern science that it has furnished this proof with very rich materials increasing daily."[6] Whereas communism was feared throughout the twentieth century as a political philosophy that would homogenize difference under the guise of equality, Engels proposes that democratic socialism should model itself on Darwin's findings that the material world is in a state of infinite variation and differentiation: that, as Engels writes, "every organic being is every moment the same and not the same [. . .] every organic being is always itself, and yet something other than itself."[7]

Engels called this Darwinian perspective on socialist problems "scientific socialism,"[8] the same phrase that Lukács uses to describe socialist realism (94), in which Lukács says that "reality is neither static nor constant; the investigator cannot exhaust its substance. It is, on the contrary, a constant flux—only revealing a definite, though never simple, direction to the eye of the trained observer" (97). Darwin in science, Engels in political philosophy, and Lukács in modernist aesthetics thus all propounded a radical idea—more radical than many twenty-first-century academic theorists writing under the influence of poststructuralism will allow—that nature is not a static, eternal essence of being but a material entity that is subject to change. Unlike Social Darwinism—founded, arguably, on capitalist ideals of liberal individualism—all three views of nature propose that the material world should be respected by the forces that would seek to contain it for ideological ends.

While Darwin, Engels, and Lukács are silent if not condemnatory on the subject of non-normative sexuality, the poet and sexologist Edward Carpenter's 1908 text *The Intermediate Sex*, a cross-disciplinary examination of non-normative sexuality, fuses Darwinian and Marxist thought in ways that support a science, politics, and aesthetics based on same-sex attraction. There, Carpenter writes that "Eros is the great leveller [sic]. Perhaps the true Democracy rests, more firmly than anywhere else, on a sentiment which easily passes the bounds of class and caste, and unites in the closest affection the most estranged ranks of society."[9] Carpenter envisions in this passage a socialist democracy guided by the biological law of "Eros," specifically its disregard for the socially constructed laws of "class and caste." For Carpenter (as for Walt Whitman, Carpenter's muse), sexual freedom entails social and economic freedom; so the more that non-normative forms of Eros like homosexuality and polyamory are disburdened of social constraints, the more that economic freedom may be realized.

Carpenter named this sexual-political theory "exfoliation," a theory that reveals Carpenter's intellectual debt not only to Whitman but to Darwin. In short, Carpenter believes that evolution occurs not only from without but also from within, such that sexual and social union allow individuals to shed layers of civilized restrictions and evolve according to their own natural laws.[10] For Carpenter, humans evolve not just as a species across time but as individuals within time, a process in "which the outer similitudes and shells, like the minute cells of an organism, are shed and die in endless multitudes with continual decay and corruption."[11] Carpenter's non-reproductive, inter- and intrasubjective "Science of Love," as he calls it, thus proposes "as in the evolution of all organic life—more and more

differentiation as the life rises higher in the scale of existence"[12] Carpenter
believes that the political group should model itself on the natural group:
The social world should be formed on the basis of common affectional
bonds and evolve organically into a differentiated mass, one wherein difference exists on a level structural field, not in a hierarchy. In its recognition of Darwin's dispassionate, unmoralized principle that nature is
subject to change, then, Carpenter's theory of exfoliation may be said to
exfoliate Darwin's theory of nature itself of Social Darwinists' misap-
propriation thereof.

When viewed in light of Forster's *Maurice*, Carpenter's theory of exfoliation may also help us to exfoliate the genre of modernist realism. In *Angel's Wings*, in fact, Carpenter expounds a theory of realism alongside his
theory of exfoliation: "We only know what we see ourselves. This is the
complete answer to the idea of an exact Realism. There is no such thing.
It is as impossible in Art as it is in Science. Every object, every scene is
inexhaustible; the person who contemplates it can only *pick out* for representation what appeals to him" (72).[13] Realism, for Carpenter, sounds remarkably modernist in that it can only make claims to universality from a
subjective perspective that, by the very example of its particular subjectivity, acknowledges the objective "inexhaustibility" of the material world: its
infinite variation and its reliance upon a range of individual perceptions,
including the perceptions of those excluded from Lukács's definition of the
"typical" and marshaled into the realm of the "exceptional." Realism, in
this view, is neither a constructed ideology imposed from without nor a
phenomenological perspective limited to subjective relativism but an epistemology that, on the proof of any individual difference, sees reality as
comprising material variation.

Both formally and topically, *Maurice* oscillates between the typical and
the exceptional by charting the gradual descent of a young man, Maurice,
from a life of heterosexual middle-class privilege to one of homosexual
lower-class ignominy. *Maurice* is a bildungsroman that defies the formal,
sexual, and economic traditions established for that genre by novels like
Jane Eyre and *Great Expectations*. Maurice's angst grows more pronounced
throughout the novel as he is educated into heterosexuality, capitalism,
and classism and as his upper-middle-class lover, Clive, rejects him for a
life of "typical" bourgeois heterosexuality. As a consequence of his exceptionality within the typical—his homoerotic feelings in a heterosexual
world—Maurice grows further isolated within his society. As the narrator
reports, "One cannot write those words too often: Maurice's loneliness: it
increased" (141).

Exemplifying Forster's self-consciousness about how such anomic despair might be regarded by critics like Lukács as decadent—and therefore
unrealistically modernist—the novel's narrator consistently describes Maurice's development in terms of reality: The more that Maurice engages his
queer feelings, the more the narrator (a rather queer consciousness itself)
indicates that both Maurice *and* his world become "real," closer to what
this novel envisions to be the differentiated texture of reality. For example, the narrator notes at the beginning of the novel that Maurice, struggling with how he conceals his queer feelings, "saw that while deceiving
others he had been deceived, and mistaken them for the empty creatures
he wanted them to think he was. No, they too had insides [. . .] As soon as
he thought about other people as real, Maurice became modest and conscious of sin [. . .] no wonder he pretended to be a piece of cardboard; if
known as he was, he would be hounded out of the world" (30). Through
free indirect discourse, the narrator, isolating Maurice's consciousness,
criticizes Maurice for his belief in a surface aesthetic: his belief that social
forms of behavior can deceive others into believing that exteriority constitutes character. For Forster, delving into Maurice's consciousness, interiority supplants the exterior and, by novel's end, actually *constitutes* the
exterior self: The narrator charts Maurice's recognition that, while reality
is limited to individual perspectives, as Carpenter says, such limits are productive, for they enforce recognition that infinite variety exists beneath
the homogeneous "cardboard" exteriors that constitute social reality. Maurice must be "hounded out of the world" by novel's end, then, not in order
to escape the social but to redefine it as being as heterogeneous as nature.

In point of fact, when Maurice falls in love with Clive, the narrator reports that "one thing in him at last was real" (40). But when Clive hauls
out his cardboard, heterosexual self again to become, as Clive says, "normal" (116), Maurice begins to backtrack from his homoerotic reality and
considers, as Clive does, marriage. This backtracking leads the narrator
to claim that Maurice "had the Englishman's inability to conceive of variety. His troubles had taught him that other people are alive, but not yet
that they are different" (161). Maurice can only learn to value differentiation from nature, then, not from society, because in society Maurice must
carry himself as the "typical" man that Lukács would have at the center of
the realist novel. Says the narrator, Maurice "was an average man, and
could have won an average fight, but Nature had pitted him against the
extraordinary" (162).

Embracing Nature's "extraordinary" burden, Maurice ends the novel
by falling in love with a lower-class man named Alec and relocating with

him in the greenwood, far away from England's urban centers. Through this development, Maurice learns to embrace natural differentiation and thus to reject social homogenization. The Victorian degeneration theorist Max Nordau might call Maurice's progress of sexual, social, and economic descent "degeneration," or the reverse of evolution, but Forster depicts this descent as Maurice's maturation, his evolution toward a more developed state of being. In Carpenter's terms, consequently, we might call *Maurice* not a novel of development but a novel of exfoliation: It charts the individual's angst-filled recognition of his or her place in nature, not in society, and the example that he or she thereby establishes for society to shed its pretensions to homogeneous sociality.

In point of fact, while Forster insists in his 1960 "Terminal Note" about the novel that *Maurice* ends happily, and while it may be true that Maurice is happier with Alec in the greenwood than he was with his urban cardboard life, the novel does not conclude with a focus on Maurice but on Clive, who is described as attempting to conceal his erotic history with Maurice from his current wife, just as Maurice attempted earlier to conceal his queer feelings from his social world (246). Although the angst of the character Maurice dissipates in the novel, then, the angst of the novel *Maurice* escalates: Its protagonist functions as a foil for social reality's intransigent homogeny, its recalcitrance in the face of nature's insistent diversity. The plot structure and the narratorial point of view through which this novel's world is conveyed thus provide a model of literary realism for modernism that proffers exceptional forms of social differentiation as typical—as a part of nature's variety—even as it mourns that nature—and the social reality that could be formed on it—are being destroyed in a rapidly industrializing, capitalist England, just as Darwin's theory of nature was being contorted by Social Darwinists for capitalist and eugenic purposes.

In its exfoliation of Darwin's theory of natural variation, then, *Maurice* manifests what Adorno would call an angst-filled feeling for nature and, thereby, a feeling for the nineteenth-century socialist philosophy founded on evolutionary science. In his notorious 1939 essay "What I Believe," after all, Forster mourns that "Science, who ought to have ruled, plays the subservient pimp" in interwar England.[14] Science plays the pimp to Social Darwinist programs like those employed by the Nazi regime, but Forster believes that science can and should rule from the basis of its dispassionate presentation of facts about the material world's variegation. Indeed, Forster claims in the essay, sounding like Engels, that science has shown us that "though A is not unchangeably A, or B unchangeably B, there can still be love and loyalty between the two."[15] Edward Carpenter similarly writes that evolutionary science had shown the modernists that "our union with Nature and humanity is a *fact*,"[16] not an ideological construction, and that "the germs of it [non-normative desire, or what he calls the "Uranian temperament"] *are* almost, if not quite, universal."[17] Rather than arguing on behalf of any sexual particularity, Carpenter's claim reorients modernism's understanding of what constitutes universal reality: Erotic difference reveals how the material world is comprised of difference, not of dominance, such that no singularity can be "quite [. . .] universal." If Eros is to be the great leveler, Carpenter suggests, it will show that there is no nature but natures, what one might call in this case queer natures. The question in *Maurice*, as in scholarly discussions of nature today, is whether those who construct social reality are prepared to acknowledge the material complexity and imaginative possibility of the nature that they oversimplify and thereby threaten to destroy.

NOTES

1. Georg Lukács, *The Meaning of Contemporary Realism*, trans. John and Necke Mander (London: Merlin Press, 1963), 66, 9. Subsequent references in the text will be to this edition.

2. Randall Stevenson, "Forster and Modernism," in *Cambridge Companion to E. M. Forster*, ed. David Bradshaw (Cambridge: Cambridge University Press, 2007), 209.

3. E. M. Forster, *Maurice* (New York: Norton, 1971), 249. Subsequent references in the text will be to this edition.

4. Theodor Adorno, *Aesthetic Theory*, trans. Robert Hullot-Kentor (Minneapolis: University of Minnesota Press, 1997), 94, 97.

5. Friedrich Engels, *Socialism: Utopian and Scientific*, trans. Edward Aveling (International Publishers, 1972), 55.

6. Ibid.

7. Ibid., 54.

8. Ibid., 77.

9. Edward Carpenter, *The Intermediate Sex* (London: George Allen and Unwin, 1908), 114–15.

10. See Edward Carpenter, *Civilisation: Its Cause and Cure, and Other Essays* (London: Swan Sonnenschein, 1891), 129.

11. Edward Carpenter, *Towards Democracy* (London: George Allen and Unwin, 1916), 493

12. Edward Carpenter, *Love's Coming of Age* (New York: Mitchell Kennerley, 1911), 147.

13. Edward Carpenter, *Angel's Wings: A Series of Essays on Art and Its Relation to Life* (London: Swan Sonnenschein, 1908), 131.

14. E. M. Forster, *Two Cheers for Democracy* (New York: Harcourt, Brace, 1951), 67.

15. Ibid.

16. Edward Carpenter, *Our Days and Dreams: Being Autobiographical Notes* (New York: Scribner's, 1916), 303.

17. Carpenter, *Intermediate Sex*, 117.

"Spectacles in Color":
The Primitive Drag of Langston Hughes

The color problem is a drag on the whole world,
not just on Negro poetry.

—LANGSTON HUGHES[1]

In a chapter titled "Spectacles in Color" that appears toward the end of his first autobiography, *The Big Sea* (1940), Langston Hughes recounts the cultural events that distinguished Harlem during the modernist period. The chapter opens with Hughes's chiastic description of the Hamilton Club Lodge Ball, "the ball where men dress as women and women dress as men" and they all assemble in a "queerly assorted throng on the dancing floor." To Hughes, the "strangest and gaudiest of all Harlem spectacles in the '20s," the ball was, in fact, a Harlem institution inaugurated in 1869 and attended annually by hundreds of East Coast denizens.[2] After four brief paragraphs describing this presumably unusual affair, Hughes asserts that "Harlem likes spectacles of one kind or another" and documents, through paratactic associations, other Harlem gatherings: a lodge parade with band members donning ornate costumes; Florence Mills's funeral procession, complete with chorus girls and an airplane-released flock of blackbirds; Countee Cullen's wedding to W. E. B. DuBois's daughter, Yolande; and the "show"-like church revivals of the Reverend Dr. George Wilson Becton.[3]

As in much of *The Big Sea*, the logical progression of this chapter's descriptions is curious: Why does Hughes initiate his discussion of Harlem cultural events—those as quotidian as funerals, weddings, and church meetings—with a drag ball? What does the seemingly subcultural phenomenon of drag have in common with these more normative, indeed often heteronormative, ceremonies? What might this writer, best known for his poetry about Harlem culture, have learned from these "spectacles in color," and how could that cultural education have informed his Harlem-based poetry?

Further investigation of "Spectacles in Color" contextualizes these questions and the role that drag culture plays in Hughes's vision of 1920s Harlem. As George Chauncey records, modernist Harlem was a "homosexual mecca," a place where, the female impersonator Earl Lind believed, "one c[ould] live as Nature demands without setting every one's tongue wagging."[4] The drag balls of the 1920s and 1930s were the safest and most visible spaces in which queers could affirm the nonnormative "Nature" that Lind describes, and they "enhanced the solidarity of the gay world and symbolized the continuing centrality of gender inversion to gay culture."[5] The balls could also be said to represent Harlem culture at large, however, because they were typically racially integrated and therefore could house the intra- and interracial multiplicity of Harlem, which was, after all, known as the "crossroad of the Negro world."[6] Drag balls attracted a sizable heterosexual audience that found the events entertaining, moreover, and the Hamilton Ball in particular was based on "conventional" masquerade balls familiar to a broader heteroerotic audience. Most important, if the drag ball can be taken as a symbol of theatricality, and if Harlem in the 1920s was a place where gay men "sought to emphasize the theatricality of everyday interactions" and where "life was lived as theatre,"[7] Hughes's "Spectacles" comports with a well-known historical account of Harlem life, lived outside the drag balls, as itself being a "spectacle in color."

That the ball was a space in which queers and straights, blacks and whites, men and women alike convened and crossed suggests why Hughes opens "Spectacles in Color" with a drag ball rather than with, say, Cullen's wedding: because it does not discriminate on the basis of ethnic markers but blurs them, the drag ball is, to Hughes, Harlem's most representative metonym. Hughes associates the ball, parade, funeral, wedding, and revival, then, through their visual practices and affective products: the parade emphasizes auditory and visual excess and the joy of celebration; the funeral was, Hughes thought, a site of performatively enjoined grieving;[8] Cullen's wedding ironically depicts a queer man pledging love to the daughter of the most prominent modernist in black America; and Becton's church performances feature "a very bad preacher" of unprecedented popularity but noted cupidity who is able to elicit sincere feeling and faith from his parishioners by deploying psychoanalytic techniques.[9] Because each of these ceremonies relies on a formal logic of visual performance to engender feeling, Hughes's association of them in "Spectacles" suggests that, to this poet, the events that define Harlem life exemplify a positive relation between artifice and nature, performance and feeling.

Given the comprehensiveness of its social portrait, "Spectacles in Color" offers a useful rubric for understanding Hughes's Harlem-based poems, for they, especially those in *The Weary Blues* (1926), characteristically cross gender, sexual, racial, and even formal lines. In this essay, I argue that, just as "Spectacles" envisions Harlem culture as a drag performance, *The Weary Blues* records a lyric history of modernist Harlem in poems that perform in drag, an aesthetic of visual crossing. This aesthetic ironically coincides with the identitarian stereotypes of African Americans and queers that were propagated by early twentieth-century sexological science and degeneration theory: namely, that blacks and queers were unnatural and degenerate because they, unlike whites and heterosexuals, exhibited a lack of racial and gender differentiation through racial miscegenation and arrested sexual development. Yet Hughes's adoption of these stereotypes in lyric and dramatic poetry countermands their pathologizing aims. While lyric and dramatic poems conventionally embody a speaker's performance of subjective feeling, when we ask of Hughes's blues poems the apparently simple question "Who speaks?" we find that the texts capitalize on their generic performativity, for their speakers are typically ungendered and unraced, which makes them read like drag performers who manipulate visual representation for affective ends. In both the blues and drag aesthetics, those ends are the chiastically linked feelings of mournful laughter and joyful sadness.

In concert with Hughes's claim that "art crosses color lines and gets around into many places where the creators of the art themselves may not be welcome,"[10] the trope of crossing and the rhetorical form of chiasmus structure *The Weary Blues*'s poetic drag performances. By this formal logic, when the poet claims that "[t]he color problem is a drag on the whole world, not just on Negro poetry," he suggests that the socially constructed problem of color (namely, the uncrossable color line, that which establishes discrete identities) retards the progress of Negro poetry and, indeed, of the whole world.[11] But if the word *drag* can be read polysemously, Hughes's claim also suggests that the color problem's establishment of seemingly fixed racial identities provides the visual resources for a sartorial drag on Negro poetry, if not on the whole world, for the color line's essentialized markers of identity are the very markers that drag performance employs to expose the incongruity between discursive renderings of racial identity and race as experienced in and on the body. To Hughes, the color problem's socially regressive drag unwittingly offers Negro poetry the subversive visual logic of drag performance: the logic of, in other words, an "art [that] crosses color lines." Hughes's observation about the color problem's drag thus simultaneously enforces and reverses evolutionary science's positivist precepts—the precepts that ground sexological and degeneration theories alike—for the poet's polysemy implies that Negro poetry can reverse the color problem's atavistic drag if it crosses the hegemonic color line by up-holding the line's visual and epistemological taxonomies only to undermine them.

From a queer perspective, to discuss Hughes's poetry in the context of blues and drag performance inevitably invokes Judith Butler's influential theory of gender performativity. For Butler, *performativity* denotes gender performance's paradoxically naturalizing and denaturalizing effects: Performance can naturalize the concept of gender in the body with repeated gestures, and it can *de*naturalize the gendered body by exposing such naturalization as constructed.[12] While providing an indispensable heuristic for understanding the gender and racial instability of Hughes's queer poetic, Butler's theory excludes the natural itself from consideration[13] and therefore cannot accommodate how Hughes's speakers feel identitarian instability as natural but not normative—as embodied, material, and subject to change but not naturalized, original, or transhistorically unvarying. Offering a "gender performance [that] will enact and reveal the performativity of gender itself in a way that destabilizes the naturalized categories of identity and desire,"[14] Hughes's poems position performance's denaturalizing effects as themselves affectively natural, proper to what Eve Sedgwick calls the "performative affectivity" produced when the "discursive performativity" central to Butler's theory is disrupted.[15] Performing identitarian instability, or queerness, as a natural feeling, *The Weary Blues* reveals how, as Rei Terada argues, "the theatricality of self-representation might seem to cast doubt on the reality of experience [but] it does not suspend or weaken emotion."[16]

As my revised approach to Butler's theory suggests, to ask that we read Hughes's poetic form as drag performative necessitates that we also examine his poetry through the lens of historical emotion. Hughes categorized

himself as one of the "regional poets of genuine realities and authentic values" and among the "lyric historians," whom he defines as writers who
recognize that "it is more profitable to know how people *feel* than it is to
know what they think."[17] Such claims invite hermeneutic attention to affect since, as Sianne Ngai contends, "the feeling calls attention to a real
social experience and a certain kind of historical truth."[18] In point of fact,
Hughes claims that writing is a process of translating "inner emotions into
exterior form"[19] and that, with "its roots deep in the nature of the universe,"
poetry records "the distilled essence of experience, the concentrated flavor of an emotion," but could be as difficult to crack as "a riddle, a new
crossword puzzle."[20] Because he regarded *The Weary Blues* as one of his
most "timely" works[21] and because that volume's ethnic crossings create a
kind of "crossword puzzle," it seems sensible to examine his first book for
Hughes's history of modernist Harlem's lyric feelings.

In keeping with the poet's own historicism, by conjoining the terms
primitive and *drag* to describe Hughes's verse, I invoke the two dominant
historical tropes, primitivism and cross-dressing, that Hughes employed
in his work. While his early poetry primitivizes Africa, Hughes centrally
primitivized what he called the "low-down" culture of the "folk." Among
the folk, as in "the primitive world," Hughes found that people "do not, as
many civilized people do, neglect the truth of the physical for the sake of
the mind. . . . [T]he barrier between words and reality is not so great as
with us."[22] To Hughes, the low-down crosses the typical "barrier" between
representation and reference, "words and reality," by attending to "the
truth of the physical." Because he (perhaps romantically) admired that the
folk "draw no color line between mulattoes and deep dark-browns,"[23] however, Hughes also finds that low- down Negro culture destabilizes visual
markers as essentializing criteria of identity.

In its blurring of visual taxonomies, the low-down exemplifies, for
Hughes, not the racial authenticity of blackness but what I call modernist
Harlem's "down-low" rejection of identitarian taxonomies to encapsulate
what Hughes broadly described as "Negro" experience, especially since,
as the poet maintains, Negroes themselves crossed many color lines.
Though Hughes himself did not use it, I employ the anachronistic term
down-low to invoke its contemporary associations with meaningfully unidentified, or queer, sexuality: Thought to originate in the African American community in the late twentieth century, the term *down-low* denotes
erotic acts that "traverse—and, more importantly, elide—hetero- and homosexual group identity."[24] Offering "an ongoing crisis in sexual and racial definition; an ongoing crisis in how discourses police male (and

unmentioned female) queers of color"[25] the down-low describes the queer practice of drag performance in *The Weary Blues*, the poems' unsettling of visual and epistemological taxonomies of identity. Accordingly, where critics have been vexed by Hughes's and his poems' ambiguous sexualities for decades, I do not attempt to resolve such ambiguity but take it as a productive site of inquiry into how these texts represent the historical feeling of nonnormative, disidentificatory experience.[26] I also mean to invoke the chiastic balance between the terms *low-down* and *down-low* because representations of race and sexuality in *The Weary Blues* are mutually constitutive. Depicting racially low-down characters on the sexual down-low, this volume invokes the primitivist and naturalist associations of the former term to suggest that an unidentified, or queer, sexuality is natural. Simultaneously, the text's down-low aesthetic, conveying how desire's lability disrupts identity, problematizes the fetishistic implications of primitivism such that the low-down comes to represent racial feeling rather than identity. More precisely yet, when low-down race and down-low gender intersect, their center is queer feeling, an affect that rejects identity and claims nonnormative experience (racial or sexual) as natural. Meeting at the crux of their chiasmus, both terms convey above all that the black queer is degenerate, *low* and *down*; given their blues context, however, the terms celebrate such degeneracy. Structured thus, the poetic performances in *The Weary Blues* co-opt pathologizing taxonomies of blacks and queers in order to debunk them even while retaining the nature-based premises of those discursive stereotypes.

Crossing Color and Gender Lines

I'm standin' at the crossroad babe I believe I'm sinkin' down.
                    ROBERT JOHNSON, "CROSS ROAD BLUES"

Because Hughes's blues poems embody Harlem's history of drag performance in their formal traversals, my analysis proceeds by crossing between Hughes's work and the historical context that it records. "Cross" is one of the most salient of the *Weary Blues* poems to invite such inquiry: Its gender, racial, sexual, and formal intersections typify the crossings that constitute the volume's structure and texture. A poetic incarnation of the Harlem spectacle in color, "Cross" was Hughes's "ace in the hole" when he "delivered [it] dramatically" at public readings;[27] such delivery was appropriate to the poem's subjects since, Hughes says, "the problem of mixed blood in America [is] a very dramatic one."[28] Perhaps inspired by Robert

Johnson's classic "Cross Road Blues," Hughes in fact set the poem to music in 1960.

Initially, "Cross" appears to be neither dramatic in mode nor erotic but to record, in seemingly lyric fashion, an ungendered speaker's plaint about his or her racial identity:

> My old man's a white old man And my old mother's black.
> If ever I cursed my white old man I take my curses back.
> If ever I cursed my black old mother And wished she were in hell,
> I'm sorry for that evil wish And now I wish her well.
> My old man died in a fine big house. My ma died in a shack.
> I wonder where I'm gonna die, Being neither white nor black?
>
> (*Collected Poems* 58–9)[29]

Structurally atypical of Hughes's *Weary Blues*, the poem's stanzas work on a metrically irregular 4-3-4-3 stress pattern, the pattern of the traditional ballad and the religious hymn. As such, the poem would seem to belie Hughes's description of its "mood" as being "that of the blues"[30] and to resemble the Cullen-McKay strain of traditional Harlem Renaissance poetry. While ballads are normatively narrative in mode, however, "Cross" is (ostensibly) lyric, given its I speaker and unapparent addressee, so the poem cannot be called a normative ballad; moreover, the poem's blues "mood" would secularize the hymn meter's religious associations. "Cross" crosses these traditional and modern forms to balance them: The ballad, the hymn, and the blues are all folk forms, after all, and each relies on structural and sonic repetition. Generically down-low, or taxonomically unstable, and low-down, or folk-based, the poem crosses genres to balance its center at spatially degenerate feeling.

Such formal traversals reflect the poem's chiastic thematics. The speaker is not gendered, nor does he or she avow a stable racial identity. Instead of stabilizing his or her race according to the culturally hegemonic one-drop rule, the speaker ends the poem by embracing racial multiplicity: He or she is "neither white nor black," a definition by negation that disrupts both binary and syncretic thought, for the speaker does not claim to be white and black at once. That the poem ends with a question therefore warrants scrutiny, for if the speaker accepted essentialized social standards of race, the point would be moot: He or she would be black. In these final lines, the speaker brandishes his or her "cross," a move most available to the queerly embodied: As José Esteban Muñoz argues, "[I]dentity practices such as queerness and hybridity are not a priori sites of contestation but, instead, spaces of productivity where identity's fragmentary nature is accepted and negotiated."[31] Using the essentialized standards of racial discourse against themselves, the speaker foregrounds his or her racially "fragmented nature" as the poem's balanced topic.

Such racial and gender instability recalls the stereotypes propounded in the early twentieth century by sexologists like Havelock Ellis, whose work Hughes read,[32] perhaps as part of his general ambition "to study sociology and history and psychology."[33] Exemplifying Ellis's claim that "the question of sex—with the racial questions that rest on it—stands before the coming generations as the chief problem for solution,[34] "Cross" is sexualized, despite its deceptively nonerotic subjects, for its apparent problem—racial crossing—occurs before the poem's action through sexual crossing. Insofar as "miscegenation, for many, typified the nonheteronormative" in America because it "symbolize[d] the violation of racialized heteronormativity and its guarantee of American (i.e., 'white') racial purity."[35] Hughes's emphasis on the mulatto figure in "Cross" simultaneously emphasizes what was to sexologists the queer figure. Both figures manifest nonnormative experiential crossings and are mutually signified, chiastically crossed and balanced with one another. As the speaker stands, like Johnson's, "at the crossroad . . . sinkin' down," his or her final question interrogates not only race but also sexuality. But to whom is that question addressed?

Recalling Hughes's claim that this poem was his most successful performance piece, I would argue that the speaker's question is not lyrically self-addressed but dramatically directed toward an apostrophized addressee: toward the dominant discourses that institutionalize standards of racial and sexual identity and that would force the speaker to be "white [or] black." The poem crosses lyric and dramatic modes, then, as Martin Ponce suggests generally of Hughes's work.[36] As a dramatic (in both senses of the term) question, the poem's concluding lines decenter identity and center the poem's queer feeling; the text's descriptive title announces this multiple focus, for "Cross" itself is cross-referenced among the poem's subjects. The speaker forgives his or her parents in the first two stanzas but still evinces anger in the final line, an affective mixture that invokes the blues: the speaker's laughter (forgiveness) cries, we could say, especially as it contemplates death. Because the word *cross* (like the poem's hymn meter) invokes the Christian cross and, therefore, suffering, and because *cross* also means "angry," the synthetic affective product of "Cross" may also be felt as opposition, one's angry revolt against suffering even as one upholds one's own experience. Affirming its speaker's "fragmentary nature" during such opposition, "Cross" epitomizes the naturally queer feeling that emerges throughout *The Weary Blues* in the chiastic link between low-down primitivism and down-low drag.

The formal and discursive traversals of "Cross" elucidate how Hughes could be deemed both "the poet laureate of his race" and the "poet 'low-rate' of Harlem" in his day.[37] A title also often applied to his coeval Cullen, "laureate" suggests that Hughes represented "his race" with some authenticity and accuracy. "Low-rate" instead suggests that Hughes became a "Sewer Dweller," as the *Amsterdam News* claimed,[38] with an "obsession for the more degenerate element" of African American culture and whose work was "a study in the perversion of the Negro," as the *Philadelphia Tribune* remarked.[39] Hughes knew of these aspersions and co-opted them: If his work must be called "degenerate stuff," the poet stoutly declared that he would don the mantle of "the 'baddest' of the bad Negroes."[40] This response and Hughes's claims that he wanted to take "*my* poetry, to *my* people" because he "wrote about Negroes, and primarily *for* Negroes"[41] concerning "the dreams and heartaches that all Negroes know"[42] imply that, through a status crossing, he authorizes himself as poet laureate because he is the poet low-rate. Hughes's Harlem poems embrace degenerate and perverse forms of life as representative spectacles in color whose degeneracy constitutes their exemplarity.

As the concluding lines of "Cross" indicate, such celebration of degeneracy was a political act in the early twentieth century. When Hughes claims that "politics in any country in the world had better be disguised as poetry"[43] he indicates how, while his later poems may be more explicitly polemical, his early verse reveals a "disguised" politics: a politics whose drag aesthetic visibly attacks sexological stereotypes. If that drag form can be associated with the veil—a sartorial object that conceals or blurs identity—*The Weary Blues* may be Hughes's implicit response to DuBois's famous characterization of African American experience as felt from behind "a vast veil," one that demarcates racial identity.[44] Instead of being naturalistically determined by that shroud, Hughes's speakers deploy the drag veil to lift the color line's veil: They don visual indeterminacy to cross the identitarian line established between one side of the veil and the other. In this way, the primitive drag of the blues, which Hughes thought the most modern and urban of black art forms,[45] offered him the means of social protest as well as the formal and affective means to claim a voice in modernism.

A Shakespeare in Harlem: Performing Historical Discourse

My man got a sissy, his name is Miss Kate He shook that thing like jelly on a plate.

MA RAINEY, "SISSY BLUES"

Set in Harlem's blues and drag culture, *The Weary Blues* invites us to pursue the historicist possibilities of Houston Baker, Jr.'s yet unheeded proposal that "Hughes may be more comprehensible within the framework of Afro-American verbal and musical *performance* than within the borrowed framework for the description of *written* inscriptions of cultural metaphor."[46] Hughes wrote many of his blues pieces to be performed, after all, and he sang his poems to himself as he composed them. His work was first performed vocally in 1925, and in 1927 Lola Wilson "danced interpretations" of his poetry.[47] In keeping with Hughes's assertion that "it was difficult for any colored person to gain entrance" into "the American entertainment field . . . except as a performer,"[48] the historical context of early twentieth-century bodily performances—which I limit here to the blues and drag—elucidates the materiality of the poetic performances in *The Weary Blues.*

Hughes has been revered in literary history as "the first and greatest poet to write in a blues form."[49] In 1927, Howard Mumford Jones contended that Hughes "contributed a really new verse form to the English language,"[50] a claim that aligns Hughes with a conventional definition of modernism as experimentation even as his primary poetic influences were democratic poets like Walt Whitman and Carl Sandburg. Hughes's adoption of the blues was in fact part of what Michael North identifies as Harlem Renaissance writers' attempt "to free a language from domination" by traditional linguistic and literary forms, but the blues's vernacular could also be viewed by racial and linguistic purists as degenerate, especially considering the early-twentieth-century transatlantic craze to standardize the English language.[51]

Given such potential degeneracy, it is surprising that, in the myriad analyses of Hughes's blues poetic, scholars have largely neglected his aesthetic's historical affiliation with queerness.[52] Baker, for instance, argues that the blues conveys "genuine reflections of the true emotional referents and experiential categories of black life" and that the form "constitutes the essence of black discursive modernism,"[53] but nowhere does he acknowledge queerness as a "true emotional" and "experiential" component of this "essence," which is striking because Hughes wrote *The Weary Blues* during a period in which queerness was often integrated into the lyrics and performances of blues songs. As Eric Garber records, "The blues reflected a culture that accepted sexuality, including homosexual behavior and identities, as a natural part of life."[54]

In point of fact, the most renowned Harlem blues singers, including Lucille Bogan, George Hanna, and Ma Rainey, performed songs featuring queer content like "B. D. Women Blues," "Sissy Man Blues," "Freakish Blues," "Sissy Blues," and "Prove It on Me Blues." Hughes's favorite singers—Ethel Waters, Alberta Hunter, Bessie Smith, and Gladys Bentley—all engaged in homoerotic behavior, and many of them openly participated in drag culture, creating what Gary Holcomb calls a culture of "drag blues."[55] In *The Big Sea*, Hughes reserves special regard for Bentley, who famously performed in a white tuxedo and top hat and whom Hughes calls "an amazing exhibition of musical energy—a large, dark, masculine lady . . . a perfect piece of African sculpture, animated by her own rhythm."[56] An "exhibition" of "African sculpture" performing in drag, Bentley encapsulates, for Hughes, the primitive drag of Harlem spectacles in color, a figure fitting the primitivist contexts in which many blues performances were staged. The most famous strip of speakeasies and clubs, establishments that Hughes considered akin to theaters,[57] was called the Jungle, for instance, where Bentley performed at the suggestively named Clam House.

This historical affinity between the blues and drag may derive from the similar affects that both aesthetics aimed to embody and to garner. As Hughes characterizes it, the blues is "ironic laughter mixed with tears,"[58] "incongruous laughter of . . . an animal sadness,"[59] paradoxes that Yusef Komunyakaa helpfully summarizes as follows: "The laughter fuses with the crying and the synthesis is affirmation."[60] This affirmation is explicitly sexualized when Hughes writes that blues songs were "gay songs because you had to be gay or die."[61] *Gay*, one of Hughes's favorite adjectives, could connote queerness in this period, though it was not a taxonomic identity category; it also meant joyful, aligned with Komunyakaa's "affirmation."[62] The word *gay* itself thus celebrates queerly sexual affect, and it is no surprise that Hughes uses it more often in *The Weary Blues* than in any of his other books.[63] If, as Hughes maintained, the blues also exhibits a "veiled weariness,"[64] then he affirms nonnormative sexual feeling, gayness, through the low-down folk and down-low "veiled" nature of the blues.

As Esther Newton records, such feeling was also central to drag performance, which often relies on a camp aesthetic, a "*system* of humor" that Newton defines just as Hughes defines the blues: "Camp humor is a system of laughing at one's incongruous position instead of crying. That is, the humor does not cover up, it transforms."[65] The ironic affect that "transforms" despair into joy is the affirmed locus of the chiastic process of gender crossing, and it is created through disidentification with oppressive forces, the sources of "crying." While Newton argues that "the drag concept implies *distance* between the actor and the role or 'act'"[66]—distance between anatomical configuration and gender performance—camp reveals how drag can imply proximity between the affects of the actor and act. The referential feeling of camp thus unsettles Newton's assertions that "all drag symbolism opposes the 'inner' or 'real' self (subjective self) to the 'outer' self (social self)" and that, most important, drag always already opposes the "'naturalness'" of gender and sexuality.[67] Instead, as Chauncey notes, gender crossing provided many queers with "a means of constructing public personas they considered more congruent with their 'inner natures.'"[68]

Insofar as "communities are to be distinguished, not by their falsity/genuineness, but by the style in which they are imagined,"[69] the affective and stylistic similarities between the blues and drag indicate how both media provided Harlem residents the means to consolidate a community. It is no accident, then, that Alain Locke characterizes his New Negro by claiming that "Negro thoughts now wear the uniform of the age,"[70] for, as Stephen Knadler contends, sartorial performance is a traditional mode of African American liberation. "A boastful parading of fashion and self-adornment," Knadler documents, "was a way for African Americans (even during slavery) to take back a measure of control over their bodies and their souls—to affirm themselves."[71]

In the Harlem Renaissance, this concern for physical spectacle coincided with writers' characterizations of the movement in scientific terms. James Weldon Johnson, for instance, viewed self-adornment as one of the most significant expressive media[72] and also declared in *The New Negro* that "Harlem is more than a Negro community; it is a large scale laboratory experiment in the racial problem."[73] A devotee of sexology, Locke similarly described Harlem as "the laboratory of a great race-welding" wherein ethnic "sentiment and experience" fuse to create a "consensus of feeling," if not of racial identity.[74]

Such fusion of the sartorial and the scientific resonates in the period's sexological work, which measured race and sexuality by somatic signs thought to yield essential information about the body's soul. Paradoxically, lack of racial and gender differentiation was the most visible sign of blacks' and queers' degeneration. As recorded in Robert Park and Ernest Burgess's

1921 *Introduction to the Science of Sociology*, which taught that "the Negro is, by natural disposition . . . the *lady* among the races,"[75] blackness was "a trope for *gender* indeterminacy."[76] At the same time, racial difference (i.e., nonwhiteness) was represented as a "queer physiognomy" in which "different citations blur together, and the people [whom sexologists] purport to represent merge into a mass of brown bodies."[77] Similarly, inspired by Charles Darwin's claim that "some extremely remote progenitor of the whole vertebrate kingdom appears to have been hermaphrodite or androgynous" (207), many sexologists explained homosexuality "as the outcome of an 'arrested development' at a stage prior to full differentiation of the sexes.[78] Given these characterizations, it follows that miscegenation was also considered degenerate because the miscegenate body would literalize the failure to differentiate between races.[79] Sexological discourse about race and queerness thus promoted what Barbara Spackman summarily calls a logic of "degenderation".[80] The nonwhite and/or queer confused binaries by fusing them, stopped short of sexual and racial differentiation, and therefore threatened the survival of the (white) race.

This idea was especially propounded by Havelock Ellis, whom Hughes not only read and wrote about but to whom he sent a copy of *Fine Clothes to the Jew* (1927), which Ellis admired.[81] While not affirming Ellis's condescending rhetoric, Hughes's poems co-opt, for instance, Ellis's claim that "where we differ from the savage, and in so differing also differ indeed from ourselves of yesterday, is that to-day we seek to contemplate sex objectively and impersonally, to disentangle it from the felted textures in which it was so tightly woven that we hardly ever saw it naked."[82] To Ellis, degenerates not only refuse to distinguish between the sexes but also cannot "perceive the distinction between real and imitation normality";[83] cross-dressing would only exacerbate this problem, but it would also suggest that, to the degenerate, "imitation" denotes one's "real . . . normality."

In point of fact, Ellis held that cross-dressers, whose practice he alternately termed "sexo-aesthetic inversion" and "eonism," were distinguished by "aesthetic emotion," by "the impulse to project themselves by sympathetic feeling into the object to which they are attracted, or the impulse of inner imitation," which is, he maintains, "the essence of all aesthetic feeling."[84] Ellis's association of gender performance and art through the locus of feeling suggests how cross-dressers, homosexual or not, might use the expressive form of "imitation" to convey the "essence" of their "inner" feeling, an affect perhaps related to the androgynous body that Darwin associates with vertebrate evolution. Recalling Locke's "uniform," Ellis's aesthetic, affective theory of transvestism encapsulates Hughes's point of intervention into sexological discourse, for the "felted textures" of sexual savages (or drag performers) suggest that degenerate subjectivity is based on sensory affect, on what is "felt" and touched ("textures").

While Hughes bears a subversive relation to Ellis, he finds a more direct scientific alignment with Louis Berman, whose 1922 *The Glands Regulating Personality* Hughes not only admired but used to understand how his own glands might regulate his personality (specifically his ambivalence toward communism).[85] A scientific text aligned with Darwin's basic theoretical principle that nature is material and mutable, Berman's study proposes that science can "assure us that human nature, in spite of its beast-brute-slave origins holds the possibility of a genuine transformation of its texture."[86] Evoking Ellis's "felted textures" with the possibility of "a genuine transformation," Berman's anti-eugenic, physiological text queerly rebuffs the idea that human nature is immutable even as it naturalistically proposes that glands and internal secretions regulate individual personality, affect, and behavior.[87] To Berman, the body determines one's personality just as any metaphysical dimension might.[88] Because he believes that the body's secretions are subject to change, however, Berman positions "the nature of the queer beings" he studies as queerly natural.[89] Indeed, he believes that cross-gender behavior is glandular and can (but need not) be manipulated; "homo-sexuality," similarly, "is not purely a psychic matter" but is grounded in the physical, and ever-changing, body.[90]

Given this performative and discursive context, Baker's proposal that "the reading or performance by human beings of a . . . graphemic record . . . constitutes *the event* and, in the process, produces (or reproduces) a meaningful text"[91] illuminates how the poetic performances of racial and gender instability in *The Weary Blues* consolidate affective experience by disidentifying with the discourses that they otherwise undermine. The poems focalize the embodied and affectively felt *"event"* that subtends the production of any textual body, sexological or literary. The texts' historical context and performative content reveal, then, what E. Patrick Johnson refers to as "not only blackness as *discourse* [performative], but also . . . embodied blackness in that moment where discourse and flesh conjoin in performance," that moment when the poems' speakers say "'I am' and are so, so real."[92] By this logic, even as the volume's poems wear referential instability on their surfaces by embracing sexological stereotypes, *The Weary Blues* always exists in historically materialist reference with the "Negro" bodies and the weary feelings that Hughes lyrically historicizes.

The Low-Down Pierrot Down-Low

The trouble with white folks singing blues is that they can't get low
down enough.

BESSIE SMITH TO LANGSTON HUGHES[93]

In his introduction to *The Weary Blues*, Carl Van Vechten advertises the
book as a collection exhibiting "an essentially sensitive and subtly illusive
nature, seeking always to break through the veil that obscures, for [Hughes],
the ultimate needs of that nature."[94] An instructive précis of what I am calling the book's chiastic aesthetic—its use of crossing on structural and
textural levels—Van Vechten's description highlights how the poetic performances in *The Weary Blues* manifest a performatively queer, "subtly illusive nature" and a nonperformative referentiality (the book tries to "break
through the veil that obscures" its "essentially sensitive . . . nature"). Van
Vechten's mention of the poet in this description also highlights the book's
first generic crossing between biography and fiction: Hughes says that *The
Weary Blues* was a personal collection,[95] but he also claims that his speakers are usually "the poor and uneducated Negro of the South,"[96] which
Hughes himself was not. Irreducible to autobiography or dramatic
character—Hughes maintained "that much of his poetry 'is in the form of
a kind of dramatic monologue,'"[97] yet most of his speakers are too vaguely
sketched to be called characters—Hughes's speakers in *The Weary Blues*,
more than in his other books (which he avows were less personal), cross a
literary line between author and speaker.

Regardless of biography, Hughes's blues poems are a hybrid of lyric and
dramatic modes: They are neither solely the personal reflections of individual speakers nor only poems voiced from speakers to addressees but are
typically both. Such crossing occurs on another generic level, for Hughes
adapts the oral tradition of the blues to the written page, "producing poems that manage to capture the quality of genuine blues in performance
while remaining effective as poems."[98] In the early twentieth century, such
transcription would surely have been deemed degenerate, given sexologists'
warnings against the failure to differentiate; indeed, the oral blues was classified as such.[99] Reflecting an aesthetic of balance, moreover, blues songs
and poems are not entirely free verse but dance, like T. S. Eliot's vers li-
bre, with the ghost of some structure. As Ponce notes, Hughes's blues is
designed on a traditional twelve-bar *aab* form that he modifies with en-
jambment.[100] The poet maintains a traditional formal reference, then, even
as he modernizes it with lineation and syntactic innovation.

Even more prominently than these formal crossings, the poems in *The Weary Blues* exhibit the racial and gender crossings that sexologists associated with primitive undifferentiation. Evinced in the book's section divisions—"The Weary Blues," "Dream Variations," "The Negro Speaks of Rivers," "Black Pierrot," "Water-front Streets," "Shadows in the Sun," and "Our Land"—Hughes's aim, as a lyric historian, is to document the history and the present-day experience of African Americans. It follows, then, that of the book's sixty-nine poems, twenty-four have no gendered speaker or erotic focus; instead, they anonymously parade, as in a pageant play, Negro history in locales ranging from Africa to the American South to Harlem cabarets.

Throughout these historical poems, the low-down folk constitute Hughes's primary locus of racial primitivism. In his 1926 essay "The Negro Artist and the Racial Mountain," after opening with a psychoanalytic account of how blacks "subconsciously" (and mistakenly) want to be white, Hughes declares that "the low-down folks, the so-called common element . . . are the majority" among Negroes and "furnish a wealth of colorful, distinctive material for any artist because they still hold their own individuality in the face of American standardizations."[101] When he claims that they also evince "the eternal tom-tom beating in the Negro soul—the tom-tom of revolt," Hughes primitivizes the folk, but he does so not to posit the essential truth of blackness but to argue that, if claimed, a common heritage can function as a "Negro" act of "revolt" against the "white world."[102] The "low-down" art form Hughes most anticipates is "the rise of the Negro theater," for he believes that folk performance can set blacks "free within ourselves," where the spatial orientation of freedom ("within") indicates the stable reference of Hughes's poetic performances: affective experience.[103] The down-low theatrical gender instability of Hughes's historical poems provides such freedom, such unidentified, natural balance.

Of the volume's forty-five other poems, only three, "Lament for Dark Peoples," "Epilogue," and "Mother to Son," announce their speakers' genders. But even these poems exhibit racial and gender indeterminacy, which indicates how no poem in *The Weary Blues* evades the sexological problem of racial or gender undifferentiation. In "Lament," the male speaker's race is unstable: He "was a red man one time" and "a black man, too" (39). Similarly, in "Epilogue" ("I, Too" in *Collected Poems*) the speaker proclaims, "I am the darker brother," but he ends the poem with the claim that "I, too, am America." Recalling the "dark" assignation of "Lament," the speaker's first self-description refuses a stable term of racial identification, and his second self-description, as "America," expands such categorical instability. The speaker's indistinct self-authorization bespeaks Hughes's engagement with sexological stereotypes and his attempt to be a representative poet, to historicize modernist Harlem's manifold voices (46).

Insofar as "racial authenticity is and is not a matter of skin color,"[104] Hughes destabilizes color itself to highlight how insufficient the category "black" (or any color) is to signify the authentic experience of the "Negro." In the "Negro" section of *The Big Sea*, for instance, Hughes recollects how, during his trip to Africa, "the Africans looked at me and would not believe I was a Negro. . . . In Africa, the word [*Negro*] is more pure. It means *all* Negro, therefore *black*." Hughes learns from this encounter that "I am not black," an astonishing claim from a poet heralded by many to be African America's representative writer. Instead, Hughes explains, to Africans "I am brown,"[105] an observation that suggests that racial multiplicity cannot be maintained in visual categories. "Realiz[ing] that most dark Negroes in America do not like the word *black* at all,"[106] Hughes opts, as the chapter title suggests, to use the term *Negro* because of its cultural and affective, rather than visually taxonomic, logic of categorization.

This representational decision is clear in the poem that opens *The Weary Blues*. Titled "Proem" and later anthologized as "Negro," the poem is framed by the refrain "I am a Negro: / Black as the night is black, / Black like the depths of my Africa" (24), lines whose syntactic organization chiastically reverses the blues's *aab* structure. A possible response to Hughes's experience in Africa, the ungendered speaker's claim that he or she is a "Negro" Because, as the colon suggests, he or she is "black" confounds Hughes's view of racial multiplicity. But the poem's interceding stanzas disrupt the equation of blackness with negritude because this speaker is many Negroes: He or she is a "slave" to "Caesar" and "Washington"; a "worker" in the "pyramids" and at the "Woolworth Building"; a "singer" "from Africa to Georgia" singing "sorrow songs" and "ragtime"; and a "victim" of "the Belgians" and "lynch" mobs in "Mississippi." The poem's transhistorical logic unsettles the speaker's stable identity as much as his or her lack of gender does, and he or she emerges by text's end just as downlow in racial, national, and historical orientation as in gender status. When the refrain returns to tell us that this "Negro" is "Black as the night is black, / Black like the depths of my Africa," then, each line's unstable simile questions, first, the colored quality connoted by the ploce "black" and, second, the colored quality of Africa's "depths." Disrupting conventional equations between negritude, Africa, and blackness, "black" emerges as one unstable visual taxon, as in "Lament" and "Epilogue," that contributes to

the speaker's racial feeling, to his or her nature as a "Negro" who has suf-
fered the history of Negro oppression.

In this context, "Lament" and "Epilogue" may be stably gendered poems, but they compound the volume's racial instability as announced in
"Proem." "Mother to Son," the only other poem with a gendered speaker,
similarly unsettles the apparent stability of its speaker's identity. Remarkably not identified by race, the speaker is gendered only by the poem's title; she then relates how "life for me ain't been no crystal stair" and enjoins
her "boy" not to "turn back. / Don't you set down on the steps / 'Cause you
finds it's kinder hard" (30). A blues poem spoken from a maternal figure to
a boy, the piece invokes the laughing-crying aesthetic historically associated with both the blues and drag; consequently, if read in the context of
not only the culture of drag blues but also the other drag blues poems in
The Weary Blues, "Mother to Son" holds more queer potential than the heteronormative implications of its familial title suggest. Familial referents
were often used among cross-dressers[107] after all, and "the mother figure
is perhaps the most prevalent familial trope in black gay vernacular and
culture."[108] Considering this context, one possible explanation for the
speaker's lack of racial (and, other than her title, gender) identity is that, as
the term *mother* denotes in drag culture, this mother is an aged, well-
respected drag queen speaking to, by the logic of the familial drag conceit, a queer youth. The potential for this queer reading further emerges
from Hughes's claim that "the papa and the mama—maybe both—are
anonymous" in blues culture.[109] While "mama" and "mother" appear to
be not only stably gendered but also gender-normative names, in the blues,
Hughes records, they actually denote anonymity, the lack of a name: identity on the down-low. Because the mother's gender and racial identity are
"anonymous" in this blues poem, "Mother to Son" foregrounds its speaker's low-down feeling.

Its potential queerness notwithstanding, "Mother to Son" is the only
Weary Blues poem to feature a gendered speaker and addressee, and "Lament" and "Epilogue" are the volume's only masculine-gendered (but racially unstable) pieces; none of these three, notably, offers much in the way
of eros. As mentioned, twenty- four poems are ungendered, unerotic historical poems. The volume's forty-two other poems could arguably be
called erotic, however, and in twenty-five of them the addressee or erotic
object's gender is identified, but the speaker's is not. In the seventeen other
erotic poems, the gender of neither the speaker nor the addressee or erotic
object is clear.[110] All but three of the poems in *The Weary Blues* are ambiguously gendered, then, and the three that are not could still be considered

ethnically performative. It is for this reason that I call *The Weary Blues* a drag ball, for the book's performance of categorical instability is coincident with the drag balls Hughes attended. When the low-down focus of the book's racial aesthetic crosses with this down-low instability, the product is Hughes's primitive drag, the drag that depicts nonnormative feeling as natural.

Hughes's draglike poems could have been read as queer in modernist Harlem, where the "hegemonic way of understanding sexuality" among the lower classes (Hughes's "folk") was "on the basis of [queers'] imaginary gender status."[111] In this period, to deviate from (or to elide) gender normativity was to deviate from sexual normativity because the popular, not to mention the scientific, belief was that "cross-dressing is generally an earmark of sexual intermediacy."[112] Nonetheless, if drag is "an allegory that works through the hyperbolic [and] brings into relief what is, after all, determined only in relation to the hyperbolic: the understated, taken-for-granted quality of heterosexual performativity,"[113] the seemingly "understated" poems of *The Weary Blues* may appear anything but draglike or queer. Indeed, Hughes's work has long been "taken for granted" as heteroerotically normative, but the overwhelmingly unstable representations of race and gender in *The Weary Blues* might more aptly be called hyperbolically unhyperbolic, which suggests that the book's ostentatious elisions of marked identity expose the hyperbolically "understated" quality of normative gender performativity. As does Hughes's queer mélange of Harlem events in "Spectacles in Color," the exaggeratedly unhyperbolic gender performances in *The Weary Blues* reveal how gender performativity itself is always draglike and all the more so when gender normativity is "taken for granted."

Buttressing this theatrical reading, Hughes makes theatricality itself a pervasive subject of *The Weary Blues*. The section title "Black Pierrot," for instance, refers to the French pantomime figure who performs in whiteface and loose white clothes. The figure evokes the minstrel tradition of blackface, then, but if the modifier "black" denotes a black actor performing whiteness, this figure would reverse the minstrel tradition; simultaneously, the figure could be a white actor performing in black-face, reversing only the Pierrot's performance, not his or her own race. The uncertainty of the figure's color again suggests, as in "Proem," the inability of the term *black* to represent racial feeling: He or she is a "spectacle in color" unlike the spectacles in black or white found in the minstrel and Pierrot traditions.

The section's eponymous poem exemplifies how, in *The Weary Blues*, racial and gender crossing balance at the center of queer feeling. With its female addressee, theatrical title, blues affect, and uncertainly gendered speaker, "A Black Pierrot," which Hughes set to music in 1950, reads like a song that Bentley, Hughes's metonym for primitive drag, might have performed. Reconfiguring the blues's *aab* structure just as in "Proem," the poem's refrain—"I am a black Pierrot:/She did not love me,/So I crept [later "wept" and "went"] . . ." (31)—emphasizes the speaker's theatrical blackness and his or her erotic rejection by a female beloved over the course of three stanzas. Each stanza procedurally accretes one line to expand the speaker's blues even as his or her "soul" is "[s]hrunken like a balloon without air." Such paradoxical accretion and depletion centers on the speaker's "once gay-colored soul," which he or she wants to redeem by "seek[ing] a new brown love," a notably ungendered and unraced figure. A synesthetic construction that emphasizes the nonnormatively affective, sexual, and spectacular nature of his or her subjectivity, the speaker's "gay-colored soul" emerges by poem's end as the black Pierrot's performative offering: In the spirit of the blues, this speaker learns to laugh in spite of his or her sadness as he or she embraces the queer possibility of unidentified erotic experience.

Performing Performativity: A Queer-of-Color Critique

I feel like . . . losing myself, to all who know who I am, in a distant city where I could live according to my queer nature.

EARL LIND, THE FEMALE-IMPERSONATORS, 74

As these poetic examples reveal, *The Weary Blues* is structured on the basis of gender, sexual, racial, and literary-historical crossings and constitutes a poetic, primitive drag ball: a spectacle in Harlem color. As such, the book challenges present-day literary-historical narratives of the Harlem Renaissance and dominant theories of performativity. Essex Hemphill's contention that Harlem Renaissance writers' racial concerns "precluded issues of sexuality,"[114] for example, misreads not only Hughes's lyric histories of queer feeling but also his lyric histories of African American experience. Similarly, Henry Louis Gates, Jr.'s claim that Richard Bruce Nugent "was the first writer who directly raised the issue of what being black and being gay might have to do with each other,"[115] while rightly recognizing Nugent's aesthetic, overlooks the imbrications of Hughes's low-down and down-low practices. Nugent himself, in fact, contended that Hughes had his "hand on the pulse" of the Harlem Renaissance more than Locke, its ostensible leader.[116] Considering his hardly down-low queerness, Nugent's observation suggests that Hughes might be representative of a Harlem Renaissance queerness that has largely been ignored, one both veiled and revealed in the form of primitive drag.

In point of fact, Nugent's cover for an issue of the otherwise conservative publication *Opportunity* published in March 1926, two months after *The Weary Blues*, depicts Harlem's "pulse" at that time as one throbbing to primitive drag. The drawing reads, provocatively, like an amalgamated rendering of Van Vechten's March 1932 photographic portrait of Hughes, whose pose in profile with the portrait of a seemingly African woman aligns the figures. Given his or her earring, headdress (the circles representing hair are large enough to be sequins or paillettes), and rouged cheeks (whether tinted by sun or by cosmetics, which may also color the lips and eye area), Nugent's figure could easily be an African man or woman; he or she is, in other words, an emblem of primitive drag, an aesthetic that Van Vechten's portrait evokes by correlating Hughes and the female figure. Moreover, the phallic palm tree in the Nugent drawing's upper-left corner sexualizes this aesthetic's setting and suggests the erotic "pulse" enlivened by gender performance, the pulse and performance on which Hughes had his poetic hand.[117]

In addition to highlighting this neglected historical feeling, Hughes's poems confound twenty-first-century distinctions between performance and performativity. In Butler's terms, "performance as bounded 'act' is distinguished from performativity insofar as the latter consists in a reiteration of norms which precede, constrain, and exceed the performer. . . . [W]hat is 'performed' works to conceal, if not to disavow, what remains opaque, unconscious, unperformable." Here performance seems to function as little more than the vehicle of performativity's dually naturalizing and denaturalizing aims, but if "the reduction of performativity to performance would be a mistake,"[118] the opposite must also hold true. The disruptive, down-low "acts" of performance in *The Weary Blues* reiterate sexological norms, but in doing so they reveal, not "conceal" or "disavow," "what remains": the feeling produced by disrupting those norms. Through their low-down, primitive quality, Hughes's performative poems remind us that *perform* means not just "pretend to do" but "do, carry out." Both pretending and doing, Hughes's poems perform to disrupt racist and homophobic understandings of nature, and they literally perform Hughes's vision of an embodied queer Negro nature. In Kimberly Benston's terms, "they comprehend diasporic consciousness," or a consciousness of crossing, "not merely as conceit but as material condition."[119]

What Hughes's poems perform of race they also perform of gender and sexuality. Insofar as "sexuality is clearly the least constrained (most affect-like) of the drives," as Sedgwick contends,[120] *The Weary Blues* performs gender instability to manifest the somatic affect of sexuality, especially its queer feelings. Against Butler's understanding of gender performativity, which fixates on discourse and epistemology, Hughes's poetry requires "asking new questions about phenomenology and affect (what motivates performativity and performance, for example, and what individual and collective effects are mobilized in their execution?)"[121] Performing as embodied and affectively natural what it performatively exposes as unstably gendered, *The Weary Blues* offers representations of gender and sexuality that cannot be accommodated by contemporary gender performativity theory, which, like much current critical thought, thrives on the motto "(you can't say it often enough) *It's not natural.*"[122]

As the epigraph from Lind indicates, such categorical opposition to nature obscures many modernists' literary and sexual innovations. When Lind claims that he went to New York because he wanted to "live according to my queer nature," he records what to many contemporary queer theorists must be a contradiction in terms, for to them, queerness has nothing to do with nature. Queerly distinguishing nature from normativity, the natural from the naturalized, the cross-dressing Lind, like Hughes's *The Weary Blues*, offers a productive paradox for rethinking literary histories of modernism and theories of sexuality by the Darwinian notion that "the nature of the universe," as Hughes calls it, is always subject to change, or queering. Neither constructionist nor essentialist nor nonreferentially queer, modernist literature like *The Weary Blues* offers what Sedgwick calls "a political vision of difference that might resist both binary homogenization and infinitizing trivialization."[123] Like the "stories" that "mingle themselves softly/in the dark shadows that cross and recross" in the *Weary Blues* poem "Aunt Sue's Stories" (*Collected Poems* 23), the spectacles in color depicted in *The Weary Blues*, its "crossword puzzles" decked out in the "felted textures" of drag and its affects, cross early-twentieth-century racial and gender lines to historicize poetically how feeling degenerate, low and down, constituted Langston Hughes's vision of the Harlem Renaissance's queer nature.

NOTES

1. Langston Hughes, *Essays on Art, Race, Politics, and World Affairs*, ed. Christopher C. De Santis (Columbia, Mo.; London: University of Missouri Press, 2002), 523.

2. Ibid., 273.

3. Ibid., 274, 276.

4. George Chauncey, *Gay New York: Gender, Urban Culture, and the Making of the Gay World, 1890–1940* (New York: Basic, 1994), 244, 201.

5. Earl Lind, *The Female-Impersonators* (1922; rpt., Amsterdam: Fredonia, 2005), 297.

6. Ibid., 246.

7. Ibid., 168; Thomas H. Wirth, Introduction to *Gay Rebel of the Harlem Renaissance: Selections from the Work of Richard Bruce Nugent*, ed. Thomas H. Wirth (Durham, N.C.: Duke University Press, 2002), 60.

8. Hughes, *Essays*, 375, 377.

9. Langston Hughes, *The Big Sea* (1940; rpt., New York: Hill, 1993), 276–8.

10. Hughes, *Essays*, 263.

11. Ibid., 523.

12. Butler uses the term "performativity" to denote both "a repetition and a ritual, which achieves its effects through its naturalization in the context of a body" (*Gender*, xv) and the "relation of being implicated in that which one opposes, this turning of power against itself to produce alternative modalities of power" (*Bodies*, 241). To distinguish my method from Butler's, however, I use the term "performativity" to refer to the disruptive properties of *The Weary Blues* and "performance" to refer to the poems' embodied, affective record of such instability. This revision of Butler's theory coincides with Sedgwick's endeavor to focus on the intrasubjective affect and phenomenology of performativity rather than, as Butler does, solely on its discursive properties as "repetition" and "relation."

13. Judith Butler, *Bodies That Matter* (New York: Routledge, 1993), 1.

14. Judith Butler, *Gender Trouble* (New York: Routledge, 1990), 177.

15. Eve Kosofsky Sedgwick, *Touching Feeling: Affect, Pedagogy, Performativity* (Durham, N.C.: Duke University Press, 2003), 68; Butler, *Bodies*, 108.

16. Rei Terada, *Feeling in Theory: Emotion after the "Death of the Subject"* (Cambridge: Harvard University Press, 2001), 31.

17. Hughes, *Essays*, 408, 507, 508.

18. Sianne Ngai, *Ugly Feelings* (Cambridge: Harvard University Press, 2005), 5.

19. Langston Hughes, *I Wonder As I Wander: An Autobiographical Journey* (1956; rpt., New York: Hill, 1993), 3.

20. Hughes, *Essays*, 319–20.

21. Carl Van Vechten, *Remember Me to Harlem: The Letters of Langston Hughes and Carl Van Vechten*, ed. Emily Bernard (New York: Knopf, 2001), 101.

22. Hughes, *Big Sea*, 311.

23. Ibid., 208.

24. Scott Herring, *Queering the Underworld: Slumming, Literature, and the Undoing of Lesbian and Gay History* (Chicago: University of Chicago Press, 2007), 196–7.

25. Ibid., 198.

26. For the most comprehensive discussion of Hughes's biographically ambiguous sexuality, see Rampersad 27, 45, 77, and Vogel. For provocative queer readings of Hughes's work, see Vogel, who analyzes the queer temporality of Hughes's first two books of poetry; Schwarz, who claims that Hughes pathologizes gender-crossing queers to valorize "'manly' and heterosexual narratives" (87); and Ponce, who attends to "the ambiguity and mobility of the 'I' emerging in [Hughes's] poems [which] point toward Hughes's fluid, gender-crossing positionality" (507). My analysis diverges from Ponce's assumption that *The Weary Blues* has a more stable "I" subject than does Hughes's later work (510).

27. Hughes, *I Wonder*, 59.

28. Hughes, *Big Sea*, 263.

29. All citations of Hughes's poems, including those from *The Weary Blues*, are from *Collected Poems*.

30. Hughes, *Essays*, 310.

31. José Esteban Muñoz, *Disidentifications: Queers of Color and the Performance of Politics* (Minneapolis: University of Minnesota Press, 1999), 79.

32. Hughes, *Essays*, 404.

33. Hughes, *I Wonder*, 204.

34. Havelock Ellis, *Studies in the Psychology of Sex*, vol. 1, (1927; rpt., Middlesex: Echo Lib., 2007), 6.

35. Roderick Ferguson, *Aberrations in Black: Toward a Queer of Color Critique* (Minneapolis: University of Minnesota Press, 2004), 34.

36. Martin Joseph Ponce, "Langston Hughes' Queer Blues," *Modern Language Quarterly* 66, no. 4 (2005): 514.

37. "Negro Poet Sings of Life in Big Cities," *Washington Post* (Feb. 6, 1927), rpt. in Tish Dace, ed., *Langston Hughes: The Contemporary Reviews* (Cambridge: Cambridge University Press, 1997), 89; "Under the Lash of the Whip: A Column of Constructive Criticism of Men and Measures in the Hope of Correcting Errors and Evils," *Chicago Whip* (Feb. 26, 1927), rpt. in Dace, 100.

38. W[illiam] M. K[elley], "Langston Hughes: The Sewer Dweller," *New York Amsterdam News* (Feb. 9, 1927), rpt. in Dace, 91–2.

39. Orrin C. Evans, "Modern Muse Presents New Book of Poems," *Philadelphia Tribune* (Feb. 12, 1927), rpt. in Dace, 92–3. These pejorative

remarks were made about Hughes's second book, *Fine Clothes to the Jew*
(1927), which is as nonnormative as *The Weary Blues* but less representative of
the "laureate" title Hughes also received. *The Weary Blues* establishes the
"low-down," "degenerate" framework on which *Fine Clothes* builds, but it also
contains the "down-low" ambiguity that fostered Hughes's canonicity as
Negro spokesman. As Hughes admitted in 1927, "'Weary Blues' will always
be the most popular book, I think. Its [sic] more 'poetically' poetic" than
Fine Clothes (Langston Hughes Papers, box 3, folder 98). Many of the poems
in *Fine Clothes* were written at the same time as those in *The Weary Blues*,
however, which suggests how cries about the former's degeneracy easily
could be applied to the latter.

40. Hughes, *Essays*, 97, 41.

41. Hughes, *I Wonder*, 42.

42. Hughes, *Big Sea*, 285.

43. Hughes, *Essays*, 408.

44. W. E. B. DuBois, *The Souls of Black Folk* (New York: Penguin, 1996),
4.

45. Hughes, *Essays*, 213.

46. Houston A. Baker, Jr., *Blues, Ideology, and Afro-American Literature: A
Vernacular Theory* (Chicago: University of Chicago Press, 1984), 97.

47. Van Vechten, 49.

48. Hughes, *I Wonder*, 328.

49. Ponce, 506.

50. Howard Mumford Jones, "Two Negro Artists," *Chicago Daily News*
(June 29, 1927), rpt. in Dace, 125.

51. Michael North, *The Dialect of Modernism: Race, Language and Twentieth-
Century Literature* (Oxford: Oxford University Press, 1994), ii, 19–20.

52. Vogel's recent "Closing Time," which examines the queer implications of cabaret settings for Hughes's poetry, is an important exception to
this critical history.

53. Baker, 73, 93.

54. Eric Garber, "A Spectacle in Color: The Lesbian and Gay Subculture
of Jazz Age Harlem," in *Hidden from History: Reclaiming the Gay and Lesbian
Past*, ed. Martin Duberman, Martha Vicinus, and George Chauncey, Jr.
(New York: NAL, 1989), 320.

55. Gary Holcomb, *Claude McKay, Code Name Sasha: Queer Black Marx-
ism and the Harlem Renaissance* (Gainesville: University Press of Florida,
2007), 111.

56. Hughes, *Big Sea*, 226.

57. Hughes, *Essays*, 301.

58. Ibid., 33.

59. Van Vechten, 12.

60. Yusef Komunyakaa, "Langston Hughes + Poetry = Blues," *Callaloo* 25, no. 4 (2002): 1141.

61. Hughes, *Essays*, 209.

62. Chauncey, 14–17, 24–5.

63. Peter Mandelik and Stanley Schatt, *A Concordance to the Poetry of Langston Hughes* (Detroit: Gale, 1975), 90.

64. Qtd. in Arnold Rampersad, *1902–1941: I, Too, Sing America* (Oxford: Oxford University Press, 1986), 140.

65. Esther Newton, *Mother Camp: Female Impersonators in America* (Englewood Cliffs, N.J.: Prentice Hall, 1972), 109.

66. Ibid.

67. Ibid., 100, 103.

68. Chauncey, 49.

69. Benedict Anderson, *Imagined Communities: Reflections on the Origin and Spread of Nationalism* (London: Verso, 1983), 15.

70. Alain Locke, "Negro Youth Speaks," in Alain Locke, ed., *The New Negro* (1925; rpt., New York: Simon & Schuster, 1992), 50.

71. Stephen Knadler, "Sweetback Style: Wallace Thurman and a Queer Harlem Renaissance," *Modern Fiction Studies* 48, no. 4 (2002): 900.

72. Ibid., 903.

73. James Weldon Johnson, "Harlem: The Culture Capital" in Locke, *New Negro*, 310.

74. Locke, 7, 6, 10.

75. Robert Park and Ernest W. Burgess, *Introduction to the Science of Sociology* (Chicago: University of Chicago Press, 1921), 139.

76. Dana Seitler, "Queer Physiognomies; or, How Many Ways Can We Do the History of Sexuality?" *Criticism* 46, no. 1 (2004): 89.

77. Julian Carter, "Normality, Whiteness, Authorship: Evolutionary Sexology and the Primitive Pervert," *Science and Homosexualities*, ed. Vernon Rosario (New York: Routledge, 1997), 80, 158.

78. Ibid., 156.

79. Chauncey, 139.

80. Barbara Spackman, *Decadent Genealogies: The Rhetoric of Sickness from Baudelaire to D'Annunzio* (Ithaca, N.Y.: Cornell University Press, 1989), 25.

81. Langston Hughes Papers, box 59, folder 1118.

82. Havelock Ellis, *Sex in Civilization*, ed. V. F. Calverton and S. D. Schmalhausen (Garden City, N.J.: Garden City, 1929), 20.

83. Carter, 166.

84. Havelock Ellis, *Studies in the Psychology of Sex*, v. 7 (Philadelphia: Davis, 1928), 27.

85. Langston Hughes Papers, box 278, folder 4574.

86. Louis Berman, *The Glands Regulating Personality* (New York: Macmillan, 1922), 17.

87. Ibid., 21.

88. Ibid., 203.

89. Ibid., 1.

90. Ibid., 226–7.

91. Baker, 104.

92. E. Patrick Johnson, *Appropriating Blackness: Performance and the Politics of Authenticity* (Durham: Duke University Press, 2003), 42, 83.

93. Hughes, *The Big Sea*, 296.

94. Hughes, *Weary Blues*, 13.

95. Rampersad, 169.

96. Van Vechten, 179.

97. Ponce, 520.

98. David Chinitz, "Literacy and Authenticity: The Blues Poems of Langston Hughes," *Callaloo* 19, no. 1 (1996): 177.

99. Carter, 170.

100. Ponce, 523–4.

101. Hughes, *Essays*, 31–3.

102. Ibid., 35.

103. Ibid., 34, 36.

104. E. Johnson, 108.

105. Hughes, *Big Sea*, 11.

106. Ibid., 103.

107. Chauncey, 291.

108. E. Johnson, 91.

109. Hughes, *Essays*, 370.

110. The twenty-five poems in the former category are "To Midnight Nan at Leroy's," "To a Little Lover-Lass, Dead," "Nude Young Dancer," "To a Black Dancer," "Song for a Banjo Dance," "March Moon," "Joy," "The South," "Young Prostitute," "Pierrot," "Sick Room," "A Black Pierrot," "Ardella," "Water-front Streets," "Port Town," "Natcha," "Death of an Old Seaman," "Beggar Boy," "Troubled Woman," "Soledad," "When Sue Wears Red," "To the Dark Mercedes," "Young Bride," "Poem (to F. S.)," and "Danse Africaine." The seventeen poems in the latter category are "The Cat and the Saxophone," "Songs to the Dark Virgin," "The Jester," "After Many Springs," "Blues Fantasy," "Our Land," "Summer Night," "Lenox Avenue: Midnight," "The White Ones," "Harlem Night Club," "Jazzonia," "Cabaret," "Poème d'Automne," "Harlem Night Song," "Suicide's Note," "Poem—to the Black Beloved," and "Cross."

111. Chauncey, 13.

112. Lind, 199.

113. Butler, *Bodies*, 237.

114. Essex Hemphill, Introduction in *Brother to Brother: New Writings by Black Gay Men*, ed. Essex Hemphill (Boston: Alyson, 1991), xxii.

115. Henry Louis Gates, Jr., Foreword in Wirth, *Gay Rebel*, xii.

116. Wirth, 5.

117. See Wirth's gloss of the Nugent image for a similar reading (*Gay Rebel*, 66).

118. Butler, *Bodies*, 234.

119. Kimberly Benston, *Performing Blackness: Enactments of African-American Modernism* (New York: Routledge, 2000), 21.

120. Sedgwick, 18.

121. Ibid., 17.

122. Ibid., 109.

123. Ibid., 108.

Epilogue: The Myth of Nature

The inventiveness of a whole range of queer historical practices
might be understood as a result of the paired necessities of having
"to fight for it" and to "make it up."

—HEATHER LOVE, *Feeling Backward*[1]

The emphasis that Barnes and Woolf place on the importance of empathic feeling at the dawn of World War II—communal feeling that is distinct from Kant's "common sense"—anticipates the direction in which the concept of queer natures developed throughout the twentieth century. It developed, I will briefly suggest in this epilogue, to the status of a communal myth. Myth is generically defined as both a falsehood and a foundational tale: It is a factually untrue story that explains inexplicable phenomena in typically supernatural terms; such stories often ground the formation of selves and communities.[2] While I have focused throughout *Queer Natures* on how the Darwinian concept of nature provided queer writers with a means of aesthetic and sexual experimentation, I am interested here in exploring how this movement from literary and self-production shifts into a process of community production.

Darwin's concept of nature became one of many mythological grounds on which modern queer communities were developed. This was a particularly urgent need in the twentieth century, wherein the sexual identities propagated by sexual science became the targets of unprecedented organized political movements like those led by Adolf Hitler and the American

134

senator Joseph McCarthy. In literature, as Christopher Nealon argues, queers' interest in forming communities is manifest in a lineage of queer "foundling" texts that evince a "movement between solitary exile and collective experience" and that are "more attuned to collective experience than to individual identity."[3] This lineage, Nealon writes, "begins to be visible around World War I and picks up momentum after World War II."[4] The myth of nature was one of many myths that allowed queers to believe in their own historicity and in the possibility of transhistorical and transnational communities that are paradoxically founded on the criterion of difference.[5]

In his long poem *The Granite Butterfly*, Parker Tyler—one of the most prolific but overlooked writers in both the modernist and postmodernist traditions—exemplifies the importance of nature to twentieth-century queer aesthetics, subject formation, and social organization. In this long poem that relates the development of a queer boy into adulthood, Tyler writes,

> So myth has always been
> A lie, the moment it was uttered
>   just as, the moment it was
> Uttered, it was also a truth:
>   it was a lie to test
> The truth, and a truth to test the
>   lie, being ambivalent toward
> Itself
>   as Narcissus is
> Ambivalent toward
>   himself, as all con-
> Cepts, once they are con-
>   ceived of as Natural
> Contradict themselves
>   Nature
> Being subject to change—[6]

Published in 1945 on the fault line separating conventional literary histories of modernism and postmodernism, *The Granite Butterfly* uses Darwinian logic to ground a new myth of sexual subject and community formation for the twentieth century. Tyler begins by defining myth in its most conventional terms: "a lie" that "was also a truth," where both lies and truths "test" each other. As false and foundational, lie and truth, myth for Tyler is "ambivalent toward/Itself" and thus serves as the ideal medium through which to convey a queer bildungsroman in epic form: For myth, being "ambivalent toward/Itself," is a queer, unstable, fluid genre.

Tyler makes this association between myth and queerness most evident when he likens myth to Narcissus, one of the queerest characters in classical mythology. Depicted as impossibly beautiful (and impossibly vain), Narcissus is the demigod who transforms into the flower species narcissus in Ovid's *Metamorphoses*, itself a collection of (often queer) myths about the changing status of nature.[7] In the concluding lines of the passage quoted previously, Tyler reveals the foundational premise of this association among myth, queerness, and nature: All natural concepts must "contradict themselves/Nature/Being subject to change." While Ovid of course relies on this principle in *Metamorphoses*, Tyler also invokes here the Darwinian principle that nature is subject to change, which shows both how queer natures have existed throughout time—from Roman antiquity through American postmodernity—and how mythopoeic Darwin's thought actually is. Darwin's nature is tantamount to a myth, Tyler implies, for it is as ambivalent toward itself as myth and Narcissus—not to mention queerness—are toward themselves.

The title of *The Granite Butterfly* reinforces this mutual interplay of science and mythopoeic aesthetics in Tyler's long poem, for the butterfly is a creature whose short lifespan metaphorizes Darwinian theory: It undergoes metamorphosis from one life form to another, all while maintaining material concreteness ("granite"). The butterfly's life is ephemeral, unstable, and depends on transformation as a central principle, but it is for those qualities no less material than "granite." This seemingly oxymoronic title is as ambivalent toward itself as Tyler's definition of myth: Myth is all the more foundational—like granite—for its butterfly-like transformations and contradictions. As these lines exemplify, Tyler mimics such transformations in his flutteringly indented and enjambed lines, which transform ostensibly "granite," or assured, words like "concepts" and "conceived" into "contradictions" by breaking them at their prefixes. All concepts are subject to change, Tyler writes, making every confident conception a contradiction.

The Granite Butterfly is one of the last of many modernist long poems—exemplified by T. S. Eliot's *The Waste Land* (1922) and Hart Crane's *The Bridge* (1930)—that aim, as Ezra Pound said, to create "the tale of the tribe."[8] Yet Tyler's poem is ostensibly autobiographical and focused upon one man's development into adulthood, for Tyler describes the poem as "a personal revival of myth, not in order to reinforce the Classical form of the Medusa and Oedipus legends" but "to convert them to my own uses because I identified certain dominant experiences in my life with these two Classical figures, and yet, so doing, to revaluate the poetic, or basic, meaning of those figures."[9] Tyler uses communal myths to ground his speaker's foundational sense of self, then, but since the poem is also a long poem, this foundational sense of self synecdochically offers a tale of the queer tribe after Darwin. It is a communal tribe founded on the myth of nature: the belief that all concepts, including sexuality and literature, are subject to change.

The idea that nature after Darwin became mythic is not a new concept in the history of science. While Paul Civello claims that Darwin "succeeded for the first time in explaining organic phenomena in natural, rather than in supernatural, terms,"[10] Darwin's theory is still a theory, as continued searches for its "missing links" suggest.[11] Darwin himself claimed that inadequate fossil evidence from the geological record constituted "the most obvious and serious objection which can be urged against the theory" of evolution,[12] which is in part why, as we have seen, Darwin called the "origin" of the species "that mystery of mysteries":[13] He knew the limitations of his naturalist practice and allowed mystery to infuse nature. Thus, although Civello is right to claim that Darwin's theory of evolution served the same function as supernatural explanations for phenomena did, it would be misleading to claim that Darwin had actually explained those phenomena in anything more absolute than theoretical terms.

Upon its publication, Darwin's theory of evolution of course came into conflict most directly with mythopoeic institutions such as organized religion. To Civello, Darwin came to have a church of his own, one that, in England and America, competed with the Christian church. The church of Positivism, in fact, of which George Eliot was a member, arose during this era, but its institutional form received little membership, whereas Darwin influenced belief more persuasively outside of an institutional setting: through the publication and private consumption of his works, much in the way literature functions. Writers such as Joseph LeConte in *Evolution: Its Nature, Its Evidences, and Its Relation to Religious Thought* (1888) found ways of assimilating Darwin's nature into conventional Christian mythology, claiming that evolution was "a process in which God Himself was immanent."[14] As a theory, Darwin's theory is open to such appropriations, just as it is open to the queer appropriation of evolutionary theory as religious myth's counterpoint: secular myth.

George Levine summarizes this mythopoeic view of evolutionary theory when he claims that Darwin's work not only challenged "the basic myths of our culture," especially creation myths, but became "a literal creation myth, and carries with it the affective weight of myth."[15] As a creation myth for the modern world, Darwin's theory of nature inspires, in the manner of myth (rather than of information), belief or disbelief. For Darwin, nature was a religion of sorts: Darwin's son William wrote, in fact, that his father's "deep sense of the power of nature may be called in his case a religious feeling."[16] Whereas Max Weber famously argued that the rise of positivist science led to the disenchantment of the modern world—it ushered in a lack of mystery and ambiguity—Levine argues that Darwin's science contributes "to a radical re-enchantment of the world," because, as I examined in Chapter One, Darwin exemplifies "the attitude of wonder that is so central, on all accounts, to the experience of enchantment."[17] Darwin's theory and prose present, Levine says, "the possibility not only of doing without transcendent consolation but of finding positive value in the 'merely' natural, and of loving it."[18] After Darwin, enchantment and myth do not require divine or supernatural forces: they require only "deep feeling,"[19] which can be produced by and about the rational as much as the irrational.

In terms of queerness, that Darwin's view of nature came into conflict with Christian teachings is clear from the most well-known denunciation of queerness, which is itself mythopoeic and literary: Paul's epistle to the Romans in the King James Bible. There, Paul writes that wicked humans

> changed the glory of the uncorruptible God into an image made like to corruptible man, and to birds, and fourfooted beasts, and creeping things.

> Wherefore God also gave them up to uncleanness through the lusts of their own hearts, to dishonour their own bodies between themselves:

> Who changed the truth of God into a lie, and worshipped and served the creature more than the Creator, who is blessed for ever. Amen.

> For this cause God gave them up unto vile affections: for even their women did change the natural use into that which is against nature:

> And likewise also the men, leaving their natural use of the woman, burned in their lust toward one another, and receiving in themselves that recompence of their error which was meet. (Romans 1:24–27)

In his contradictory rhetoric of nature, Paul anticipates degeneration theorists' contradictions about the concept, for he claims that God punished humans who went "against nature" because they "changed" God's "image" into something closer to material nature: "corruptible man, "birds," and so on. Paul calls this conversion a metamorphosis of "the truth of God into a lie," for humans began to worship each other more than a supernatural force: They came to believe in the myth, the "lie," of not a supernatural deity but of "the lusts of their own hearts." Paul's naturalist rhetoric here clearly commits the naturalistic fallacy, so his condemnation of men and women who commit the "vile affections" of burning "in their lust toward one another" is nothing but a moral condemnation. While this point may seem obvious, heterosexual reproduction is so often taken to be the "natural use" to which bodies should be put that oppressive, moralizing "recompense" by this mythopoeic logic of nature continues to threaten queers through the twenty-first century.

The "lie" "against nature" that humans tell about God in Romans is the very lie that Darwin propounded in his theory of evolution. Throughout the twentieth century, Paul's view was easily rejected on Darwinian grounds: as Raymond Williams claims, modernism affirmed "the humanist and secular—and, in political terms, liberal and later socialist—proposition that human nature was not, or at least not decisively, unchanging and timeless, but was socially and culturally specific."[20] Derived from Darwinian thought, this secular belief becomes one salient example of how modernists use "classical myth and literature as a source of symbolic, self-valuable units of meaning"[21]—what T. S. Eliot called "the mythical method."[22] As I will explore in a future project, and as anticipated by the texts by Audre Lorde and Juliana Spahr that I will explore here, postmodern writers extend the modernists' mythical method through the aesthetic of magical realism. Both the mythical method and magical realism find mythical thought in largely secular texts, and even when those texts are religious, writers queer the myths' normative aims to create the strangest of foundational texts: texts that found the paradoxical concept of a queer community.

Max Horkheimer and Theodor Adorno's *Dialectic of Enlightenment* anticipates how aesthetics like the mythical method and magical realism might proliferate throughout the twentieth century, at least on the basis of a myth of nature, and how Darwinian science might usher in that modern myth. Horkheimer and Adorno argue that the rise of positivist science and technology in the nineteenth and twentieth centuries threatened what had theretofore been nature's status as a myth. They urge modern subjects to return to nature's mythic status as a remedy for what Weber calls "the disenchantment of the world," which Horkheimer and Adorno label "Enlightenment's program."[23] They write that "on their way toward modern science human beings have discarded meaning. The concept is replaced by the formula, the cause by rules and probability."[24] If enchantment is "meaning," the modern world of science and industry is, for Horkheimer and Adorno, meaningless.

The Enlightenment program wanted, Horkheimer and Adorno maintain, "to dispel myths, to overthrow fantasy with knowledge," and to reject those "who substituted belief for knowledge."[25] Kant himself evinces such a program in *Critique of Judgment* when he avers that

> deliverance from superstition is called *enlightenment*, because although this name belongs to deliverance from prejudices in general, yet superstition specially (*in sensu eminenti*) deserves to be called a prejudice. For the blindness in which superstition places us, which it even imposes on us as an obligation, makes the need of being guided by others, and the consequent passive state of our reason, peculiarly noticeable.[26]

Kant's displeasure with mythopoeic thinking—here, superstition—is that it "makes the need of being guided by others [. . .] peculiarly noticeable." Superstition makes the subject vulnerable to humility, in other words, so enlightened thought proposes that humans dispel mythopoeic thinking and master nature so that they can camouflage their frailties.

Yet, in keeping with their typically paradoxical logic—and the title of their book—Horkheimer and Adorno claim that modern society has itself actually "relapse[d] into mythology" because of "the fear of truth which petrifies enlightenment itself." By "truth" Horkheimer and Adorno mean "intellectual history" and "current reality." Positivist science becomes mythology, they claim, because it is afraid of "departing from the facts," which "is exactly the same as the fear of social deviation." "Myth," for Horkheimer and Adorno, thus means "false clarity," that which is "obscure and luminous at once."[27]

Modern society's myth—its false clarity—is that it thinks of the world only in terms of facts: Such facts obfuscate "truth" because, Horkheimer and Adorno maintain, there are some thoughts and truths that are obscure, unknowable, unrepresentable. As products of this myth, Horkheimer and Adorno pessimistically claim, "art, literature, and philosophy must conform today" to false clarity, for Enlightenment thought has "taboo[ed] any thought which sets out negatively from the facts and from the prevailing modes of thought as obscure, convoluted, and preferably foreign."[28] Mythopoeic thinking—that which explains phenomena not through facts but through uncertainties, through fictions—has thus been replaced for Horkheimer and Adorno by the myth of science. The problem with modern myth is thus not that science and technology "are obtusely liquidating metaphysics "but that these things are themselves becoming metaphysics, an ideological curtain."[29]

Central to the Enlightenment's myth is "society's domination over nature."[30] As we have already seen Adorno maintain in Chapter One, Horkheimer and Adorno write that "the subjugation of everything natural to the sovereign subject culminates in the domination of what is blindly objective and natural."[31] The only goal of scientific research into nature, they claim, is "how to use it to dominate wholly both it and human beings. Nothing else counts. Ruthless toward itself, the Enlightenment has eradicated the last remnant of its own self-awareness."[32] And it is only thought that "does violence to itself," they maintain, that "is hard enough to shatter myths."[33] Such violence derives in Horkheimer and Adorno's opinion "from human fear," especially "a horror of myth" itself, for "humans believe themselves free of fear when there is no longer anything unknown."[34] The mythically unknown of nature, Horkheimer and Adorno claim, is unsurprisingly the most fearsome to humans: "For civilization, purely natural existence, both animal and vegetative, was the absolute danger."[35]

While their insights into the disenchanted status of nature are compelling and certainly shed light on works like Tyler's—and, we will see, Lorde's and Spahr's—Horkheimer and Adorno also propound a fairly reductive understanding of science. They claim that

> science is repetition, refined to observed regularity and preserved in
> stereotypes [. . .] In technology the adaptation to lifelessness in the
> service of self-preservation is no longer accomplished, as in magic, by
> bodily imitation of external nature, but by automating mental pro-
> cesses, turning them into blind sequences [. . .] The camouflage used
> to protect and strike terror today is the blind mastery of nature, which
> is identical to farsighted instrumentality.[36]

Nothing could be further from Darwin's evolutionary theories than Horkheimer and Adorno's caricature of science. While it is true that some forms of positivist science study "repetition" and enforce "stereotypes," Darwin studies variation and mutation, the antitheses of repetition and the stereotypical. Darwin is not interested in "the blind mastery of nature," moreover, but in allowing nature its mystery: in admitting humans' powerlessness to comprehend nature's infinite variety. Horkheimer and Adorno's views of myth can seem equally reductive, for they claim that "myth is already enlightenment, and enlightenment reverts to mythology."[37] With this chiasmus, Horkheimer and Adorno attempt to equate mythopoeic thinking with instrumental, rational thinking: Both myth and enlightened thought aim, in their view, to subsume objectively mysterious and natural phenomena within ordered frameworks. They write that "myth sought to report, to name, to tell of origins—but therefore also to narrate, record, explain."[38] In such myths, they claim, "myth becomes enlightenment and nature mere objectivity," such that "mythical nature" becomes tantamount to "enlightened mastery of nature."[39] Most myths of nature, Horkheimer and Adorno maintain, reduce rather than respect nature's infinite variety and obscurity.

While this may be true of the examples that Horkheimer and Adorno present—especially Homer's *The Odyssey*—*not* all mythopoeic thinking is interested in vaunting the subject and giving him or her control over nature. In their regard for nature's infinitely unknowable variety, for example, Ovid's *Metamorphoses* and Darwin's evolutionary theories decenter the masterful subject and place power in the hands of sexual feeling (Ovid) and nature (Darwin). Moreover, mythopoeic literature must be distinguished from much positivist mythology because the former claims its self-awareness as myth—as, in other words, a falsehood—whereas the latter often makes truth claims that justly accrue Horkheimer and Adorno's decrials. Not all myth is enlightenment, then, or at least not the kind of enlightenment that fuels the fire of reductionist scientific mythologies.

Ultimately, Horkheimer and Adorno condemn myths that fuel the Enlightenment project, those that "became a teaching" rather than experiences themselves, those that rejected "the ambiguous meanings of mythical thought"—in short, those that were no longer literature.[40] What Horkheimer and Adorno mourn in the loss of the myth of nature is the loss of metaphysical inquiry into "substance and quality, activity and suffering, being and existence."[41] They mourn the qualitative modes of life—including feelings—that were supplanted by quantitative, scientific modes that conceived of "the world as a giant analytical judgment."[42] With such judgment, any qualitative mode of experience is reduced, Horkheimer and Adorno aver, to "illusion; modern positivism consigns it to poetry."[43] What modern myth lacks is thus its literary quality: It lacks ambiguity, imprecision, implication, and above all the humility of the subject before the autonomy of the object. In lacking its literary dimension, modern myth is also "estranged" from nature, even as it manifests a "blind and mutilated" version thereof.[44]

The kind of myth that Horkheimer and Adorno want to revive is a myth wherein stories are "directly identical with elements"; one that bears "regard for differences"; a myth closer to magic and ritual; a myth that works through "mimesis," or the sacrifice of the self to the object, "not through an increasing distance from the object"; a myth wherein the foundational falsehoods that myths tell do not aim to master nature but allow nature to master myth.[45] Indeed, what Horkheimer and Adorno want is a literary myth of nature not unlike Darwin's own: one wherein "representation gives way to universal fungibility," one that "appears supple in its substitution of one thing for another," one that recognizes "amorphous nature."[46] Rather than on a rigid structuralist schema, Horkheimer and Adorno's myth of nature works on the logic of figuration, on the logic of literature, and perhaps literary science like Darwin's. Darwin's myth of nature and the literary texts that reshape it thus disprove Horkheimer and Adorno's lament that "the principle of immanence, the explanation of every event as repetition, which enlightenment upholds against mythical imagination, is that of myth itself."[47] Not all myths of nature are created alike, Darwin reveals, nor are their natures.

The sciences that Horkheimer and Adorno condemn are less like Darwin's evolutionary science and more like contemporary genetic inquiries into the etiology of sexual identity. I have already argued in this project's introduction that such inquiry is wrongheaded for political but especially scientific reasons.[48] Whereas Dean Hamer, one of the most influential contemporary genetic researchers into homosexuality, proclaims that "the implication" of Darwin's writing "is that even sexuality most likely has a significant genetic component,"[49] Darwin nowhere writes of discrete sexualities. While Hamer recounts a variety of theories that have been constructed to align queerness with Darwin's theory of evolution—ranging from the idea that the gay gene increases the reproductive capacity of those who carry it (meaning, of course, that homosexuals would not be exclusively homosexual, thus discounting the possibility of a gene for homosexuality) to E. O. Wilson's "altruism theory" that queers are very helpful to those who do reproduce—all of these alternatives are theories.[50] And none of them, strangely, includes the most viable theory—Darwin's—recourse to which could propose that, because nature is mutable, and because sexual feeling is a part of nature, all sexuality will be mutable and no discrete sexuality will exist in nature.

Limited by their tendentious adherence to the falsehoods of socially constructed categories of sexual identity, scientific theories about sexuality are postulates of belief and feeling, not incontrovertible, universally true knowledge claims.[51] For knowledge and belief may be distinguished, Charles Altieri claims, by the fact that, whereas knowledge relies on factual and verifiable information, "the beliefs may be themselves influenced by the specific flow of feelings, so rather than helping us identify the emotion they become aspects of complex states that are quite difficult to characterize."[52] Beliefs are feelings that we take to be true, even as we have no other evidence for their truth than the biophysical record of those feelings in the body. This view accords with William James's argument in *The Varieties of Religious Experience* (1902) that religious belief is based in the body—the very same theory he held for feeling in *Principles of Psychology*—which can have feelings about immaterial phenomena as much as it can about those that are material.

For his part, Hamer actually does draw a distinction between knowledge and belief when he admits that his scientific perspective is one that places faith in the latter: "As a geneticist, to be blunt about it, I don't really give a damn what label anyone uses, or even what they do, or with whom. I care about what they feel inside."[53] If Hamer were studying people's feelings, rather than trying to link the discursive content of those feelings with other discursive constructs—such that *I feel like a homosexual* tendentiously proves that homosexuality is a natural kind—genetic science might have different stories to tell about feeling bodies and their beliefs. Unfortunately, Hamer's belief is circumscribed by discursive constructs of sexuality (what constitutes sex, gender, and sexual identities), whereas it could be expanded by attention to bodies and their pleasures.

That genetic studies are based on theories and beliefs does not mean, however, that genetic inquiry is without value, for what it demonstrates is a scientific belief in the biological structures of sexuality. Whereas science has proven universally that penicillin cures syphilis, for example, it has proven only its own belief in the existence of a gay gene; yet this is itself a fascinating historical fact. By searching for the gay gene, genetic scientists are chasing a myth—and to say as much is not an insult. It is instead to suggest that genetic scientists are creating literary histories of their own mythopoeic beliefs about sexuality and that these beliefs have circulated throughout the twentieth and twenty-first centuries as an influential form of secular myth.

As I demonstrated in Chapter One, sexual science has relied on literature since its inception, but it has also relied on mythic literature specifically and on mythopoeic thinking. Foucault points to such reliance when he records that sexology combined "the great evolutionist myths with the recent institutions of public health."[54] As Lombroso experienced a backlash against his theory of atavism, he exhibited this belief when he claimed, "What do I care whether others are with me or against me? I believe in the type. It is my type; I discovered it; I believe in it and always shall."[55]

Sigmund Freud is, of course, one of the most influential sexologists to have used a mythopoeic perspective in his practice—especially with the myth of Oedipus—though he was also more explicit about using it than current geneticists. Even Foucault himself, Bullough writes, was "engaged in the process of constructing his own myths of the past, which might or might not be true."[56] The literary quality of and reliance upon mythic thinking in sexology reveals, in sum, Edward Stein's claim that "our confidence that we have advanced a great deal in our understanding of sexual orientation compared to Aristophanes and his fellow celebrants in *The Symposium* is premature."[57]

That belief is grounded in feeling does not justify any belief or feeling on moral grounds. Simply because belief can be referred to the feeling body does not mean that one *should* hold any belief. After all, one could argue that the Nazis firmly believed, and felt, that queers were degenerate and deserved persecution. The untenability of such a belief is a question of morality, not science. When it comes to political matters, one can, and should, judge beliefs on the basis of their moral value. As a literary history, *Queer Natures* has set those judgments aside—though not claimed them unimportant—to analyze instead how modernist writers attempted to depoliticize concepts such as nature and sexuality that have throughout history been oversaturated with moral and political imputations. My interest in this epilogue is not to justify or condemn particular beliefs but to analyze how and why nature specifically served as a source of mythical belief in the materiality of sexual and aesthetic feeling for queers throughout the twentieth century and, departing from the modernists that I have studied in this project, to analyze how it even became a source of political organization.

Simon LeVay—who, like Hamer, has conducted influential research into the genetics of sexuality—remarks that "beliefs about the causation of homosexuality clearly *do* influence attitudes toward gay people. Therefore, research that attempts to find the cause of homosexuality is inherently a social and political enterprise as well as a scientific one."[58] LeVay is right to emphasize that scientific belief has political ramifications; it has, in fact, grounded gay liberation political movements throughout the twentieth century. For example, when the character Oswald in Edward Prime-Stevenson's 1906 novel *Imre: A Memorandum* declares of his queerness, "'I had no disease! No. I was simply what I was born!'"[59] he epitomizes the most common belief that stems from scientific research into sexuality: "I was born this way." As one of the most salient mottos of modern gay liberation movements, this claim is often meant to communicate a politics of exoneration: *I was born this way, so don't persecute me.* With such intention, this claim commits the naturalistic fallacy by assuming that recourse to biology can expedite political liberation.

But "I was born this way" can also simply be a statement of subjective feeling and belief, outside of politics, that nonetheless offers the grounds for political organization. From this view, the feeling (not the etiological content) of "I was born this way" cannot be challenged on scientific grounds—if anything, it can only be supported by them. As a felt belief (rather than a knowledge claim), "I was born this way" is a mythic statement because it is both false and foundational: It is a lie about etiology that tells the truth about sexual feeling. The statement is false because its etiological pronouncement cannot be verified scientifically; and it is foundational insofar as it records the sensational embodiment of queer feeling. Thus, when a queer person cries, *Listen, I was born this way, this is how I feel,* one can of course simply reply, *That's nice. How do you know?* But this question, however apt in a literal sense, misses the sophistication of this person's claim. For that person is actually saying: *My subjective feeling is the root of my belief, and what I know I know from my body alone.* As the texts that I have analyzed in the preceding chapters reveal, this biophysical claim is, in its apolitical manifestations, a very modernist one: It is made by John Marcher and Melanctha, by the speakers of Langston Hughes and D. H. Lawrence's poems, by Matthew O'Connor and Miss LaTrobe.

When uttered in a politically performative context, the "I" of "I was born this way" is not just a lyric "I." It is a synecdoche for the queer community at large, a community compromised as much as it is consolidated by the criterion of difference. In the late twentieth and early twenty-first centuries, *I was born this way* has been the rallying cry of this community: It was shouted in the 1960s and could be heard as recently as the 2008 protests against California's Proposition 8, a proposition to abolish gay marriage. In its recourse to a myth of nature, *I was born this way* can also be heard in a range of modern queer literature. For now, Audre Lorde's *Zami: A New Spelling of My Name* (1982) and Juliana Spahr's *The Transformation* (2007) serve as instructive examples.

Zami documents the rise of gay and lesbian communities throughout the twentieth century in locales ranging from New York to Cuernavaca to Carriacou, an island in the West Indies. Lorde records the creation of these communities from the perspective of her protagonist, Audre, whose peripatetic movement throughout the text leads her to join a series of queer enclaves. Even though she ultimately leaves each of those communities— for a variety of reasons, including economics, race, and sexuality—Audre declares at text's end that "every woman I have ever loved has left her print upon me, where I loved some invaluable piece of myself apart from me— so different that I had to stretch and grow in order to recognize her. And in that growing, we came to separation" (255).[60] Audre acknowledges the impossibility of queer community formation, but in the same stroke she claims that such fracture helps her to develop her own foundational sense of self.

In *Zami*, the self is thus founded on the myth of community: the lie that communities are stable, coherent, and self-unifying entities. As she watches those communities fracture because difference always compromises any community's identity, Audre comes to believe only in "the house of difference" (226), a paradoxical concept of home and community wherein the only criterion for inclusion is otherness. In *Zami*, the myth of community founds the self's own mythic coherence. Indeed, despite its autobiographical content—Audre is clearly Audre Lorde—*Zami* is not Lorde's autobiography: It is instead what Lorde calls a "biomythography," a narrative that mythologizes the facts of biographical life (the text concludes, for instance, just before Lorde's 1962 marriage to Edward Rollins, with whom she reared two children). The "new spelling of my name" referenced in *Zami*'s title encapsulates this mythic relation between self and community: Though its mythic references are transcultural, *Zami* relies above all on the myth of *Zami*, which is "*a Carriacou name for women who work together as friends and lovers*" (255). All of the women in *Zami* are, in this sense, *Zami*: Given that synecdoche can work as a part-whole or a whole-part relationship, *Zami* is a synecdoche simultaneously for the queer communities that Audre joins and leaves and for Audre herself.

That the term *Zami* derives from the language of Carriacou is central to the text's myth of nature, for Audre regards that island as her "home," whereas she never actually visits it. Carriacou is the island from which Audre's parents immigrated to the United States, and Audre hears stories about the island that make it assume for her the status of myth: "*How Carriacou women love each other is legend in Grenada, and so is their strength and their beauty* [. . .] *Carriacou*, a magic name like cinnamon, nutmeg, mace, the delectable little squares of guava jelly each lovingly wrapped in tiny bits of crazy-quilt wax-paper" (14). The source of sexual "legend," Carriacou is also for Audre the source of feeling about the body and sensation: her descriptions of food, as in this quotation, are throughout the text as "lovingly wrapped" as the Carriacou guava jellies.

Carriacou represents, then, a "truly private paradise" for Audre (14), where "private" connotes not only her selfhood but her body and its feelings, especially the sexual feelings that connect her to evanescent social networks. Carriacou's mythic status—it is a place that "was not listed in the index of the *Goode's School Atlas* [. . .] I never found it, and came to believe my mother's geography was a fantasy" (14)—offers Audre the source of a mythic belief in the nature of queerness, its sensational grounding in the material body. When Audre says in the text's final paragraph that "once *home* was a long way off, a place I had never been to but knew out of my mother's mouth. I only discovered its latitudes when Carriacou was no longer my home" (256). She relates how the myth of Carriacou provided the means to construct an ideal of home that she could never reach. Once she actually reached places that felt like home—her various queer communities—Audre came to depend all the more on that original myth: By realizing that home cannot be stabilized in practice, she discovers her mythic home's "latitudes."

Zami's final sentence then summarizes how this myth resonates in the material body: "There it is said that the desire to lie with other women is a drive from the mother's blood" (256). Though ostensibly an essentialist claim—one that sounds very much like *I was born this way*—*this* sentence actually propounds a mythic claim about the somatic nature of queerness. As she has all along with Carriacou lore, Audre acknowledges that this idea is a legend—"there it is said"—even as she places this sentence directly after her realization that she has "discovered" Carriacou's "latitudes": that she has found a way to root her belief in what constitutes "home." What constitutes home, for this queer woman, is naturally encoded in "the mother's blood": "the desire to lie with other women." "Lie" here functions polysemously, as Audre relates how her relationships with women often ended on the basis of lies, exemplified by her relationship with Muriel. But, just as myths are lies that tell the truth, so too do these lies tell the truth of queerness's nature: It is a lie about "the blood" that tells the truth about "desire."

As a biomythography, *Zami* is an anomalous text in the history of American literature: No other text, to my knowledge, has been described with that generic category. Juliana Spahr's *The Transformation* is similarly anomalous, for it can at best be described as a prose poem, even as it is also a piece of aesthetic and academic criticism and an environmentalist polemic. Like Tyler's and Lorde's, this text is also autobiographical, as Spahr notes in its appended notes section (which reinforces its academic quality—and its modernist quality, after *The Waste Land*). *The Transformation* resonates with many of the texts that I have examined in *Queer Natures*—its title alone recalls the metamorphoses of Tyler's *The Granite Butterfly*—but in style it most resembles "Melanctha" and even alludes to its debt to Stein.[61] Given to present participles and antecedentless pronouns, the text combines modernist spatial form and postmodern pastiche and encapsulates how queer natures aesthetically and epistemologically evolve over the twentieth century and into the twenty-first.

The Transformation explores a wide range of subjects, but two of its abiding interests are queerness and nature. In the former case, the text charts the progress of three lovers—two men and one woman—as they move around the globe. Sounding like Stein, Spahr writes that "two of them had been a couple for many years. This relationship was intense and variable and intellectually driven. One of them had met another. This relationship was intense and variable and passionate. Two of them had assumed that one of them would no longer be one of them. But it did not work out that way" (14).

Although the relationship remains "intense and variable" in its triadic form, Spahr emphasizes here that the third member adds a "passionate" ingredient to the original couple's "intellectually driven" bond. It is such feeling that unites the trio throughout their relationship: Moving from bed to bed, they "would have to think about which bed had been the bed for waking. Or which skin had been the most touched of the skins [. . .] What smell. What feeling. What satisfaction" (15). What the trio, rather than the dyad, generates is thus an aesthetic pleasure in sex—"feeling" and "satisfaction"—rather than intellectual comportment alone.

In their pursuit of feeling, the trio generates a new feeling: the feeling of being outsiders and of having "few models to turn to" (16). They consider labeling themselves "perverts" (20) and "queer" (173), but they reject those terms because no members ever have anything but heterosexual sex (15). The trio consequently "avoided words to describe their relation because words felt wrong" (18). As discursive constructs do not account for the kind of "felt" relationship that the trio experiences, *The Transformation* becomes "a story about realizing that they cannot shrug off this they and so a story of trying to think with it. A story of how much this realization of being a they changed them and a story of embracing this change," a change inspired in part by "an island in the middle of the Pacific and how it changed them" (21).

Transformation, in this text, thus occurs through two primary means: queer feeling (among the trio) and nature (the island). What the island represents for the trio is ultimately an Adornian concept of nature as a wound: "it was an island of both great environmental beauty and of great environmental destruction" (27). Nature, the trio comes to find, has a "fearful symmetry" that is "both beautiful and horrible" (34). As they recognize that "chemical factories" and "billowing smokestacks" have irrevocably transformed nature's beauty, the trio feels about the natural world an "emotion that combined intense, awful loss with a recognition of continuing and endless beauty despite, perhaps even caused by the loss." As we have seen, what Spahr calls "human-induced horrible beauty" (35) Adorno calls simply "natural beauty"; I have called it a degenerate version of Kant's sublime.

What their feeling for nature ultimately generates for the trio is a feeling of humility. As Spahr writes, self-consciously invoking Stein's pleasure in grammar, the trio will not regard itself in the nominative but only in the accusative: and "negotiating this accusative they not only changed them and their bodies, but it also changed their thought patterns. They liked this change" (48). It is only through their humility, their refusal to master nature, and their acceptance of being mastered by natural feelings, that the trio achieves a sense of humanity: They believe "in the hope that a catalogue of vulnerability could begin the process of claiming their being human" (214).

In line with Adorno's aesthetic theory of the object, Spahr's "they" renounce their subject positions, regard themselves as objects, and try repeatedly to understand their relationship in terms of nature. When explaining their relationship, for example, "they kept resorting to metaphors of nature, as if that would make them natural. But the metaphors of nature always failed them. Everything happens somewhere in nature" (18). Spahr suggests here that post-Darwinian nature's queerness—its non-identical relationship to itself—cannot offer the trio discursive explanations or exoneration because "everything happens somewhere in nature." Insofar as "they too were trying to escape from large systems, from limitations on relation" (33), the trio's struggle—and, one could say, *The Transformation*'s struggle as well—is to represent queer feeling through discourse in ways that accord with nature directly, not metaphorically.

The text opens, in fact, by claiming that "flora and fauna grow next to and around each other without names. Humans add the annotation [. . .] and as they do this they read into them their own stories" (13). *The Transformation* laments this anthropomorphic impulse toward naturalization and attempts to unite nature and human discourse through the conduit of feeling. In its nod to modernism, *The Transformation* admires "writing of fragmentation, quotation, disruption, disjunction, agrammatical syntax, and so on" because that writing—which sounds very much like modernist writing, that which emphasizes discourse's gaps—is so sensational and anti-discursive. Spahr writes, "really what it was was that they felt this writing

in their body. They felt certain sensations" (63). Literary discourse—
discourse that exposes the affective gaps in rational language—is for
Spahr, as for the modernists she imitates, the way to represent the queerness of nature, one that, even when represented, is always changing. As the
trio feels, such writing "entered into their body and changed it" (64).

Because "they" and the text itself refuse to naturalize the trio's queer
feeling, *The Transformation* also documents how that feeling is coincident
with negative feeling: "So it is also a story of finding an ease in discomfort. And a catalogue of discomfort" (22). Rather than politicize their
feelings—for they have no political group or queer community to join—
"they were, they are, defined by the just accusations of others and intimate
with one another inside this accusation" (23). As the modernists do with
negative aesthetic judgments of their sexual feelings, the trio subverts negative judgment—"accusations"—and carves out space within such feeling
to feel degenerate: to regard themselves in "the accusative." Again reminiscent of the modernists, the trio's degenerate feeling is queer not only
for its sexual content but also for its affective indeterminacy, for they are
always "flipping back and forth between love and confusion, acceptance
and alienation, fascination and anger" (87).

It is such queer feeling, combined with negative feelings about nature,
that inspires the trio's elevation of aesthetic and sexual feeling to mythic
heights. Using the same terms—"intense and variable"—with which she
describes the trio's relationship, Spahr writes that "the beauty of the island was so intense and so variable that it entered into their brain as a drug
and they were high on it and only able to see it as intense and wonderful,"
a feeling always compromised and informed by their seeing it as "at risk
and colonized" (30). As in Adorno's *Aesthetic Theory*, the myth of natural
beauty in *The Transformation* is a lie about beauty that tells the truth of
nature's violation: It is a myth that, Spahr insists, must be recognized *as* a
myth, as a "drug," in order for its salutary affective content, nature's "horrible beauty," to be felt. Sounding very much like Adorno, Spahr writes
that such feeling is best conveyed in the modernist style of fragmentation,
which feels like a mythically "trance-inducing chant" (188), and that it is
the only kind of feeling that could inspire a politics of nature, queer or not:
"they liked to think of these emotions as the beginning of a politics of some
sort, as the baby steps that would move them to action" (72).

As Spahr's example suggests, in their affection for the myth of nature,
queers in the twentieth and twenty-first centuries would still qualify as degenerates by late nineteenth-century standards—indeed, they would
more than ever. Talbot notes how an "occult conception of degeneracy is

even yet a part of American folklore,"⁶² a claim with which Nordau could be expected to agree because he targets mysticism—"the habit of looking on everything inexplicable as supernatural"—as one of the primary signs of degeneracy.⁶³ As an umbrella concept for mythical thinking, mysticism is the most emotional state of degeneracy, for its ecstatic emotions "accompany every strong and excessive functioning of the nerve-cells, every extraordinary and violent decomposition of nerve-nutriment."⁶⁴ It is, in fact, mysticism that Nordau most associates with sexual feeling, likening it to the "ecstasy" that one experiences in religious feelings.⁶⁵ As he claims, "mysticism is, as we know, always accompanied by eroticism, especially in the degenerate, whose emotionalism has its chief source in morbidly excited states of the sexual centres."⁶⁶

Many of the attacks against *Degeneration* were targeted at Nordau's decrial of mysticism, and he was certainly open to them because he, in characteristically contradictory fashion, also claimed that "repudiation of dogma, the negation of a supersensuous world" is also a sign of degeneracy.⁶⁷ What this epilogue has demonstrated is that Nordau's dissociation of nature and mysticism—he claims that "science does not compete with theology and metaphysics"—overlooks the fact that science is itself theoretical and offers explanations for phenomena that cannot always be verified empirically.⁶⁸ As Sander Gilman claims, "Science creates fictions to explain facts, and an important criterion for endorsing these fictions is their ideological acceptability."⁶⁹ Not all science is fiction, of course—again the example of antibiotics comes to mind—but general theories like evolution, which are, as Darwin himself admits, rife with missing links, are fictions of a kind even as they explain natural phenomena such as biological change. Science is, as the philosopher of science Karl Popper called it, "vulnerable knowledge"⁷⁰—but its vulnerability as knowledge only intensifies the strength of the feelings and beliefs that scientific inquiry engenders. It is precisely their vulnerability—their openness to change—that has made feelings and beliefs about queer natures such a vibrant locus of literary production throughout the twentieth and twenty-first centuries.

NOTES

1. Heather Love, *Feeling Backward* (Cambridge: Harvard University Press, 2007), 130.

2. Michael Bell, *Literature, Modernism and Myth* (Cambridge: Cambridge University Press, 1997), 1.

3. Christopher Nealon, *Foundlings: Lesbian and Gay Historical Emotion Before Stonewall* (Durham, N.C.: Duke University Press, 2001), 8.

4. Ibid., 4.

5. While this is not the forum to explore this concept in detail, see Michael Warner's Introduction to *Fear of a Queer Planet* (Minneapolis: University of Minnesota Press, 1993), vii–xxxi, for more information about the paradoxical qualities of a "queer community." I have begun to explore the problem of the queer community and its relation to myth in "Making Modernism New: Queer Mythology in *The Young and Evil*," *ELH* 76, no. 4 (Winter 2009).

6. Parker Tyler, *The Granite Butterfly* (Orono, Maine: National Poetry Foundation, 1994), 45.

7. Ovid, *The Metamorphoses of Ovid*, trans. Allen Mandelbaum (New York: Harcourt, 1993), 97.

8. Michael Bernstein, *The Tale of the Tribe* (Princeton, N.J.: Princeton University Press, 1980), 8.

9. Tyler, *Granite*, 136.

10. Paul Civello, *American Literary Naturalism and Its Twentieth-Century Transformations* (Athens: University of Georgia Press, 1994), 7.

11. Searches for transitional fossils—those that demonstrate how species have evolved over time—continue to this day. As of this writing, the most recent discovery that adds fuel to the fire of Darwin's theory was announced in May 2009: the fossil of a 47-million-year-old primate, *Darwinius masillae*, or "Ida" ("MISSING LINK FOUND: New Fossil Links Humans, Lemurs?," *National Geographic Online*, 19 May 2009, 12 August 2009, http://news .nationalgeographic.com/news/2009/05/090519-missing-Jink- found.html). As we have seen, however, Darwin claimed that a complete knowledge of evolutionary history would never be found because so much data is irretrievable (*Origin* 132; *Descent* I: 36). We learn more and more about the material bases of Darwin's theory with each new empirical discovery, then, but in doing so we only confirm belief in, not absolute knowledge of, his theory. See George Levine, *Darwin Loves You: Natural Selection and the Re-enchantment of the World* (Princeton, N.J.: Princeton University Press, 2006), for a discussion of debates about the speculative versus informational qualities of Darwin's theory (86–7).

12. Charles Darwin, *The Origin of Species* (1872; rpt., London: Collier MacMillan, 1962), 308.

13. Ibid., 25.

14. Civello, 16.

15. George Levine, *Darwin Loves You: Natural Selection and the Re-enchantment of the World* (Princeton, N.J.: Princeton University Press, 2006), 17, 141. Darwin's contemporaries themselves noted this new creation myth. For example, in *Man's Place in Nature* (1863), a theory of evolution that

parallels Darwin's theory of descent, Thomas H. Huxley opens his account of evolution by aligning it with other mythological creation myths. Thomas H. Huxley, *Man's Place in Nature* (1863; rpt., New York: Dover, 2003), 9.

16. Qtd. in Levine, 31.

17. Levine, 22, 24.

18. Ibid., 130.

19. Ibid., xvi.

20. Raymond Williams, *The Politics of Modernism* (New York: Verso, 2007), 84.

21. Ibid., 68.

22. T. S. Eliot, *Selected Prose of T. S. Eliot*, ed. Frank Kermode (New York: Farrar, Straus & Giroux, 1975), 178.

23. Theodor Adorno and Max Horkheimer, *Dialectic of Enlightenment*, trans., Edmund Jephcott (Stanford: Stanford University Press, 2002), 1.

24. Ibid., 3.

25. Ibid., 1.

26. Immanuel Kant, *Critique of Judgment*, trans. J. H. Bernard (Mineola, N.Y.: Dover, 2005), 102.

27. Adorno and Horkheimer, xvi–xvii.

28. Ibid.

29. Ibid., viii.

30. Ibid., xvii.

31. Ibid., viii.

32. Ibid., 2.

33. Ibid.

34. Ibid., 10, 22, 11.

35. Ibid., 24.

36. Ibid., 149.

37. Ibid., viii.

38. Ibid., 5.

39. Ibid., 6, xviii.

40. Ibid., 5, 23.

41. Ibid., 3.

42. Ibid., 72, 20.

43. Ibid., 4–5.

44. Ibid., 31.

45. Ibid., 5–7.

46. Ibid., 7, 24.

47. Ibid., 8.

48. For a thorough review of post-WWII sexology, including but not limited to genetic research, see Vern Bullough's *Science in the Bedroom: A*

History of Sex Research (New York: Basic Books, 1994). Even this research—including Alfred Kinsey's emphasis on interviews (173)—has a highly literary emphasis. Only William Masters and Virginia Johnson's studies of physiological arousal—somatic stimulation—seem to analyze feeling in a way coincident with William James's theory that feeling is embodied (196–209). By making sex a matter of the body rather than solely the mind, Masters and Johnson eliminate the possibility that discursive constructions of identity tendentiously bias the studies—they suggest that the experience of sexual feeling, not its biological origin, should be the locus of sex research.

49. Dean Hamer and Peter Copeland, *The Science of Desire: The Search for the Gay Gene and the Biology of Behavior* (New York: Simon & Schuster, 1994), 26.

50. Ibid., 180–6. Such theories are moreover subject to the naturalistic fallacy: Wilson, for example, proposed his altruism theory as a means of arguing "that homosexuality is normal in a biological sense" (*On Human Nature* [Cambridge: Harvard University Press, 1978], 149).

51. Edward Stein, *The Mismeasure of Desire: The Science, Theory, and Ethics of Sexual Orientation* (New York: Oxford University Press, 1999), 196, 221.

52. Charles Altieri, *The Particulars of Rapture: An Aesthetics of the Affects* (Ithaca, N.Y.: Cornell University Press, 2004), 11.

53. Qtd. in Joan Roughgarden, *Evolution's Rainbow: Diversity, Gender, and Sexuality in Nature and People* (Los Angeles: University of California Press, 2004), 250.

54. Michel Foucault,. *The History of Sexuality, vol. I, An Introduction*, trans. Robert Hurley (New York: Vintage, 1980), 54.

55. Qtd. in Daniel Pick, *Faces of Degeneration: A European Disorder, c. 1848–1918* (Cambridge: Cambridge University Press, 1989), 121.

56. Bullough, 245.

57. Stein, 348.

58. Simon LeVay, *Queer Science: The Use and Abuse of Research into Homosexuality* (Cambridge: MIT Press, 1996), 5.

59. Edward Prime-Stevenson, *Imre: A Memorandum*, ed. James J. Gifford (Orchard Park, N.Y.: Broadview, 2003), 95–6.

60. Audre Lorde, *Zami: A New Spelling of My Name* (Freedom, Calif.: Crossing Press, 1982), 255. Subsequent references in the text will be to this edition.

61. Juliana Spahr, *The Transformation* (Berkeley, Calif.: Atelos, 2007), 79. Subsequent references in the text will be to this edition.

62. Eugene S. Talbot, *Degeneracy: Its Causes, Signs and Results* (New York: Scribner's, 1898), 2.

63. Max Simon Nordau, *Degeneration* (1895; rpt., Lincoln: University of Nebraska Press, 1993), 64.

64. Ibid., 63.

65. Ibid., 64.

66. Ibid., 188.

67. Ibid., xxiv, 5.

68. Ibid., 108.

69. Sander Gilman, *Difference and Pathology: Stereotypes of Sexuality, Race, and Madness* (Ithaca, N.Y.: Cornell University Press, 1985), 28.

70. Bullough, 294.

PART II

Queer Mythologies

Fast Books Read Slow:
The Shapes of Speed in
Manhattan Transfer and *The Sun Also Rises*

Speed of itself is not dangerous but the inability to stop is dangerous.

—C. S. ROLLS, co-founder of Rolls Royce Ltd.[1]

Festina lente [Hurry slowly].

—MOTTO OF ALDUS MANUTIUS, 16th-century publisher

Historicizing Speed and Narrative Space

F. T. Marinetti, founder of the Italian Futurist movement, programmatically declared in 1909 that, because it must yoke the period's unprecedented speed technologies for aesthetic purposes, modern art "can only be violence, cruelty, and injustice."[2] In 1915, Marinetti extended this imperative to humanity itself: "one must prepare," he insisted, "for the imminent and inevitable identification of man with motor."[3] Based on such pronouncements, a considerable body of scholarship has taught us that early 20th-century speed technologies are historically imbricated with violence; that modernist aesthetic movements, like Futurism, fueled this relationship; and that subjectivity is at stake when a culture accelerates beyond the ability to stop.[4] Foremost among such scholarship, Stephen Kern's *The Culture of Time and Space, 1880–1918* (1986) and Paul Virilio's *Speed and Politics* (1977), while methodologically divergent texts, concur that, especially between the world wars, technological innovations in the automotive, film, radio, and martial industries "created a 'cult of speed' for a generation that wanted 'to conquer time and space,'"[5] if not "to annihilate time and space."[6] By these accounts, the advent of cultural products ranging from pocket watches to Futurist literature manifested a desire for speeds that could not only contract but imperil the time and space of modernism.[7]

While we have learned much from such histories about the effects of fast travel, fast sex, fast machines, and, in the case of Futurism, fast literature on modernist culture, we have learned much less about how the modernist attempt to conquer and/or annihilate time and space influenced literary production in traditions other than Futurism.[8] How fast did literature become, after all, and what role did it play in the culture of violent acceleration and its antagonism toward time and space? Did modernist novels, for instance, contribute to the "violence, cruelty, and injustice" that Marinetti describes? Or was it possible to participate in the culture of speed while upholding an ironic view thereof? As Michael North asks, "In what way could modernist works of art derive their own sense of exhilarated technical freedom from social conditions that also seemed to mean oppression and even experiential paralysis?"[9] Endeavoring toward "technical freedom" by harnessing technology, in other words, did fast novels create or relieve Marinetti's mechanized man, what Virilio calls the "man deprived of a specific place *and thus of his identity*"?[10]

One way of answering these questions is to consider the most famous form of interwar modernist novels, what in 1945 Joseph Frank deemed "spatial form,"[11] an umbrella term designating the techniques with which writers disrupt the linear, chronological sequence intrinsic to narrative. Interrupting narrative diachrony with synchronic reflexivity, spatial form techniques include analepsis, prolepsis, parataxis, leitmotifs, fragmentation, and juxtaposition, among other familiar modernist formal experiments as typified in James Joyce's *Ulysses* or Virginia Woolf's *Mrs. Dalloway*. Useful though it is, Frank's theory has been assimilated so readily into critical discourse that few scholars have asked why spatial narratives pervade modernist literature.[12] If it is true, as Frank says, that "changes in aesthetic form always involve major changes in the sensibility of a particular cultural period,"[13] how might the interwar conflict between speed, technology, and space illuminate why spatial form was amenable to modernist writers?[14] In short, if novels became fast during this period, may that also explain why they became spatial?

John Dos Passos' *Manhattan Transfer* (1925) and Ernest Hemingway's *The Sun Also Rises* (1926) offer responses to these questions because they are both spatial form novels preoccupied with speed and violence; moreover, Dos Passos and Hemingway served noncombatant roles in WWI and were throughout their careers troubled by the relationship between speed and politics.[15] Whereas Futurist doctrine might have licensed the destruction of time and space, *Transfer* and *Rises* mimetically reproduce the effects of speed technology at the levels of narrative structure and texture to create literary space, an imaginative sphere of reflection and deliberation, in a culture where technology depleted physical space, both literally and perceptually.[16] A comparison of these novels confirms literary histories that align modernist texts with technological innovation, then, even as it unsettles beliefs that modernist writers either embraced or rejected technology so uncritically that they vaunted or derided speed as the mechanism with which to "conquer" or "annihilate time and space." For interwar writers like Dos Passos and Hemingway, the desire to conquer by means of technology was deeply vexed; indeed, if "there was sharp debate about the meaning and value of speed" at the turn of the century,[17] Dos Passos and Hemingway saw both sides and maintained subversive views toward the technologies that inspired their novels.[18]

A critically neglected relation between speed and space inheres in the very notion of spatial form, which is so-called because its techniques fracture linear temporal progression and omit causal connections, much in the way that speed technologies like the telegraph, movie camera, and even reading machines did in other media.[19] The logical gaps produced by such speed-based techniques "place a greater burden on readers' synthesizing power than do more conventional temporal narratives,"[20] however, a burden that slows readers' responses and produces literary space. This hermeneutic deceleration coincides with Kern's claim that the processes and technologies that acceleration displaces, even if they once were fast, become slow at the moment of their displacement. Modernist technologies, says Kern, "speeded up the tempo of current existence and transformed the memory of years past, the stuff of everybody's identity, into something slow."[21] This dialectic between fast and slow velocities relates crucially to literature, particularly if we accept that literature affects and informs "the stuff of everybody's identity." If acceleration always implies deceleration, I argue that the literary products of speed culture slowed (and still slow) readers' responses to those texts by virtue of their stylistic acceleration, for readers must reduce their reading speed to provide the logical connections and information that the fast texts elide.[22] Mimetically reproducing speed at the levels of narrative structure and texture in order to spatialize readers' responses, *Transfer* and *Rises* exemplify how and why the temporally fast novel may also be spatially vast.

As a metaphorical version of space, the spatial novel's vastness is a product of the reader's imagination, but it is no less material than physical space because of its imaginative location. As Maurice Blanchot describes, literary space's referenced materials are psychic and affective, not extra-personal: "the work is a work only when it becomes the intimacy shared by someone who writes it and someone who reads it, a space violently opened up by the contest between the power to speak and the power to hear."[23] Manifesting "a space violently opened up by" representational ac-celeration, *Transfer* and *Rises* decelerate readerly speed and offer a psychic location where time moves slower than in the texts' represented worlds and, by most historical accounts, in modernist readers' lived realities.[24] If, as Virilio posits, "duration was survival" for the deracinated modernist subject—the subject for whom technologies like the armored car created a world where, literally and perceptually, "earth no longer exists"[25]—novels like *Transfer* and *Rises* aid survival by slowing time and producing literary space as a replacement for physical and reflective space.

After analyzing these texts' spatiality through formal and reader re-sponse analyses, I will explore the social and philosophical alternatives to speed culture that *Transfer* and *Rises* provided for the early 20th century. Martin Heidegger's notion of ontological dwelling and Michael Seidel's conception of postexilic eminence—a theory that exile's dialectical rela-tion to stasis and motion creates imaginative space—elucidate that, since modernist narrative spatializes and thereby expands time, it reclaims the present moment as one of deliberation, not instantaneousness—individualization, not automation. For Dos Passos and Hemingway, the modernist spatial novel functions as a bulwark against the dehumanizing effects of modern speed culture by, paradoxically, subjecting readers to speed as mimetically produced in narrative. What most histories of mod-ernist narrative do not consider is how many spatial form techniques are mimetic representations of acceleration, not deceleration.[26] One of my goals, then, is to suggest through the instances of *Transfer* and *Rises* that our literary historical record of modernist spatial form is incomplete if we do not consider how the factor of velocity in its structural, thematic, and reader-response dimensions contributed to that aesthetic phenomenon.

Spatial Acceleration

Dos Passos' *Manhattan Transfer* is a characteristic example of Frank's spa-tial narrative; in fact, with its multilinear plot, fractured character focus, neologisms, and free indirect discourse, *Transfer* is a spatial novel *par ex-cellence*, very much in the Joyce/Woolf tradition. Less frequently regarded as but nonetheless spatial, *The Sun Also Rises* established what many critics believe became the preeminent literary style of the mid and late 20th century, one featuring paratactic sentence structure, unattributed dialogue, concentrated use of leitmotifs, and an objective "reporterly" tone.[27] Where Dos Passos' novel appears ideal for an analysis of speed and space,[28] however, *Rises* may initially seem less so, for its terse prose and trim plot make the novel read much more quickly than most texts in the high modernist tradition; indeed, as Italo Calvino remarks, a "bare résumé," a "laconic" style, and "economy of expression"[29] all characterize fast narrative, and all are trademarks of Hemingway's novels. But such speedy prose is the precise target of my analysis, for while one may dash through the syntactically bare sentences of *Rises*, the reader with any goals toward thematic comprehension is sure to get stuck in the novel's logical gaps.

Both *Transfer* and *Rises* reproduce speed stylistically and thematically to achieve their spatial forms, yet Dos Passos and Hemingway displayed ambivalence about the cultural promise of speed technology. Dos Passos, for instance, was "politically and socially mistrustful of the very techniques he put to such innovative use" in his novels, for he feared that visual media would supplant literary media and that technological innovations like film and radio would sever human contact.[30] Historically contextualized, Hemingway's well-known iceberg technique—a notably spatial metaphor that describes narrative form—exposes a similar ambivalence, for the author was surely aware when he developed the concept just before composing *Rises* that an iceberg's imperceptible motion and submerged content had foundered one hallmark of speed technology: the Titanic.[31] Rather than speed along as their syntax does, Hemingway's novels attempt, as Laura Godfrey claims, "to create pictures or landscapes reminiscent of the beauty and simplicity of Cézanne."[32] While they may seem strange bedfellows for their stylistic dissimilarities, then, *Transfer* and *Rises* exemplify a wide range of speed-based literary techniques that modernist texts concerned with speed employed to spatialize time—"to create pictures or landscapes"— and to counteract the violence of inexorable velocity.[33]

As David Mickelson avers, one of the clearest methods with which the novelist can "approximate a static present [is] by fragmenting the narrative."[34] Such fragmentation is one of *Transfer*'s most salient qualities; at first glance, however, the novel's structure appears deceivingly symmetrical. Divided into three sections of five, eight, and five chapters, respectively, the novel would seem to contain a linear narrative because of its balanced organization and chronological progression from pre- to active to post-war states. Each chapter begins with epigraph-like descriptions that resemble dramatic stage directions, however, distinguishing each chapter as a scene or episode. As in *Rises* (but perhaps even more dramatically), these episodes are linked only through juxtaposition, not causal connection. Chapter titles, for instance, rarely refer to the epigraphs that follow them; more often, these titles refer to other chapters' epigraphs, as with "Rollercoaster," which describes not its own epigraph but the preceding chapter's. Such cross-reference contorts the plot's trajectory from linearity to circularity.

This effect multiplies if we take the novel's epigraphs to resemble chapter headlines (which are, in more literal form, also strewn throughout the text). As Marshall McLuhan argues in "Speed of Cultural Change" (1958), a brief analysis of how writers "accep[t] the technological challenge" of speed as "strateg[ies] of culture," "when news begins to come in so fast that it can't be spelled out, can't be organized editorially, then the editor has to package it in capsulated form by new methods as best he can, and he tosses the final package to the audience and says 'Do it yourself, I have collected the data, it is up to you to put it together.'"[35] *Transfer*'s fractured chapters, epigraphs, and literal newspaper headlines resemble this technique of technological mimesis, for as "fast" as information arrives that "it can't be spelled out," the reader must "do it" him or herself—must collect the fast information as slowly as possible, must "put it together" into something slow.

Spatial breaks that resemble poetic white space further splinter *Transfer*'s narrative beyond its three-section, eighteen-chapter structure. Very few of these breaks (whether within or between chapters) continue a primary thread or storyline; instead, the breaks act as "cuts" between scenes, which has led some to label Dos Passos' technique a "camera eye" after the *U. S. A.* trilogy's Camera Eye sections, which track many plot lines simultaneously.[36] What Gérard Genette would call "*implicit* ellipses, that is, those whose very presence is not announced in the text and which the reader can infer only from some chronological lacuna or gap in narrative continuity,"[37] the novel's spatial breaks, associated with speed technologies like the camera, slow readers' responses by eliminating necessary logical connections between episodes. The cuts accordingly fracture the text's ostensibly linear symmetry and indicate a recursive cycle of departure and return from physical localities, states of war, and states of mind.

The novel's recursion structurally mimics its characters' recursive habits, for, as the character George Baldwin laments, it seems that all the characters "'can do is go round and round in a squirrel cage'" (*Transfer*, 220). Dos Passos' juxtaposition technique is therefore mimetic insofar as the accelerating culture he depicts is, Virilio muses, one in which "the ancient inter-city duel, war between nations [. . .] have suddenly disappeared, giving way to an unheard-of opposition: *the juxtaposition of every locality, all matter.*[38] While perhaps not as fully realized as the globalized world Virilio envisions, Dos Passos' Manhattan is a conglomeration of snapshots, disparate matter fused, localities, and moments joined (however incongruously) into an impressionistic sensation of life ever-accelerating and discombobulating. In terms of the reader's response, when conventional causal/temporal connections are severed so recursively, "'the reader becomes disoriented and is forced to concentrate on the identification of new aspects of situation.'"[39] The text thus becomes a space that the reader must enter to make logical connections, as the juxtaposed plot lines enforce a hermeneutic of simultaneity, not linear chronology.

Unlike *Transfer*'s splintered story line, *Rises'* plot is more singularly focused, though only ostensibly linear. Because this focus is portioned into disparate, unlinked episodes, however, it still achieves a more spatial than temporal orientation. In fragmented first-person novels like Hemingway's, after all, "the reader is confined almost exclusively to the perspective of the experiencing self. The functional moment is 'now,' not 'then,' and this gain in immediacy is necessarily accompanied by a loss in coherence."[40] Divided into three books and twenty-four chapters, *Rises* resembles this description, particularly since its chapter endings and beginnings are not linked causally, as seen in Book I. Chapter V, for instance, ends with Jake's vague dismissal of Cohn—"We talked about one thing and another, and I left him to come to the office" (*Rises*, 47)—but Chapter VI does not open in the office: "At five o'clock I was in the Hotel Crillon waiting for Brett" (*Rises*, 48). The chapter break disrupts rather than enhances temporal progression, and the reader is left to ponder what happened in the gap between Jake's dismissal of Cohn and his pursuit of Brett and what significance, if any, that gap might bear on the novel's themes.

Compounding such disparities, *Rises'* three books are not symmetrically divided: Book I contains seven chapters, Book II eleven, and Book III only five. This final book, which constitutes only twenty pages of the entire novel, comes as a particularly abrupt, or fast, ending given the attenuated pace of Book II, which is one hundred and fifty-three pages long. Such disproportion among the books and chapters spatializes the diegesis because "the arrangement of episodes is structured more by juxtaposition or parataxis than by temporal progression."[41] Appropriately enough, since, for Jake, "life only came in flashes" (*Rises*, 219), *Rises'* episodes resemble snapshots or short films. From the vantage point of the end of the novel, the reader, too, can see the preceding episodes as quick flashes, for Book III defies any conventional promise of a "neat" conclusion in which clipped endings are resolved, or wounds are sutured. Despite its uneven structural speed, then, *Rises'* organization resembles Jake's description of "the man and the bull and the cape" in the Spanish arena: They "were all one sharply etched mass. It was all so slow and controlled" (*Rises*, 221). The arena, like the novel, is a picture, a space.[42]

Like their plot structures, both novels' narrative voices and character foci are spatially dispersed. According to Ivo Vidan, when narrative voice is disrupted, "the inner time continuity does not proceed in its natural order and is instead problematized both by the order substituted for it and by the way the reader's consciousness experiences the problematization."[43] Because Jake narrates the novel, *Rises* exemplifies such problematization: The narrative world is primarily a subjective representation of Jake's experience. This subjective focus spatializes the reading process, for the reader's challenge in such novels is to differentiate between mimetic and subjective depictions of the narrative world.[44] The reading process is slowed, then, as the reader experiences the novel not as a picture of an external narrative world but as a picture of the narrator's mind.

As an intrusive (rather than detached) narrator, Jake insists upon such subjectivization. Time after time, Jake abruptly inserts himself into otherwise objective descriptions, disrupting the diegesis and the reader's perceptions of the narrative world. To start with, Jake does not view himself as "literary"—"Braddocks was his literary friend. I was his tennis friend" (*Rises*, 12)—yet he "writes" the novel we read. Unsurprisingly, then, Jake judges himself as an unreliable narrator: "Somehow I feel as if I have not shown Robert Cohn clearly" (*Rises*, 52). He also acknowledges that he strays from his own narrative ends: "That has nothing to do with the story" (*Rises*, 102). These intrusions do not, of course, undercut the novel's literary value simply because Jake doubts his own abilities. Rather, as Wolfgang Iser describes, such disruptions increase the literary work's value for the reader because they evoke "the possibility that we may formulate ourselves and so discover what had previously seemed to elude our consciousness."[45] When we launch ourselves into the space, what Iser would call the "gaps"[46] that Jake creates with his self-doubt, we engage the literary text on a personal, creative level and are forced to investigate our own responses to such "incompleteness." As Adrian Bond aptly claims, "By the novel's conclusion, we have entered into an experience which approximates Jake's own. As readers of the novel we too, like Jake, its writer-reader, are frustrated; like him, we try to find what we know is missing."[47]

In contrast to this single character focus, Mickelson observes that spatial-form novels "may also offer a picture of society" and cites *Manhat-*

tan Transfer as a primary example. Novels of this type characterize a society in a static picture, refusing development in the same way that novels with an individual subject do. For each type, "the procedure is the same: a large number of congruent segments make up a static whole."[48] In *Transfer*, as aforementioned, Dos Passos does not provide a single plot-line or a standout protagonist like Hemingway's Jake. Jimmy Herf and Ellen Thatcher, the only characters we follow from novel's beginning to end, are *Transfer*'s protagonists if any human characters are, but their identities are so interlaced with other characters' to make even their plotlines difficult to follow.

To accomplish this character blending, in addition to crosscutting from plotline to plotline, Dos Passos repeats (or at least approximates) names for many of his characters in an unusual form of leitmotif. For example, Jimmy (or Jimps) Herf, a major character, shares his name with James Merivale, a minor character; their common name becomes so confusing that it beguiles even their cousin Maisie: "'There cant [sic] be two Jameses can there?'" (*Transfer*, 100). Similarly, two minor characters are named Joe: Joe O'Keefe and Joe Harland, whose names sonically resonate with the names of two other minor characters, Gus McNeil and George Baldwin. Conversely, though to the same spatializing effect, Dos Passos repeatedly changes some characters' names. Congo becomes Armand, Jake Silverman has five aliases (*Transfer*, 348), and Ellen is referred to as Ellen, Elaine, Ellie, and Helena, all with three surnames: Thatcher, Oglethorpe, and Herf. Ellen's panoply of titles, particularly if confused with two minor characters' names, Elsie and Nellie, is ironic given Ellen's mother's anxiety to have her child "labeled" when she is born, lest she be mistaken for another baby (*Transfer*, 7). Indeed, labels, or names, do not serve their conventional narrative function in *Transfer*—rather than being signs for specific character referents, names are signs that resist referents. As a spatial technique, this name (con)fusion slows the reader's progress in proportion to how quickly these characters slip in and out of the novel's fractured plot.

For our readings of Jimmy and Ellen, this name slippage is most problematic because the characters' nominal associations with minor characters resist the reader's attempt to focus on the pair as protagonists. Thus, more than Jimmy and Ellen, perhaps, as A. C. Goodson argues, *Transfer*'s protagonist seems to be Manhattan itself.[49] While I do believe that Jimmy and Ellen are vital characters to the novel, Goodson's argument is useful if, insofar as Manhattan is *Transfer*'s central character, all of the other characters emerge as isolated attributes of this larger focus. From this perspective, the novel's polyvocality (the range of dialects as well as the sheer number of different voices represented) does not emphasize character as much as it emphasizes a lack of, or a space for, character. In point of fact, throughout the text, groups of characters are typically mentioned as a homogeneous mass—"'People are all the same'" (*Transfer*, 37)—or as impersonal synecdoches: "sudden jetbright glances of eyes under straw hats, attitudes of chins, thin lips, pouting lips, Cupid's bows" (*Transfer*, 153). The text's narrative voice (which varies wildly, including third limited, second person, and free indirect discourse) compounds this homogeny via, paradoxically, heterogeneity, for no single narrative voice claims authority.

For all their indistinction, then, Manhattan's residents seem "in the juggled parti-colored crowds like people invisible" (*Transfer*, 302), people indistinct. *Transfer*'s world is a place where, as Ellen describes, "'everybody in the world is always at the same place at the same time'" (*Transfer*, 182), but no one is ever singularly present. Challenged by the polyvocality and character indistinction which result from the speed with which characters move in and out of the diegesis, the reader must read *Transfer* as a gap-laden space and insert him or herself into the text as the only "present" consciousness that can fill those gaps.

Like plot and narrative voice fragmentation, the leitmotif functions spatially because it forces the reader to pause in order to connect moments of repetition throughout the text. In *Rises*, leitmotifs such as impotence and consumption (of alcohol, cigarettes, and food) structurally halt time through recursive repetition and reproduce the effects of speed technology insofar as "the progressive possibilities of the new visual media give way to isolation, impotence, and retrogression."[50] As much subject to those feelings as Jake, who "had that feeling of going through something that has all happened before" (*Rises*, 70), the reader feels a paradoxical sense of vertigo and stasis as Jake and his friends move within the same fixed grooves, as a bullfighter might circle a bull. Moving from bar to bar and country to country, the group revolves around the same ideas, the same motifs. Even the book's title and epigraph from Ecclesiastes imply this cyclical motion.

Rises' leitmotifs structurally reinforce the novel's characters' attempts to live in the present because memories of the past (the war) and fears of the future (speed) constantly threaten that presentness. As Robert Cohn—whom Jake describes as "really very fast" (*Rises*, 1)—says, "'I can't stand it to think my life is going so fast and I'm not really living it [. . .] Don't you ever get the feeling that all your life is going by and you're not taking advantage of it?'" (*Rises*, 18–19). Brett, too, feels shackled by an overweening personal velocity: "'How can I stop it? I can't stop things'" (*Rises*, 187).

Swept away—stripped of their agency—by speed culture, Hemingway's characters try to anchor themselves in the present with repetitive actions, like alcohol consumption, which allows Jake and his ilk to numb the trauma that they experienced in the war. One of those changes is, of course, that Jake is impotent; and since his perspective controls narrative time, the only present into which the group can escape is, ironically, an impotent one.

From writing to fishing to sex, the characters' activities seem perpetually adumbrated by disappointment. Cohn, for example, says, "'I can't get this second book going,'" to which Jake responds, "'That happens to everybody'" (*Rises*, 45). Jake's fish, too, are "smaller" than Bill's, "'all about the size of [Bill's] smallest'" (*Rises*, 125). Even Jake's dreams are at one point impotent: "'I don't think I dreamt'" (*Rises*, 129). And to Jake, as to perhaps his readers, "'All countries look just like moving pictures'" (*Rises*, 18)—his world is a simulacrum, an incomplete version of the original. Jake thus offers us a "moving picture" of *Rises*' world: a world ironically paralyzed by its repetitive motion and a place that the reader must actively enter to comprehend, for it is otherwise not affectively "moving" but "sterilized" by Jake's everywhere-projected impotence.[51]

Like these leitmotifs, Jake's descriptions, paratactic though they may be, often circle around a single point, launching from a thesis to which, after a paragraph or two of tangential description, he returns. Chapter XIX, for instance, opens with Jake's observation, "In the morning it was all over. The fiesta was finished." Following two paragraphs that describe ancillary events (Jake showering, children cleaning up fireworks, Jake sitting at a café table), Jake returns to this point as though he had never left it: "The fiesta was over" (*Rises*, 231). A digression that Genette labels a "descriptive pause" in the novel's "duration"—the relationship between the temporal length of represented events and the text's own length—the intervening description slows narrative time even as it speeds through several events.[52] Because "repetition" and "digression" are "techniques for slowing down the course of time,"[53] Jake's digression between repeating his main point creates a spatial moment for reflection after the frantic commotion of the fiesta.

Such competing velocities stylistically and thematically reinforce *Transfer*'s spatiality as well. Insofar as "the style of spatial form often drifts away from closely representational, denotative language,"[54] the novel's language not only drifts but surges with speed-imitative techniques like neologisms, alliteration, and syntactic inversion: "down the avenue lamps were coming on marking off with green shimmer brickpurple blocks of houses; chimney pots and water tanks cut sharp into a sky flushed like flesh" (*Transfer*, 6).[55] Lacking standard punctuation like commas and lubricated by alliterative fricatives, this passage's words flow fast and are typical of *Transfer*'s literary texture. In keeping with the author's goal to "record the fleeting world the way the motion picture film recorded it,"[56] the readerly impression of such syntactic speed is that the novel's narrators are moving so quickly that their perceptions meld into one another, creating an over-whelming synesthetic sensorium. Insertions of found literature reinforce this record of ephemerality: Intermingling passages from advertisements, newspaper clippings, and songs within the narrators' musings, Dos Passos imitates how subjects moving through Manhattan might catch mere glimpses (like Jake's "flashes") of information around themselves. Such in-formation is all the harder to understand, of course, because the narra-tors' apparent physical and perceptual speed strips the information of its context.

As a consequence of this sensory bombardment, Mickelson's claim that "complicated syntax, an unusual vocabulary, or elaborate imagery all slow the reader's progress"[57] proves true with *Transfer*'s style, for as fast as words are combined, contorted, or inserted (without context) in the novel, the reader must slow his or her progress to absorb the condensed sensory in-formation. In fact, as Oliver Sacks contends in "Speed" (2004), his analysis of the neurological causes of subjective perceptions of acceleration, while the physical world may move at great velocities, a person in such circum-stances may find him or herself "in a suddenly enlarged and spacious timescape, where he has all the time he needs."[58] The exigencies of physi-cal speed—literary or otherwise—can create a phenomenological decelera-tion of time into what Sacks aptly calls a timescape: a sense of time that becomes spatialized, slower and roomier than the speedy external forces impinging upon, and creating, that slow interior space.[59] As *Transfer* indi-cates, to refuse such a timescape is to risk becoming, like Ellen, "'just numb'" (*Transfer*, 267) to the violent external experience of acceleration.

Thematically, too, the notion that speed elides time recurs so often in *Transfer* that it emerges as one of the text's central themes.[60] Characters repeatedly complain that they "'never have time any more'" (*Transfer*, 58) or that they "'dont [sic] know what to do about time'" (*Transfer*, 132). Time is so accelerated, in fact, that the characters' lives lack temporal synchron-icity. Schedules do not coincide, for example, as when Jimmy and Ruth eat breakfast and lunch simultaneously (*Transfer*, 135). The characters even age at different rates, as during the "Steamroller" chapter, where Ellen has aged from an infant to a married woman yet Bud is still twenty-five, the same age he was during Ellen's infancy (*Transfer*, 121–2). This lost time seems directly related to the city's perpetual motion: Upon his first arrival in

New York, for instance, Jimmy observes that "'after you've left the ship you can still feel the motion,'" which causes his legs to ache (*Transfer*, 71). Tellingly, Jimmy's mother calls this aching "growing pains" (*Transfer*, 71), suggesting that, in speed culture, even biological growth is painfully accelerated as a result of constant motion.

Dos Passos emphasizes that the pain caused by such velocity is ineluctable, beyond the characters' control. As an unnamed real estate agent, a character rendered incidental by the novel's menagerie of characters, proclaims, "'We are caught up Mr. Perry on a great wave whether we will or no, a great wave of expansion and progress [. . .] All these mechanical inventions [. . .] they're leading somewhere'" (*Transfer*, 15). Although he does not name this ominous "somewhere," the agent then picks up a ram's skull, the remains of an animal killed to clear construction land. This juxtaposition of a depersonalized character with a product of speed culture's violence indicates that speed in *Transfer* is a personally and environmentally violent force. Anticipating Virilio, in fact, Elmer describes how the fast pace of Manhattan makes daily life seem like it takes place "in the middle of a battle just like in the war" (*Transfer*, 331). In contrast to its apparent section divisions into pre-, active, and post-war states, *Transfer* is, for all its fragmentation, a mimetic depiction of one single war zone: speed culture.

As indicated earlier, many of the spatial-form novel's techniques may be grouped under the term *parataxis*, a syntactic mode evident in both Dos Passos' and Hemingway's fiction, most famously in the latter's.[61] As Kern records, "The need for speed, clarity, and simplicity" in the technologically innovative journalistic profession "shaped a new 'telegraphic' style. No doubt Hemingway's simplification of the English language was in part a consequence of his experience as a foreign correspondent."[62] *Rises*' characteristically short, clipped sentences (particularly in its dialogue) could be said to imitate the technology of speed culture, then, but they also subvert that culture because parataxis slows readerly comprehension: "After the Great War," Eric Rabkin argues, "culture may have been fragmented but [. . .] Hemingway's failure to make logical connections forces his readers to actualize in their own minds [. . .] a coherent value system."[63] By this account, Hemingway's parataxis creates space where a cultural obsession with speed, technology, and its resulting warfare eliminate it.[64]

Most conspicuous in his long description of the running of the bulls (*Rises*, 200), Jake's diction is predominantly paratactic: monosyllabic, repetitious, and logically disjunctive. Once a reporter like Hemingway, Jake seems to have gleaned his compositional technique from speed culture, for he simplifies through omission even the most complicated of subjects. His description of Pedro Romero's bullfighting, in fact, metaphorizes his (and Hemingway's) paratactic writing style:

> Romero's bull-fighting gave real emotion, because he kept the absolute purity of line in his movements and always quietly and calmly let the horns pass him close each time. He did not have to emphasize their closeness [. . .] Romero had the old thing, the holding of his purity of line through the maximum of exposure, while he dominated the bull by making him realize he was unattainable, while he prepared him for the killing. (*Rises*, 171–2)

To Jake, as to Hemingway, "real emotion" is achieved through implication and evasion, "not hav[ing] to emphasize"—through the near but never completed approach. Hence Jake's simple descriptions which, for all their simplicity, designate underlying complexity. In response to Bill's comment that good writing is full of "'Irony and Pity'" (a modernist revision of Aristotle's definition of tragedy), for instance, Jake describes his breakfast as "coffee and buttered toast. Or, rather, it was bread toasted and buttered" (*Rises*, 119). The "purity" of this description contains Bill's irony and pity ("the killing," or the tragedy), for Jake's attention to such mundane details— that he would take the time to contemplate two nearly identical descriptions of the same thing—suggests a torpor, a stasis that only the most frustrated, but most reflective, lives could contain. The reader shares this frustrated reflection, for the effect of such repetitions is "one of slow-motion progression, two steps forward and one step back."[65]

In a similarly paratactic yet emotionally fraught description of his own body, Jake withholds the nature of his war wound. He only records that, "undressing, I looked at myself in the mirror of the big armoire beside the bed. That was a typically French way to furnish a room. Practical, too, I suppose. Of all the ways to be wounded. I suppose it was funny. I put on my pajamas and got into bed" (*Rises*, 38). The reader never really knows the "way" Jake is "wounded" because Jake evades, though does not avoid, the subject. His non-sequiturs about the mirror imply that he is trying to distract himself from his wound just as his circumlocution distracts the reader. Paradoxically, such wandering focus (focus in motion) invites our attention to the evaded subject and consequently slows our progress, for, in order to feel the "real emotion" of Jake's description, we must focus not on what we are reading but on what we are *not* reading. In this sense, Jake actually emphasizes through omission the subject he ostensibly wants to de-emphasize—his focus lies in his gaps, which the reader is burdened to fill.[66] So where Bill urges Jake to be ironic and pitiful in a more ostentatious "New York" style (Bill sings his entreaty, in fact), Jake and Hemingway already achieve both qualities with reporterly parataxis. Employing speed culture's techniques to undercut its dehumanizing effects, *Rises'* author and protagonist reveal that language designed to eliminate "real emotion" may, ironically, produce it.[67]

Long passages of un- or rarely attributed dialogue in *Rises*, like the exchange among Jake, Brett, and the Count (*Rises*, 37), similarly slow the reader's progress: While the lack of tags may initially increase reading speed, it finally forces the reader to provide the attributions that Hemingway omits. When Jake tells Brett, "'When you talk to me you never finish your sentences at all,'" Brett's response—"'Leave 'em for you to finish. Let any one finish them as they like'" (*Rises*, 65)—indicates the manner in which unattributed dialogue creates Iserian gaps for the reader. Hemingway knowingly gouged his novel with such gaps, for in an early draft of *Rises* he writes that "none of the significant things are going to have any literary signs marking them. You have to figure them out by yourself."[68] While the absence of "literary signs" remains in the final text, Hemingway's ultimate omission of these sentences creates a gap about gaps in the novel; for the speedy reader, Hemingway's iceberg runs treacherously deep.

The dialogue's lack of tags also spatializes the characters, who tend to blend together when speaking: "A kind of echolalia comes to inhabit the text as one character repeats the other, as their voices merge; become indistinguishable."[69] In narratologically paratactic fashion, no individual voice seizes authority, making the characters seem, as Jake tells us, "writers and artists [. . .] too many" (*Rises*, 25). If, as Robert Lamb contends, dialogue among Hemingway's characters involves "a kind of shorthand that would make their conversation incomprehensible to an outsider (or reader),"[70] such dialogue creates a space that readers must enter to "finish" the characters' ideas "as they like"—though with much effort and to no ultimate conclusion.[71]

Compounding this spatiality, non sequiturs pock *Rises'* dialogue, most commonly in the forms of oblique non-responses to questions (*Rises*, 85) and narrative interruptions of dialogue. At the end of Chapter IX, for instance, Robert asks, "'Did you get my line, Jake?'" to which Jake's following narration, which concludes the chapter, omits any response: "The cab stopped in front of the hotel and we all got out and went in. It was a nice hotel, and the people at the desk were very cheerful, and we each had a small good room" (*Rises*, 95). Rushing past Jake's answer to and even his thoughts about Cohn's question, the narration's first sentence consists of

Hemingway's typically fast, monosyllabic words shot out, as if by a machine gun, without standard, decelerating punctuation. Mimetic because the sentence describes vehicular and pedal motion, these techniques exemplify Hemingway's "paratactic syntax and his use of non-standard English [which] were a politics of form that expressed the damage done to language" by WWI.[72] Here that damage resembles human disconnection and apathy, since Jake appears to have neglected Cohn's attempt at communication and since each resident of the hotel, metonymy of transience, stays in his or her own room. The chapter's last sentence diverges from the penultimate sentence's syntax, however, and features Hemingway's characteristic use of polysyndeton and commas to describe space. Because the paratactic clauses are coordinated but not subordinated, they stack upon one another and create a picture: As Trodd observes, "written in a staccato rhythm, without subordination, the sentences achieve stasis through structure. Events pile up and the result is a sense of eyewitness."[73] The chapter closes with a spatial sentence about space, which leaves the reader room to wonder about the gaps in communication between the narrative's characters—gaps produced, one might venture, by the speedy sentence transporting the reader from Cohn's question to the hotel.

In both *Transfer* and *Rises*, perhaps the most pernicious effect of speed culture is its recursive motion: For all their acceleration, the texts' characters appear to be static. In *Transfer*, for instance, Bud and Ellen want to move to the "center" of things (*Transfer*, 24, 267), but like Yeats' "center" that "will not hold," Manhattan has no center at which to arrive, for speed culture cyclically pulls people to and from centrality. A leitmotif in the novel, this speed-induced "static circularity" surfaces in images like "a doublefaced word [that] clinked like a coin: Success Failure, Success Failure" (*Transfer*, 303), which haunts Jimmy and other characters. Here the cliché "whatever goes up comes down" (*Transfer*, 351–2) is transformed by speed culture's ruthless economy as a cycle that leads some to suicide (Stan) and others to exile (Jimmy). The difference between these two characters' fates seems to be that Jimmy rejects the notion of success (and, therefore, its vicious cycle) while Stan embraces it. Stan, like Bud (who does not age), is stuck in speed culture: "'I cant [sic] decide what I want most, so my motion is circular, helpless and confoundedly discouraging'" (*Transfer*, 176). This circular motion discourages Stan to the point that he (evoking Hemingway's Jake) elects sterility, for he believes that "'procreation is an admission of defeat'" (*Transfer*, 210); such motion is finally so discouraging that Stan kills himself. In contrast, Jimmy escapes the monotony of circular motion because he knows what he wants: to fail. For Jimmy, "'to fail [is] the only sublime thing'" (*Transfer*, 175), where failure may be read as the rejection of speed culture's elusive standards of success via progress.

Jimmy's escape from Manhattan's speed culture, particularly contrasted with Ellen's fate, undergirds our overall conception of the modernist novel's spatial function. If *Transfer* primarily focalizes Manhattan's effects on its residents, Jimmy and Ellen represent the poles of such effects. By novel's end, Ellen remains in Manhattan, swept up by speed culture (and perhaps replaced by Anna, her doppelganger—another instance of character elision), while Jimmy escapes it. Jimmy and Ellen's fates are of particular import for, despite my earlier qualifications, the couple is more individualized than most of *Transfer*'s characters, which Dos Passos emphasizes by showing how Jimmy and Ellen, unlike Stan, want to escape the city. This desire is, in fact, what initially brings the couple together (*Transfer*, 179). Coincident with their exilic longings, Jimmy and Ellen want to be artists, creators of some sort. Ellen learns early in childhood that "'we need construction and not de-struction in this world'" (*Transfer*, 18), an iconoclastic notion in her blurred culture which gives her a sense of autonomy: As a child she runs and daydreams "'because [she] wanted to'" (*Transfer*, 55), and later she has a successful career as an actress. Jimmy similarly dreams of an iconoclastic life: Contrary to his mother's and his Uncle Jeff's wishes, he daydreams about blue-collar life (*Transfer*, 80) and seeks to escape his journalistic profession as soon as he enters it (*Transfer*, 121). Jimmy and Ellen appear more individualized, then, because they (and their readers) know what they want: to leave Manhattan and to create.

Jimmy and Ellen's fates diverge, however, in relation to their resistance to mass media and the speed culture that engenders it. Despite their successful exile during the war, Jimmy and Ellen return to New York, at which point Ellen seems to resign herself to speed culture, losing her exilic dreams, while Jimmy wants to leave again. The couple's involvement with the media grounds this exilic disparity, for, upon their return, Jimmy leaves the journalistic profession while Ellen enters it. Jimmy quits his reporter job because, like Eliot's typist in *The Waste Land*, he becomes a part of his machine: He seems like "'a goddam traveling dictograph,'" "'an automatic writing machine'" (*Transfer*, 344), so much so that he confesses that "print itches like a rash inside me. I sit here pockmarked with print" (*Transfer*, 354). Jimmy says he is, as a reporter, "a parasite on the drama of life, reporter looks at everything through a peephole. Never mixes in" (*Transfer*, 320). Overwhelmed by this peripheral (though, paradoxically, central) position in speed culture, Jimmy declares, "'I've got to chase myself'" (*Transfer*, 384), as though he were only a shadow of himself, a copy of the original Herf text. Dehumanized thus, Jimmy flees his profession to save, rather than to chase, himself—to regain his "faith in words" (*Transfer*, 366). Ellen, in contrast, concedes to such dehumanization, for she takes a job with a magazine and cannot escape "the fagging memory of the office, the smell of it, the chirruping of typewriters, the endlessly repeated phrases, faces, typewritten sheets" (*Transfer*, 372–3). Having relinquished her iconoclasm to speed culture, Ellen's only autonomy is over the machine she has become: "she kept winding up a hypothetical dollself and setting it in various positions" (*Transfer*, 374). Considering *Transfer*'s preponderance of mass media text, metonymic of speed, part of the novel's spatiality—its function as a space for self-creation—is its challenge to readers to resist, unlike Ellen, the thrall of media messages in favor of the literary artifact itself.[74]

Given this challenge, it follows that *Rises* and *Transfer* privilege literary writing over journalism. The novels' emphases on journalism, in fact, create lacunae for the literary artist. In *Rises*, Bill says Jake is not a writer but "'only a newspaper man. An expatriated newspaper man'" because, as aforementioned, Jake's writing lacks those "literary" qualities of irony and pity (*Rises*, 119). Moreover, *Rises*' artists and writers do not create anything during the narrative, consumed as they are by motion. In *Transfer*, the artist is similarly regarded as "'a useless fardel on society'" (*Transfer*, 361): Insinuated by Dos Passos' omission of literary (as opposed to mass media or pop culture) texts from his found text insertions, one character distinguishes "'newspaper work'" from Jimmy's desire "'to write'" (*Transfer*, 359), just as Bill does Jake's in *Rises*. Characters who can produce the novels' valued form of writing—the literary—are thus notably absent from both texts' narrative presents even as Jake and Jimmy threaten to fill those gaps in the future.

As a result of these literary lacunae, both *Rises* and *Transfer* thematize literature as a curative for speed-induced vertigo. For Jake, reading functions as a sort of Dramamine: "I did not want to shut my eyes because the room would go round and round. If I kept on reading that feeling would pass" (*Rises*, 151). Reading offers Jake stable experience in an unstable world, for, after reading, "It would seem as though it had really happened to me. I would always have it" (*Rises*, 153). Because he recognizes literature's importance as a space for self-construction, Jake fills *Rises*' artistic lacuna by writing the text of *Rises* itself. Indeed, contrary to Bill's accusation, Jake *is* a writer because he has achieved the purity of line (and concomitant irony and pity) that Hemingway models as proper literary technique. As an artifact of Jake's consciousness, *Rises* testifies to Jake's ability to break from the circular, static motion that he depicts in the novel. Jimmy, although he has not yet achieved it, similarly seeks lasting experience through literary pursuits. His longing for space, after all, motivates his exile at novel's end: "If we only had more space, he was muttering; we live cramped in our squirrelcage [. . .] Space space cleanness quiet; the words were gesticulating in his mind as if he were addressing a vast auditorium" (*Transfer*, 329). Here Jimmy anticipates the kind of clean, well-lighted space that Hemingway's Jake achieves with literary writing. That Jimmy's words echo so in his imagined auditorium (itself echoing Iser and Hemingway's "arenas") intimates that he has discovered the space for his own self-creation: the space of literature. Jimmy's exile, then, constitutes his endeavor to fill *Transfer*'s literary-art lacuna.

I do not mean to suggest, however, that either *Transfer* or *Rises* ends in any traditional, closed fashion. If the spatial novel's ending "provides a sudden, definitive, almost arbitrary break in the potentially endless cycle evident in" the rest of the narrative,[75] *Transfer* and *Rises*' conclusions are typically spatial. Jimmy's response to the question "'How fur ye goin?'"/"'I dunno. . . . Pretty far'" (*Transfer*, 404) and Jake's question "'Isn't it pretty to think so?'" (*Rises*, 251) are confoundingly quick, pithy conclusions for such dense narratives, particularly given Jimmy's uncertainty and Jake's interrogative. Exiles that they are, both Jimmy and Jake are also in motion at their novels' endings, thus perpetuating the recursions established in the rest of each novel even as the texts seem to conclude. As a result, readers must engage in cyclical reading, for "the disparity" between each narrative's preceding cycles and abrupt conclusion "forces a rereading ('reflexive reference') of the earlier material; the reader is thrust back into the story once more to correlate the work's seemingly discontinuous sections."[76] As with the other spatial techniques that I have discussed, fast endings of this sort slow the reader's progress, for we must return to the novel just when we've thought we've finished it. It is because of this enforced hermeneutic that I read these novels' endings optimistically. While these readings are, of course, products of my own creative engagement with the texts, such engagement is, I argue, the spatial novel's offering to the subjects of modern speed culture. Because both Jimmy and Jake exile themselves to literary pursuits—because they seek space within their space-less speed cultures—*Transfer* and *Rises*' endings allegorize the processes that their readers must enact to engage these texts.

Imaginative Space: Speed War's Safe Zone

As I alluded to earlier in my discussion of Kern's dialectic, the reading processes required of modernist spatial novels are ultimately processes of
self-formation and -reclamation. Insofar as Kern describes the "stuff of
everybody's identity" as something "slow," Heidegger's notion of dwelling,
which Virilio posits as antithetical to speed culture,[77] and Michael Seidel's
conception of postexilic eminence[78] clarify how modernist novels' deceleration of hermeneutic speed via stylistic acceleration creates space for such
self-construction. For Heidegger, human beings can only "Be" when they
"dwell," where dwelling is defined as "to be set at peace [. . .] to remain at
peace within the free, the preserve, the free sphere that safeguards each
thing in its essence. *The fundamental character of dwelling is this sparing.*"[79]
By this logic, Heidegger contends that "the way in which you are and I am,
the manner in which we humans *are* on the earth, is *buan*, dwelling."[80]
Humans can dwell anywhere, then, so long as this "free," or self-preserving,
space is constructed: "Space is in essence that for which room has been
made, that which is let into its bounds [. . .] by virtue of a locale [. . .] *Accordingly, spaces receive their essential being from locales and not from 'space.'*"[81]
To Heidegger, "locales" are human "buildings," which he conceives in both
literal and metaphorical terms: They are human constructions built for
self-sparing, whether those constructions be edifices, songs, or novels.
"Building thus characterized is a distinctive letting-dwell," and human
beings provide themselves the space in which to dwell "when they build
out of dwelling, and think for the sake of dwelling."[82]

If we view the modernist novel as a kind of Heideggerian building, we
begin to see how the fast yet spatial narratives I am discussing create space
for human dwelling—space in which human beings dehumanized by speed
culture can reclaim their humanity, can autonomously "Be." Heidegger anticipates this cooption of technology for reflective purposes, in fact, when
he argues that one is not confined "to a stultified compulsion to push on
blindly with technology or, what comes to the same, to rebel helplessly
against it and curse it as the work of the devil. Quite to the contrary, when
we once open ourselves expressly to the *essence* of technology we find ourselves unexpectedly taken into a freeing claim."[83] Viewed as an inevitable
component of modern existence, technology can liberate human beings
from the "will to mastery," for "the essence of technology must harbor in
itself the growth of the saving power."[84] Indeed, to Heidegger, art and technology can serve one and the same purpose insofar as they derive from
the same Greek word, *techni*.[85]

In point of fact, as David Harvey observes, Heidegger supported "a counter-myth of rootedness in place and environmentally-bound traditions as the only secure foundation for political and social action in a manifestly troubled world,"[86] which suggests how the modernist novel concerned with speed served in its own time (and, certainly, may serve in our own time) not only humanistic but political and social functions. Harvey describes the period *entre deux guerres* as one in which "the trauma of world war and its political and intellectual responses" incited "the search for a myth appropriate to modernity," a myth that would "redeem us from 'the formless universe of contingency' or, more programmatically, to provide the impetus for a new project for human endeavor."[87] This need fell squarely on the shoulders of aesthetic modernists, for "the fading of unified Enlightenment beliefs and the emergence of perspectivism left open the possibility of informing social action with some aesthetic vision."[88] Modernist writers' reactions to speed are part of this socio-aesthetic action, for their texts, public commodities, could influence readers in the same way that they were produced: by slowing time and regaining "dwelling" space. If speed culture violently deracinates people from the land, and if it metaphorically annihilates the land itself, modernist subjects could secure their political and social acts in the space of literature.[89]

One might ask at this point how *Transfer* and *Rises* could propose "building," something stationary, as a remedy for speed if Jimmy and Jake are in motion at their novels' conclusions. Here Michael Seidel's notion of postexilic eminence expands our understanding of the Heideggerian building.[90] To Seidel, the exile's "building" is the imaginative construct yielded by the exile's motion. For this reason, Seidel claims that "the space of the exilic leap"—which he sees as a particular quality of early 20th-century fiction, and as we have seen is a primary component of *Transfer* and *Rises*—"is a powerful, perhaps even constitutive, metaphor for the genesis and disposition of narrative itself."[91] When the exile moves, his or her "imagined outland is a version of the inland; the possible a version of the previous."[92] So for the writer in motion, as modernist writers like Dos Passos and Hemingway were during this era and as Jimmy and Jake are by their novels' ends, motion itself must be part of the imaginative construction, the "previous," even as that construction proposes decreased motion as "the possible." Thus, Seidel argues that neither stasis nor perpetual motion, home nor exile is the exile-writer's "dwelling" space: The writer must oscillate between these states, for "it is almost as if the imagination requires the impediments of time or distance to activate it."[93] Per Heideggerian dwelling, the exile's "exile becomes his sovereignty."[94] Exile—the space between native and foreign land, stasis and perpetual motion—is where selfhood materializes, for "imagining, in this sense, may be the only tangible property of the narrative estate."[95] For writers deracinated by speed culture, Seidel's "unreal estate" is their "building"—literary narrative is the re-placement of space annihilated by speed, and it is a certain site of the modernist subject's dwelling.[96]

Seidel's exile model also illuminates Virilio's contention that stasis is a perniciously tempting "safeground" in speed culture: "In a social configuration whose precarious equilibrium is threatened by an ill-considered initiative," Virilio avers, "security can henceforth be likened to the absence of movement [. . .] we impose the new belief that a body's inability to move is not really a serious problem."[97] In this model, "The war machine is now not only all of war, *but also becomes the adversary/partners' principal enemy* by depriving them of their freedom of movement."[98] Virilio's sarcasm in these passages demonstrates that, for him, stasis in speed culture is tantamount to death—that, in a culture where speed is so powerfully destructive, speed can only be combated with speed. At the same time, however, Virilio insists that "running toward your Death [. . .] killing your Death" is tantamount to "'Death killing Death.'"[99] Using speed as a weapon against speed is, in this view, like slitting one's wrists *and* throat: It is a gesture suicidal twice over.

What Virilio's pessimistic double bind proposes is that speed must be countered by a reduction of speed—by a decrease in velocity, if not a total "absence of movement." The "warrior" opposed to the speed war can never stay still, nor can he/she attempt to fight acceleration with acceleration. Rather, this warrior must, as the modernist novelist, adopt the techniques of speed to recreate space: By Seidel's phrase, to engender "postexilic eminence," the exile must move ("exile") and stop ("post") in endlessly recurrent cycles. For Virilio and Seidel, as for Kern, motion slowed (though not stasis—motion must always be prefigured in this formulation) yields subjectivity regained. The threats to subjectivity that Virilio warns against, then, only highlight the importance of Seidel's model of motion-based inspiration, and they clarify the modernist novelist's strategy of employing speed (motion) to create space (stasis).

The ambiguous endings of *Manhattan Transfer* and *The Sun Also Rises* epitomize this oscillation between motion and stasis, for each predicts future motion—transference and rising—even as the narratives reclaim present space, as implied by *Transfer*'s titular subway transfer stop and *Rises*' static alternative to "also." *Rises* links exile and literature saliently, in fact, when Jake observes that Cohn thinks "South America could fix it and he did not like Paris. He got the first idea out of a book, and I suppose the second came out of a book too" (*Rises*, 20). Jake's irony implies that neither solution is entirely adequate: that the exile must search for inspiration both at home and afar; in stasis and in motion; in "moving pictures." As he tells Robert, "'You can't get away from yourself by moving from one place to another'" (*Rises*, 19); indeed, as a result of motion, one reconstitutes self, or space. But if the only way to be present is to slow time enough to re-claim space, the only way to avoid being overrun by the larger speed cul-ture is to abandon space as soon as it is claimed. In this sense, *Transfer* and *Rises* do not simply attack speed culture, for they are products thereof: With-out that culture's threat of violent velocity, the texts—and the spaces that they provide—would not exist in their current form. In concert with Hei-degger's belief that "man becomes truly free only insofar as he belongs to the realm of destining and so becomes one who listens, though not one who simply obeys,"[100] Dos Passos and Hemingway maintain critical dis-tance from the very technologies they use not "to conquer" or "to annihi-late" but to *create* "time and space." The paradoxes that I hope to have illuminated are that *Transfer* and *Rises* create space because and in spite of the culture of speed and that their literary spaces served not only aesthetic but socio-political purposes in the face of that culture's violence.

NOTES

My thanks to Glenn Brewer, James Landau, Mark McGurl, Michael North, Jessica Pressman, and the anonymous reader at *JNT* for their advice about and support for this essay.

1. Qtd. in Stephen Kern, *The Culture of Time and Space, 1880–1918* (Cambridge: Harvard University Press, 1986), 113. This quotation resonates all the more since Rolls, a pioneer of aviation, ballooning, and motoring, died in an airplane accident.

2. Filippo Tommaso Marinetti, *Teoria e Invenzione Futurista*, ed. Luciano De Maria, Vol. 2 of *Opere di F. T. Marinetti* (Milan: Arnoldo Mondadori, 1968), 13.

3. Marinetti, *Teoria e Invenzione*, 256.

4. In "On Speed and Ecstasy: Paul Virilio's 'Aesthetics of Disappear-ance' and the Rhetoric of Media" (*Configurations* 10.1 [2002], 129–48), Sandy Baldwin argues against fatalistic accounts of speed like Virilio's and con-tends that one's perception of speed produces ecstasy, an aesthetic product akin to Benjamin's aura. Relying upon the notion that, as evidenced by paratactic syntax, "the efficacy of speed accumulates disappearance in an increasingly delirious experience of the world, an increasing loss of reality"

(142), Baldwin suggests that, "if not exactly a perception of what disappears," we encounter with speed "at least an experience of its lack. Vanished perception leaves inert and apathetic bodies, which turn nonetheless into a source of experience. Our nonexperiences become the basis for subjectivity in new media environments" (135). By relying upon disappearances and nonexperiences, however, Baldwin aims only to redeem the absent, to affirm the negative while preserving the authority of absence and negation: "Speed names what comes aesthetically from beyond all codes, what can only be metaphorized and thus cannot be named, naming a paradoxical movement of movement. The thematization of speed provides a terminology for the prediscursive immediacy of an experience we all share without being able to talk about it" (144). It is my contention that Dos Passos and Hemingway are, in the modernist tradition, very much interested in recouping a subjectivity based on literary experience, not pure nonexperience, an experience that we can "name" or at least identify by considering the formal properties of their texts.

5. Kern, *The Culture of Time and Space*, 111.

6. Paul Virilio, *Speed and Politics*, trans. Mark Polizzotti (New York: Semiotext(e), 1986), 62.

7. Virilio explains his more radical position by claiming that the "dromological evolutionism of the 1920s" encouraged speed-based warfare to, "from lack of space, spread out into Time" (Virilio, *Speed and Politics*, 55). That survival was, however, short-lived: "Contraction in time, the disappearance of the territorial space [. . .] causes the 'present' to disappear in the instantaneousness of decision" (141). Based on the Heideggerian concept of dwelling—that if "'to be is to inhabit' [. . .] not to inhabit is no longer to exist" (78)—Virilio asserts that a culture in constant motion is a culture doomed to nonexistence. Hence modern warfare's preoccupation with fast weapons and fast death: "Sudden death is preferable to the slow death of he who is no longer welcome, of the reject, of the man deprived of a specific place *and thus of his identity*" (78).

8. Virilio cites Futurism as the figurative origin of a modern mentality that had its end, violence, prefigured in its beginning, speed: "Futurism in fact comes from a single art—that of war and its essence, speed" (Virilio, *Speed and Politics*, 62). This art is, for Virilio, "the origin of a totalitarian language of History [. . .] the mutual effort of the European States, then of the world, toward the absolute essence of foreign or civil war (speed)" (118). One might subject Dada to a similar analysis, for that aesthetic movement founded itself upon timed automatic writing experiments wherein artists created their work as quickly as possible (Malcolm Cowley, *Exile's Return* [New York: Penguin, 1994], 206–7).

9. Michael North, *Camera Works: Photography and the Twentieth-Century Word* (Oxford: Oxford University Press, 2005), 151.

10. Virilio, *Speed and Politics*, 78.

11. Joseph Frank, *The Idea of Spatial Form* (New Brunswick, New Jersey: Rutgers University Press, 1991).

12. Admittedly, Frank attempts to historicize the form by noting how "the feeling of loss of control over the meaning and purpose of life amidst the continuing triumphs of science and technics" contributed to the spatial impulse (Frank, *The Idea of Spatial Form*, 58), but his analysis suggests that writers repudiated "science and technics" altogether to create a world of myth alone (63–4). While I agree that Frank's analysis of myth pertains to many modernist texts, many other texts, like *Transfer* and *Rises*, foreground myth less than they do the very technologies that Frank argues they eschewed, which suggests that modernist spatial form arose in other ways paradoxically related to the social conditions that writers aimed to mollify.

13. Frank, *The Idea of Spatial Form*, 10.

14. Since Frank coined the phrase "spatial form" in his 1945 essay "Spatial Form in Modern Literature," spatial form theory has offered fertile ground from which to analyze narrative technique regardless of historical period. Novels like *Tristram Shandy* (1759–66) and *Adam Bede* (1859), with their self-conscious writer-narrators, accordingly confound the assertion that spatiality is a particularly 20th-century narrative technique. In his reassessment of "Spatial Form," in fact, Frank argues that "the emergence of spatial form in twentieth-century narrative should no longer be regarded as a radical break with tradition" (*The Idea of Spatial Form*, 120) but, instead, as an explosion of inchoate tendencies anticipated in earlier literature. While I concur with these assessments, I nonetheless believe that spatial form and its theoretical coinage in 1945 illuminate a historical problem peculiar to modernist literature: the problem of the modern subject's contention with overweening velocity. In his "Introduction: Spatial Form and Narrative Theory," Jeffrey Smitten acknowledges as much when he says, "The reader's capacity for reflexive reference is taxed far more by many late nineteenth- and early twentieth-century narratives than by others. More of the synthesizing, the discovery of narrative syntax, is left to the reader; there are more and greater gaps to be filled in" ("Spatial Form and Narrative Theory," *Spatial Form in Narrative*, ed. Ann Daghistany and Jeffrey R. Smitten [Ithaca, New York: Cornell University Press, 1981], 22). This preponderance of "slowing" narratives suggests a preoccupation with speed particular to the 20th century.

15. Dos Passos and Hemingway were famously preoccupied with technological innovation; when analyzing those preoccupations' political

roots, however, critics typically align Hemingway with the "cult of speed" and position Dos Passos against it. Comparing the authors may seem counterintuitive, then, especially since Hemingway's lifelong obsession with masculinity can be associated with speed technology, and since Hemingway publicly impugned Dos Passos' liberalism during the Spanish Civil War (see George Packer, "The Spanish Prisoner," *The New Yorker* [Oct. 31, 2005]: 82–7, 85). As evidenced by their interwar novels, however, Dos Passos' and Hemingway's political views of speed were much more alike in the 1920s than we might assume, for their concerns with technology produced very similar tensions between their novels' formal and thematic ambitions. In "John Dos Passos' *Rosinante to the Road Again* and the Modernist Expatriate Imagination" (*Journal of Modern Literature* 21.1 [1997]: 137–50), Donald Pizer suggests Dos Passos' and Hemingway's interwar political connection when he observes that "both writers began with the premise that modern life, as epitomized by American civilization, was largely devoid of the meaning necessary for the full life of the spirit. And although one writer stressed, within this premise, the baleful effects of an industrialized and mechanized society and the other the inadequacy of conventional beliefs in a world of this kind, both subscribed to the idea that the war was the fullest expression of the destructive emptiness of early twentieth-century life" (149). Useful though it is, Pizer's association minimizes the role of technology in Hemingway's literary politics. In her analysis of how Hemingway used technological aesthetics to mitigate the horrors of WWI, however, Zoe Trodd corrects this misprision by claiming that, after the war, Hemingway used "a camera-eye aesthetic that re-embodied reality and expelled the ghosts [of the war]. This aesthetic was often multi-focal. Imitating film rather than single-shot photography, it rejected all apparently coherent and exclusive ways of perceiving the world, and asked readers to 'mistrust all frank and simple people, especially when their stories hold together'" (Zoe Trodd, "Hemingway's Camera Eye: The Problem of Language and an Interwar Problem of Form," *The Hemingway Review* 26.3 [2007], 8). For more on modernist formal politics, see Marianne DeKoven, "The Politics of Modernist Form" (*New Literary History* 23.3 [Summer 1992], 675–90).

16. John Dos Passos, *Manhattan Transfer* (Boston: Houghton Mifflin, 1925); Ernest Hemingway, *The Sun Also Rises* (New York: Scribner, 1926). Subsequent citations of *Manhattan Transfer* and *The Sun Also Rises* will appear as *Transfer* and *Rises*, respectively.

17. Kern, *The Culture of Time and Space*, 100.

18. In *The Condition of Postmodernity* (London: Blackwell, 1990), David Harvey echoes Kern's sentiment when he posits that "the pressing need to confront psychological, sociological, technical, organizational, and political

problems of massive urbanization was one of the seed-beds in which modernist movements flourished" (25). Of those various problems, my focus in this essay is on modernist writers' overlooked confrontation with the problem of speed.

19. For more information on these speed technologies, see North's *Camera Works* and Jessica Pressman's forthcoming study of the modernist reading technology called the taschistoscope.

20. Smitten, "Introduction," 21.

21. Kern, *The Culture of Time and Space*, 129.

22. My claims about readers' responses to these texts are, of course, theoretical and not empirical, a scholarly limitation and advantage intrinsic to reception theory.

23. Maurice Blanchot, *The Space of Literature*, trans. Ann Smock (Lincoln: University of Nebraska Press, 1982), 37. Blanchot claims that spatial form's "originality cannot be grasped in terms either of geometrical space or the space of practical life" (qtd. in Frank, *The Idea of Spatial Form*, 127). Instead, he argues, art provides a "power to substitute for space the unmalleable, lifeless profundity of the imaginary" (48).

24. Mickelson describes this process in terms similar to Virilio's and Kern's postulations about the dialectic of velocity: "We see here a corollary to Heisenberg's Uncertainty Principle: an author can delineate with precision either the velocity (time) or the position (space) of a subject, but not both. The accuracy of their measurement is inversely proportional, since any gain in one dimension is matched by a loss in the other" (David Mickelson, "Types of Spatial Structure in Narrative," in Daghistany and Smitten, eds., *Spatial Form in Narrative*, 77). By narratively decelerating a world that was rapidly accelerating, modernist novelists delineated time with "imprecision" and, by Mickelson's formula, could therefore produce space. He describes this production as "an alternative to the *Bildungsroman*," for the spatial-form novel "offers a *Bild*, a picture; it portrays someone who has *already* developed" (65).

25. Virilio, *Speed and Politics*, 55, 62.

26. See David Hayman, *Re-Forming the Narrative* (Ithaca, New York: Cornell University Press, 1987). Hayman suggests this neglected area of study when he notes that "high modernist fiction [. . .] is characterized by fine-tuned and delicately balanced ironic productions that toy with the 'kinetic' but maintain a cautious balance by confining motion to the formal tensions within the artifact and by refusing both definition and the absolute conclusion" (20). Beyond this claim, however, Hayman does not pursue the issue of speed; rather, like many contemporary scholars, he focuses on modernist representations of time. In "'Absolutamente necesario': The

Express Train in Malcolm Lowry's *Under the Volcano*, Chapter Twelve"
(*Modernism/Modernity* 12.2 [2005], 209–28), Pam Kuhlken does attend to the
spatial form of Lowry's novel by considering, in part, the factor of speed, but
she does so on the assumption that speed in modern culture and Lowry's
novel indicate when "technology replaces God and rapid progress governs
trade and justice; velocity itself becomes the goal" (217); "by definition," she
says, "speed will accelerate, creating the need for new images and models
that help us understand the nature of velocity" (225). As evidence of such
pure acceleration, Kuhlken remarks that, in the 21st century, "as technology
caught up to the speed of light, human experience was left behind" (218), a
claim that not only ignores phenomenological views of experience but that,
most important, neglects the decelerating possibilities of velocity. As
Transfer and *Rises* reveal, speed need not "by definition" inevitably "accelerate"; and not only that, speed may decrease through its ostensible technological (or stylistic) increase, a paradox which pressures the definition of
speed upon which Kuhlken relies for her analysis.

    27. Robert Paul Lamb, "Hemingway and the Creation of Twentieth-
Century Dialogue," *Twentieth Century Literature* 42.4 (1996), 453.

    28. Dos Passos' 1935 essay "The Writer as Technician" (*Modernism: An
Anthology of Sources and Documents*, ed. Vassiliki Kolocotroni, Jane Goldman,
and Olga Taxidou [Chicago: University of Chicago Press, 1998], 545–8)
suggests as much when the author links writing, speed technology, and
politics in his theory of "the writer as technician." Arguing that "the process
[of writing] is not very different from that of scientific discovery and
invention," Dos Passos suggests that the pace of his writing changed in
tandem with the speed of technological change: "In a time of confusion and
rapid change like the present, when terms are continually turning inside out
and the names of things hardly keep their meaning from day to day, it's not
possible to write two honest paragraphs without stopping to take crossbear-
ings on every one of the abstractions that were so well ranged in ornate
marble niches in the minds of our fathers" (545). Completing the link in his
work among writing, speed, and politics, Dos Passos claims that "a writer, a
technician, must never, I feel, no matter how much he is carried away by
even the noblest political partisanship in the fight for social justice, allow
himself to forget that his real political aim, for himself and his fellows, is
liberty" (546).

    29. Italo Calvino, *Six Memos for the Next Millennium* (New York: Vin-
tage, 1993), 33, 36, 37.

    30. North, *Camera Works*, 142, 148. For further examples of Dos Passos'
early opposition to speed technology, see his 1916 essays "A Humble
Protest" and "Against American Literature."

31. In *A Moveable Feast* (New York: Simon & Schuster, 1996), Hemingway explains his iceberg theory as a "theory that you could omit anything if you knew that you omitted and the omitted part would strengthen the story and make people feel something more than they understood" (75). See Hemingway's *Death in the Afternoon* (New York: Scribner, 1932) and George Plimpton's "The Art of Fiction: Ernest Hemingway" (*Conversations with Ernest Hemingway*, ed. Matthew J. Bruccoli [Jackson: University Press of Mississippi, 1986]) for more information about Hemingway's iceberg technique.

32. Laura Gruber Godfrey, "Hemingway and Cultural Geography: The Landscape of Logging in 'The End of Something,'" *The Hemingway Review* 26.1 (2006), 60. Hemingway compared himself to Cézanne, in fact, and noted that he "learned how to make a landscape from Mr. Paul Cézanne" (Lillian Ross, "How Do You Like It Now, Gentlemen?" *The New Yorker* [May 13, 1950], 41). He also claimed of art that "unless you have geography, background, you have nothing" (qtd. in Godfrey, 49).

33. In this respect, *Transfer* and *Rises* are rather like the prose narrative counterparts to Pound's *The Cantos* and Eliot's *The Waste Land*, insofar as those two long poems represent modernist models of spatial accretion and deletion, or what Ronald Schleifer calls the modern crisis of abundance and parsimony (Ronald Schleifer, *Modernism and Time* [Cambridge: Cambridge University Press, 2000], 18).

34. Mickelson, "Types of Spatial Structure," 73.

35. Marshall McLuhan, "Speed of Cultural Change," *College Composition and Communication* 9.1 (Feb. 1958), 17.

36. A. C. Goodson, "*Manhattan Transfer* and the Metropolitan Subject," *Arizona Quarterly* 56.1 (2000), 91.

37. Gérard Genette, *Narrative Discourse*, trans. J. E. Lewin (Ithaca, New York: Cornell University Press, 1980), 108.

38. Virilio, *Speed and Politics*, 136.

39. Reimer Bull qtd. in Mickelson, "Types of Spatial Structure," 73.

40. Mickelson, "Types of Spatial Structure," 75.

41. Mickelson, "Types of Spatial Structure," 75.

42. Recalling Hemingway's bullfighting arena, Wolfgang Iser calls the literary text "something like an arena in which reader and author participate in a game of the imagination," a game which the author depends upon, "for the text only takes on life when it is realized" by the reader's "active and creative" engagement with the text (Wolfgang Iser, *The Implied Reader* [Baltimore: Johns Hopkins University Press, 1974], 274–5).

43. Ivo Vidan, "Time Sequence in Spatial Fiction," Daghistany and Smitten, eds., *Spatial Form in Narrative*, 134–5.

44. Mickelson, "Types of Spatial Structure," 71.

45. Iser, *The Implied Reader*, 294.

46. Iser, *The Implied Reader*, 280.

47. Adrian Bond, "The Way It Wasn't in Hemingway's *The Sun Also Rises*," *The Journal of Narrative Technique* 28.1 (Winter 1998), 69.

48. Mickelson, "Types of Spatial Structure," 72.

49. Goodson, "*Manhattan Transfer* and the Metropolitan Subject," 92. Tellingly, in his essay Goodson misattributes many of Ed Thatcher's experiences to Bud Korpenning (92–3). While regrettable, this hermeneutical error demonstrates the challenges that Dos Passos' spatial techniques pose to even the most presumably attentive readers. Paradoxically (though surely unintentionally), Goodson's errors also buttress his argument that Manhattan itself is *Transfer*'s only clearly delineated character.

50. North, *Camera Works*, 147.

51. On repetition's spatiality, Robert Lamb describes Gertrude Stein's influence on Hemingway in tellingly "spatial" terms: "Hemingway was working toward applying the principles of repetition that he had learned from Gertrude Stein and James Joyce. Stein's theory of repetition was designed to provide synchrony in, and remove linearity from, narrative, as the three justifications she advanced for repetition—beginning again, using everything, and the continuous present—make clear" (Lamb, "Hemingway and the Creation of Twentieth-Century Dialogue," 462). Indeed, in her lecture "Poetry and Grammar," Stein rejects commas by the following logic: "Why if you want the pleasure of concentrating on the final simplicity of excessive complication would you want any artificial aid to bring about that simplicity" (*Look at Me Now and Here I Am: Writings and Lectures 1909–45*, ed. Patricia Meyerowitz [New York: Penguin, 1971], 132). She writes of her sentences, too, that "they had become something that was a whole thing and in so being they had a balance which was the balance of a space completely not filled but created by something moving as moving is not as moving should be" (135).

52. Genette, *Time and Narrative*, 95. While Genette's theory of narrative speed regards solely the internal speed of the narrative—the relation between events' lengths and the text's length—instead of the reader's perceptual speed, his observations nonetheless offer a useful starting point for considering the factor of velocity in narrative terms. As Genette explains, "By 'speed' we mean the relationship between a temporal dimension and a spatial dimension (so many meters per second, so many seconds per meter): the speed of a narrative will be defined by the relationship between a duration (that of the story, measured in seconds, minutes, hours, days, months, and years) and a length (that of the text, measured in lines and in pages)" (88). Because "the quantity of information is solidly in inverse ratio

to the speed of the narrative" (166), he says, descriptive pauses slow narrative time while summary and ellipsis accelerate it (95).

53. Calvino, *Six Memos*, 46.

54. Mickelson, "Types of Spatial Structure," 72.

55. Dos Passos seems conscious of this stylistic spatialization, for in *Transfer* he alludes to other modernist spatial texts like Eliot's *The Waste Land* ("'please I'm in a hurry if you dont mind'" [*Transfer*, 84]) and Proust's *Remembrance of Things Past* ("'Mother.' She wasn't in the sittingroom. He was terrified. She'd gone out, she'd gone away. 'Mother!'" [*Transfer*, 85]).

56. Qtd. in Trodd, "Hemingway's Camera Eye," 12.

57. Mickelson, "Types of Spatial Structure," 72.

58. Oliver Sacks, "Speed," *The New Yorker* 80.23 (Aug. 23, 2004), 63.

59. Provocatively, Sacks also contends that such reactionary timescapes may "become so ingrained as to be almost second nature, no longer in need of conscious effort or decision. One level of brain activity may be working automatically, while another, the conscious level, is fashioning a perception of time, a perception which is elastic, and can be compressed or expanded" (Sacks, "Speed," 63). While I cannot support or critique Sacks' medical view of such reactions, his notion of a trained, "second nature" response to speed is salient in the context of my argument in that the modernist novel may not only allow the modern subject brief reprieve from speed culture but may actually train him or her with neurological defenses against it.

60. North argues that, in the *U.S.A.* trilogy, "Dos Passos' characters seem so singularly incapable of choice or agency in part because there is no time for it; swept along from one discontinuous moment to the next, they are in a state of constant, bewildered surprise" (North, *Camera Works*, 149), which suggests that this central theme is a leitmotif running throughout Dos Passos' work.

61. Kern helpfully sources the modernists' predilection for this style in technological innovations: "The technology of speed affected newspaper reporting and modified the language of journalistic communication. Because economy of expression produced monetary savings, reporters were inclined to write their stories with the fewest possible words. The telegraph also encouraged the use of unambiguous words to avoid any confusion, and the language of journalism came to be more uniform" (Kern, *The Culture of Time and Space*, 115).

62. Kern, *The Culture of Time and Space*, 115.

63. Eric S. Rabkin, "Spatial Form and Plot," *Spatial Form in Narrative*, ed. Daghistany and Smitten, 97.

64. Importantly, Rabkin observes that fragmentation is "the most obtrusive but not the only manifestation" of parataxis (Rabkin, "Spatial

Form and Plot," 99); in this sense, *Transfer*'s fragmentary plot and character portraits are also paratactic techniques that create hermeneutical challenges.

65. Trodd, "Hemingway's Camera Eye," 15.

66. Rabkin confirms this claim when he contends that Hemingway's use of "antecedent-less pronouns forces the reader to suspend—for lack of knowledge—any judgments about the description [. . .] He must suspend the activity of constructing a synchronic story until more information is supplied" (Rabkin, "Spatial Form and Plot," 96).

67. In 1821, the Italian poet Giacomo Leopardi, as translated by Calvino, makes a similar claim when he opines that "speed and conciseness of style please us because they present the mind with a rush of ideas that are simultaneous, or that follow each other so quickly they seem simultaneous, and set the mind afloat on such an abundance of thoughts or images or spiritual feelings that either it cannot embrace them all, each one fully, or it has no time to be idle and empty of feelings" (Calvino, *Six Memos*, 42).

68. Qtd. in Trodd, "Hemingway's Camera Eye," 14.

69. Peter Messent, *New Readings of the American Novel* (Singapore: Macmillan, 1990), 125.

70. Lamb, "Hemingway and the Creation of Twentieth-Century Dialogue," 462.

71. Curiously, despite his otherwise thoughtful analysis, Lamb never mentions Hemingway's frequent omission of dialogue attributions. In fact, Lamb observes an opposite trend: "unnecessary identification tags" (Lamb, "Hemingway and the Creation of Twentieth-Century Dialogue," 456). While I agree that Hemingway employs this technique as well, I find his unattributed dialogue more stylistically noteworthy, particularly as it informs spatial theory. Ironically, despite Lamb's omission of this technique, he "tags" (attributes) two long passages of Hemingway's dialogue to aid readers of his own essay (Lamb, "Hemingway and the Creation of Twentieth-Century Dialogue," 458, 471). At least implicitly, then, Lamb acknowledges the difficulty posed by Hemingway's lack of attributions

72. Trodd, "Hemingway's Camera Eye," 10.

73. Trodd, "Hemingway's Camera Eye," 13.

74. Hemingway's reporterly parataxis and Jake Barnes' and Jimmy Herf's transitions from journalism to more "artistic" literary production call into question the role of the media within modernist narrative. Virilio, in fact, views the mass media as a prime agent (and product) of the speed war: "Unleashed in the 1920s, the de-neutralization of the media paves the way for what has been called 'the war of the domestic market,' a massive ideological campaign addressed directly to the family puzzle that it claims to put together, even to reinvent, as an 'infinite receptacle for consumer goods.'

This campaign will very quickly become a veritable animal domestication of the American citizen" (Virilio, *Speed and Politics*, 110). Virilio attributes such "domestication," or de-individualization, to the media's invasion of individual privacy: "Everyone suddenly found himself exposed to the scrutiny of his neighbors, compared with the Identikit portrait of the ideal American consumer" (111). In *Modernity at Large: Cultural Dimensions of Globalization* (Minneapolis: University of Minnesota Press, 1996), Arjun Appadurai similarly contends that modern communication technologies and "the media create communities with 'no sense of place'" and engender a world characterized by "rootlessness, alienation, and psychological distance between individuals and groups" (29). By riddling people's private lives with public messages (as Dos Passos' integration of advertisements into his narrative mimetically reveals), speed culture's media acted like a flashing bulb on modern subjects (like Jake's "flashes"), sourcing self-illumination in an authoritarian external force.

75. Mickelson, "Types of Spatial Structure," 76.

76. Mickelson, "Types of Spatial Structure," 76.

77. Virilio, *Speed and Politics*, 78.

78. Michael Seidel, *Exile and Narrative Imagination* (New Haven: Yale University Press, 1986).

79. Martin Heidegger, *Basic Writings* (New York: Harper Collins, 1993), 351.

80. Heidegger, *Basic Writings*, 349.

81. Heidegger, *Basic Writings*, 356.

82. Heidegger, *Basic Writings*, 360, 363.

83. Heidegger, *Basic Writings*, 330–1.

84. Heidegger, *Basic Writings*, 313, 334.

85. Heidegger, *Basic Writings*, 339.

86. Harvey, *The Condition of Postmodernity*, 35.

87. Harvey, *The Condition of Postmodernity*, 30–1.

88. Harvey, *The Condition of Postmodernity*, 31.

89. Again, the provision for such action seems particular to early 20th-century literature for, as Ivo Vidan states, in modern fiction "there is something that distinguishes from the traditional model not only novels which grow on the principle of an organized system of imagery, but also those which have a distorted chronology. There is wider room for subjective interpretation, for deliberate *construction*" (Vidan, "Time Sequence," 134, emphasis added). In "The Difficulties of Modernism and the Modernism of Difficulty" (*Critical Essays on Modernism*, ed. Michael J. Hoffman and Patrick D. Murphy [New York: Macmillan, 1992]: 104–14), Richard Poirer concurs with this idea, defining modernism as "an attempt to perpetuate the

power of literature as a privileged form of discourse. By its difficulty it tries, paradoxically, to reinvoke the connections, severed more or less by the growth of mass culture, between the artist and the audience" (105). While I do not mean to suggest that Dos Passos and Hemingway wrote their novels with such political commentary in mind, I do suggest that their novels nonetheless served a political purpose—by slowing the reading process through ironic imitation of speed culture's acceleration, *Transfer* and *Rises* comment upon that culture's destructive effects.

90. To be more precise, Seidel's notion in some ways duplicates Heidegger's, for in *Heidegger and the Issue of Space* (University Park: Pennsylvania State University Press, 2003), Alejandro Vallega characterizes Heidegger's thought in terms very similar to Seidel's. Heidegger, says Vallega, exhibits "exilic thought," or an epistemology that recognizes neither stasis nor motion as exclusive elements of being but represents "an experience of thought that remains in the evanescent lightness and density of its finite transformative passage, a passage that belongs to thought's alterity in the up-rooting transfigurative enactment of its essential temporality or historicity" (8). Vallega also notes that Heidegger believed that "life, bodies, communities, things, words, numbers, thoughts, feelings and states of mind, our imagination—all these occur not just temporally but also spatially" (10); the imagination, in other words, was as viable a space to Heidegger as geometric or extra-personal space. See Blanchot, *The Space of Literature*, 10, 52, for further discussion of exilic space.

91. Seidel, *Exile and Narrative Imagination*, 1.

92. Seidel, *Exile and Narrative Imagination*, 3.

93. Seidel, *Exile and Narrative Imagination*, 6. In his analysis of spatial novels, Eric Rabkin concurs with Seidel on this notion of recursion, as he claims that "spatial form may be thought of as a tendency, but in ordinary languages it is never fully achieved" (Rabkin, "Spatial Form and Plot," 81). Rabkin argues that the spatial novel can never be entirely synchronic, even though spatial techniques allow us to "more or less approach synchronicity." After all, the story underlying every plot is by its nature diachronic—it is a series of chronological events that the reader eventually arranges into diachronic fashion, no matter how a plot defamiliarizes it (81). Even the act of reading—one's eyes moving across the page—is diachronic. Thus, "we never achieve" total synchronicity (81), just as the exile never fully arrives home.

94. Seidel, *Exile and Narrative Imagination*, 16.

95. Seidel, *Exile and Narrative Imagination*, 5.

96. Appadurai, citing Fredric Jameson's notion of modern "nostalgia for the present" (qtd. in Appadurai, *Modernity at Large*, 29–30), concurs with

Seidel's privileging of the imagination. For in a world where the present speeds by too quickly to experience it, "the imagination is now central to all forms of agency, is itself a social fact" (31). For the modern subject, then, agency, or individual autonomy, is *located* in the imagination.

97. Virilio, *Speed and Politics*, 125.
98. Virilio, *Speed and Politics*, 148.
99. Virilio, *Speed and Politics*, 21–2.
100. Heidegger, *Basic Writings*, 330.

Making Modernism New:
Queer Mythology in *The Young and Evil*

Instead of narrative method, we may now use the mythical method.
It is, I seriously believe, a step toward making the modern
world possible for art.

—T. S. ELIOT, *"Ulysses*, Order, and Myth"[1]

Literature is and was and is and was.

—PARKER TYLER TO EZRA POUND, letter dated September 18, 1933

Queer Mythology?

Although it has largely eluded critical attention, Charles Henri Ford and
Parker Tyler's 1933 novel *The Young and Evil* has come to be known among
some scholars as one of the first proto-queer texts in American letters. Joseph Allen Boone, most notably, argues in his *Libidinal Currents* (1998)
that the novel "deliberately carves out an alternative niche for itself within
the modernist tradition" by using "modernist style [to] encod[e] explicit gay
content."[2] Boone's reading helpfully highlights that *The Young and Evil* depicts a group of young men and women in the late 1920s Greenwich Village community who engage in an array of non-normative sexual
experiences and that the text relates these experiences through a proto-
typically high modernist aesthetic of formal experimentation. Featuring
poetic lineation, spatializing parataxis, stream-of-consciousness narration,
and surrealist imagery and thematics, *The Young and Evil* reads at various
moments like Gertrude Stein's *Three Lives* (1909), Djuna Barnes's *Nightwood* (1936), and Ezra Pound's *The Cantos* (1970). Such likenesses are unsurprising since Ford and Tyler were friends with Stein, Barnes, and Pound,

and since they edited and managed the little magazine *Blues*, which Ford and Tyler described as "a magazine of modernism" that "afforded modernism to everyone."[3] More surprising is that, given the authors' professional and personal intersections with so many canonical modernists, Ford and Tyler's literary achievements have been widely overlooked.

One reason for *The Young and Evil*'s obscurity may, ironically, be due to the very attributions that Boone uses to champion the novel: Despite its experimental style, *The Young and Evil* has seemed all too "niche," too focused on an "outcast queer fringe" to be considered as a representative modernist text.[4] Such a reading is counterintuitive, however, because the novel's queerness undergirds its most consummately modernist ambitions: to renovate myth for modern purposes and to create folklore for a burgeoning ethnic community.[5] Grounding hallmark modernist texts like T. S. Eliot's *The Waste Land* (1922) and James Joyce's *Ulysses* (1922)—the novel that incited Eliot to promote a "mythical method" for modernist literature in his 1923 essay "*Ulysses*, Order, and Myth"—myth traditionally aims to convey cultural universals and ideals. Folklore, in contrast, records the beliefs, customs, and idioms of particular, or ethnic, groups, as epitomized in novels like Younghill Kang's *The Grass Roof* (1931) and Zora Neale Hurston's *Their Eyes Were Watching God* (1937). Together, myth and folklore comprise the aesthetic goals and content of much canonical modernist literature and offer two formal instances of literary modernists' more widespread anxiety to reconcile cultural unity and pluralism. When Eliot propounds his "mythical method," for example, he requests that modernist writers "manipulat[e] a continuous parallel between contemporaneity and antiquity," or particularity and universality, which is, he maintains, "a goal toward which all good literature strives."[6]

By the standard of Eliot's mythical method, *The Young and Evil* would seem to qualify as a paradigmatic modernist text, perhaps even as "good literature." Consider the novel's opening paragraph: "Well said the wolf to Little Red Riding Hood no sooner was Karel seated in the Round Table than the impossible happened. There before him stood a fairy prince and one of those mythological creatures known as Lesbians. Won't you join our table? they said in sweet chorus."[7] In less than fifty words, the paragraph invokes at least five mythological references: the fairy tale "Little Red Riding Hood," Arthurian legend via "the Round Table," "a fairy prince," "mythological creatures" ethnographically identified as "Lesbians," and a kind of Greek "chorus." Such allusions associate the novel with a seemingly unrelated group of transcultural mythologies, a mixture that queers the text's relation to "impossible" myth, or Eliot's "antiquity," from the outset. Set in a Greenwich Village bar, the paragraph simultaneously evokes the novel's folkloric properties, what Eliot would call its signs of "contemporaneity." As George Chauncey's 1993 study *Gay New York* documents, most of these mythological allusions function as gay code in the early twentieth century: Riding Hood likely refers to a drag queen; "wolf" denotes a conventionally masculine man who had sex with younger and more effeminate men; the prince's "fairy" status refers to effeminate gay men (thus queering the fairy tale itself as an ethnic genre) who "established the dominant public images of male sexual abnormality" in early twentieth-century New York; and the lesbians, evidently, specify homosexual women, including perhaps the famous Greenwich Village club owner Eve Addams, evoked in the novel's first—and self-consciously mythic—working title, *Eve's Adam.*[8] Set at a table at the popular Greenwich Village restaurant the Round Table, the paragraph establishes the text's ambition to depict a historically queer community much like the actual community of Greenwich Village at the same time that it dehistoricizes this community as mythic: These modern queers are the age-old "mythological creatures" that already inhabit the western mythopoeic tradition. Co-opting that tradition from a sexually ethnic perspective, *The Young and Evil* positions itself within and without western folklore's dominant mythologies.[9]

Rather than "encoding explicit gay content," then, as Boone maintains, *The Young and Evil*'s modernist techniques would appear to reveal that content. The novel accordingly disrupts critical narratives that relegate queerness to a "niche" realm of scholarly and literary interest and those that, like Eliot's and many modernists', appear to align the mythic with the heteronormative.[10] *The Young and Evil* implicitly poses the question: Can myth be queer? If so, what would be the literary and social consequences of a mythology that posits queerness not as tangentially "alternative" but as central to literary modernist experience? As Karel, one of the novel's focal characters, asks of the nature of desire, "Where is the line between the strange and the common?" (Ford and Tyler, 175), or the line between "strange" ethnic experience and "common" universal experience? To explore this question, we may similarly ask: Where, in a disciplinary sense, is the line between our "common" literary history of modernism and Ford and Tyler's "strange" novel?

In *Foundlings* (2001), Christopher Nealon opens inquiry into these questions when he observes that an ethnic version of queer experience, "more attuned to collective experience than to individual identity, begins to be visible around World War I and picks up momentum after World War II."[11] While Nealon analyzes what he calls queer "foundling" texts of this period that evince a "movement between solitary exile and collective experience," I take this movement another step to reveal how Ford and Tyler's text shuttles between two collective, and to them similar, experiences— those of the queer community and of literary modernist culture at large— to blur the line between the strange and the common, the queer and the mainstream, in American modernism.[12] Where the ethnic specificity of its folklore depicts a queer modernist subculture, *The Young and Evil*'s mythic allusions and structure universalize that subculture's experience into an exemplary myth for and about literary modernism.[13]

Integral to the question of whether myth can be queer is the question of whether community can be queer. As Michael Warner has suggested, the concept of a queer community is paradoxical, for queerness is by most definitions anti-communitarian.[14] As with the relation between myth and queerness, *The Young and Evil* takes this paradox as one of its central subjects: The idea of a queer community is, for this novel, itself a queer myth that foregrounds the tensions between the particular and universal that any myth must engage. When Karel, for example, says that "the ultimate value of any particular experience or any of its parts would have to be related to a whole" in works of art (Ford and Tyler, 126), he and another character, Louis, describe the relation between "particular" and "whole" as dialectical rather than teleological: In response to Louis' mythic, and queer, claim to be "waiting for the day . . . when I can destroy all definitions," Karel, representing a folkloric position, declares, "but until then . . . they are the most that matters" (Ford and Tyler, 112). Adhering at times to "definitions," Ford and Tyler historicize the local communities and ethnic traditions that formed around the criterion of sexual difference throughout the twentieth century, even as they acknowledge such a criterion as paradoxical. The authors' queer mythology and historiography expose, in other words, that trying to create a community based on difference—trying to relate any "particular" difference to an undifferentiated "whole"—is at best a fantastical endeavor. Such a project seems sympathetic, in the end, to Warner's claim that "heteronormativity can be overcome only by actively *imagining* a necessarily and desirably queer world."[15] The myth of a queer community is, for this novel, the precondition for imagining in art the very concept that it depicts as a fraught construction in historical reality.

Based on this attempt to imagine a community outside the limits of practicable reality, *The Young and Evil* primarily employs two antirealist literary forms: spatial narrative structure and surrealist imagery and thematics. These aesthetics are most modernist in their opposition to late-nineteenth-century literary realist and naturalist traditions. Where Ford and Tyler thought those aesthetics to universalize lived experience through positivist forms and heteronormative themes, *The Young and Evil*, lodged in the "until then" time between realist definitions and their queer destruction, records the "particular experience" of a queer subculture even as it aims to destroy the definitional coherence of that subculture in order to universalize its folklore as myth.[16]

It is perhaps this self-generating mythic and folkloric quality that led Gertrude Stein to remark on the novel's dust jacket that *"The Young and Evil* creates this generation as *This Side of Paradise* by Fitzgerald created his generation. It is a good thing, whatever this generation is, to be the first to create it in a book." As with her notorious characterization of Hemingway's "lost generation" after *The Sun Also Rises*, what Stein means by "this generation" is unclear—even to herself, which is curious because she made several revisions to *The Young and Evil* during its composition.[17] Stein could simply mean to denote the thirteen-year gap between the novels' publication dates, but more likely she means to highlight the Fitzgerald novel's creation of a disillusioned and normatively heterosexual generation and the Ford and Tyler text's creation of a vibrant, polymorphously queer generation.

Ezra Pound similarly thought Ford and Tyler capable of creating a new generation when he wrote to Ford in 1929 that "every generation or group must write its own literary program."[18] In spite of this encouragement, Pound would also tell Tyler five months prior to the novel's publication that "nothing new what bloody ever has been said or thought on the subject" of what he calls "bhoogery" since "the death of Martial. And it simply can NOT be discovered 2000 years later."[19] Responding to the exigency of this heteronormative claim, Ford and Tyler use Pound's 1929 advice to subvert his 1933 reprimand. In accord with Tyler's avowal that "literature is and was and is and was," these authors believed that they could make literary and sexual modernism new by saying something old: by infusing literature that was into literature that is, and vice versa. As Tyler responded to Pound's unencouraging letter, "Antiquity doesn't hold any patents on homosexuality: there is plenty in the modern fauna and flora—so much— that doesnt fit into the greekvase pattern—not to speak of some freshening of myth."[20]

"Freshening" the very tradition of "myth" with which Pound derided their effort (and which, in *The Cantos*, he used to make his own modernist myth), Ford and Tyler thus co-opt Pound's "MAKE IT NEW" credo to create a book not "at the margins of official modernist practice," as Boone maintains, but aligned with many modernists' primary concern: how to "mak[e]

the modern world possible for art."[21] The authors do so by creating an ethnically queer "generation" whose exemplarity signifies mythically: For
"whatever this generation is" that Ford and Tyler depict, Stein avers, it is
most important that they "create it in a book." Using the literary imagination to reform old myths, to document ethnographically new folklore, and
to create the mythic possibility of a queer community, Ford and Tyler make
good on Stein's ambiguous designation of their novel's generation, which
could be the human generation or the queer American generation of the
1930s, one that itself defies categorization. Given the text's generically dual
ambitions, we would most appropriately say that it does both at once. Understanding this duality may, I propose, enable contemporary literary historians to make modernism new, since Ford and Tyler's effort to renovate
that movement has for so long escaped critical regard.

Making It Mythopoeic

To understand Ford and Tyler's use of the word in application to their
novel, the slippery and now critically unfashionable term *myth* requires further delineation at this point. As Michael Bell observes in his *Literature,
Modernism and Myth* (1997), because myth "means both a supremely significant foundational story and a falsehood," the term always indicates that
"there is a multiplicity of possible human worlds" at the same time that it
seems to affirm one world view.[22] Rather than try to resolve this definitional paradox, I aim, as Bell does, to examine mythopoeia, or mythmaking, in *The Young and Evil* as the "underlying outlook that creates myth;
or, more precisely again, sees the world in mythic terms."[23] By describing
the text as mythopoeic, a word that Tyler used to describe his 1945 long
poem *The Granite Butterfly*, I attempt not to verify the truth-value of universalizing mythic claims but to examine how and why, from a literary-
historical perspective, Ford and Tyler found literary and cultural value in
a mythopoeic stance that could elicit a "supremely significant foundational
story" for modernism even as it recognizes that such universality is defi-
nitionally also a "falsehood."[24]

A section from the eighth canto of *The Granite Butterfly* clarifies how
Ford and Tyler aimed, throughout their careers, to tell the "lie" of "myth"
in order to record a non-naturalist "truth":

> So myth has always been
> A lie, the moment it was uttered just as, the moment it was
> Uttered, it was also a truth: it was a lie to test

The truth, and a truth to test the lie, being ambivalent toward
Itself
   as Narcissus is
Ambivalent toward himself, as all con-
Cepts, once they are conceived of as Natural
Contradict themselves
   Nature
Being subject to change—[25]

Anticipating Bell's definition, Tyler admits here that "myth has always been/A lie" even as "it was also a truth." Against beliefs in a universally heteronormative "Nature," the poet harnesses myth's generically ambivalent status to posit the rather Darwinian claim that "Nature" is always "subject to change," to queering, which Tyler emphasizes by alluding to Narcissus, one of the queerest characters in classical mythology.[26]

Despite its hallmark irony and pessimism, modernism is rife with mythopoeic texts that tell the lie of cultural universalism. While such lies often took the form of heteronormativity, queer modernist texts like *Nightwood* and Marcel Proust's *A la recherche du temps perdue* (1927) also, as Joseph Frank argued in 1945, "transmut[ed] the time world of history into the timeless world of myth. And it is this timeless world of myth, forming the content of so much of modern literature, that finds its appropriate aesthetic expression in spatial form."[27] Taking Frank's lead, E. W. Herd posits that mythopoeic literature characteristically features "totality, in the sense of a representation of a universally valid reality in a series of images; timelessness [and] the transformation of an apparently real or realistically described situation into a struggle against invisible forces . . . which are inaccessible to man and incapable of rational interpretation."[28] G. R. Manton would add to this definition "the desire to link the present with the past," a project that involves the phenomenal ambitions of historiography but that transforms such detail into the timeless noumena of myth.[29]

Manton's definition echoes Friedrich Nietzsche's seminal view of history, established in "On the Uses and Disadvantages of History for Life" (1874), wherein Nietzsche argues that "a living thing can be healthy, strong and fruitful only when bounded by a horizon," by which he means that one must assume a dialectical approach to one's sense of history. Recalling Eliot's definition of the mythical method, Nietzsche declares that "*the unhistorical and the historical are necessary in equal measure for the health of an individual, of a people and of a culture.*"[30] If we may exchange the term *unhistorical* for *mythopoeic* and the term *historical* for *folkloric*, and if, as Bell does, we recognize Nietzsche's thought as central to modern mythopoeia, we may begin to see how the dually mythopoeic and folkloric aims of Ford and Tyler's novel are part of a widespread—if variously manifested— metaphysical and aesthetic preoccupation with the relationships among "*the health of an individual, of a people and of a culture*" in the early twentieth century.[31]

The Young and Evil engages this historical dialectic with formal experiments that rupture what Eliot calls "narrative method," or the techniques of literary realism, and create, after the mythical method, abstract-universal depths beneath particularized surfaces. Such experiments repudiate realism's attempts to represent a universalized reality through empirical evidence alone and suggest that universalization can only be mythic: in other words, "a supremely significant falsehood."[32] The most apparent of such features is what Frank would call the novel's spatial form, created by the text's montage-like structure, recursive plot, unidentified narrative voices, and lack of a central narrative thread or central characters. At the structural level, for instance, chapter divisions disrupt temporal continuity, as between chapters 13 and 14, the former ending with Julian and Karel (the text's protagonists if it has any) discussing metaphysics in Karel's room, the latter opening with Julian, Karel, and Frederick cruising Broadway. Karel's lament for Louis and his desire for death in chapter 13 are thus spatialized and rendered ephemeral by the paratactic cut to chapter 14's campy banter. The time elided between chapters—indeed, the time during which narrative action occurs at all—thus recedes from focus as the narrative emphasizes how characters fill the various spaces, including metaphysical spaces, in which they find themselves.

The Young and Evil's characters fill those spaces with internal reflections more than they do with external actions. The novel largely omits external character detail, in fact, and what detail it offers serves less to delineate specific identities than to interrogate human experience in a symbolic fashion. Karel, for example, is so concerned with his appearance that he sets an "endurance record in front of the mirror" (Ford and Tyler, 32), but the narrator reports little of how he appears other than that "Karel was like a tall curved building only much smaller. He was wearing a dark green, the color of the rings around the holes, hat with an upward sweep on the left side. His overcoat seemed to fit him desperately." Narrated with free indirect discourse from Julian's third-person-limited perspective, this passage reveals more about Julian's interior consciousness and his habit of looking "in the mirror from various angles" than it does about Karel's external appearance (Ford and Tyler, 26). As seen through a funhouse mirror, Karel appears entirely out of proportion in the opening simile: both tall and curved, small and large as a building.[33] The ungrammatical appositive in the passage's second sentence similarly disrupts Julian's mimetic report about Karel's external appearance—his dark green hat—to mimic the digressive nature of Julian's consciousness: When he thinks of "dark green," Julian recalls how he initially envisioned Karel as having a "slightly orange face containing eyes with holes in them" (Ford and Tyler, 15). Instead of providing a realistic picture of Karel—an orange-faced, diminutive, curved building with green-ringed eyeholes is more aptly a surrealist vision—this passage provides a realistic picture of Julian's "desperately" subjective reception of Karel and anticipates the stream-of-consciousness technique that the novel most centrally employs as an alternative to external description.

The Young and Evil does not disregard surface aesthetics, then, but represents surfaces as indices of interior thoughts and feelings rather than exterior identities. When Karel claims that "sentimentality" is "a willingness to believe in form without substance" (Ford and Tyler, 32), he vocalizes how the novel formally rejects a realist narrative tradition associated with sentimental literature and embraces form as substantial.[34] Karel encapsulates this position when he later insists that his "tears [are] real": He is not "the sort of person to weep for nothing—for effect," nor is the novel (Ford and Tyler, 213).[35] Tyler explained this depth model of surface aesthetics to Pound, claiming that "the boys in our book while supericially sktched in as CHAracters show a special type of contemporary psychic action in relation to their several embraces of the homosexual image."[36] The novel's characters are rendered in minimal detail, Tyler claims, so that they can manifest internally "psychic," not externally plot-based, "action," related specifically to "the homosexual image," a symbol of queerness.

Adhering to a contemporary predilection for recognizing modernist formal and sexual experimentation as performative and non-referential, Boone nevertheless argues that *The Young and Evil* "avoids representing states of interiority" and "offer[s] characterizations singularly devoid of psychological depth."[37] Like its author Tyler, however, the novel invites us to read its characterological voids as representing "psychological depth" when, for instance, Karel claims that even "bracelets can become symbols," or figures with both literal and figurative referents (Ford and Tyler, 38). Like Tyler, Karel seems to instruct the reader to interpret the novel's exteriors symbolically: not as just "for nothing—for effect" but for mythic "depth." This symbolic aesthetic is central to the novel's mythopoeic status, for mythological literature generically relies upon the challenge that symbol presents to the ostensible realism of surface-based aesthetics: "as with the symbol in general," Tzvetan Todorov claims, "mythology is *at once* general and particular, it is *and* it signifies."[38]

The character Theodosia's representation and role in *The Young and Evil* most consistently exemplify the substance lurking beneath the text's queer surfaces. Despite Karel's and Julian's repeated attempts to write poetry, Theo's passages are the text's most lyrical and most expressive: With her "disquieting beauty, sarcasm, violated eyes," Theo invites Julian to wonder, for example, "where bottomless places are and their reality," places where "even reality [seems] a little forced" (Ford and Tyler, 35). Plumbing such depths, Theo constitutes the narrative's affective center, yet the novel provides even less detail about her as a character of action and appearance than it does about Karel, Julian, Gabriel, and Louis. Theo's function in the novel is most universalizing, then, for the text's abrupt shifts to her point of view at the ends of chapters 3, 6, and 9—the passages in which Julian mourns his loss of Karel (3) and Theo mourns her loss of Julian (6 and 9) and a sailor named Jack (6)—provide the metaphysical underside to the physical, exterior loss that so many characters experience throughout the narrative.

In chapter 6, for example, Julian—whom Karel has just left for Louis because Julian "made things lopsided" (Ford and Tyler, 71)—attempts to find the depth of his loss in the surfaces around him: "He looked around the room to see what was missing. He could find a wrong space nowhere and was sad. Then he thought he saw what he had lost," a "temporary illusion" that is finally only a kind of concealer for pain "that could be concealed by something else" (Ford and Tyler, 72). Recalling Karel's claim about form and substance, surface becomes depth for Julian through the associative symbol of concealer: The next several pages consist of his musings about "*murderpiss beautiful boys* [who] *grow out of dung*" (Ford and Tyler, 74), boys whose exterior beauty belies their deeper decrepitude but to whose veneers Julian is nonetheless happy to be attracted so as to feel their "closetomeredder smell" (Ford and Tyler, 76). Julian's acknowledgement that surface can yield affective depth (he later "knew that people had to forget appearances") triggers an abrupt transition to a short passage about Theo and Jack, characters rendered as no more than metonymies (Jack is described only in blazon) for the kind of ephemeral love that Julian has just embraced (Ford and Tyler, 167). While Theo's loss is hetero-erotic (and one whose end echoes the "Nausicaa" chapter of *Ulysses*), Julian's is homoerotic; the novel's paratactic juxtaposition of the two privileges neither, however, indicating how human desire, loss, and the dialectic between surface and depth that creates symbols are the chapter's—and the novel's—central subjects. As Julian says, "beckoning is the same as becoming" in this queer worldscape (Ford and Tyler, 97).

Like its desirous characters, the novel's plot works toward no teleological or ontological end; instead, it is built upon a series of betrayals, losses, and vagrancies. "Pack what you have and leave with me" is a sentiment repeated so often (in both speech and action) that it becomes a narrative leitmotif, framing the text thematically and structurally (Ford and Tyler, 110). Whereas naturalist novels like *Sister Carrie* (1900) typically used such emotional and spatial peripatetics for tragic purposes, however, *The Young and Evil* portrays betrayal, loss, and vagrancy as means toward ontological becoming. They suggest periodically arrested progress, recursive rather than linear motion, which Karel lauds when he learns that Julian has left Theo and is "not living with anyone now." "Things do become don't they Karel said" (Ford and Tyler, 109), suggesting that one "becomes" by refusing ends: "if we do not move, we will not get anywhere" (Ford and Tyler, 22). because such movement is so often recursive, it assumes what the novel's characters think to be a metaphysical depth: "'Again' thought Julian is more tragic than remorse" (Ford and Tyler, 137). As it does with symbols, meaning in *The Young and Evil* accumulates through "again": through association and repetition, both of which occur with circular, not linear, motion. The novel's second working title after *Eve's Adam*—*Love and Jump Back* (chapter 11's title in the final text)—encapsulates this recursive, synchronic structure and texture.

The novel's plot does, of course, contain various conflicts and narrative threads, but those threads are multifarious, not singular or linear, as demonstrated by the final chapter, which concludes with an unexpected Dracula's kiss when Louis bites Karel for refusing to leave Julian. Other than Louis' examination of Julian's teeth in the previous chapter (Ford and Tyler, 203), nothing in the diegesis anticipates this gothic ending—nothing other, that is, than the bite's mythic resonance, which it shares possibly with "Little Red Riding Hood" and more certainly with Bram Stoker's *Dracula* (1897), a text that Leslie Fiedler believes created perhaps the most popular myth of the twentieth century.[39] This inconclusive conclusion, which opens rather than closes the book, echoes Fiedler's claim that "primal myth . . . has no proper Aristotelian beginning or end—only an indefinitely extended middle."[40] The novel's "middle" is extended through its "end" as the text closes mid-action: The narrative concludes with Karel's scream, omitting information about whether or how that scream stops. If anything, this "end" reinforces the narrative's foreclosure of realist sentimentality—Louis dams Karel's tears with a bite—and its embrace of what we will later see is a surrealist fusion of desire and death.[41]

In microcosmic fashion, chapter 8 perhaps best exemplifies *The Young and Evil*'s mythopoeic structure and texture and encapsulates how, at the levels of form and theme, the novel depicts the queer community itself as a mythic construction, a collective imaginable only as fragments. Titled "Letter," the chapter is a Dear John missive from Karel to Julian and constitutes only a single page in the novel. Paratactically inserted between chapter 7 (which ends with Gabriel in Theo's room) and chapter 9 (Julian walking to Theo's), the letter disrupts any diachronic progression and emphasizes the atemporal affect, not the action, of Karel's abandoning Julian. On the textural level, this emotion is created through Karel's use of present participles and antecedentless pronouns, a technique that bears the imprint of Stein, Ford's sometime mentor. The letter opens ambiguously: "It is not that. That wasn't the making of it. It's the unmaking. It is the unmaking of us. It is not that I am talking about: I am talking about us" (Ford and Tyler, 85). In the first two sentences, "it" has no antecedent—and while in the next two sentences "it" refers to "the unmaking," in the following sentence Karel says that that "it" is not the "it" he is talking about. The accumulated effect of these ambiguous pronouns—and the participles among which they are situated—is to queer the concrete identity of Karel's subject and to spatialize Karel's emotion about the facts he cannot nominalize.

Recalling Nietzsche, Karel's emotion is finally one of ecstasy at the promise of creative destruction. He realizes (like Joyce's Molly Bloom) that "we were only being yes apart, not together, and that is the making of it": For Karel, fracture—saying "yes" to "apart"—is the origin of "making," whether the making of writing—the letter itself—or of sexual union. Karel synthesizes these topics when he writes that his departure "is good too for I am loving him, I am finding out again with someone entirely different oh so much so that there is nothing now but the writing of it" (Ford and Tyler, 84). Karel's leaving produces a new union with Louis, yet Karel says that their bond, like his breakup with Julian, must be represented in "writing": It can only be imagined in the writing of the letter, which is itself part of the writing of *The Young and Evil*. "Letter" as a whole thus indicates that queer union is a myth—foundational in the imagination but a falsehood in reality—and that this myth structures the unstructured queer community. When even Julian later recognizes that he "was separated from the others and he was in it" (Ford and Tyler, 105), he realizes how, in the world of *The Young and Evil*, separation is the precondition for inclusion.

In point of fact, when Karel leaves Julian to pursue Louis, he finds Louis "turning queer so beautifully gradually and beautifully like a chameleon like a chameleon beautifully and gradually turning," where the passage's chiastic syntax implies that "turning queer" also involves "queer turning," the very kind of betrayal that Louis later commits against Karel (Ford and Tyler, 124). Presentist like chapter 8 with its Steinian participles and chiastic spatiality, Karel's description alludes to chapter 3's aria of "Theodosia finding queer, saying I love you," where loving another is synonymous with recognizing that other's queerness (Ford and Tyler, 35). Gesturing self-referentially to chapters 3 and 8, Karel's "turning" passage universalizes the feeling of labile and multi-directional desire as an atemporal affect and disperses it across the novel's diegesis. Encapsulating the novel's thematic and structural sensibilities, Karel's aestheticization of promiscuous desire (Louis' turning is "beautiful") moreover reinforces his belief in "Letter" that queer union requires aestheticization. Recalling Stein's reminder that "whatever this generation is" that Ford and Tyler represent, "it is a good thing . . . to be the first to create it in a book," Karel's letter endorsing polyamory and promiscuity reveals how queer collectivity can only be mythologized, aestheticized: represented "in a book" of queer mythology.

Taken together, these anti-realist formal techniques indicate how *The Young and Evil* attempts to create a mythic vision of human desire and experience—a vision that they are inevitably queer, or unstable—and why, from a historical standpoint, such a universal vision, even if granted as a "falsehood," was "supremely significant" to queer authors writing in the wake of literary realism and naturalism.[42] Where naturalist literature is concerned with "the apparently unassailable supremacy of the natural sciences," after all, and where those sciences in the late nineteenth century typically pathologized queer sexuality in medical cases that often became legal (if not forensic) cases, literary modes that enabled one to bypass the tyranny of the quantifiable in favor of the qualitative seemed logically amenable to writers whose queerness was all too quantified and not qualified enough.[43] Tyler in fact claimed that *The Young and Evil* would not "contribut[e] anything to textbook knowledge of homosexuality" because "homo information is not homorendition; there is plenty of homo information unaided by poetic insight but psychologically psychology never had any interest for me nor would mere transcribed orgy." "The main point" of the novel, he maintained, "is NOT whether there are any new 'scientific' conclusions but whether there are any new phenomena."[44]

The Young and Evil exhibits Tyler's anti-positivist program when Karel asks Gabriel how it would feel "to consider meaning instead of being meant": to consider representing oneself rather than being the object of representation. Instead of a naturalist predilection for quantifiable experience—"being meant"—Karel endorses a mythopoeic appreciation of qualitative experience: For "meaning" as an ongoing process, a present participle and a gerund; for "new phenomena," in Tyler's words, rather than "scientific conclusions" (Ford and Tyler, 45). Julian pointedly satirizes the aesthetic of "being meant" when he decries Bernard Shaw and Thomas Hardy: He campily reflects that, had he "been born as ugly . . . or as old" as them, he "should have *had* to be a genius," suggesting that his own life falls outside of deterministic ontological and literary genealogies (Ford and Tyler, 108). Julian later extends this satire to sexology by calling Karel a "degenerate!" (Ford and Tyler, 115) for wanting a kiss and then by cheering his queer compatriots with a faux-eugenic toast: "To universal castration said Julian" (Ford and Tyler, 116).

These explicit affiliations of the nineteenth century with pathologizing dispositions toward queerness indicate how and why Ford and Tyler represent queer experience with modernist formal experimentation: They create a spatial novel whose nonlinear structure and texture mirror its nonlinear subjects, especially the nonlinear directions of queer desire. Ford and Tyler thus adhere to Eliot's mythical method insofar as myth must "ignore simple verisimilitude," Margaret Dalziel contends, in order "to shed light on man's deepest questionings about himself and his place in the universe."[45] Here Dalziel assumes that human beings' questionings are so "deep" that they escape explicit surface representation and realist conclusions; they require, instead, illumination (but not pat answering) through implication and suggestion—through, as Karel says, "forestalling realization" (Ford and Tyler, 25) but not mythologization, for "stars are the reasons for men-bewildered words" (Ford and Tyler, 17). In *The Young and Evil*, cosmic illumination and mortal confusion are the source and the end of literary endeavors, "words."

Queering Modernist Mythopoeia

While Ford and Tyler challenge nineteenth-century literary aesthetics and their socio-political implications with mythopoeia, they also question the essentialist assumption that the most popular modernist myths' "deepest questionings" are common to humanity. Freud's psychoanalytic rendition

of the Oedipus myth—a rendition that became perhaps the most influential myth of the twentieth century, especially its early half—epitomizes the
need for such scrutiny. Despite his relatively benign attitude toward homosexuality, Freud interprets the myth in a heteronormative, clinical framework and creates a foil for homosexual identity formation. In his search
for the etiology of sexuality, Freud isolates the Oedipus myth's exclusion
of same-sex desire as an explanation for why such desire is abnormal and
therefore potentially remediable.[46]

Freud's powerful interpretation of Sophocles' *Oedipus Rex* demonstrates
how idealist visions of mythic totality were, in the early twentieth century,
especially regarding sexuality, contentious at best. Such ideals were sourced,
after all, in scientifically based fears of degeneracy and atavism, fears of
and obsessions with origins made most famous by Max Nordau's 1895 positivist polemic *Degeneration*. Julian epitomizes Ford and Tyler's opposition
to this precedent in his response to a character named Rector, an academic
who asks Julian why Julian should exist: "I'm not asking you Julian said to
account for your birth or anyone else's" (Ford and Tyler, 90). Instead of the
etiology of subjectivity or of desire, Ford and Tyler are, like the surrealists,
interested in how desire shapes reality to produce the mythic in the surreal.
In fact, Ford and Tyler make their most overt critique of Freud in reference
to E. E. Cummings's surrealist play *Him* (1927), which Julian calls "comic"
and "the most important event in American literary history": "America
doesn't know how to be comic [Julian] called; it knows only how to be
Freudian" (Ford and Tyler, 111). Working against the Freudianization of
America, Ford and Tyler engage myth to universalize queer experience and
to propose that modernist myth can and must account for kinds of experience too readily overshadowed by heteronormative modernist mythopoeia.

For Ford and Tyler, Freud's inadequate mythopoeic account of queerness may derive from his clinical desire to see the conscious mind regulate
the unconscious, whereas in myth, as Herd translates Hermann Broch's
famous claim, "Conscious effort never affords access to that sacred realm."[47]
In *The Young and Evil*, conscious and unconscious efforts to create myth
must be fused, and such fusion is predicated on the latter's ability to refashion the former (Freud, of course, prescribes the opposite). One of the
more salient examples of this need to reform established myths is in the
text's myth of dollness, evoked early on in chapters 1 and 2—which reference, after Henrik Ibsen, a "Doll's House"—and later troped in chapter 13,
"I Don't Want to be a Doll."[48] In each instance, characters create and
ironize the myth of the queer as an effeminized doll to reinforce a universal human desire for myth and to emphasize the particular queer need for

myth to be reconceived. Just as Ibsen's Nora challenges Coventry Patmore's myth of the Angel (or Doll) in the House, so too do Karel and Julian escape the ontology of dolls, or stereotypes easily taxonomized, easily housed. But unlike Nora, whose doll status is ready-made based on popular heteronormative Victorian mythology, Karel and Julian must first be made dolls by Ford and Tyler's conscious invocation of the myth: The queer characters must be included within a heteronormative mythology in order to unmake it.

The novel relates Karel's and Julian's repudiations of the myth of dollness in stream-of-consciousness passages that foreground the unconscious mind's associative logic and that allocate narrative authority to Karel and Julian. Whereas the myth of dollness propounds a falsehood about exterior identity, *The Young and Evil* offers a myth about the foundational possibility of interior subjectivity. For both men, it is upon being abandoned by lovers that they abandon the myth of dollness. When Julian rejects him, for example, Karel descends into a childhood reverie and remembers that his family "SNATCHED" away his dolls because they thought "only little girls" should play with them (Ford and Tyler, 23). Repudiating these "many large people not being very kind" (Ford and Tyler, 20), Karel declares that he will ignore others' "saying you are the darling of the Doll's House" and the injunction that "I AM TO STAY INDOORS," inside the closet of heteronormative myth (Ford and Tyler, 24). Karel proclaims instead that he "shall go further into that other house," one wherein he can "use high heels over their corpses" (Ford and Tyler, 20). In that queer house, Karel longs for a doll of Kermit Roosevelt, Theodore's son, whose image evokes for Karel a homoerotic vision of Lancelot (Ford and Tyler, 24). Rejecting his family's heteronormative rejection of his queerness, Karel fashions a queer mythology—a Lancelot who might desire him—to escape the Doll's House myth.

Julian later has a similar epiphany about his own ontological development when, weary of his fleeting sexual encounters, he finds depth in the surface of dollness by repudiating gay versions of dollness. "I am not a fairy doll," Julian announces, because "a doll does not believe in itself he thought it only believes in its dollness." At this point Julian views his homosexuality not just as a quantifiable, naturalist surface marker but as a "fetich" that accumulates substance by being a "habit." Reinforcing the novel's principle that surface acquires depth through iteration, Julian embraces his sexuality—not his dollness—as "a symbol of power," a symbol of universal desire but not "a specific symbol" of homosexual dollness (Ford and Tyler, 170). Both Karel and Julian refashion the Doll's House myth of identity, then, to represent queer desire in mythic terms, those that express queers' particular interiority (through stream-of-consciousness) and their connection to common visions of human universality (through the myths of Lancelot and the Doll's House). In this way, the queer men can feel, as Julian later reflects, that they "had captured the myth and had not been captured by it" (Ford and Tyler, 87).[49]

The Young and Evil consciously invokes myths to reshape them with unconscious processes, then, a technique that bears comparison to Joyce's *Ulysses*, a novel that, Bell maintains, "dissolves the dualistic assumptions of the word 'consciousness' itself."[50] For Bell, "Joyce's use of ancient myth is integral to a celebration of human life as transformed by the power of the human imagination"—so his conscious deployment of myth is a means of manifesting the unconscious already everywhere in the world.[51] Part of this effort, Bell contends, is to bring Dublin "disinterestedly into being"; as we will see, Ford and Tyler similarly bring a queer world into being without subjectively qualifying that world on any moral basis.[52] While I do not wish to suggest that *The Young and Evil* imitates or achieves the same goals as *Ulysses*—the American ban on which was lifted in 1933—Bell's claims about the latter are salient for the former insofar as *The Young and Evil* invokes Joyce not only formally (as in chapter 9's catechism) but by bearing fictional (and historically incorrect) witness to his death (Ford and Tyler, 202). A parallel worth bearing in mind, then, is that, since Joyce envisions the universal (western consciousness) via the particular (Dublin), not at the expense of either (Irish politics figures largely in his project), and since myth generically functions when retold and reconceived, Ford and Tyler may well envision their novel as carrying Joyce's torch, retelling a universal myth through an ethnic lens.[53]

Part of this retelling involves Ford and Tyler's departure from dominant modernist myth-makers' relationships to personality and time. Peter Nicholls characterizes Joyce's late work, for example, as attempting "to avoid a narcissistic individualism by restoring art to the public sphere."[54] Informed by modernist theories of impersonality, this stance holds that most literary representations of subjective consciousness exclude the public—and not only the contemporary public but the universal, atemporal public manifested in tradition and history. The impersonal thus functions as the ideal medium for accessing history in either its temporal or atemporal manifestations, a view that extends from T. S. Eliot's assertion in "Tradition and the Individual Talent" (1919) that "the progress of an artist is a continual self-sacrifice, a continual extinction of personality."[55] This claim echoes Tyler's contention that the individual spirit, not the personality, is the conduit for mythic collectivity: Literature arises, he says, "from the desire to differentiate the personal experience; the operation of the universal or 'human community' factor is automatic and concomitant, and is not present in isolatable integers."[56] Ford and Tyler, however, like Joyce, simultaneously eschew the privilege that Eliot, in *"Ulysses,* Order, and Myth," places on the mythic past to devalue the present; likewise, they refuse myth as a means for returning to a primitive origin in the past.[57] Instead, Ford and Tyler incorporate the past (mythic allusions) into the present (Greenwich Village) to redeem, by fusing, both temporal zones.

This temporal blend resonates with many modernists' concerns about the relation between art and life. Like Nietzsche, who, Bell notes, "assimilated the dualistic elements of life and art so completely that they ceased to be separably apparent," which is "an important clue to the metaphysics of literary modernism at large," Ford and Tyler see life as inextricably bound with art.[58] As voiced by his character, Horace Zagreus, in *The Apes of God* (1930), however, Wyndham Lewis maintains precisely the opposite position: *"the real* should not compete with creations of Fiction. There should be two worlds, not one."[59] For Ford and Tyler, Lewis's Schopenhauerian vision polarizes the very concepts that, in their view, create myth when fused. It is no surprise that Lewis includes homosexuality among "the child-cult, artistic amateurism," and—the source of his central attack against *Ulysses* in *Time and Western Man* (1927)—"the time-cult" as modern trends that engage the subjective, the personal, at literature's expense.[60] It is therefore equally unsurprising that Ford and Tyler critique Lewis in their novel when Julian remarks that Lewis "has no better word for the behavior of the organism than negative," an objection that Julian raises in defense of Stein's fusion of "writing" and "walking," creating and being— activities that are, for these artists, "the same" (Ford and Tyler, 98).

Surreal Desire

Unlike most Anglo-American modernists, Ford and Tyler's mythic vision emerges from their association with the surrealist movement. In 1940, Ford founded the surrealist magazine *View,* for which Tyler served as associate editor and to which André Breton—in spite of his public stance against homosexuality—conceded the demise of his own journal, *VVV.*[61] The writers' interest in surrealism began much earlier, however: Tyler was fluent in Jean Cocteau during the twenties, and Ford's time in Paris in the early thirties and his association with Stein, Barnes, and Pavel Tchelitchew (the latter two with whom he had relationships) provided him access to the surrealists, among other avant-garde groups.

Louis Aragon's description of the surrealist aesthetic may best convey how *The Young and Evil* exhibits that movement's philosophy. In *Paris Peasant* (1926), Aragon observes how, walking on the Passage de l'Opera, "the reality of the outside world and the subjectivism of the passage" fuse, a perceptual state that Aragon enjoins the reader to embrace: "let us pause in this strange zone where all is distraction, distraction of attention as well as of inattention, so as to experience this vertigo." For it is in this state of epistemological vertigo that one can rend the "interior boundaries of [one]self" to gain "access to a hitherto forbidden realm that lies beyond [one's] human energies."[62] Surrealist vertigo is the zone between—at the nexus of—conscious and unconscious states, states of "attention as well as of inattention," and it is notably a "realm" whose "forbidden" qualities connote the non-normative "human energies" of queerness.

"Vertigo" may in this sense be the most apposite term to denote the effect and affect of *The Young and Evil*, as is evident in chapter 7, "Napoleon and the Merry-Go-Round." At the beginning of the chapter, Gabriel, who has just been abandoned by Louis, walks through Union Square Park. Gabriel is drunk, so the park feels to him like "a merry-go-round" where "people picked up their legs like racehorses"; it is a vertiginous urban center that "was turning so fast now that it made him dizzy" (Ford and Tyler, 81). After righting himself, Gabriel avoids the Union Square subway and walks to Theodosia's apartment. On the way, he feels "something . . . pulling him up by the scalp" even as he remains grounded (Ford and Tyler, 82). Upon his arrival at Theo's, these surrealistic gestures become most vertiginous. First, Gabriel sees Theo's eye in the crack of the bathroom door:

> Gabriel stopped with his lips apart and looked at the slit showing her one eye. He was silent and seemed to be impelled towards the thin horizontal shaft that had an eye at the top. He was running after it (through a tunnel) and the thing was on the end of a train leaving him running as hard as he could; in the darkness he stumbled, he was pitching forward and his face would be smashed; he was falling forward, he made no resistance and was shocked into consciousness like if an alarm clock had gone off. His eyes focused and it was Theodosia's breathing close face that he saw. (Ford and Tyler, 83)

Here the subway trip that Gabriel consciously avoided manifests unconsciously in the vertiginous and eroticized terms of a "slit" and a "horizontal shaft that had an eye at the top," which becomes a "train" in a "tunnel." Theo's room is now the merry-go-round, as Gabriel's vertigo reorients a vertical shaft separating door from frame into a horizontal shaft beckoning him toward Theo. When he reaches Theo, Gabriel prepares to perform cunnilingus on her, but he is thwarted when he sees "a nude woman walk up behind him. She kicked his head off. He saw his head whirl brilliantly from his shoulders. His head was a bottle whirling in the sun. He could see the blood gushing from his headless trunk. It gushed like vomit." This surrealistic vision of Gabriel's projected feelings is prompted by his literally having projected vomit (presumably on Theo). Gabriel's conscious activity thus catalyzes and fuses with unconscious activity—which is "shocked into consciousness"—to create a surreal vision that ends as would the most vertiginous ride on the merry-go-round of unrealizable desire (Ford and Tyler, 84).

The surrealist quality of such disorienting passages may derive from the fact that, as Ford records, *The Young and Evil* was written "roughly unconsciously enough to escape being officialized modernism."[63] As Breton maintained, composing "roughly unconsciously," or automatically, is central to the surrealist aesthetic: "*automatism* alone is the dispenser of the elements on which the secondary work of emotional amalgamation and passage from the unconscious to the preconscious can operate effectively."[64] By the standards of this theory, Ford and Tyler may be said to have achieved a surrealist "emotional amalgamation" by writing their novel "unconsciously," automatically, and then consciously revising it, as Ford did for a year in Paris. Rather than being the means by which the novel "escaped being officialized modernism," automatic writing aligns *The Young and Evil* with surrealism's official aesthetic philosophy.

Surrealism's preoccupation with collapsing states of consciousness may have been attractive to Ford and Tyler because it offers an alternative to determinist models of literary realism and naturalism. As Nicholls describes, "For the Surrealists, the novel as a form is not flawed by description alone, but by a sense of determinism and fatality, by a species of logic which leaves us subservient to reality as it is."[65] For queers, being "subservient to reality" was often literally, let alone metaphysically, fatal in the early twentieth century; surrealism provided Ford and Tyler the techniques to elude such subservience, at least aesthetically, with its conception of an unconscious that exceeds the limits of naturalist particularity. *The Young and Evil*'s queer roundelay represents a surreal version of the unconscious, which Breton describes as a promiscuous force that "refuses itself nothing," that moves "from one object to another, never valorizing among the objects any but the last one."[66] Considering Breton's public stance against homosexuality, however, that Ford and Tyler use surrealist techniques to construct their queer vision also indicates how they seized the queer lacuna in official aesthetics to make modernist conceptions of myth new. Their novel may in this sense best represent the surrealist vision to "discove[r] objects which, because they have no clear use, offer a lifted horizon where we may read the promise of a *shared* will to change."[67]

Ford and Tyler locate the queerest potential of surrealism in the movement's focus on desire as a mediating force not only between consciousness and unconsciousness but also between life and death. The passage that invokes the text's final title offers a salient example of this concept: Almost in passing, Karel notices that Louis's face, which "was dark, even morbid," "attracted because it was evil and young" (Ford and Tyler, 49).[68] Expressing the surrealist theme that desire is bound with death, Karel's "attraction" for Louis is based on the latter's "morbid," "evil," and "young" qualities. In *The Young and Evil*, as an unnamed narrator states, "the macabre is not omitted from any universe" because the threat of death renders all desire, including the "young," universally macabre and, therefore, unstable (Ford and Tyler, 161). Unfulfilled desire thus motivates the novel's spatial plot and characters, as Julian notes of himself: "His blood he felt was many engines; his heart was chasing them" (Ford and Tyler, 108). The heart chases so promiscuously and so unteleologically, in fact, that the text's diegesis elides sexual activity—what Tyler calls "mere transcribed orgy"— in favor of desirous interactions, from the banal to the bawdy (Ford and Tyler, 52, 162). Instead of actualizing sex, "whose shadow," a narrator reports, "is death" (Ford and Tyler, 207), *The Young and Evil* envisions a world comprised almost wholly of desire.

The surreal proximity between desire and death constitutes, for this novel, the mythic grounds on which a queer community might exist. As Karel thinks, "The possibility of hate is all love needs to complete it. . . . Hatred and love at once raise love above earth" (Ford and Tyler, 195). When love acknowledges its own possible destruction in hatred, Karel thinks, then love becomes mythic, numinously "raise[d] above earth." Karel extends this sentiment later when he asks "is [want] affection or something mystic?"—a question to which the novel answers "[b]oth" when Karel observes that "accident is that for which we are insufficiently prepared and inevitability is that for which we are even more insufficiently prepared. Louis has left me" (Ford and Tyler, 176–77). It would seem that Karel's reference to "accident" here is his "affection" for Louis, his desire to unite with him, because "inevitability" refers to their union's fracture; yet Karel ironically says that he is more unprepared for that inevitability than for the accident. Even though he knows that fracture is inevitable, Karel retains the myth that union will not break so that he can turn accidental "affection" into "something mystic": "both are divine Karel said accident and inevitability" (Ford and Tyler, 176), both the myth of affection and its real dissolution. Complementing its vertiginous logic, this epiphany ends in a surreal vision: "birds of plumage screamed through the room" (Ford and Tyler, 177).

Ethnic American Folklore

For all its screaming "birds of plumage," however, this passage still takes place, as most of the novel's mythopoeic moments do, in locations like "the room," here a particular apartment that Karel keeps in early twentieth-century Greenwich Village. As its opening paragraph establishes, *The Young and Evil* wants to document an ethnic community in which sexual desire attains a mythic status, so its most mythopoeic moments coexist with its most folkloric moments, those instances in which the novel historicizes itself and the community it portrays. Such communal descriptions locate the novel's myth within a folkloric tradition, for, as Manton claims, myths that "seem to be merely of literary interest must once have had . . . a context"—a social, extra-literary context.[69] This emphasis on social context allows myth, according to Erich Fromm, to serve one's "need to overcome [one's] feeling of separateness," the same "need" that, Nealon records, became acute to queers during this historical period.[70]

The novel enables the individual to overcome his or her "feeling of separateness" by depicting a universally queer world—one that, paradoxically, maintains a feeling of separateness as a criterion for inclusion within it. It is the falsehood, the practicable impossibility, of such a world that constitutes, in Ford and Tyler's vision, the foundational reality of New York's queer community at the turn of the century. The text aims to show, as Julian does, that "America is so Greek but doesn't know it" (Ford and Tyler, 135)—where "Greek" is code for queer—and that "ninety-five percent of the world is just naturally queer" (Ford and Tyler, 159), and it does so by defeating all expectations of stable identity, individual or communal. As Boone argues, "Ford and Tyler's goal is *not* simply that of replacing the traditional boy-meets-girl formula with an equally reductive boy-meets-boy plot." Instead, the novel's overall lack of plot notwithstanding, formations of desire in *The Young and Evil* are "queer in the contemporary sense"—they are so variously and non-hierarchically conceived that they destabilize binary *fin-de-siècle* configurations of sexuality.[71] As Julian remarks, blurring textual art and life, the "heart [is] a question mark" in this novel: Desire is a queer question, not a stable period (Ford and Tyler, 137).

None of the text's characters resists blurring sexual taxonomies, not even members of normative social institutions, including a magistrate (Ford and Tyler, 191), policemen, and doctors (Ford and Tyler, 41). That these figures transgress in the novel the very boundaries that they maintain in 1930s America is crucial to the novel's anti-naturalist stance, since the threat of the normative social is otherwise felt throughout the text: Parties are always close-curtained (Ford and Tyler, 33); Louis, Karel, and Frederick are arrested (Ford and Tyler, 41, 186); and Gabriel, Karel, and Frederick are attacked by gangsters and sailors (Ford and Tyler, 46, 182). Indeed, in the world of *The Young and Evil*, "Something is always threatening trade," as Julian campily quips, where "trade" is code for prostitution (Ford and Tyler, 39).

Ford and Tyler ameliorate this threat by mythologizing the New York queer community, converting the threat of violence into the resource for a desire that never reaches its aims. Chapter 11's drag ball exemplifies how the novel mythologizes the historical queer community of 1930s New York, for its "dancefloor was a scene of celestial flavor and cerulean coloring no angelic painter or nectarish poet has ever conceived" (Ford and Tyler, 152). "Lit up like high mass" (Ford and Tyler, 152), the drag ball, a regionally ethnic event in modernist New York, offers a transcendent locale that, once concluded, looks like "the garden of Eden" after the Fall (Ford and Tyler, 168). The chapter contains a poetically lineated passage whose lines begin and end with phrases that connect them to contiguous lines but that fracture any logical connection among the lines' speakers or their sentiments:

> confessed his love for a man so I didn't stand up and wave the flag I just
>   sat there you know me Mabel and
> smiled Mr. Schubert get OFF my face I can't see the CONtract the wine
>   came up and he looked at my intellect so often go
> out of the way of a big truck and put my hand over my cunt like
> this just too bad isn't it buttercup scalps (Ford and Tyler, 158)

At the level of external action, as Christopher Looby contends, such lines depict how "interested glances are skipping promiscuously from person to person" on the dance floor and perhaps even mimic "the acoustic effect of turning abruptly in relation to another moving dancer's utterance and hearing it first in one ear and then in the other."[72] At the level of internal action, however, the passage's resemblance to stream-of-consciousness narration but lack of a single narratorial "I" also converts such sensorial information into a collective stream-of-consciousness, offering arguably the most unifying collective moment in the novel. A utopian vision of what might constitute a queer community, the drag ball is a mythic event that unifies a variegated population, even as its conclusion, like that of the Edenic Fall, will mark that community's dissolution.

In Ford and Tyler's historiography, then, the myth of a queer community founds the very real Greenwich Village community that formed around the criterion of sexual difference in the early twentieth century. Ford claimed, after all, that "nothing is invented" in the novel, a statement that highlights the text's self-historicizing impulse.[73] Part of that impulse is purely geographical because, as one narrator says, books "about the Village . . . are bound to be ninety percent/lies" (Ford and Tyler, 157). Specific addresses of the neighborhood's gay meeting places accordingly abound, offering a cartography that locates folklorically the environment in which the text's myth is born. To some scholars, this dual function actually reproduces the historical status of the two regions in which Ford and Tyler wrote *The Young and Evil*: Greenwich Village and the Left bank, arguably the first coherent and self-identifying queer communities in western civilization.[74] For while those communities were sites of what, for this essay, constitutes the "particular"—the sexually non-normative—they were more precisely defined, according to Jamake Highwater, as "artistic ghettos" where "the basis of commonality was neither linguistic [n]or ethnic" but "based on difference."[75]

Representative of how the novel shuttles between the historical particularity of Greenwich Village and the mythic universality of the sexual-aesthetic, this conflation of the queer with the artistic via the broad category of "difference" enables the novel's myth to include—indeed to centralize—the queer within communal myth by simultaneously transcending such particular focus under the auspices of the aesthetic. Highwater's concept of the "artistic ghetto" coincides, after all, with how *The Young and Evil* and, indeed, a generation of queer texts depict everyday life, sexuality, and art as inextricably bound. Writing during the ascendance of psychology and anthropology—two disciplines that sought to correlate the individual and the community through quasi-scientific means—Ford and Tyler join a group of queer writers at the turn of the century who were attempting to, in Chauncey's words, "create gay histories," or historical communities within which they could locate themselves, even if it meant telling the anachronistic and mythopoeic "lie" about "sexuality" as a transhistorical phenomenon.[76]

Suggested by this anachronism, the most striking feature of Ford and Tyler's historiography is its literary rather than positivist nature. In keeping with Heather Love's claim that "the inventiveness of a whole range of

queer historical practices might be understood as a result of the paired necessities of having 'to fight for it' and to 'make it up,'" many early
twentieth-century queers attempted to discover a lineage of "homosexual"
writers in literary history so as to place themselves within "an honorable
tradition."[77] Writing against the heteronormative tradition of American
folklore, such writers create what could be called a mythopoeic historiography, one that claims its historical falsehoods (Shakespeare was not, Michel Foucault's constructionist legacy has taught us, homosexual) as
foundational for the formation of twentieth-century queer communities.
Because gays found themselves unrepresented in "the family-centered oral
traditions available to other disenfranchised groups," they created literary
histories that would represent their lives, often through "individual and
idiosyncratic readings of texts" and through the creation of gay argot,
which Chauncey argues "fostered their sense of collective identity" and "allowed men to see themselves as participants in the dominant culture by
enabling them to see themselves in the interstices of that culture."[78]

The Young and Evil's ethnic argot most notably includes campy, bawdy
humor in the form of double entendre. In response to Louis's request for
a cigarette, for instance, the text reads, "Have one Julian said offering his
package. Have something to eat" (Ford and Tyler, 31), where "package" refers to much more than Julian's cigarette case, and the "something" to eat
connotes phallic food, like the hot dogs and bananas Karel and Julian have
just consumed (Ford and Tyler, 28). Such coded humor may seem to be
the stuff of folklore, not myth, but the accumulated effect of this double-
talk is to evoke the dichotomy between states of consciousness integral to
the novel's surrealist vision: Operating on two semantic levels, code, pun,
and double entendre may be said to work first on the level of folklore but
second on the level of myth. When Julian asks "what is divine besides
slang," accordingly, he suggests that slang is literally a medium for accessing the divine (Ford and Tyler, 134). As a folkloric document composed in
the style of the mythical method, then, *The Young and Evil* marks a crucial
queer turning point for American modernism: It establishes a historically
inchoate tradition of gay folklore, creates a new queer (rather than specifically gay) myth for that folklore, and inserts itself into the dominant folklore of modernist literature. For Ford and Tyler, folklore must be mythic
because history is itself a myth, as Tyler claimed of Pound's early *Cantos*:
"[I] am inclined to doubt efficacy of your idiom as HISTORY," he says, for
"the best parts Ive seen are always those which depend least for meaning
upon the strictly contemp. frame."[79] Tyler suggests that the queer modernist need to "*feel historical*," as Nealon says, manifested itself not only as

a queer need for personal and ethnic history but as a modernist need for universal history, one accessed in this novel through the conduit of queer desire.[80]

The Young and Evil also marks a historical turning point for queer literature because it diverges in style and subject from most other gay-themed American novels in the thirties, the majority of which ended with the queer protagonist's ignominious death, a formal trait that Chauncey associates with writers' desires to placate potential censors.[81] Ford and Tyler's novel does not end with the protagonist's death (in part because it has no protagonist), however, nor does it bow to convention to avoid censorship. Circumnavigating those heteronormative pressures, just as Joyce did with *Ulysses*, the authors had the book published by the Obelisk Press in Paris. The publication and partial creation of the novel in Paris' queer community (perhaps more developed than any in New York) indicates how Ford and Tyler distinguished themselves from other queer American writers even as they attempted to represent those writers' communities through a transnational vision. In doing so, they establish a tradition of queer mythopoeia that a range of late twentieth-century British and American texts including Jeanette Winterson's *Oranges Are Not the Only Fruit* (1985) and Gil Cuadros's *City of God* (1994) recognize, modify, and retell themselves.[82]

From its narrative outset, *The Young and Evil* invites such folkloric transmission. Just after being immersed in the "strange" (and strangely familiar, or "common") world of the Round Table, Karel is beckoned by a "nice fat old bullfrog" who "had a fresh cup of tea to offer Karel." At the bullfrog's request, Karel then "repeat[s] an old nursery rhyme he learned as a child," retelling a common myth in a strange locale (Ford and Tyler, 11). Recalling the animal-populated tea party in Lewis Carroll's 1865 *Alice in Wonderland* (Louis and Karel's names indeed recall that text's author), Ford and Tyler refashion popular fairytale tropes with gay code: The bullfrog, akin to the "horrid ogre" that Karel later encounters (Ford and Tyler, 13), might be a "troll" (itself a mythological reference), or an unattractive gay man, and the "tea" (a reference to "tea rooms," or restrooms in which gay men have sex) is likely a sexual advance, if not its product. The novel's first page thus thematizes and structuralizes the necessity to tell, remake, and retell popular, universal myths for the benefit of a particular community's folkloric tradition.

Self-consciously modernist, Ford and Tyler seem to cry "MAKE IT NEW" throughout such passages, but they make Pound's cry coyer and queerer: "Won't you join our table? they said in sweet chorus." Requesting recognition of the queer community's "table"—which is, to its authors, simultaneously modernism's—*The Young and Evil* "makes new" the often heteronormative ends to which Eliot's "mythical method" was put. If modernism was dominated, as Tyler claimed, by writers "who arent MEN enough to be FAIRIES," Ford and Tyler wrote like fairies, or queers whose historical moniker reverberates mythically.[83] In doing so, Ford and Tyler offer a "sweet" invitation to their modernist peers and to modernist schol-ars alike to sit at their table and to wonder whether the line between the strange and the common in American modernism isn't much thinner than they've recognized.[84]

NOTES

1. T. S. Eliot, "*Ulysses*, Order, and Myth," in *Selected Prose of T.S. Eliot*, ed. Frank Kermode (New York: Farrar, Straus & Giroux, 1975), 178.

2. Joseph Allen Boone, *Libidinal Currents* (Chicago: University of Chicago Press, 1998), 255–6. Throughout this analysis, I will oscillate between using the terms *gay* and *queer* because scholars like George Chauncey have documented on a social/historical level what they call New York's gay male community, one that had not congealed entirely into a particularly defined homosexual community but that was nonetheless structured on the criterion of sexual difference. See Chauncey, *Gay New York* (New York: Basic Books, 1993). On the formal and thematic level of *The Young and Evil*, however, that uncongealed community is more aptly described as queer. That is, the novel historicizes the gay male communities that historians have recorded but finds in their uncongealed particularity—their polymorphously queer, not just homosexual, population—the mythopoeic resources to offer a queer vision of humanity at large, part of what I am arguing is the novel's fluctuation between folkloric (particular) and mythic (universal) functions.

3. Charles Henri Ford and Parker Tyler to *The English Journal* in 1931, Charles Henri Ford Papers, YCAL MSS 32, Beinecke Rare Book and Manuscript Library, Yale University, box 2, folder 176. As their comments about *Blues* indicate, Ford and Tyler wrote in a period that they self-consciously called modernism. In contemporary literary historiography, of course, the category *modernism* does not signify a monolithic aesthetic movement. Accordingly, I do not aim to simplify a variegated period under the rubric of this historical term but to examine how Ford and Tyler conceived of the period: as a movement of formal and experiential (especially sexual) experimentation. As my introductory examples suggest, such experiments in *The Young and Evil* most typically resemble a high modernist aesthetic, one allied with texts by James Joyce, T. S. Eliot, Gertrude Stein, William Faulkner, and Djuna Barnes and distinguished from, say, those by Willa Cather, F. Scott Fitzgerald, and D. H. Lawrence.

4. Boone, 264.

5. I use the term *ethnic* to denote the qualities or characteristics of a particular group. While Michael Warner claims in the Introduction to *Fear of a Queer Planet* (ed. Warner [Minneapolis: University of Minneapolis Press, 1993], vii–xxxi) that "people tend not to encounter queerness in the same way as ethnic identity" (xvii), twentieth-century queer writers' use of mythology to create literary and historical communities tells a different story, especially about the role that mythological literature plays as a mediating force in the paradoxical construction of a non-identitarian community. For several uses of the term *ethnic* to refer to the queer community, see Chauncey, 271–99; Gayle Rubin's "Thinking Sex: Notes for a Radical Theory of the Politics of Sexuality" in *The Lesbian and Gay Studies Reader*, ed. Henry Abelove, Michèle Aina Barale, and David Halperin (New York: Routledge, 1993), 3–44; and Richard Rodriguez's chapter "Late Victorians" in his *Days of Obligation: An Argument with My Mexican Father* (New York: Viking, 1992), 26–47.

6. Eliot, "Ulysses, Order, and Myth," 177, 176. Ford and Tyler invoke Eliot twice in the novel, in fact, which suggests their unsurprising awareness of his importance to modernist aesthetics (Ford and Tyler, 39, 176). For a helpful critical examination of Eliot's "*Ulysses*, Order, and Myth," see Denis Donoghue's "Yeats, Eliot, and the Mythical Method," *The Sewanee Review* 105 (1997): 206–26.

7. Ford and Tyler, *The Young and Evil* (New York: Masquerade Books, 1988), 1. Hereafter cited parenthetically by author and page number.

8. Chauncey, 34. An entire essay could be devoted to how Ford and Tyler queer the mythological texts to which they allude in the novel, beginning with Julian's composition and destruction of a story about Adam and Eve: Just as Ford and Tyler discard the text's first title, so too does the text discard one of the most heteronormative tales in western mythology (Ford and Tyler, 88–89). The allusion to Riding Hood also exemplifies such queering, for, by situating Riding Hood in the queer world of the Round Table, the authors expose the sexual non-normativity inherent but often overlooked in that fairytale. As related by Charles Perrault, female homo-eroticism and drag propel the text's plot: Red's "mother was beyond reason excessively fond of her, and her grandmother yet much more"; so much more, in fact, that Red doesn't pause when the person she believes to be her grandmother beckons Red to "come into bed to me." Instead, Red "un-dressed herself, and went into bed" and offers a rather erotic blazon of her grandmother before the wolf devours her ("Little Red Ridinghood," *The Classic Fairy Tales*, ed. Iona and Peter Opie [New York: Oxford University Press, 1980], 122, 125). The wolf is able to do so only, of course, because he

has, anticipating Ford and Tyler's drag queen, imitated both Red and the grandmother's voice and worn the grandmother's clothes.

9. Apart from those cited elsewhere in this essay, the novel's other explicit mythical allusions include references to satyrs and naiads (Ford and Tyler, 12), "Goldilocks and the Three Bears" (Ford and Tyler, 13), *Arabian Nights* (Ford and Tyler, 17), Jesus (Ford and Tyler, 17), Cinderella (Ford and Tyler, 17, 135), Prometheus (Ford and Tyler, 26, 48), Helen of Troy (Ford and Tyler, 136), and the headless horseman (Ford and Tyler, 171), but I would contend that the text's various invocations of modernist writers are also mythopoeic: They attempt to mythologize the contemporary literary scene through formal juxtaposition with traditional mythological allusions.

10. Eliot's insistence upon mythical literature's "way of controlling, of ordering . . . the immense panorama of futility and anarchy which is contemporary history" (177) in *"Ulysses*, Order, and Myth"* exemplifies such normativity, for he hopes that the mythical method will allow the ostensibly orderly past to control the ostensibly chaotic (and therefore meaningless) present. Eliot's lament for unsullied, reproductive heterosexual relations in *The Waste Land* suggests the heteronormative assumptions behind this aesthetic, even if his own support of often queer texts like *Ulysses* and *Nightwood* betrays those assumptions. Although Heather Love has recently argued for the centrality of mythology to queer experience in *Feeling Backward: Loss and the Politics of Queer History* (Cambridge: Harvard University Press, 2007), esp. 5, 133, 135, most accounts of literary mythology rely upon a heteronormative framework similar to Eliot's. See especially Leslie Fiedler's *Love and Death in the American Novel* (New York: Stein and Day, 1966), which purports to study an interracial, "homoerotic" mythic bond between men in the American realist narrative imaginary but which renders that myth asexually homophilic when Fiedler claims that delibidinized attraction marks "a general superiority of the love of a man for man over the ignoble lust of man for woman" (369). For Fielder's reliance upon Sigmund Freud's heteronormative Oedipal myth, see *Love and Death*, 382, 390.

11. Christopher Nealon, *Foundlings: Lesbian and Gay Historical Emotion Before Stonewall* (Durham, N.C.: Duke University Press, 2001), 4.

12. Nealon, 8.

13. In his *More Man Than You'll Ever Be* (Bloomington: Indiana University Press, 1989), Joseph Goodwin argues that folklore functions in a "subculture as a means of communication and identification, as an aid to subcultural cohesion" (xiv) and, beyond the subculture, as "a framework for ordering experience" that may "requir[e] disorganization and restructuring of our existing concepts of reality" (79). Folklore thus serves a double function of cohesion (for the subculture) and disruption (of the dominant

culture), precisely the double function I am describing of *The Young and Evil*'s mythology. All myths were at some point folkloric, of course, but some myths—especially biblical and classical myths—have assumed such universal status in western societies that they appear deracinated from their folkloric traditions. Ford and Tyler seize upon such false universalization to root their text's literary critique and co-option of mythology.

14. Warner, xxv.

15. Warner, xvi; emphasis mine.

16. Where Eve Kosofsky Sedgwick's terms *universalizing* and *minoritizing* might be useful to consider in this context (Sedgwick, *Epistemology of the Closet* [Berkeley: University of California Press, 1990], 40), as Boone does (see Boone, 252–3), I prefer the terms *mythic* and *ethnic* because they more comprehensively describe not only the sexual-historical but the literary-formal aims of Ford and Tyler's project.

17. About *The Young and Evil*, Ford writes to Stein on December 20, 1932 that "you are most good. I like the new words much better and am sure Parker will appreciate the change too" (Ford to Stein, Gertrude Stein and Alice B. Toklas Papers, YCAL MSS 76, Beinecke Rare Book and Manuscript Library, Yale University box 107, Folder 2119). Ford notes that Stein made changes to drafts of the novel's chapters "Siege" and "High Heels Over Their Corpses" (presumably revised as "Chapter Two: Julian and Karel" in the final text [*Y*, 20]) (Charles Henri Ford Papers, Harry Ransom Center, University of Texas at Austin, box 7, folders 3 and 12). See Stein and Alice B. Toklas's *Dear Sammy*, ed. Samuel M. Steward (Boston: Houghton Mifflin, 1977) for a humorous variation on Stein's evaluation of the novel's "first" accomplishment (34).

18. Pound to Ford, February 1, 1929, Charles Henri Ford Papers, Beinecke Rare Book and Manuscript Library, Yale University, box 2, folder 144. Authors' often idiosyncratic spelling and punctuation in correspondence have been preserved here and throughout this essay.

19. George Bornstein, "Eight Letters from Ezra Pound to Parker Tyler in the 1930s," *Michigan Quarterly Review* 24 (1985): 13.

20. Tyler to Pound, October 14, 1934, Ezra Pound Papers, YCAL MSS 43, Beinecke Rare Book and Manuscript Library, Yale University, box 53, folder 2400.

21. Pound, *The Cantos of Ezra Pound* (New York: New Directions, 1970), 265; Boone, 264.

22. Michael Bell, *Literature, Modernism and Myth* (Cambridge: Cambridge University Press, 1997), 1, 37.

23. Bell, *Literature*, 2.

24. Parker Tyler, *The Granite Butterfly* (Orono, Maine: National Poetry Foundation, 1994), 74. For further examination of the various definitions of

the term *myth* and the ways it has been used in literary criticism, see Bell, *Literature*, 4, 12; Eric Gould's *Mythical Intentions in Modern Literature* (Princeton: Princeton University Press, 1981), esp. 6–14; Lynda D. McNeil's *Recreating the World/Word: The Mythic Mode as Symbolic Discourse* (Albany: State University of New York Press, 1992), esp. 260–1; and *Myth and Literature: Contemporary Theory and Practice*, ed. John B. Vickery (Lincoln: University of Nebraska Press, 1966), esp. 3–136.

25. Tyler, 45.

26. For just one example of Ford's later attempts to refashion conventional myths for modern purposes, see his late film *Johnny Minotaur* (1971).

27. Joseph Frank, *The Idea of Spatial Form* (New Brunswick, N.J.: Rutgers University Press, 1991), 63–64.

28. E. W. Herd, "Myth and Modern German Literature," in *Myth and the Modern Imagination*, ed. Margaret Dalziel (Dunedin: University of Otago Press, 1967), 69.

29. G. R. Manton, "The Making of Myth," in *Myth and the Modern Imagination*, 16.

30. Friedrich Nietzsche, "On the Uses and Disadvantages of History for Life," *Untimely Meditations*, trans. R. J. Hollingdale (Cambridge: Cambridge University Press, 1983), 63.

31. Bell, *Literature*, 35.

32. For an extended discussion of the relationship between realism and mythology, see Gregory L. Lucente's *The Narrative of Realism and Myth: Verga, Lawrence, Faulkner, Pavese* (Baltimore: Johns Hopkins Univ. Press, 1981), esp. 41–53.

33. My thanks to Glenn Brewer for his help with thinking through this disorienting description.

34. Christopher Looby examines this tension between the queer novel and the genre's historical affiliations with romance and sentimentalism. See Looby, "The Gay Novel in the United States 1900–1950," in *A Companion to the Modern American Novel 1900–1950*, ed. John Matthews (Oxford: Wiley-Blackwell, 2009), 414–36, esp. 414–15.

35. Ford claims something similar of himself when he writes to Pound on 15 August 1927, "I may not understand. I may not know. but I feel with no false emotion" (Pound Papers, box 17, folder 746).

36. Tyler to Pound, 18 September 1933, Pound Papers, box 53, folder 2400.

37. Boone, 261.

38. Tzvetan Todorov, *Theories of the Symbol*, trans. Catherine Porter (Ithaca: Cornell University Press, 1982), 210.

39. See Fiedler, *What Was Literature?* (New York: Simon & Schuster, 1982), 136.

40. Fiedler, *What Was Literature?*, 132.

41. In a metatextual speech, Karel suggests how this spatial plot is mythopoeic: Referring to Gabriel and Louis, he says that "they are the secret of the night but so am I and so the siege is begun. No castles have fallen nor ladies been abducted for today we are too subtle for that. I'm going to the library" (Ford and Tyler, 196). In a novel filled with psychic and emotional conflict, or "siege," the characters are too "subtle" for the plot conventions of traditional narrative. Abjuring convention, the text fulfills its promise, like many high-minded modernist texts, to be a novel bound for "the library" rather than the bedside table.

42. See Jamake Highwater's *The Mythology of Transgression* (Oxford: Oxford University Press, 1997), 56, for a discussion of realism's naturalization of myth's unnaturalizable impulses.

43. Herd, 53.

44. Tyler to Pound, 18 September 1933, Pound Papers, box 53, folder 2400.

45. Dalziel, "Myth in Modern English Literature," in *Myth and the Modern*, 29–30.

46. See Freud's *Three Essays on the Theory of Sexuality*, trans. James Strachey (New York: Basic Books, 1962), 6, wherein Freud describes homosexuals as inverts, *pace* Havelock Ellis. Freud's position on homosexuality is notoriously ambiguous: While he does break from nineteenth-century sexology in his claim that "inverts cannot be regarded as degenerate" (4), for instance, he still assumes that an invert's self-loathing indicates the possibility and need for "being influenced by suggestion or psycho-analysis" (3n)—that is, cured—without questioning the social pressures that might produce such loathing. While Freud might share some good will about queer sexuality with Ford and Tyler, then, his vision is restricted by the etiological and normalizing aspects of his psychoanalytic project. For further information about Freud and myth, see Bell's cogent analysis of Freud's mythopoeic retelling of Oedipus in *Literature*, 17.

47. Herd, 63. Ford seems all too aware of the risks of attempting to create myths consciously: In his diary, he criticizes Genet for this very habit. See Ford, *Water From a Bucket: A Diary 1948–1957* (New York: Turtle Point Press, 2001), 61.

48. Boone notes that the Doll's House was a "gay speakeasy" in modernist New York (256), but the text's references to the Doll's House are also biographically derived: As Ford records in his diary, the "Doll House" was, in his youth, "originally a kind of playhouse built for children" but in which Ford and his friend Tim would have sex (5–6). The novel's Doll House is a folkloric reference to a gay bar, then, and a central symbol in Ford's sexual

biography, a heteronormative toy that he and his friend refashioned for the purposes of queer pleasure.

49. Tyler later made this necessity to refashion classical myths central to *The Granite Butterfly*: "The 'realistic' narratives involved in this poem become *original* mythopoeic thought automatically using classic-myth labels as easy indices . . . (imaginative card-index system?)" (74). Tyler reiterates this thought in a letter to Robert Graves, describing the poem as "a personal revival of myth, not in order to reinforce the Classical form of the Medusa and Oedipus legends" but "to convert them to my own uses because I identified certain dominant experiences in my life with these two Classical figures, and yet, so doing, to revaluate the poetic, or basic, meaning of those figures" (136). See Barnes's *Nightwood*, ed. Cheryl J. Plumb (Normal, Ill.: Dalkey Archive Press, 1995) for further examination of the relationship between queerness and the figure of the doll (118, 123) and, incidentally, Little Red Riding Hood (69).

50. Bell, *Literature*, 69.

51. Bell, *Primitivism* (London: Methuen, 1972), 47.

52. Bell, *Literature*, 87.

53. See Manton, 15. In his *Modernisms* (Berkeley: University of California Press, 1995), Peter Nicholls describes *Ulysses'* "major narrative form [as being] taken from Homer's *Odyssey* and supplemented by a wealth of internal correspondences and codes" (254), the kind of structure, I am arguing, on which *The Young and Evil* is based: Pre-established mythic frameworks are modified—and thus expanded into new myths—via coded language and narrative spatialization.

54. Nicholls, 251.

55. Eliot, "Tradition and the Individual Talent," in *Selected Prose*, 40.

56. Tyler to Pound, 29 January 1933, Pound Papers, box 53, folder 2399. In the novel, Karel delivers a political speech that conveys a similar sentiment. See *The Young and Evil*, 264–5.

57. Eliot, "*Ulysses*, Order, and Myth," 177–8.

58. Bell, *Literature*, 24.

59. Wyndham Lewis, *The Apes of God*, ed. Paul Edwards (Santa Barbara, Calif.: Black Sparrow Press, 1981), 253.

60. Nicholls, 262.

61. See Steven Watson, Introduction in Ford and Tyler's *The Young and Evil*, xxii–iii (my pagination).

62. Louis Aragon, *Paris Peasant*, trans. Simon Watson-Taylor (London: Picador, 1980), 101.

63. Watson, Introduction, ii.

64. Andre Breton, *Manifestos of Surrealism*, trans. Richard Seaver and Helen R. Lane (Ann Arbor: University of Michigan Press, 1972), 230. Again,

this fusion of unconscious and conscious literary techniques resembles Joyce's aesthetic in *Ulysses*. As Bell describes it, "Although the *techniques* are highly self-conscious, their *meaning* is not directly stated, and the potentially philosophical questions embodied in the successive narrative techniques remain precisely that, embodied, and are resistant to any systematic discursive account" (*Literature*, 69).

65. Nicholls, 284.

66. Breton, *Communicating Vessels*, trans. Mary Ann Caws and Geoffrey T. Harris (Lincoln: University of Nebraska Press, 1990), 287.

67. Nicholls, 289, emphasis mine. For further examination of the relationship between surrealism and myth, see Northrop Frye's *Reading the World: Selected Writings, 1935–1976*, ed. Robert D. Denham (New York: Peter Lang, 1990) and Herbert S. Gershman's "Surrealism: Myth and Reality" in *Myth and Symbol: Critical Approaches and Applications*, ed. Bernice Slote (Lincoln: University of Nebraska Press, 1963), 51–60.

68. Tyler describes his vision of evil in Nietzschean terms: To him, evil indicates "whoever rejects labels and methods and systems, even nominal rights and privileges, in order to uncompromisingly create its own individual good" (Watson, i). Coupled with Djuna Barnes's evaluation of the novel as rejecting conventional morality—"their unresolved acceptance of any happening is both evil and 'pure' in the sense that it is unconscious" (quoted in Watson, i)—Tyler's idea that evil denotes that which falls outside the realm of morality echoes the text's queer, or antinormative, aesthetic and metaphysic.

69. Manton, 12.

70. Quoted in Manton, 13. However, during the 1950s—the most popular decade for both mythopoeic and New Critical scholarship—many scholars dismissed the idea that historical context was relevant to mythic texts. See Lucente, 32.

71. Boone, 253.

72. Looby, 442–3.

73. Watson, iii.

74. See Highwater, 169.

75. Highwater, 170.

76. Chauncey, 283. For just a handful of modernist examples of such projects, see John Addington Symonds's sexological treatises *A Problem in Greek Ethics* (1883) and *A Problem in Modern Ethics* (1891); Edward Carpenter's anthology *Ioläus* (1908); and Blair Niles's *Strange Brother* (1931).

77. Love, 130; Chauncey, 284.

78. Chauncey, 283, 287.

79. Tyler to Pound, 12 February 1934, Pound Papers, box 53, folder 2400.

80. Nealon, 8. This discussion accords with Michael Pina's contention that "history has become the supreme myth of the modern age," though it deviates from Pina's pessimistic conclusion that this is in practice "the myth of no myth" ("The Archaic, Historical and Mythicized Dimensions of Aztlán," in *Aztlán: Essays on the Chicano Homeland*, ed. Rudolfo A. Anaya and Francisco A. Lomelí [Albuquerque: University of New Mexico Press, 1991], 44, 28). Ford and Tyler acknowledge that the secular belief in history as a discourse of truth constitutes a new source of mythopoeic thought in the twentieth century, and they accordingly practice historiography as mytho- poeia: They tell lies about history, especially about the transhistorical nature of sexuality, in order to create the grounds for new forms of belief.

81. Chauncey, 324–5. See James Levin's *The Gay Novel in America* (New York: Garland Publishing, 1991), esp. 36, for an analysis of how *The Young and Evil* diverges from gay novels in this period.

82. Boone remarks that, historically, the queer vision of *The Young and Evil* had little political or social efficacy. He singles out Karel's privileging of the individual spirit over the material masses and argues that it is indicative of "the failure of the sexually fluid alliances arising in interwar New York City" to create a coherent political vision such that queers "lacked any organized or conscious *sexual* politics beyond the politics of pleasure or the politics of art" (Boone, 265). This claim highlights the paradoxical nature of the queer community—that it is a group only insofar as it is fractured—and how mythology might best imagine that paradoxical construction in literature. Although Karel's stance may not function for a stable political group, it constitutes, if this novel's folklore is to be believed, the ground of a real historical group's founding mythology. For a mythic text like *The Young and Evil*, the focus is always, Boone says, "in the present-tense, lived experi- ence of daily world-making" (265); in that sense, the novel's myth succeeds every time it is read and worlds are thereby remade on a "daily," if not permanent, basis.

83. Tyler to Pound, 25 February 1933, Pound Papers, box 53, folder 2399.

84. In his much-contested *A Place at the Table* (New York: Simon & Schuster, 1994), Bruce Bawer writes that contemporary gays and lesbians must choose between little (ethnic) and big (universal) tables of cultural orientation, and he argues that they should choose the latter: "Certainly most homosexuals don't want to be relegated to that little table. We grew up at the big table: we're at home there. We want to stay there" (70). Unlike Bawer's assimilationist and dualistic position, Ford and Tyler's "invitation" suggests that the little table of American modernism was its big table: The two collapse into one simultaneously ethnic and universal vision of queer modernism.

American Failurism:
Hart Crane's *The Bridge* and
Kenneth Burke's Paradox of Purity

The Paradox of the Pure Long Poem

Since its publication in 1930, Hart Crane's most famous work, *The Bridge*, has so consistently been deemed a failure that any critical engagement with the long poem seems to necessitate consideration of what precisely its failures are. Most typically, the term "failure" has been applied in a generic sense, especially because Crane, working within a literary tradition which posits that the long poem should be a national epic, claimed in a 1923 letter to Gorham Munson that *The Bridge* would be "a mystical synthesis of 'America.' History and fact, location, etc., all have to be transfigured into abstract form that would almost function independently of its subject matter."[1] In his 1930 review of the poem, Yvor Winters established a critical precedent that Crane failed to meet this mythic benchmark: "the 'destiny' of a nation is hard to get at in the abstract," Winters claims, "since it is a vague generality [. . .] It reduces itself [. . .] to the most elementary and the least interesting aspects of the general landscape."[2] Three years later, Crane's friend Waldo Frank similarly contended that the "disadvantageous esthetic" of *The Bridge* is that "Crane's cosmos . . . has no Time:

and his person-sense is vacillant and evanescent."[3] The earliest reactions to Crane's poem as a failure thus ironically indicate that Crane universalized experience—made his "mystical synthesis"—so well that he particularized experience, or engaged "history and fact, location, etc.," not at all.[4]

With Derek Savage's 1944 evaluation of Crane, the critical trend shifted from calling *The Bridge* a failure in the most pejorative sense to deeming the poem a "failure—if a glorious one." To Savage, Crane's dense poetics are "glorious," but, echoing Winters and Frank, his themes fall short because the poem does not achieve "an integration of personality and society, of the inner and outer worlds."[5] Most famously, in 1952, R. P. Blackmur expanded upon Savage's precedent and contended that *The Bridge* evokes the "exciting splendor of a great failure,"[6] a notion that Edward Brunner explores in *Splendid Failure*, his remarkable 1985 historicist study of Crane.[7] While these critics still focus on the poem's failings, they, unlike Winters and Frank, pose the text's product as a paradox: *The Bridge* is not just a failure but a "glorious, splendid" one.

Unlike recent Crane criticism that would repudiate this discourse of failure as a dry well of scholarly inquiry, I suggest that the curious fusion of myth, splendor, and failure in the critical discourse about *The Bridge* still presents some of the most crucial questions that arise when we scrutinize the poem and its status as a modernist text. What, after all, does this oxymoronic construction of "splendid failure" actually mean? Are the words coterminous, or do they designate a part of Crane's work as splendid and another a failure? The paradoxical description also begs the question of what a successful long poem, a truly "mystical synthesis," would look like, particularly in modernism. For if, as Michael Bernstein posits, the modern long poem aims to create "the tale of the tribe"[8]—a phrase that Ezra Pound borrowed from Rudyard Kipling to describe his own long poem, *The Cantos* (1970)—one of the first questions that any writer of the long poem must ask him or herself is how an epic tale can represent successfully a tribe, or group, especially a national group. The poet's answer to this question depends, of course, upon his or her sense of what constitutes that national tribe: If the poet views the nation as a failed union, could a long poem actually succeed because it embodies such failure?

Reinvigorating the discourse of failure about *The Bridge* from a literary historical standpoint, I contend that, like most writers of the modern long poem, Hart Crane acknowledged the problem of—and, for him, the impossibility of—creating a representative tale of the American tribe. Unlike other writers, however, Crane harnessed the long poem's generic incapacity to universalize experience as his poem's central structural and thematic principle. Where scholars like Christopher Nealon are quick to distinguish what "are the failures, and not the foundations, of the poem,"[9] then, I argue that the poem's generic "failures" are themselves the "foundations" upon which it succeeds—succeeds, that is, according to Crane's particular strain of American modernism, one that views failure as a mode of relation between the particular and the universal. Crane shared this view of failure with his friend Kenneth Burke; in fact, the two men were part of a group of writers that, in 1928, Gorham Munson deemed "The Younger Generation," a set that also included Waldo Frank, E. E. Cummings, Jean Toomer, Malcolm Cowley, and Munson himself.[10] As members of this vital if overlooked set of American modernists, Crane and Burke came to understand America as a failed unity and to appreciate such failure as a kind of ideal. Contrary to the critical tide around his poem, then, Crane's engagement in *The Bridge* with this failurist relationship between the particular and the universal—a relationship that Burke would later call "the paradox of purity"—reveals a strain of modernism that claims the failure of unity as an aesthetic and philosophical ambition for modern American literature.

Many evaluations of modernist literature begin with Theodor Adorno who, in *Prisms* (1981), argues that a dialectic model is a necessary foundation for any successful twentieth-century work of art. In Adorno's view, "A successful work [. . .] is not one which resolves objective contradictions in a spurious harmony, but one which expresses the idea of harmony negatively by embodying the contradictions, pure and uncompromised, in its innermost structure."[11] As helpful as Adorno's proposition has been to modern scholarship, Burke's conception of the relationship between the particular and the universal, or Adorno's "contradiction" and "harmony," actually anticipates Adorno's dialectic model and provides a historically useful tool with which to understand the logic of Crane's long poem in a specifically modernist context. Deemed "the paradox of purity," Burke's theory, established in 1945's *A Grammar of Motives*, holds that

> paradox may be implicit in any term for a *collective* motivation, such as a concept of class, nation, the 'general will,' and the like. Technically, it becomes a 'pure' motive when matched against some individual locus of motivation. And it may thus be the *negation* of an individual motive. Yet despite this position as dialectical antithesis of the individual motive, the collective motive may be treated as the source or principle from which the individual motive is familially or 'substantially' derived in a 'like begets like' manner.[12]

In the Burkean model, one cannot replace the "individual" with the "collective," or the "human" with the "cosmic" (the terms with which Waldo Frank describes Crane's philosophic poles ["Foreword" xiv]),[13] without effacing the individual. To make such a replacement does not solve the problem of the individual's imperfection: It simply negates, or fails, it into the absence of particulars—into the "pure" collective One. Paradoxically, however, the individual depends upon the collective for its existence, as the latter is the utopian paradigm of the former: The collective is the model from which the individual derives and to which it aspires.

Alongside Adorno's model of unharmonious literature, Burke's paradox of purity seems like a response to the problem posed by the "tale of the tribe" theory of the long poem. Where the latter posits collective unity as possible, the former acknowledges it as impossible and even ethically and aesthetically unacceptable. For Burke, the collective ideal is both the source and the failure of the real; reality is the failure of the ideal insofar as it is imperfect; and, therefore, both the real and the ideal must fail for either one to exist. In his "General Aims and Theories," Crane echoes this line of thought when he posits that the poet "must, of course, have a sufficiently universal basis of experience to make his imagination selective and valuable. His picture of the 'period,' then, will simply be a by-product of his curiosity and the relation of his experience to a postulated eternity."[14] Here Crane seems to be working backward, regressing from the transcendental to the material world to comprehend the transcendental. As Burke notes, however, the universal negates "selective" experience: Once one has witnessed the universal, the world ceases to be particular. Prior knowledge of the universal, as Crane seems to want, then precludes the need to experience the particular.

For decades, scholars have drawn upon Crane's apparent contradiction in this essay as evidence of the poet's failure to understand his own poetics, a failure that they then ascribe to *The Bridge* as a whole. By the terms of the paradox of purity, however, Crane is not only aware of his contradiction but employs it to complicate our notions of his "period" in a particularly modern, American way. After all, Crane only seeks a "sufficiently" universal basis of experience, a "postulated" eternity, which is neither universal nor eternal at all—it is sufficient, approximated, but not complete. Such incompleteness, or failure of the universal, is in fact what he says gives rise to the "selective and valuable [. . .] by-product" of experience. As a version of the paradox of purity, Crane's response to the absolutist problem of the modern long poem is to employ the quest for the universal as a means of undermining that quest, thus producing, in dialectic fashion, particulars that any final achievement of the universal would efface.[15]

For Crane, then, myth—one of the generic ambitions of the long poem—is not a poetic or philosophic end but a means to debunk absolutism as a solution for the problem of connection, of union, in the ephemeral material world. The "splendid" result of myth's failure in *The Bridge* is thus Crane's view that human connection cannot be conceived in either mythic (ideal, communal) or real (imperfect, individual) terms. It is rather best represented by a Burkean dialectic between these two poles in which the failure of one pole yields the possibility of the other.

Burke's model thus additionally reveals how, contrary to critical opinion, "splendid" and "failure" operate coterminously in *The Bridge*. Failure is not only a product of the poem but is, more important, a component of it in the way that Adorno describes. And while Burke's theory was published fifteen years after Crane's poem, Crane met Burke in 1923, the year that he began work on *The Bridge*. Because the two think quite similarly about the relationship between the particular and the universal, and because Crane claims that, while he had "sharp arguments with Burke" and other friends about *The Bridge*, he remained "very fond of Burke" and appreciated his input,[16] we may assume that the affinity between these men had important intellectual and artistic repercussions for both. The paradox of purity illuminates *The Bridge* and the failurist aesthetic of these American modernists, then, regardless of whether Crane consciously employed such a theory to write the poem.[17] Moreover, that Burke's theory coincides with Adorno's indicates how Crane and his generation already operate within a dominant definition of modern art. My aim in this essay is to unveil Crane and Burke's contribution to that definition as exemplified by Crane's failurist response to the problem of the modern American long poem, a response that might help us to distinguish this poet's strain of modernism especially because, as Nealon records, Crane is most often noted for his "unassimilability to literary-historical narration."[18]

As I will demonstrate in the next two sections, the paradox of purity operates most saliently in two rhetorical devices, catachresis and homographesis, which expose how, through failed linguistic and sexual unions, Crane creates connections with disconnection in *The Bridge* and so embodies the beauty, or success, of failure. Both devices and the poem's representations of desire exemplify how Crane's attempts to idealize human experience expose the limits of idealization, for, according to the paradox of purity, once ideal forms are established, impure forms multiply from them. Insofar as any long poem aims to create a myth, or an ideal representation of a community, we can see how such impurities are built into the epic project, as the word "myth" denotes both a cultural ideal and a half-truth. Crane embodies this generic paradox in various acts of "bridging," the poem's structural and textural connective principle and itself a manifestation of the paradox of purity: For a bridge may connect two things only insofar as their distance is maintained—and as one approaches either end of the bridge, one must get further away from (must fail in proximity to, recognition of) the other. Crane affirms this dialectic, the "antiphonal [. . .] swing"[19] between human and cosmic poles as his long poem's poetic and ethical goal.

Crane's historical position at the eve of American Romanticism and the dawn of modernism—which, as Thomas Yingling notes, is also the "historical threshold when homosexuality began to be articulated as an identity through Western cultures"[20]—indicates how the long poem's form offers an ideal mode for Crane to explore the paradox of purity in the realms of poetics and desire. As a queer writer attempting to write the tale of the tribe, Crane was confronted with poetic and sexual transition— instability—even as his project demanded that he stabilize those fluctuations. By integrating linguistic and sexual failure into his epic to demonstrate the modern long poem's inability to unify a fragmented world, Crane turns the long poem project against itself to produce particulars like, as Crane paradoxically called them, "moments in eternity"[21] and queer desire that, in the first case, contradicted the modern long poem's universalizing aims and, in the second case, could not be named in modern discourse at large. Crane's subversion of the long poem project is thus a peculiar effort to affirm experience—to envision America's failure to create a national unity as the successful production of a multiplicity of ephemerally divine particulars.[22]

The Paradox of Pure Language

As suggested by *Transmemberment of Song* (1987), Lee Edelman's excellent study of Crane's catachrestic rhetoric, Crane's poetics exemplify how the paradox of purity undergirds *The Bridge*. In Edelman's view, "Crane's poetry [articulates] what could be identified as an ideology of catachresis,"[23] a title under which he groups anacoluthon, chiasmus, and catachresis: a collection of rhetorical devices (to which I add puns) that disrupt rather than establish semantic connection. With this framework, Edelman argues that, through an "ideology of catachresis,"

> Crane's poetry self-consciously undertakes to subvert the apparently literal or referential aspects of its language so as to gesture toward the disjunction between language and its referent and thus toward the productive primacy of rhetoric itself—that is, toward the primacy of rhetoric and its structures over the psychological or thematic content that those structures necessarily produce.[24]

Here Edelman encapsulates how Crane's disruption, or failure, of linguistic connection actually produces meaning beyond what words normatively convey. Helpful though these claims are, however, Edelman unnecessarily devalues the literal in this formulation and attributes "productive primacy" to disruptive rhetoric and its structures. Opposed to this devaluation, I suggest that productive primacy for Crane resides in the process, or dialectic, of signification, for signs and their referents must first be read literally (or absolutely) in order for them to fail. As signs meant to communicate meaning, words rely upon the perception that they exist in one-to-one, or absolute, correlation with their referents. When Crane bridges words together in ways that defy absolute meaning, he simultaneously relies upon our presumption that absolute meaning will exist: As Burke's paradox of purity would have it, the presumption must preclude in order to produce the failure. Crane must therefore work within normative linguistic structures in order to disrupt them: To do otherwise, to write only from the site of disruption, would be to negate meaning altogether rather than to multiply it.[25] In this way, Crane's use of failure in his dialectic produces polysemy, which undercuts ambitions toward all hierarchical meaning, including Edelman's primacy of rhetoric, as dialectic is by definition the failure of hierarchy. For Crane, then, rhetoric is not a poetic end unto itself: It is a necessary means to the end of signification's failure, where "end" in this phrase signifies both the goal of making absolute signification fail and the cessation of total referential failure, the failure that Edelman and like-minded queer critics would seem to value.[26]

Examination of nearly any portion of *The Bridge* reveals Crane's engagement with the paradox of purity on this linguistic and its corollary thematic levels.[27] As Crane did in his compositional process, we may profitably start with the poem's final section, "Atlantis." If we recall Crane's February 1923 letter to Munson, we may expect to find traces of the poet's search for a synthesis, or mythic unity, in this section of the poem, as it was the piece, then titled "Finale," that prompted the letter. In the poem's published incarnation, however, we find not mythic unity but the paradox of purity in action. Consider stanza six:

> From gulfs unfolding, terrible of drums,
> Tall Vision-of-the-Voyage, tensely spare—
> Bridge, lifting night to cycloramic crest
> Of deepest day—O Choir, translating time
> Into what multitudinous Verb the suns
> And synergy of waters ever fuse, recast
> In myriad syllables,—Psalm of Cathay!
> O Love, thy white, pervasive Paradigm . . . ! (56–7)

Coming "from gulfs unfolding," the bridge's song (with both the bridge and Crane as choristers) misnames from the stanza's opening line. Initially, "gulfs" seems to denote the literal gulf across which the Brooklyn Bridge unfolds, but the catachrestic attribution of motion to a static object (whether the gulf or the bridge—the syntax implies both) explodes this literal reading, for the gulf may also be an abyss, the absence of a literal referent, or a gap in meaning. A gulf, in this sense, is literality's failure, and it is from this failure that the bridge's song unfolds. As the bridge catachrestically "lifts" night to the crest (echoing the Proem's "terrific threshold" [4]) of deepest day, again the static object moves, now to fold time in on itself rather than to bridge space. Space is here conflated with time, in fact, as the day is measured in spatial terms.

The effect of such misnaming is, per the paradox of purity, to presume myth only to negate it—to produce not synthesis but "synergy," fusion where the sum is more than its parts. When, for instance, "time" becomes a "Verb" (a proper, or absolute, noun), Crane posits an absolute to produce not universals but infinite particulars, for the Verb is "multitudinous," a dispersal that the paradoxically "fuse[d]" waters "recast/In myriad syllables." The catachrestic notion of an absolute verb demands such fragmentation, for verbs imply motion, not the stasis of nominalized eternity. Similarly, by describing his song as the "Psalm of Cathay"—a reference to "Ave Maria," the section of *The Bridge* that relates Columbus's voyage to discover Cathay—Crane ascribes to his bridging project the history of misnaming upon which America was founded, as Columbus believed that he had landed in Cathay, not North America. Titling his final poem after a similarly mythical land, Atlantis, Crane carries on the American, Whitmanian tradition of seeking one thing only to find something else, for Cathay and Atlantis symbolize the failure of names—words—to concretize reality in absolute terms. Their failure to do so makes them fecund myths—myths, which misnamed, continue to misname, and thereby continue to produce unexpected meaning, what Nealon calls "the unfulfilled aspects of the name."[28] So long as he invokes the absolute—that "white," or pure, "pervasive Paradigm"—Crane can produce such otherwise unexpected particulars.[29]

This stanza's "multitudinous Verb" recalls the goal that Crane establishes in his "General Aims and Theories" to produce with his poetry "a single, new *word*, never before spoken and impossible to actually enunciate." Rather than attempt to idealize words' meanings, Crane admits that this new word will be "an active principle in the reader's consciousness henceforward."[30] Consistent with Burke's formation, Crane knows that the apparent singularity of his "single, new *word*" will give rise to its active, or fluctuating, nature in the reader's consciousness. What Crane hopes is that by positing words as absolute he will disrupt their singularity, make them active, and that the reader will henceforward approach words in this new, de-idealized way. It is for this reason that after *The Bridge* was published, Crane called the poem "a diagram or 'process'"—not an affirmation of the absolute but "an affirmation of experience."[31]

Accordingly, in the same letter, Crane famously distinguishes his poem from Eliot's 1922 long poem, *The Waste Land*, which, for Crane, is not a positive but a negative depiction of experience. The final stanza of "Atlantis"—and, thus, the reader's final impression of *The Bridge* as a whole—encapsulates this procedural affirmation of experience through myth's misnaming:

> So to thine Everpresence, beyond time,
> Like spears ensanguined of one tolling star
> That bleeds infinity—the orphic strings,
> Sidereal phalanxes, leap and converge:
> —One Song, one Bridge of Fire! Is it Cathay,
> Now pity steeps the grass and rainbows ring
> The serpent with the eagle in the leaves . . . ?
> Whispers antiphonal in azure swing. (58)

Characteristically, the stanza opens with absolutism: "Everpresence, beyond time" and "one tolling star" extend into "One Song, one Bridge of Fire!" as the bridge's towers and strings catachrestically "leap and converge." Just as the waters that fuse in stanza six, however, this convergence is not synthetic but synergistic, for the ostensibly unnatural fusion produces the real: grass, serpent, eagle, leaves. The word "sidereal" itself manifests this synergistic process, for it denotes something starlike, but its catachrestic modification of "phalanxes," the bridge's towers, fractures this literal reading and connotes (indeed, bridges) two words that derive from sidereal: "consider" and "desire," the former etymologically a turning toward the stars, the latter a turn away from the stars for something else. Stripped of their literal meaning, the bridge's sidereal phalanxes thus embody the very process of failure upon which *The Bridge* is built: the dialectic of turning toward and away from the absolute.[32]

The figure of the serpent and the eagle, a trope common to both Shelley and Nietzsche, is also a symbol of this dialectic and indicates how Crane bridges two dominant Romantic and modern poetic theories. Like the universal and the particular or the Romantic and the modern, the serpent and eagle are conventional enemies; their fusion is always concomitant with the threat of violence or fracture. But where the modern Nietzsche, for instance, uses the trope to laud the real over the absolute, and where the Romantic Shelley uses it to invoke the eternal, Crane undercuts both positions with his final line, demanding procedural vacillation between the two poles rather than a stable hierarchy between them.[33] When "whispers" catachrestically "swing" through poem's end—as hints (whispers) of the absolute (Cathay) swing between antiphonal poles of the cosmic and human—Crane claims the paradox of purity as his poetic bridge, for the final line opens the poem to interpretation rather than Romantically closes or modernly dissolves it.

Finally, recalling Nietzsche's notion of destructive creation, this stanza's violent imagery—"spears," "bleeds," "phalanxes," posited as absolute ("thine Everpresence")—violates the ideal in order to produce the real: "one tolling star / That bleeds infinity." Where the poet seeking transcendence would attempt union with the single star, the One, Crane uses his ostensibly eternal bridge to pierce the absolute and therefore multiply the real infinitely: Destruction, or failure, is used for creation. Crane in fact called his new *word* "a kind of word-grenade," suggesting how his theory of language presumed violence, a kind of failure of unity, as a necessity for polysemy.[34] If his goal in *The Bridge* is to "splinter[ ]space" (35), where space implies an absolute limitlessness, Crane does so with the shrapnel of his word-grenades.

Importantly, as aforementioned, Crane views fragmentation, or disconnection, as transcendent—a catachrestic idea of its own kept in constant oscillation rather than in hierarchical stability throughout the text. This idea is introduced in the visionary "Proem," *The Bridge*'s first section, which, when considered with "Atlantis," structurally bookends the long poem, for they are the piece's most visionary sections. At the end of the "Proem," Crane implores the bridge to "Unto us lowliest sometime sweep, descend / And of the curveship lend a myth to God" (4). The bridge, progenitor of myth, is asked here to "lend" (which, rather than "give," implies myth's provisionality) a myth to God; but as the previous line's syntax demands, this God is not a higher being but "us," humanity. Myth is thus deracinated from its presumed divinity and scattered "unto us." But because this naming is also misnaming—it creates, after all, a broken myth—we, like Crane by writing *The Bridge*, must become myth's progenitor by lending myth back to the bridge, and so on in dialectic fashion. This dialectic is, of course, reiterated at the poem's end in the "antiphonal . . . swing" (58) of "Atlantis."

On a textual level, then, Crane's ostensibly most visionary sections of *The Bridge* are actually visions of the paradox of purity. And that Crane wrote *The Bridge*'s final section in 1923 before any other section and then revised it in 1926 when the rest of the poem was near completion suggests how the paradox of purity also informed his poem as an active, structural principle throughout the composition process. For, if we regard the 1923 "Finale" as Crane's synthetic, mythic vision, as Edward Brunner insightfully reads it,[35] the missing part of the poem—the bridge to what would be "Atlantis"—represents the human material that the final visionary poem effaced from the beginning. In point of fact, Crane all but stopped working on the poem for nearly three years, suggesting that his "Finale" vision had depleted his epic resources.[36] Realizing that his long poem could not be composed only of vision, Crane produced the remaining parts of *The Bridge* in the summer of 1926 precisely because his 1923 myth of "Finale" negated them. The poet reveals as much in a letter to Waldo Frank in June 1926 when he confesses that "the validity of a work of art is situated in contemporary reality to the extent that the artist must honestly anticipate the realization of his vision in 'action.'"[37] In dialectic fashion, once these "action" sections were near completion, Crane revised his mythic "Finale" to reflect more fully the representations of material experience that would now precede it. After these portions were written, Crane produced "Cape Hatteras," wherein Edelman contends "'darkness' or demystified knowledge" predominates.[38] Written with longer lines than the rest of the sequence and ending in a homoerotic embrace, this section is also Crane's most explicit nod to Walt Whitman, Crane's forerunner in homoerotic verse. If "Cape Hatteras" then represents Crane's descent back into the "demystified" real after revising his myth, we can see how the paradox of purity informed Crane's compositional process: Myth's failure produced the real, which then revised myth, which then reproduced the real.

On a similar structural level, the section divisions of the long poem disrupt its "tribal" ends for, as many critics have noted (most disparagingly),

The Bridge is basically a sequence of lyric poems. Winters, for instance, contends that *The Bridge*'s "structure [. . .] is lyrical; but the poem is not a single lyric, it is rather a collection of lyrics on themes more or less related and loosely following out of each other."[39] Blackmur concurs with Winters, arguing that Crane "used the private lyric to write the cultural epic; used the mode of intensive contemplation, which secures ends, to present the mind's actions, which have no ends. The confusion of tool and purpose not only led him astray in conceiving his themes; it obscured at crucial moments the exact character of the work he was actually doing."[40] To Winters and Blackmur, Crane's epic poem is undone by its lyrical qualities: A mythic end is sought by a lyrical mind that cannot secure ends. On the contrary, however, by combining lyric and epic, subjective and objective modes in his poem, Crane reveals how each genre informs (by structurally failing, or clashing with) the other: The structural conflict illuminates, not obscures, his work in *The Bridge*.

On both textual and structural levels, then, Crane's pure misnaming is foundational to his long poem's revolutionary poetic project. His successful use of failed tropes transfigures our exclusive notions of essentialist and constructionist views of language. As Edelman would have it, Crane's polysemous language is idiosyncratically modern, an example of "a modernity that can claim priority over the literature of the past to the extent that it can find its power, and even its pathos, in the undoing of the metaphysical illusions of a transparent literary language."[41] While this undoing itself is not so unusual within modern poetics (Stein and Cummings certainly undo stable signification), Crane's verse is distinctive—perhaps more than Edelman realizes—in that it privileges neither transparent nor opaque language, language from the past or the present: It oscillates between, borrows from, bridges the two.

The Paradox of Pure Sexuality

In addition to this broader poetic project, Crane's catachrestic poetics inform his long poem's personal project on cultural/thematic levels as well. Though he does not examine the subject, Edelman suggests as much when he argues that "there can be no doubt that Crane's catachrestic ideology was deeply informed by his sexuality, and that one of the things it aspired to do was to find a language whereby Crane might articulate a desire for which no 'proper' language existed."[42] If metaphor has an "apparently 'natural' quality" of joining things in "an innocent error of language, a justified deviation," after all, catachresis "has the air of something dangerous and disreputable."[43] For Crane, in other words, the failure of linguistic union is analogous to the failure of sexual union, making his broken language assume specifically referential and political significance. Especially for homosexuality, still the love that dare not speak its name in the 1920s, and for unfulfilled, broken erotic unions of any kind, catachresis opens space for poetic expression of unidealized, "disreputable" desire, or desire that the myth of heterosexual union would efface into namelessness. Where Crane at once seems to laud this latter myth by naming it, he simultaneously fragments it into the former.

While he does not use it in application to Crane, Edelman proposes the concept of "homographesis" in his second eponymously titled book (1994), and it is a concept that illuminates the paradox of pure sexuality that we see operating in *The Bridge*. As Edelman defines it, homographesis is the "inscription of 'the homosexual' within a tropology that produces him in a determining relation to inscription itself,"[44] where this "tropology" is represented by homographs, or words that read the same graphically but different semantically. Insofar as they "articulate identity only in relation to signs that are structured, as Derrida puts it, by their 'non-self-identity,'" written representations of sexuality are, for Edelman, homographs, for they seem to constitute sexuality categorically "to name a condition that must be represented as determinate, as legibly identifiable, precisely insofar as it threatens to undo the determinacy of identity itself; it must be metaphorized as an essential condition, a sexual orientation, in order to contain the disturbance it effects as a force of dis-orientation."[45] That is, per the paradox of purity, writing that attempts to essentialize sexuality in an identity formation in fact fractures that formation; rather than hierarchize sexuality into value-loaded, essentialized categories, homographesis levels sexual experience, de-essentializes it even as it seems to make sexuality pure. Most accurately, then, the homograph operates queerly, for its central effect is to destabilize normative sexuality, whether hetero- or homo-.

Edelman's homograph illuminates how Crane enscripts, denies, and broadens representations of hetero- and homosexuality with his catachrestic language; as with his catachresis hypothesis, however, to be useful for Crane's work, Edelman's trope must be evaluated in light of the paradox of purity. For the goal of Crane's language is not simply to disrupt or to deny the essential: *The Bridge* is, again, a poem about bridging, not about arrival at the destinations of unity or fragmentation.[46] To Crane, the space of sexual contradiction is where queer sexual experience and, for that matter, any sexual experience resides: It is the space where failure is success, where the failed attempt at union is tantamount to union, for the latter annihilates the attempt, the real, and therefore multiplies it beyond its originally intended absolute signification. In fact, Edelman's reliance upon what he calls "the logic of metaphor"[47] as an essentializing rhetorical device—the anti-homograph—recalls Crane's own "logic of metaphor," which he proposes in his "General Aims and Theories" as "the genetic basis of all speech," one "which antedates our so-called pure logic."[48] Essentialized as "genetic," this logic of metaphor cannot help but break, as we have seen it do in *The Bridge*, into the logic of catachresis, or the illogic of metaphor. This illogic is thus homographic: It names the unnamable by, paradoxically, seeming not to name it all. Crane's poetics are, in this sense, culturally heterodox, for in writing the homograph, the poet resists heterosexist demands to make homosexuality a visible, discrete, essentialized identity category which, as Edelman posits, may "call into being a variety of disciplinary 'knowledges' through which homosexuality might be recognized, exposed, and ultimately rendered, more ominously, invisible once more."[49] Crane's homograph is a reaction against the heterosexist myth of essentialized sexual identity (if not experience), the myth that would silence "homosexuality" by demanding that it speak.[50]

If, as Thomas Yingling contends, early twentieth-century American heteronormativity "made homosexuality an inadmissible center from which to write about American life,"[51] it follows that the most explicit representations of sexual desire in *The Bridge* seem to be within heterosexual dyads. In "The Dance," for instance, the virginal Pocahontas is Crane's most obvious figure of female sexuality, but any sexual union with her is from the start problematized by her depiction as "virginal." Perhaps because of this "pure" status, Pocahontas is also posed as a figure of destructive creation: "She spouted arms; she rose with maize—to die." Here Pocahontas is allegorized as the American landscape, whose "mythical brows" the poem's speaker (who speaks for both himself and America as a whole) then "saw retiring—loth,/Disturbed and destined, into denser green." Figure of her own chastity and of America's topographical virginity, Pocahontas reluctantly but ineluctably "retires" her virginal myth into failure, violation. As she does so, the speaker observes that this myth's violation proves fecund for insight into the temporal world, that "denser green," where the speaker observes that "there was a veil upon you, Pocahontas, bride—/ O Princess whose brown lap was virgin May" (19). Recording how Pocahontas is being transported under a veil to Maquokeeta, her partner in heterosexual union, the speaker suggests that Pocahontas is under the illusion that her virginity, the myth of both land and woman that all are "loth" to see retire, will not suffer the violation that it does later in the poem. Of course, it is because of this enforced blindness—this mythic effacement of reality—that the later violence must occur.

Accompanying Pocahontas on a voyage down the river to Maquokeeta's dance, the speaker is confronted with images of fleeting revelation, of eternity dissolving into particulars: He "learned to catch the trout's moon whisper" but then "saw that fleet young crescent die;" he saw "one star, swinging, take its place, alone" which then "bled into the dawn." For all his moments of ascension ("I gained the ledge"), the speaker simultaneously drops back into the world ("[I] knew myself within some boding shade" [20]). These cycles of ascent to the eternal and descent to the particular portend the resulting climactic dance of all three figures' union and fragmentation. Initiated by the concurrently violent and sexual image of "a distant cloud" that "Siphoned the black pool from the heart's hot root," this dance, a flurry of "fingers," "hair," "fangs," and "tongues" that "thinly busy the blue air," is at once as sexual as it is violent (20). Indeed, Maquokeeta dances only to "know death's best" as "Pocahontas grieves" his (but not only his) incipient violation. As it is the effort of the "Medicine-man" to manifest the "snake that lives before, / That casts his pelt, and lives beyond," the dance is, like *The Bridge* itself, the attempt to realize myth with the prior knowledge that such effort must eradicate the particular, here literally Maquokeeta's life.

As Crane wrote that he was depicting "the conflict between the two races in this dance,"[52] Maquokeeta's death is at once his death at the hands of America's conquerors and the death of his religious myth via Christian colonization. And, at first, the apocalyptic imagery used to describe his sacrifice—"Flame cataracts of heaven in seething swarms / Fed down your anklets to the sunset's moat" (22)—ostensibly brings union to the sexual/ cultural ritual, as the particular violently melts into the universal. The dance also becomes the speaker's ritual, however, as he claims "I, too, was liege" to myth. Maquokeeta's death is thus a sacrifice that yields further particularization and further failure of myth, for the speaker's dance is the dance of the American conqueror, as he "surpassed the circumstance, danced out the siege!" (21). "Circumstance," Maquokeeta, is overcome (or violently "surpassed") for the mythically proportioned "siege" of Native American land.

Through these cycles of failure, "The Dance" becomes the violation of Maquokeeta's ritual *and* Pocahontas's virginity, for the speaker's own brutal violation in stanza seventeen produces the "escorts" who "Flickering, sprint up the hill groins like a tide" (21). Where the land is both America and Pocahontas, and where, as the land, her "smile" was once "steep, inaccessible" (20), the dance yields the violation of Pocahontas's myth (her virginity) and produces the particular (the land that she becomes). As the then "bride immortal in the maize!," "virgin to the last of men . . ." (22), Pocahontas is reendowed through violation with the purity of myth; as the ellipsis anticipates, however, she is made pure only that she may be violated cyclically. Pocahontas and Maquokeeta's union is therefore not union at all—the sexual charge of the dance leads to union's violation. Heterosexuality in the poem is thus the homographic embodiment of the paradox of purity: It is the failure, not the affirmation, of heteronormativity.

This failure is not only heteroerotic, however: As we have already begun to see, Maquokeeta and Pocahontas's violent union and resulting disconnection homographically allows the speaker to manifest failed homoerotic union. For, when he "screamed from the stake;/I could not pick the arrows from my side" (21), the speaker reenacts his own violent and sexual union with the phallic burning stake and penetrating arrows in a kind of imitation of the queer icon St. Sebastian. The colonially identified speaker, the mythic conqueror, is now himself sacrificed to produce the particular: As the failed heteroerotic union did, the speaker's failed homoerotic union produces images of more violent sexuality in the escorts who violate Pocahontas-America's groin-hills, a violation that perpetuates violation for the purposes of experiential fecundity. In fact, bearing in mind the poem's epigraph—

> Then you shall see her truly—your blood remembering its first
> invasion of her secrecy, its first encounters with her kin, her chieftain
> lover . . . his shade that haunts the lakes and hills (19)

—we see how, from the beginning of "The Dance," heterosexual rape (Pocahontas's) is simultaneously and homographically homosexual rape, Maquokeeta's and the speaker's. As the descendants of Columbus allegorically "invade" Pocahontas by way of land, they also sexually "encounter" Maquokeeta, who functions synecdochically for the male Native Americans slain in the conquest and population of America. Through Pocahontas-America, the agents of heterosexual violation become the agents of homosexual violation. The homographic failure of the former gives rise to the latter.[53]

The allegorical dynamic here, as throughout "The Dance," is between failed sexual union and failed cultural Union: With its history of misnaming, cultural genocide, and heterosexism, Crane's mythic America fails cultural Others, and it is the poet's task to redeem this failure as the potential source of experiential "affirmation" for those others. In his first reaction to Waldo Frank's *Our America* (1919), Crane, in fact, reveals his disdain for nationalistic, or mythic, visions of America: "This extreme national consciousness bothers me [. . .] so thoroughly logical or propagandistic."[54] For Crane, America fortunately failed as a myth—"fortunately" because that myth may now successfully produce non-normative experience. As "The Dance" ends with the image of "The serpent with the eagle in the boughs," we are reminded as we are later in "Atlantis" of the fecundity of violent union for Crane—a fecundity surely troubling in a postcolonial context but, for this modernist, one way of thinking through his era on behalf of the culturally heterodox (23).

In contrast to this reading, Brunner interprets "The Dance" as Crane's paean to Native American culture, in which "the masculine and the feminine are absolutely dependent upon one another. When the two interact, there is harmony; if the two are kept apart, the result is disarray and confusion." Brunner then reads the final image of the "serpent and the eagle in the boughs" as confirmation of "the perfect union of man and woman, a union that guides passivity and calms violence."[55] As we have seen, however, the poem indicates just the opposite: Evidenced by Pocahontas's remaining mythically virginal even past her rape, a virginity that invites rather than "calms violence," the goal of absolute "harmony" produces, for Crane, "disarray and confusion" precisely because readers such as Brunner think such harmony is a goal that, like the poem, is "so simple [. . .] that its point has been easy to overlook," a point which inheres in that "perfect union of man and woman." Viewing this heterosexual "point" as "a lasting truth in an essentialized form, something elemental, undeniable," Brunner offers the kind of heterosexist reading that Crane's homographic poetry disrupts.[56]

"Three Songs" offers a similarly ostensible focus on the myth of heterosexual union, and the sequence parallels "The Dance" for its portrayal of that myth's failure by way of violence. Brunner encapsulates this failure when he argues that in all three songs "the contortions people create for themselves are efforts to avoid pain which only create additional pain."[57] The sequence's first lyric, "Southern Cross," offers the most salient example of this procedural failure and fecundity. There, the speaker initially claims that his object of desire is "nameless," but eight lines later he names her "Eve! Magdalene! / or Mary, you?" and later "simian Venus" (40). As he admits to naming the unnamable, the speaker knows his naming is catachrestic. The figures of Eve, Mary Magdalene, Mary (either Magdalene or the Mother of God), and Venus (both human, "simian," and goddess) evoke the multifarious results of this misnaming: They are at once the fallen and the saved, the lover and the celibate, the woman and the goddess.

Because of these contradictions—the failure to identify his object of desire—the speaker's "call—falls vainly on the wave" (40). "Mary" may then be the most apposite name for this figure because, to the speaker, *all* desire washes out with the sea, *mer, mere, mar*, Mary.[58] When the speaker then exclaims that this dispersion gives him "answer all within one grave!" (40), he admits to desire's failure, its grave—but because of that failure he also rejoices at the only moment when his desire is fulfilled, or answered. This figure's failure to reciprocate desire except from the grave also gives rise to "the lithic trillions of your spawn" (41). Recalling Aphrodite's birth from Uranus's castrated genitals and her conveyance to shore by "lithic" shell, this "unnatural" spawning of humanity saves those trillions from drowning in the sea but imbues them with the legacy of failed desire—the same failure, of course, upon which America was founded. And, as in "The Dance," Uranus's castration by his son Cronos again reveals how homoerotic contact—contact that always involves failure, here violence—exists homographically one layer through (not hierarchically beneath or above) the failure of heterosexual union, the most obvious (but not most important) subject of "Southern Cross."

Sexuality in *The Bridge* is not only violent, however; it is also ephemeral, denoting the failure of union's permanence. Occurring most often between men, like the homoerotic contact in "The Dance" and "Southern Cross," this desire produces only brief encounters, the fleeting glances of queer union. In "The Harbor Dawn," for instance, sexual union is poised on the threshold between waking and dreaming—it is the ideal of "*my tongue upon your throat—singing/arms close; eyes wide, undoubtful*" sought "before day claims our eyes" (10). As ephemeral as day and night, sexual union, a dream of "undoubt," fragments into "a tide of voices," "signals dispersed in veils" that "meet you listening midway in your dream" (9). As Pocahontas's veil symbolizes virginity and its concurrent violation, so too do these voices invoke and violate myth: For "if they take your sleep away sometimes/They give it back again" in dialectic fashion (9).

Importantly, as in "The Dance," the city surrounding the harbor is sexually allegorized; unlike "The Dance," however, Manhattan is allegorically masculine with its phallic "Cyclopean towers" (10). These catachrestic projections of the speaker's desire onto the city, cloaked as that desire is in the fog of his sexual dream, thus homographically disrupt the bracketed lines that "whisper antiphonally" throughout the section.[59] As a sequence, these lines together read "400 years and more . . . or is it from the soundless shore/of sleep that time/recalls you to your love, there in a waking dream to merge your seed/with whom? Who is the woman with us in the dawn? . . . whose is the/flesh our feet have moved upon?" (9–10). Interspersed throughout the speaker's erotic "waking dream," these lines read both hetero- and homoerotically, an ambivalence indicated by the speaker's uncertain question "with whom?," which conveys both anonymous and uncertainly gendered sex. This uncertainty undercuts (but does not wholly negate) the apparent heteroeroticism of the speaker waking with a woman at dawn; yet, with the feet moving upon flesh in the following line, a sexualized (and somewhat violent) contact with the "flesh" of masculine Manhattan, this woman is homographically polysemized as the possible negation of a homoerotic dream. As in "Southern Cross," this woman could be lover or anti-lover: Hers could be the ovum with which the speaker's seed merges, or she could metonymize heteronormative reality, the force which disrupts the speaker's homoerotic vision where seed merges with seed. Both possibilities are produced by Crane's effacement of identifiable particulars from this erotic vision.

"Cutty Sark," too, features a homoerotic waking dream in the form of a brief encounter with a sailor. After the opening epigraph from Melville, Crane's predecessor in homoerotic maritime literature, the speaker recollects when

I met a man in South Street, tall—
a nervous shark tooth swung on his chain.
His eyes pressed through green glass
—green glasses, or bar lights made them
so—
    shine—
        GREEN—
                eyes—
stepped out—forgot to look at you
or left you several blocks away—(27)

Remarking that the sailor is "tall" and that his nervousness is displaced onto his pendulous, phallic "shark tooth [. . .] chain," the speaker sexually sizes up the man in a brief encounter that climaxes with eye contact, emphasized by the slow, dashed build-up to the all-caps ejaculation "GREEN." As he does for Crane's shorter lyrics, John Vincent would likely call this sexual failure (ejaculation) "exhaustion," a trope through which he claims that Crane makes failure a valuable "place of its own, not simply an absence of life force or enthusiasm."[60] I would expand Vincent's claim, however, to suggest that sexual failure is not just entropic or fluidic release but, rather, one step in a cyclical motion of release and reconstitution. Instead of Vincent's figurative nonreproductive homoerotic orgasm, Crane's failure is more like a (catachrestically) reproductive homoerotic orgasm—a "little death" that breeds the possibility of more pleasures rather than just the pleasure of the single, final little death itself.

Evidence for this claim becomes clear when the sailor of "Cutty Sark" disappears from the speaker's view and the speaker's identity homographically fractures into "you," a replacement for the universal "one." As in "Harbor Dawn," sexual identity—its taxonomic essentiality—becomes uncertain, effaced; this is true for both the speaker and his object of desire, as the man is anonymous. This effacement is the kind of reproductive orgasm I suggested previously for, as we have seen, Crane strips names of absolute signification in order to multiply meaning. As Michael Warner contends of anonymous sex, "What one relishes in loving strangers is not mere anonymity, nor meaningless release. It is the pleasure of belonging to a sexual world, in which one's sexuality finds an answering resonance not just in one other, but in a world of others."[61] Thus, where through broken tropes Crane deracinates words from one meaning to a world of meanings, so, too, does he communize love relations through their brokenness, their failure to signify in absolute ways (permanence, consummation, or named partners). The ejaculation in "Cutty Sark" is the failed source of such multifarious experience. This is a particularly revolutionary move for Crane, especially as "self-hatred was common in homosexuals of Crane's time, who could find no way of fulfilling their desires without violating the image of the ideal, spiritual relationship which had been constructed for homosexual love."[62] Through homographesis, Crane celebrates anonymous sex, the unideal, and thus changes the cultural meaning (signified) associated with this act (signifier).

Brunner notes that "Cutty Sark" "has been derided as a self-indulgent poem, a stray insertion that deviates from more important themes."[63] The notion of self-indulgence, while meant derogatorily here, is a relevant concern considering that Crane wrote that he "would like to establish [his poetry] as free from [his] own personality as from any chance evaluation on the reader's part," though he grants that "this is, of course, an impossibility."[64] This impossibility arises because of Crane's paradoxically pure erotics, his effort to universalize desire as heteroerotic, which infuses his poetry with, not "frees" it from, a kind of desire that Crane was intimately familiar with: transitory homoerotic union, especially with sailors, the kind of love that kept Crane "broken in pieces most of the time"[65] but that also enticed him, just as the speaker of "Cutty Sark" is lured by the sailor's "wicker-neat lapels, the/swinging summer entrances to cooler hells" (29). Paradoxically de-purifying his epic by positing it as purely impersonal, the poet's claim to depersonalize his verse may thus be seen as a move to inscribe his own experience in *The Bridge* precisely because he purports not to.[66]

"Cutty Sark" may well be self-indulgent for Crane, then, but its themes are no less important than any other in the long poem. For, what failed homoerotic union means to Crane, failed Union means to America—and, consequently, to the myth of Crane's *Bridge*. The sailor's disappearance in "Cutty Sark" parallels, in fact, the disappearance of the ship fleets that once represented the spirit of conquest, the spirit of American myth, as the epigraph to the next poem, "Cape Hatteras"—a quotation from Whitman—reveals: "The seas all crossed, weathered the capes, the voyage done" (31). As American myth fails, sexual myth rises anew.

Sexual experience, for Crane, is thus one of the last bastions of myth and its failure that once inhered in the discovery of America. And as suggested in a letter to Waldo Frank, in which he relates his ecstasy in "walking hand in hand across the most beautiful bridge of the world" with his male lover, the literal Brooklyn Bridge of *The Bridge* is the conduit that Crane uses to connect and disconnect that myth to and from reality.[67]

The Modern Long Poem's Modernisms

Given how the poem's rhetoric and thematics inform one another through Burke's paradox of purity, we can see more clearly how the critical rhetoric of failure surrounding *The Bridge* is itself a fortunate misnaming. For a final glance at such misnaming, consider Alan Trachtenberg, who asks, "How else are we to understand the epic proportions of *The Bridge* except as the poet's quest to find himself in American history—to discover and disclose the poetic self as the center, the redemptive consciousness of the history as a totality?" Trachtenberg then answers his own question by granting that he speaks "of the conception of the poem, not its realization," the former being a quest for transcendence, the latter that quest's failure.[68] Trachtenberg's question is itself a better answer than the one he provides, however, for, by his own formulation, the poem's conception already anticipates its realization. If Crane's goal is to posit the poetic self as the center of history as a totality even as he admits that he can only "kno[w] moments in eternity,"[69] the resulting failure of the poetic self to be the center of history reveals itself as the successful achievement, not the failure,

of the poem's conception: To glimpse the particularized "moment" by failing the whole of "eternity" is, for Crane, the modern American epic poet's
achievement.

Indeed, according to Adorno, Crane successfully fulfills his long poem
project precisely because he fragments the universal into particulars. If, as
writer of the tale of the tribe, the epic poet may be viewed as a kind of cultural critic, Adorno's description of the dialectical cultural critic in *Prisms*
aptly describes Crane, poet of *The Bridge*. For, unlike the transcendent
critic, beholden to absolutes, or the immanent critic, invested wholly in
particulars, Adorno's dialectical critic must, as Crane does, wear idealism
as a pose, "as socially necessary appearance," in order to excavate "the
meaning which that existence [idealism, "culture"] has exterminated."
Thus, like Crane, who shuttles between the cosmic and the human, "the
dialectical critic of culture must both participate in culture and not participate. Only then does he do justice to his object and to himself."[70] By
writing into *The Bridge* both his culture's and his own failures to realize
myth, Crane "does justice" to his depiction of the American tribe and himself; he demonstrates how the long poem cannot succeed in its mythic
effort—cannot succeed, that is, without recognizing the impossibility of
any myth to idealize experience.

Crane's dialectic criticism warrants comparison with Eliot's and Pound's
criticism in their respective long poems in order that we may witness in a
larger cultural scope the importance of the paradox of purity to Crane's
contribution to modernism, particularly since Crane valued those writers'
work so highly. Importantly, while all three poets engage the problem of
writing the tale of the tribe, it would be difficult to say that any of them
effects such a totality; a comparison, then, shows how each writer's response to the long poem's generic problem exposes a different facet of
modernism. As we have already seen, Crane thought Eliot's *The Waste Land*
altogether too negative: Whether as an immanent critic invested in criti-
cizing the particulars of the "Unreal City" or as a transcendent critic shoring fragments against his ruins with the universalizing chant "Shantih
shantih shantih," or "the peace that passeth understanding," Eliot does not
embrace myth's failure as a dialectical critic, for he leaps from one pole to
the other without valuing the gap, the bridge, in between.[71] Holding his
transcendent ideal up to the imperfect world as criticism in its most negative sense, Eliot is at times either a transcendent critic or an immanent
critic—but, unlike Crane, not both at once.

While Crane's opinion of Pound's long poem is unknown—little of it
was written before Crane's death in 1932—he very likely read the "Three

Cantos" published in *Poetry* magazine in June, 1917. In those poems, although Pound purports to "give up th' intaglio method,"[72] or the imagist aesthetic of focusing on particularized experience, his final achievement may be described as the intaglio method *in extremis,* for *The Cantos* is an encyclopedia of particulars at the expense of transcendent vision. Indeed, Pound's admonition to Browning to "avoid speech figurative / And set out your matter / As I do, in straight simple phrases"[73] suggests his opposition to Crane's "figurative" aesthetic: For where Crane shuttles between the universal and particular, Pound, as an immanent critic, hordes "simple" particulars in order to criticize them on a material basis.

The differences among Crane's, Eliot's, and Pound's responses to the problem of the modern long poem illuminate how another modernism existed alongside and perhaps in reaction to Eliot and Pound's; as he wrote in 1921, after all, Crane was "only interested in adding what seem[ed] to [him] something really *new* to what *has* been written."[74] For this reason, where Crane could admire Eliot's and Pound's work in 1922, he could, in the same year, proclaim that "the poetry of negation is beautiful" but that he still tries "to break away from it. Perhaps this is useless, perhaps it is silly—but one *does* have joys. The vocabulary of damnations and prostrations has been developed at the expense of these other moods, however, so that it is hard to dance in proper measure."[75] Perhaps by 1923, and certainly by 1930, Crane had found his "proper measure" in the rhetorical and thematic manifestations of the paradox of purity. Building his *Bridge* with the pure myths of national, linguistic, and sexual union only to precipitate them into impure particulars, Crane constructs a long poem that affirms the fleeting joys of experience by failing the ideals to which they aspire— aspiration that is simultaneously the failure of experience's permanence. As a successful artifact of failure, Crane's poem offers a Burkean model of modernism in the paradox of purity, for its success owes to Crane's recognition that failure generically inheres in the modern long poem project itself.

NOTES

1. Hart Crane, *The Letters of Hart Crane,* ed. Brom Weber (Berkeley: University of California Press, 1965), 124.

2. Yvor Winters, "The Progress of Hart Crane," in *Hart Crane: A Collection of Critical Essays,* ed. Alan Trachtenberg (Englewood Cliffs, N.J.: Prentice Hall, 1982), 25–26.

3. Waldo Frank, "An Introduction," *The Collected Poems of Hart Crane,* ed. Waldo Frank (New York: Liveright, 1946), xxii–xxiii.

4. Even before *The Bridge* was published, Allen Tate, in his introduction to *White Buildings*, Crane's first book of verse, anticipated a problem with how Crane negotiated the ideal and the real. For him, Crane's "faults [. . .] lie in the occasional failure of meeting between vision and subject. The vision often strains and overreaches the theme." Allen Tate, "Introduction to *White Buildings*," in *Hart Crane: A Collection of Critical Essays*, ed. Trachtenberg, 22.

5. Derek Savage, "The Americanism of Hart Crane," in *Hart Crane: A Collection of Critical Essays*, ed. Trachtenberg, 42, 48.

6. R. P. Blackmur, "New Thresholds, New Anatomies: Notes on a Text by Hart Crane," in *Hart Crane: A Collection of Critical Essays*, ed. Trachtenberg, 64.

7. Edward Brunner, *Splendid Failure: Hart Crane and the Making of "The Bridge"* (Urbana: University of Illinois Press, 1985).

8. Michael Bernstein, *The Tale of the Tribe: Ezra Pound and the Modern Verse Epic* (Princeton, N.J.: Princeton University Press, 1980), 8.

9. Christopher Nealon, *Foundlings: Lesbian and Gay Historical Emotion Before Stonewall* (Durham, N.C.: Duke University Press, 2001), 46.

10. For references to Munson's term "The Younger Generation," see *The Letters of Hart Crane and His Family*, ed. Thomas S. W. Lewis (New York: Columbia University Press, 1974), 267; and Jack Selzer, *Kenneth Burke in Greenwich Village* (Madison: University of Wisconsin Press, 1996), 43.

11. Theodor Adorno, *Prisms*, trans. Samuel and Shierry Weber (Cambridge: MIT Press, 1981), 32.

12. Kenneth Burke, *A Grammar of Motives* (Berkeley: University of California Press, 1969), 37.

13. Frank, "An Introduction," xvii, xxiv.

14. Hart Crane, "General Aims and Theories," in *Hart Crane: A Collection of Critical Essays*, ed. Trachtenberg, 14.

15. In "For the Marriage of Faustus and Helen" (1922–23), perhaps his first attempt at a long poem (as it bridges the length and focus of lyric and epic poetry), Crane anticipates the guiding principle of *The Bridge*: "*There is the world dimensional for / those untwisted by the love of things / irreconcilable . . .*" (Crane, *Collected Poems*, 94). Here Crane posits the material world as irreducibly at odds with absolutism, for even when reduced down to their fundamental elements, "things irreconcilable" are found in the "world dimensional." Where some would be "twisted," or ill at ease, with the inability to make the imperfect perfect, Crane celebrates things irreconcilable, or imperfect. His love of them, in fact, sends him back into the dimensional world, not in search of a transcendental realm.

16. John Unterecker, *Voyager: A Life of Hart Crane* (New York: Farrar, Straus and Giroux, 1969), 304.

17. Most critics agree that Burke was one of Crane's closest friends; unfortunately, as such intimates, the two wrote few letters to one another and mention each other only briefly in letters to others. We do know that the men met by 1923, though the exact date of their introduction is unclear: Jack Selzer speculates that they met "probably in 1921 (when Crane was corresponding with [Matthew] Josephson) and certainly by 1922 when Crane's close friend Munson first collided with Burke in connection with *Secession*" (Selzer, *Kenneth Burke in Greenwich Village*, 83). The written record belies Selzer's certainty, however, as Crane proclaims in a letter on November 7, 1922: "I wish I could be in New York to talk to [Burke], especially lately do I feel an intense need for contact and conversation with the right sort of people" (Crane, *The Letters of Hart Crane*, 104). At the very least, then, we know that Crane craved Burke's company in '22, particularly since as early as 1920 Crane had been reading and admiring Burke's work in the little magazines (Crane, *The Letters of Hart Crane*, 36). More confidently, we can confirm Selzer's claim that "by the spring of 1923, Burke was incorporating Crane into his circle of friends and entertaining Crane at Andover" (Selzer, *Kenneth Burke in Greenwich Village*, 83). In 1923, Burke published Crane's "For the Marriage of Faustus and Helen" in *Secession*, for which Burke served as editor, and he sublet Crane's Greenwich Village apartment in the winter of 1923–24. What this patchy record shows is that Crane greatly admired and respected Burke even if it doesn't show that Crane (or even Burke himself yet) knew of the paradox of purity as such. That the theory came out of this group of writers and is manifest in both Crane and Burke's work is most important for our understanding of this strain of modernist thought.

18. Nealon, *Foundlings*, 25.

19. Hart Crane, "The Bridge," in *The Collected Poetry of Hart Crane*, ed. Waldo Frank (New York: Liveright, 1946), 58. Throughout this essay, I cite Crane's verse by page, not line number; further citations of *The Bridge* will be given parenthetically in the text.

20. Thomas Yingling, *Hart Crane and the Homosexual Text* (Chicago: University of Chicago Press, 1990), 68.

21. Crane, *The Letters of Hart Crane*, 93.

22. Parker Tyler's long poem *The Granite Butterfly* (1945) would profit from examination under similar terms, as Tyler explicitly acknowledged in a 1946 letter to Kenneth Burke that Burke's paradox of purity exemplifies the long poem's overall goals. Parker Tyler, *The Granite Butterfly* (Orono, Maine: National Poetry Foundation, 1994), 121. It is no coincidence, I think, that one of Tyler's aims with his long poem was to depict a homosexual man's emergence from his family's Freudian dynamics—a more explicitly

heterodox ambition than Crane's, but the difference between the two poems' engagement with homosexuality vis-à-vis the paradox of purity might itself be a valuable source of exploration.

23. Lee Edelman, *Transmemberment of Song: Hart Crane's Anatomies of Rhetoric and Desire* (Stanford: Stanford University Press, 1987), 8.

24. Edelman, *Transmemberment of Song*, 5.

25. The work of Futurist and Dadaist writers are salient examples of purely destructive uses of language.

26. In his essay "Hart Crane's Smile" (*Modernism/Modernity* 12, no. 4 [2005]: 629–58), Michael Snediker seems to suggest as much when he claims that, as opposed to the death-driven "fetishization of self-shattering [that] has inspired if not monopolized most queer readings of Crane" (2), Crane's ecstasy "amounts not to the apotheosis of positive feeling, but the mistranslation of positive feeling for an age whose skepticism would distrust that feeling's self-commitment" (4). I concur that Crane counters his age's skepticism with particularized and self-committed affect, but I would add to Snediker's analysis the mythic "apotheosis" by which he values such particulars in *The Bridge*, a poem Snediker does not analyze.

27. Because Edelman has already cleared so much ground regarding Crane's rhetoric, I have chosen to analyze the following passages in ways that expand upon Edelman's thesis without repeating it. To do so, I have first chosen passages that Edelman does not analyze as fully as some others. More important, however, I have constructed my readings in ways that reveal how Crane's use of the paradox of purity challenges Edelman's devaluation of the literal in his analysis of catachresis.

28. Nealon, *Foundlings*, 51.

29. Importantly, Crane's tone in this passage—ecstatic, exclamatory, as throughout *The Bridge*—reinforces this impression of transcendence just so that his words' ever-fragmenting meanings can subvert it. Crane's broken language similarly clashes with, or fails, his controlling prosodic structures: iambic pentameter and frequent, though irregular, end rhymes. As with his rhetoric, in tone and prosody, too, then, Crane makes catachrestic combinations to multiply rather than to stabilize meaning.

30. Crane, "General Aims and Theories," 16.

31. Crane, *The Letters of Hart Crane*, 353, 351.

32. Nealon extends a like-minded reading of this passage to the materiality of the poem itself: "The name, the star, will always turn out to be part of a constellation, or circuit, whose entire light will flood perception, leading the poet right back to another round of attempt, another star—during which it will collapse back into the particular thing he has produced, like some fragrant incense, a song: a poem" (Nealon, *Foundlings*, 55–6).

33. For examples of how Nietzsche and Shelley employ this trope, see Frederick Nietzsche, *Thus Spake Zarathustra*, trans. Thomas Common, ed. Manuel Komroff (New York: Tudor, 1934), 320; and William Butler Yeats, *Selected Criticism*, ed. A. Norman Jeffares (London: Macmillan, 1964), 53–57.

34. Qtd. Edelman, *Transmemberment of Song*, 223.

35. Brunner, *Splendid Failure*, 23–28.

36. Brunner, *Splendid Failure*, 99.

37. Crane, *The Letters of Hart Crane*, 260.

38. Edelman, *Transmemberment of Song*, 192.

39. Winters, "The Progress of Hart Crane," 23.

40. Blackmur, "New Thresholds, New Anatomies," 53.

41. Edelman, *Transmemberment of Song*, 5.

42. Edelman, *Transmemberment of Song*, 43. That Crane wrote some of *The Bridge* from the home in which one of his male lovers, Emil Opffer, and the overseer of the Brooklyn Bridge's construction, Washington Roebling, at different times lived suggests how intimately connected sexuality and culture were for Crane and his long poem project.

43. Edelman, *Transmemberment of Song*, 12.

44. Lee Edelman, *Homographesis* (New York: Routledge, 1994), 9.

45. Edelman, *Homographesis*, 10, 14.

46. Nealon helpfully glosses Crane's process under the term "history," which he describes as "some potent relation between the large and the small, the apprehensible and the abstract in experience" (Nealon, *Foundlings*, 30). Very much in sympathy with Nealon's view, I endeavor in this essay to particularize the historical milieu—via Burke and the Younger Generation—out of which this process-based "history" arose in American modernism.

47. Edelman, *Homographesis*, 20.

48. Crane, "General Aims and Theories," 16.

49. Edelman, *Homographesis*, 4.

50. As should be clear from this description, Edelman's central quarrel in *Homographesis* is with the codification of identity categories of sexual experience. Nowhere do either Edelman or Crane refuse the essential or non-discursive quality of sexual experience as such; indeed, Crane's strategy seems to be one of illuminating the non-discursive through the failures of discursive identification.

51. Yingling, *Hart Crane and the Homosexual Text*, 27.

52. Crane, *The Letters of Hart Crane*, 307.

53. Tellingly, Crane "was particularly impressed with the thinking of [P.D.] Ouspensky," who in his 1912 *Tertium Organum* contends that "'there are certain aspects' of our phenomenal existence 'in which we come into

direct contact with eternity . . . These are death and love'" (qtd. in Joseph
Warren Beach, "Hart Crane and Moby Dick," in *Hart Crane: A Collection of
Critical Essays*, ed. Trachtenberg, 77). Recalling Stevens's contention that
"Death is the mother of beauty," Ouspensky's conflation of death, or life's
failure, with love as temporal life's two contacts with transcendence reveals
how for Crane love is always proximal to failure—a proximity, however,
which yields momentary transcendence, just as death for Stevens yields
beauty.

54. Crane, *The Letters of Hart Crane*, 27.

55. Brunner, *Splendid Failure*, 154, 159.

56. Brunner, *Splendid Failure*, 155.

57. Brunner, *Splendid Failure*, 147.

58. This is one of Crane's most indelible and important themes, of
course, as it undergirds much of his sequence "Voyages" and comprises the
central theme of one of his last poems, "The Return," where "the sea [. . .]
sheared/Back into bosom—me—her, into natal power . . ." (159).

59. These whispers may be a reaction against American heteronormativity, which Crane labels in a 1923 letter as "these American restrictions [. . .]
where one cannot whisper a word" (Crane, *The Letters of Hart Crane*, 122).

60. John Vincent, *Queer Lyrics: Difficulty and Closure in American Poetry*
(New York: Palgrave Macmillan, 2002), 147.

61. Michael Warner, *The Trouble with Normal* (Cambridge: Harvard
University Press, 2002), 179.

62. Robert K. Martin, *The Homosexual Tradition in American Poetry*
(Austin: University of Texas Press, 1980), 122.

63. Brunner, *Splendid Failure*, 142.

64. Crane, "General Aims and Theories," 16.

65. Crane, *The Letters of Hart Crane*, 26.

66. While Crane's friends in the Younger Generation seem to have been
relatively accepting of Crane's homosexuality, Burke says in a letter to
Malcolm Cowley, "I vaguely remember Munson once telling me that Hart
got angry at parties because, since the mood was generally heterosexual, he
felt subtly excluded" (*The Selected Correspondence of Kenneth Burke and
Malcolm Cowley*, ed. Paul Jay [New York: Viking, 1988], 331). That Crane
could resent the pressure of heterosexism among even his closest peers
indicates the degree to which Crane's sexuality was an important factor in
his social, intellectual, and artistic lives.

67. Crane, *The Letters of Hart Crane*, 131.

68. Alan Trachtenberg, Introduction to *Hart Crane: A Collection of
Critical Essays*, ed. Trachtenberg, 10.

69. Crane, *The Letters of Hart Crane*, 93.

70. Adorno, *Prisms*, 31, 33.

71. T. S. Eliot, *The Waste Land and Other Poems*, ed. Frank Kermode (New York: Penguin, 1998), 62, 69.

72. Ezra Pound, "Three Cantos," *Poetry* 10, no. 3 (June 1917), 113.

73. Pound, "Three Cantos," 118.

74. Crane, *The Letters of Hart Crane*, 67.

75. Crane, *The Letters of Hart Crane*, 285.

The Cruelty of Breeding:
Queer Time in *The Waste Land*

If T. S. Eliot's poem *The Waste Land* was to have a queer theoretical future, it would seem to have found it in Lee Edelman's polemic *No Future*, wherein Edelman defines queerness primarily by its defiance of reproductive futurity.[1] A remarkably short long poem written in the epic tradition—that which, Pound said, was meant to offer "the tale of the tribe"[2]—*The Waste Land* catalogues a litany of nonreproductive sexual figures throughout classical and contemporary history and myth. Among the text's characters who ostensibly live in the early twentieth century, the character Lil has multiple abortions, inciting her friend to ask her "what you get married for if you don't want children"[3]; the typist and young man carbuncular engage in casual, mechanical sex (62); and Mr. Eugenides, reputedly homosexual, propositions one of the poem's speakers for a weekend tryst (61). The poem's mythical figures are even more plentiful: References to queer icons like Adonis and Narcissus emerge amidst a refrain about Philomela, who with her sister Procne served Tereus's son to him for dinner; Dido, too, who burns to death in lust for a man she cannot possess, reminds one speaker of desire's eternal "burning," as does Cleopatra (64); and an ironic reference to the *Pervigilium Veneris*, a poem meant to celebrate fertility and marriage, appears in truncated and plaintive form in the poem's concluding bricolage (76). For such a relatively short poem, *The Waste Land* compiles an awfully long list about reproductive lack.

Because this monument of modernist poetry announces itself to be about waste, it's tempting to nominate these instances of nonreproductive erotic relations as the poem's titular subject. If *waste* denotes *lack, that which has not been fulfilled or completed*, what is wasted, what is lacking in *The Waste Land* is reproductive futurity; the tale of this tribe is that it has no future. Scholarly tradition since the poem's publication has regarded this truism as the poem's lament, as the object of its melancholic litanies: *The Waste Land* longs for the return of the Fisher King, yearns for vegetation rites to be completed, and moans that modernity has no heroes or rites left to fruc-tify the land. When the poem is read in the light of World War I, this view is particularly persuasive, because, as David Jones reminds us in his long poem *In Parenthesis*, Eliot's title invokes the European battlefield that soldiers called "the Waste Land."[4] As Elizabeth Freeman records in her book *Time Binds*, World War I set modernity into a "queer time" by laying waste to the lives of millions of men, especially young men. In terms of heterosexual reproduction, if not martial nationalism, these men's lives were wasted because they ended before what Freeman would call their "chrononormative" end: before they could be put to reproductive use.[5]

The Waste Land bears the wounds of such lack both formally and topi-cally, from its paratactic structure and texture to its direct references to the war. Something is certainly missing in the waste land, but it is not, I will argue today, reproductive sexuality. Rather, reproductive sexuality is the inevitable precondition for what is actually wasted in this land. The poem's first section, "The Burial of the Dead," announces as much:

> April is the cruelest month, breeding
> Lilacs out of the dead land, mixing
> Memory and desire, stirring
> Dull roots with spring rain.
> Winter kept us warm, covering
> Earth in forgetful snow, feeding
> A little life with dried tubers. (53)

Allusively invoking Chaucer's celebration of springtime fertility in the Pro-logue of *The Canterbury Tales*, the first line of *The Waste Land* declares that this space is eternally fruitful: Set into the present participle and modify-ing both what precedes and follows their caesuras and enjambments, *breed-ing, mixing, stirring, covering*, and *feeding* depict a fecund land. What Eliot calls in *Sweeney Agonistes* the "brass tacks" of life—"birth, copulation, and death"[6]—are fully polished in *The Waste Land*.

If this stanza declares that reproductive futurity is not lacking in *The Waste Land*, to what does the title's *waste* refer? Remembering that *waste* can also denote *excess, that which has been or cannot be used*, I would argue that the poem distinguishes between two kinds of waste, both of which are measured in relation to the chrononormativity eternalized in the opening stanza. Reproductive time tells us that that which is historical, that which is in time, that which can be properly used in time, is that which is put to reproductive use. Anything that defies such use is excess, or waste. The poem's nonreproductive figures would by this logic not be signs of lack but signs of excess: that which breeding cannot use and for which modernity has no use. *Waste* in this view is an autoantonym that produces its antithesis: It is a word in constant dialectical relation to itself, constantly antagonizing itself, which is also its own other. What *The Waste Land* lacks is a time for its excess of queer figures, and what Eliot seeks is a time for queerness. He finds it, I will argue, in the timelessness of myth.

In alternately negative and positive terms, queerness has long been associated with the excessive and useless, in fields ranging from Christian theology to evolutionary biology. In its survey of queer figures throughout time and space, *The Waste Land* depicts reproductive time as wasteful, as laying waste to a queer history for which it cannot find time. Eliot ritually revives these "withered stumps of time" (56), this "heap of broken images" (53), this detritus of chrononormativity through allusive rituals that both invoke and create myths out of a queer past that the cruelty of breeding always promises to forget. "April is the cruelest month," then, *because* of its "breeding": because it breeds too much, not too little; because it produces on the logic of normativity that which cannot be put to use. I argue today that *The Waste Land* is a polemical prayer against the wasteful on behalf of useless waste, even as it grants that such a polemic and such a prayer will be eternally necessary. Indeed, while the poem opens with what Judith Jack Halberstam and others have called the logic of straight time, it also disrupts that time by moving from spring to winter and later to summer.[7] Temporally disjunctive, the stanza disrupts the logic of chrononormativity from the outset, even as it uses breeding's cruelty as the precondition of such disruption. The infernally eternal state of reproduction—not its threatened obsolescence—breeds the present into an eternal dialectic between states of the past and the future, between "memory" and "desire." Rather than in the reproductive teleology of

April alone, *The Waste Land* exists in a dialectical queer time that, like the poem's titular *waste*, simultaneously propels, reverses, and freezes the motion of heterotemporality. The cruelty of breeding is, in other words, the agon upon which queerness will always rely and through which queerness can find its time in myth.

As Michael Bell describes in *Literature, Modernism and Myth*, Eliot's preoccupation with myth in *The Waste Land* typifies modernist aesthetics in texts ranging from Barnes's *Nightwood* to H. D.'s *Paint It Today*. In such texts, Bell claims, the term *myth* denotes a foundational falsehood: a narrative that offers noumenal explanations of phenomena and that establishes communal rites, customs, and identities.[8] Eliot invokes such myths through the temporally anachronistic trope of allusion, and he creates, in the text's temporal disjunctions, its timelessness. Eliot thus makes a myth of modernity in the poem itself, what Maud Ellman calls "a sphinx without a secret."[9] Given the queerness of Eliot's myths, we might call this poem's mythology queer, a sphinx with an open secret. Even Pound, when nominating the poem as modern art's most important artifact to date, wrote Eliot that the piece was "by the Uranian Muse begot," where "Uranian" is a *fin-de-siècle* mythical reference to queerness.[10]

But how exactly can a myth be queer, if myths delineate normative structures and if queerness defies normativity? What would it mean for queerness to exist outside of but always in antagonistic relation to time? Like the tensions inherent in Eliot's renditions of waste and temporality, this very tension between myth and queerness distinguishes *The Waste Land* within queer modernism and, I will finally suggest, elucidates the mythopoeic practices of contemporary queer theoretical inquiry that have gone under the name of historiography alone.

In his 1922 essay about Joyce's *Ulysses*, Eliot describes an aesthetic method that can convey the tensions inherent in the concept of a queer mythology. Remarking on Joyce's invocation of Homer's *Odyssey*, Eliot calls this method "the mythical method," which he describes as the process of "manipulating a continuous parallel between contemporaneity and antiquity." Distinguished from what he calls the "narrative method," an aesthetic dependent on linear teleology, the mythical method provides the poet "a way of controlling, of ordering, of giving a shape and a significance" to "contemporary history": a way of innovating time, "contemporary history," by locating it outside of but nonetheless contiguous to reproductive temporal structures.[11]

Joseph Allen Boone and others have claimed that Eliot's emphasis on "order" here and in other writings demonstrates how "'The Wasteland [*sic*]'" and "the New Critical practice instituted by Eliot" "support a very traditional metaphysics of textual coherence, however complexly figured, and a conservative politics of individual autonomy, however fragmented."[12] Such views have portrayed Eliot himself as queerness's agon, yet one need only consider the fisting, coprophilia, sadism, masochism, and countless other non-normative sexualities that pervade Joyce's "Circe" episode to know that Eliot was not suggesting that Joyce had tidied up queerness in his novel by ordering "contemporaneity" with the mythical method.

Eliot had defined his sense of order three years earlier in his essay "Tradition and the Individual Talent," wherein he claims that myth, that which is out of time, must disrupt, not organize, that which is in time. To have what he calls "the historical sense" and "tradition," the artist and the critic alike must, Eliot argues, have "a sense of the timeless as well as of the temporal and of the timeless and of the temporal together." This disruptive temporality, Eliot says, is what constitutes order: "Whoever has approved this idea of order, of the form of European, of English literature, will not find it preposterous that the past should be altered by the present as much as the present is directed by the past."[13] Order, history, and tradition are, for Eliot, temporally non-normative: Like *waste*, they are autoantonyms that depend upon their antitheses, as Eliot writes in his essay on Joyce, to "mak[e] the modern world possible for art."[14] Indeed, as he writes in "Tradition," "To conform merely would be for the new work not really to conform at all; it would not be new, and would therefore not be a work of art."[15] Order and chaos are for Eliot much like the mythical Apollonian and Dionysian impulses were for Nietzsche: Neither attempts a positivist, or what Nietzsche calls Socratic, rendering of history. The Apollonian order simply gives the Dionysian a frame to shatter and a framework through which to understand that shattering.[16]

Eliot thus describes modernist art as dialectically temporal, what Joseph Frank might call spatial.[17] The modernist work disrupts linear time to create a space, a textual location, wherein motion takes place perpetually. For Eliot, that space is not only the "Unreal City" (55, 61, 67) that pervades the poem but of course the titular *Waste Land* itself. Eliot's separation of the words *waste* and *land* forces them into dialectical relation and emphasizes that *waste* is a concept subject to time, specifically chrononormative time. For Eliot, what has been wasted is the queer past, and he creates with the tropes of parataxis and allusion a space for that past in which corpses sprout and raped women sing. Eliot asks us in "Tradition" to live in "what is not merely the present, but the present moment of the past [and to be] conscious, not of what is dead, but of what is already liv-ing."[18] Unlike April and its breeding, *The Waste Land*'s paratactic allusions produce rather than reproduce the past in the present, disrupting the nor-mative present with the queer order of the past, with the waste that time has bred and breeds.

A funeral, as Ellman has called it,[19] and a resurrection ritual, *The Waste Land* is a textual space in which queerness has an eternal life. To revise my opening claim, then, about the poem's future in Edelman's *No Future*, it may be that *The Waste Land*'s future exists in the agonistically hopeful responses to Edelman's book, responses like Heather Love's *Feeling Back-ward*, José Esteban Muñoz's *Cruising Utopia*, and Freeman's *Time Binds*.[20] While these writers all grant that queerness must oppose the reproduc-tive future, they also argue that queering the past requires a gesture toward futurity: toward the hope that queerness is somewhere, perhaps everywhere; toward a mythical future in the past that Eliot tropes as the "Unreal City" of queer community. As a historical community, that pol-ity must, as the poem must, as queer time itself must, rupture and fail the telos of unity, but it is through such failure, what we might call spoilage, that the waste that is *queerness* is redeemed from being wasted, which is to say annihilated by history.

In such redemption, queerness lives in myth. The dialectical process of union and fracture that constitutes the mythical method and queer my-thology alike envisions the utopia of unity as a continual effort without telos. In Muñoz's terms, Eliot's modernism is a utopic dystopia, one wherein desire is inevitably unfulfilled, a disappointment that operates as a precon-dition of non-normative politics and aesthetics.

One recurring feature of myths across time and space is that produc-tion can occur, in fact most often occurs, without reproduction: From biblical resurrection tales to classical creation myths, the production of novelty derives less often from heterosexual union than from that union's failure or absence. This is most often the case in classical tragedy, which may be the queerest genre in all of literary history insofar as it ritually emplots the heterosexual nuclear family's destruction for the sake of pro-ducing the cathartic affects of pity and fear. From Orestes and Clytemnes-tra to Agave and Pentheus, the Greeks inaugurated one of the West's most longstanding aesthetic traditions with an art form that fractures chrono-normativity. Tragedy is itself cruel *to* breeding; it produces rather than regulates queerness; it is a voluminous archive of our queer mythologies.

One of the queerest classical tragedies is nominated by Aristotle as the paradigm of Western drama and by Freud as the paradigm of sexual ontogenesis: *Oedipus the King*, a tale of parricide and incest whose plot unfolds through temporal disjunction. In this play, queer time disrupts reproductive time, as Oedipus must learn his past despite his relentless desire to plunge into the future. Like every tragic hero, Oedipus must learn his past and his mistakes "too late" to change the past but not too late to see the future.[21] Yielding to the queerness of his past, Oedipus curses his children, Antigone and Ismene, and becomes through, not in spite of, such acts a revered prophet by the time of *Oedipus at Colonus*, one who can see the future on account of how acutely he feels the queer past.

Oedipus's belatedness is the time of tragedy and, I would argue, the time of queerness. Rather than being anticipatory, something not yet here, as Muñoz argues, queerness is something always already past, something eternally, mythically, out of time, which is to say out of the regulatory logic of straight time. Rather than the last call that Lil hears in *The Waste Land*'s "Game of Chess," "HURRY UP PLEASE ITS TIME" (59), queerness is *the last call for time itself*, the last call for futurity, the eternally recurring last call for the chrononormative ends of time. In the spatial terms that its recursions demand, queer time in *The Waste Land* is a future always looking and, in Heather Love's terms, "*feeling* backward." It is a land in which the future-oriented "desire" is always "mixing" with "memory" in relation to, not with or against, the normative trajectories of breeding (53).

I've detoured here through *Oedipus the King* to anticipate how Eliot himself invokes that play's queerest character, Tiresias, in *The Waste Land*. Tiresias narrates the typist and young man carbuncular's sexual liaison in the second section of the poem. The epitome of this poem's nonreproductivity, Tiresias seems by chrononormative terms a tragic figure: He can't reproduce, so his life is wasted, just like the lives of the typist and young man he oversees. This tragic spoilage is concomitant with Tiresias's queer excess, however: He can't reproduce because he is intersex, an old man with wrinkled breasts, made so through the ostensibly punishing hand of Juno. But as in most classical creation myths, punishment here has a beneficent flipside, just as I am suggesting both *waste* and *tragedy* do for Eliot. Like Oedipus, Tiresias becomes a prophet because he is queer; because he knew too much, having occupied both male and female bodies prior to occupying their liminal form. In his allusion to Ovid and Sophocles, Eliot invokes this seer as a metonym of queer modernity, one who has "foresuffered all on this same divan or bed" (62). Eliot does not waste this queer character, even as he is clearly waste, or useless, on reproductive terms. On the contrary, Eliot claims in his notes that Tiresias "sees" the "substance of the poem" (72): a substance, that, we have seen, is excessively nonreproductive. Though Tiresias's wrinkled breasts cannot nourish the children of the reproductive future, they can and do nourish the queer community of *The Waste Land*.

When one of the poem's speakers asks at poem's end, then, "Shall I at least set my lands in order?," the poem answers "yes" on the terms of Eliot's mythical method (69). As it does with Tiresias, the poem orders itself by disordering time, by placing its myth against time and within time. With the responding line "these fragments I have shored against my ruins," *The Waste Land* anticipates its own rupture, its own incompletion, its own queering. The fulcrum in this line is the preposition "against," which could denote, in conventional queer terms, *opposition*: The speaker trades fragments for ruins, opposing the former against the latter. Alternatively, in Eve Kosofsky Sedgwick's notion of the reparative,[22] "against" could mean "in contact with": fragments layered beside, near, *with* ruins. Simultaneously oppositional and cohesive, lacking and in excess, the speaker, like the poem as a whole, disrupts the utopia of totality, laying waste to the myth of completion and shoring the waste of history's spoilage against the ruins of time.

Eliot's poem typifies how queers throughout the twentieth century, ranging from Hart Crane to Audre Lorde, used mythology to find a time for queerness out of time. But it also exemplifies how our own queer methodologies, if they are to be "against" time—to be critical and reparative at once—might rely more on Eliot's New Critical mythic method rather than the New Historicism's historiography alone. From *erotic* to *sodomy* to *lesbian* to *onanist*, the Western language of sexuality has long been inflected with mythical roots. But the figurehead of contemporary historiography, Michel Foucault, famously argues that the sodomite was baptized in the cleansing waters of sexology.[23] Through this process, the mythical queer became the historical *homosexual*, and his eroticism became secular, channeled through Foucault's discursive triumvirate of pedagogy, medicine, and law. Offering the sexual component of our larger histories about modernity's secularization, Foucault claims that these secular institutions replaced religion as the primary site of sexuality's articulation. As social constructionist theory has taught us, however, and as Rictor Norton has argued most explicitly, the *homosexual* is itself a construct, a noumenous explanation for inexplicable phenomena: in other words, a myth.[24] As Freud—the other exemplar of contemporary queer methodologies, the psychoanalytical—demonstrates most saliently, the transitional bridge between the *ars erotica* of religion and the *scientia sexualis* of modern sexuality is thus the very bridge that Eliot uses to move between past and present, male and female, fragmentation and unity in *The Waste Land*. Through the bridge of myth, queer scholars themselves offer mythopoeic historiographies, what Freeman calls "erotohistoriographies,"[25] to cull the waste that positivist histories of time have wasted. Rather than placing queerness in time, a time for which it was always too late, such reparative criticism locates queerness out of time.

I've repeated throughout this talk as a kind of refrain that *The Waste Land* has a queer future in the theoretical texts of our immediate present, which is my own way of ritually repeating Love's claim in *Feeling Backward* that, if queer figures of the past are to have a future, "*we are that future*,"[26] "we" being the interpreters of artifacts. In ritualizing this claim, however, and in allowing ourselves to harbor and enliven the detritus of history, I suggest that we ourselves become waste lands and practice its ritual methods: We create history as myth, as the utopian space in which waste might reside since it will never, after all, reside in time. Queers are too late for time, so we can stop trying to catch up with it. History is what creates our waste; it is the impulse of mythopoeia, queer time, to find lands, spaces, for that waste.

In this room, in our scholarship, in our classrooms, we create a space for queerness not by insisting upon its historicity but by accepting, like Eliot, the inevitability of chrononormativity, the brass tacks of breeding, and the inevitable waste of that time. In this agonistic relationship to time itself, we shore waste against the ruins of temporality. Returning ritually to our literary and theoretical documents, we make of those documents sacred texts that offer foundational falsehoods about the queerness for which time will never have time. These rituals are our burials of the dead, what Eliot calls in "What the Thunder Said" "what have we given": "The awful daring of a moment's surrender/Which an age of prudence can never retract/By this, and this only, we have existed/Which is not to exist in our obituaries" (68). Our queer practices are our efforts to surrender ritually both to the cruelty of breeding and to its waste: We accumulate that waste into a heap of broken images, not into obituaries and the brass tacks of facts; we accumulate that waste into myths that time can never retract. While time makes waste of us, Eliot teaches us, we make waste lands of ourselves.

NOTES

    1. Lee Edelman, *No Future: Queer Theory and the Death Drive* (Durham, N.C.: Duke University Press, 2004).
    2. Ezra Pound, *Guide to Kulchur* (New York: New Directions, 1970), 194.

3. T. S. Eliot, *The Waste Land*, in *Collected Poems 1909–1962* (New York: Harcourt Brace & World, 1963), 59. Further page references to *The Waste Land* will be given parenthetically in the text.

4. David Jones, *In Parenthesis* (New York: New York Review Books, 2003), x.

5. Elizabeth Freeman, *Time Binds: Queer Temporalities, Queer Histories* (Durham, N.C.: Duke University Press, 2010), x–xii.

6. T. S. Eliot, *Sweeney Agonistes*, in *Collected Poems 1909–1962* (New York: Harcourt Brace & World, 1963), 119.

7. J. Jack Halberstam, *In a Queer Time and Place: Transgender Bodies, Subcultural Lives* (New York: New York University Press, 2005); José Esteban Muñoz, *Cruising Utopia: The Then and There of Queer Futurity* (New York: New York University Press, 2009), 17, 22, 24–25; Freeman, *Time Binds*. See also the special issue of *GLQ* on "Queer Temporalities," ed. Elizabeth Freeman: *GLQ* 13, nos. 2–3 (2007).

8. Michael Bell, *Literature, Modernism and Myth: Belief and Responsibility in the Twentieth Century* (Cambridge: Cambridge University Press, 2006), 1.

9. Maud Ellman, *The Poetics of Impersonality: T. S. Eliot and Ezra Pound* (Cambridge: Harvard University Press, 1988), 91.

10. Qtd. in Wayne Koestenbaum, *Double Talk: The Erotics of Male Literary Collaboration* (New York: Routledge, 1989), 120.

11. T. S. Eliot, "*Ulysses*, Order, and Myth," in *Selected Prose of T. S. Eliot*, ed. Frank Kermode (New York: Harcourt Brace Jovanovich, 1975), 177.

12. Joseph Allen Boone, *Libidinal Currents: Sexuality and the Shaping of Modernism* (Chicago: University of Chicago Press, 1998), 6.

13. T. S. Eliot, "Tradition and the Individual Talent," in *Selected Prose of T. S. Eliot*, ed. Frank Kermode (New York: Harcourt Brace Jovanovich, 1975), 38, 39.

14. Eliot, "*Ulysses*, Order, and Myth," 178.

15. Eliot, "Tradition and the Individual Talent," 39.

16. Friedrich Nietzsche, *The Birth of Tragedy*, trans. Shaun Whiteside (New York: Penguin, 2003), 60

17. Joseph Frank, *The Idea of Spatial Form* (New Brunswick, N.J.: Rutgers University Press, 1991).

18. Eliot, "Tradition and the Individual Talent," 44.

19. Ellman, *The Poetics of Impersonality*, 93.

20. Heather Love, *Feeling Backward: Loss and the Politics of Queer History* (Cambridge: Harvard University Press, 2009); Muñoz, *Cruising Utopia*; Freeman, *Time Binds*.

21. Sophocles, "Oedipus Rex," in *The Oedipus Cycle*, trans. Dudley Fitts and Robert Fitzgerald (Boston and New York: Mariner Books, 2002), 66.

22. Eve Kosofsky Sedgwick, *Touching Feeling: Affect, Pedagogy, Performativity* (Durham, N.C.: Duke University Press, 2003), 123ff.

23. Michel Foucault, *The History of Sexuality: An Introduction*, Vol. I, trans. Robert Hurley (New York: Vintage Books 1990), 43.

24. Rictor Norton, *The Myth of the Modern Homosexual: Queer History and the Search for Cultural Unity* (London: Cassell, 1997).

25. Freeman, *Time Binds*, 95ff.

26. Love, *Feeling Backward*, 40.

Essays

The Ancients and the Queer Moderns

Scott Herring

> You ought to be ashamed, I said, to look so antique.
> (And her only thirty-one.)
>
> —T. S. ELIOT, *The Waste Land*

One of Sam See's significant achievements was his queering of the ancient/ modern divide. However contested, this division has been a persistent attribute of modernism given its supposed break from the old. We encounter this assertion in journalism such as the *Austin Chronicle*'s review of a 2003 Harry Ransom Center exhibition, "Make It New: The Rise of Modernism," which proclaims that "for if nothing else, modernism means a break with the old, with the past, scorning your father's Matthew Arnold."[1] This assured claim also reappears in online research papers for undergraduate students seeking a readymade thesis. "Modernist literature," a purchasable piece from Essayworld tells us, "is a break from the old ways of writing from the 19th Century."[2] Well before this maxim became a downloadable premise for the matriculating, it found a home in scholarship that cast modernism's break as a rejection of that which had come before: the Victorians, the generations prior, even the ancients. Writes Matei Calinescu in *Five Faces of Modernity* (1987): "Since the mid-eighteenth century the 'ancient/modern' opposition has generated countless broadly historical and eventually typological antitheses, without which the whole evolution of the modern critical consciousness would be incomprehensible."[3] In a similar vein, Harry Levin ushered out a "receding, temporally superseded or sea-changed" modernism with his *Memories of the Moderns* (1980): "Writers first declared themselves as Moderns when they were breaking away from the authority of the Ancients."[4] We could keep going back: The *Oxford English Dictionary* formalized this divergence years before the advent of modernist literary criticism when it defined *ancient* as that "which existed in, or belonged to, times *long* past, or early in the world's history; old" as well as a term "contrasted with *modern*."[5] To these two interlaced binaries I would add antiquity/modernity, whereby the former connotes "the quality of being old (in the world's history) or ancient," "old age (of human life)," and "the period before the middle ages, the time of the ancient Greeks and Romans."[6]

I take no issue with an adjective such as "typological" to characterize divergence between the ancient and the modern. I pause over a word choice such as "opposition." Ingrained into the English language, old/new, ancient/modern, and antiquity/modernity have indeed proven indispensable to both expert and layperson accounts as one of modernism's standard character traits. Yet "antitheses" that mark both historical periods as well as chronological lifespans can grow hazy—even affable—when pressed. As my epigraph suggests, a modernist ur-text such as T. S. Eliot's *The Waste Land* (1922) incorporates British working-class slang to describe a thirty-one-year-old female as "antique."[7] Similarly, W. B. Yeats's "Sailing to Byzantium" (1927) conjures a return to later Antiquity as its male persona longs to become "But such a form as Grecian goldsmiths make / Of hammered gold and gold enamelling."[8] If space permitted, I could detail how scholars have studied other experimentalists such as James Joyce, E. E. Cummings, and H.D., each of whom modernized classicism.[9] As these select instances attest, the ancient/modern split can look less like a mano a mano *querelle* and more like a profitable alliance. While it indisputably functioned as an aesthetic and historical distancing device, the ancient/old was as much a vehicle for magnifying what counted as the modern/new. Observes Michael North in reference to modernist authorship at its height: "many admitted—or even insisted—that what seems new is really only the old come back again."[10]

This was especially the historical case for queer moderns and their emergent avant-gardes, a topic central to See's scholarship. While influential sexologists such as Richard von Krafft-Ebing rejected Antiquity's sex/gender systems in texts such as *Psychopathia Sexualis*—"we are certainly far beyond sodomitic idolatry, the public life, legislation and religious exercises of ancient Greece"—others embraced these bygone cultures for queer ends.[11] In a discussion titled "Gay Folklore," historian George Chauncey's *Gay New York* tells us that twentieth-century queers sought "to claim that heroic figures from the past were gay."[12] To support this claim Chauncey cites Edward Carpenter's *Ioläus: An Anthology of Friendship* (1902) for championing a "'poetry of friendship among [the] Greeks and Romans'" as well as Blair Niles's *Strange Brother* (1931), which characterizes Roman emperor "[Julius] Caesar . . . as homosexual."[13] Strikingly, *Gay New York* reproduces a "Certificate of Membership in the Ancient Order of Pansies of America" dated 1936.[14] At a flash point when men desiring other men began to identify themselves with previously undreamed-of appellations such as *pansy* (the *OED* originates this subcultural term at 1922), Anglophone queers also characterized themselves as participants in newfangled forms of Antiquity. Something unprecedented—homosexual gatherings during the 1920s and '30s—figures as exquisitely old given its phantastic attachment with the distant past. As Chauncey's research into urban queer modernity as well as my passing references to modernist literatures suggest, ancient/modern and old/new are not inherently oppositional. Proponents of a great historical divide have found it as useful for their arguments as much as those who historiographically worry it.

These opening thoughts crossed my mind as I sat with See's prose—writing as incandescent as any gold mosaic in latter-day Constantinople. Within this framework of ancient novelty and novel ancients his scholarship makes a lasting contribution to the field of queer modernist studies in particular and queer theory in general. Doubtless other interventions exist, but See's commitment to querying modernism's restless desire for new subjectivities and collectivities in relation to older forms of being proves unwavering. Disputed, confirmed, or both, modernity's visions of Antiquity presented See with a helpful resource for observing how early twentieth-century sexual cultures cited ancient times—however historically inaccurate, epistemologically uninformed, or chronologically ill-defined. As this essay discusses, See's writings canvassed topics such as queer temporality, subcultural development, the experimental pleasures of antiquity, cross-racial modernist youth cultures, and non-normative modes of aging during the conventional period of avant-gardes in western Europe and the United States. Christopher Looby and Michael North reproduce his thought on these matters under this collection's rubric of "Queer Mythologies," and I supplement their editorial organization to illuminate how See queerly ponders the new/old divide that informs modernism. A meticulous deconstructionist and an adept archivist who refused to privilege historicism over formalism, See keenly attended to interruptions *and* connections within whatever counted for oldness in modernism. At the same time, his writings addressed polysemic meanings of a not-so-ancient antiquity for queer moderns in order to "make literary and sexual modernism new by saying something old" (this and subsequent quotations and references are to the essay "Making Modernism New: Queer Mythology in *The Young and Evil*," included in this volume).

To support these insights I concentrate on two interconnected writings: first, See's article on Charles Henri Ford and Parker Tyler's *The Young and Evil* (1933) published in 2009; second, a talk on *The Waste Land* delivered at a 2011 meeting of the Modern Language Association of America. As we observe See mulling over the ancient/modern divide in modernist literary studies, the interpretive payoff for this field of inquiry becomes clear. Less transparent but equally impressive is the light these contributions to modernist scholarship shine on strains of U.S.-based queer theory, especially its subfield of queer temporality studies. See was, first and foremost, a literary theorist of sexual modernity who embraced a long view of the twenty-first century, and so following my assessments of these two pieces I detail their afterlife in a few contemporary queer theorizations that rely on modernists who relied on the ancients.

I

See appreciated the rhetorical possibilities of undoing binaries via post-structuralist close readings, and there is no surprise that his 2009 *ELH* article on *The Young and Evil*—a novel ostensibly about modern youth—has much to say about old ancients. His paragraphs overflow with deconstructive twists and turns of phrasing: "inconclusive conclusion," "within and without," a "depth model of surface aesthetics," to name but three instances. This interpretive strategy was a sound choice to approach Ford and Tyler's novel, for it allows See to unsettle binaries between old/new embedded within urban queer communitarianism as well as to toy with ascendant/descendent conceptions of an aesthetic movement well established by the early 1930s.

For those unfamiliar with this text, some contextual background may be in order. As Steven Watson observes in his introduction to the novel's 1988 reprint, "*The Young and Evil* appeared in August, 1933, in an edition of 2500 copies. Its dust jacket bore quotes from [Gertrude] Stein and [Djuna] Barnes, each sounding her characteristic note. [. . .] Stein declared '*The Young and Evil* creates this generation as *This Side of Paradise* by Fitzgerald created his generation.'"[15] Part of this innovative creation, See notes, is the literary documentation of Manhattan queer life as the novel's characters venture into cafés, drag balls, and bedrooms, and onto city sidewalks. There is little plot nor, See discerns, any lead character. But the novel remains notable for tracking queer subcultures as the hetero-/homosexual binary suffused medical, legal, and popular middle-class discourses. See's essay, then, is of a piece with historicist scholarship by Chauncey, Lisa Duggan, Siobhan Somerville, and Marlon Ross that has traced the intricacies of modern sexual typologies in the first third of the twentieth-century United States.

And not. According to See, the authors of *The Young and Evil* "tell lies about history, especially about the transhistorical nature of sexuality, in order to create the grounds for new forms of belief." "Ford and Tyler join a group of queer writers at the turn of the century," he finds, "who were attempting to, in Chauncey's words, 'create gay histories,' or historical communities within which they could locate themselves, even if it meant telling the anachronistic and mythopoeic 'lie' about 'sexuality' as a transhistorical phenomenon." At the same time that See identifies an empiricist version of twentieth-century sexual modernity, his essay is equally interested in how tried-and-true modernist literary techniques—surrealist imagery, non-realist characterology, and, especially, "mythopoeia, or mythmaking"—enabled Ford and Tyler to prevaricate and conjure these new sexual relations. Building on modernist literary critics such as Joseph Allen Boone, Christopher Nealon, and others, See finds that *The Young and Evil* historically constructs queer transhistoricism. Claiming that the novel does Eliot's "*Ulysses*, Order, and Myth" one better, he insists "that modernist myth can and must account for kinds of experience too readily overshadowed by heteronormative modernist mythopoeia." Hence See's opening moves argue that Ford and Tyler draw upon "the fairy tale 'Little Red Riding Hood,' Arthurian legend via 'the Round Table,'" and Biblical ur-narratives such as the Garden of Eden to "reform old myths" and bring into fictive being unanticipated sexual typologies. Within this framework, the novel's characters and its setting become as legendary as Alice Mitchell, the pairing of Gertrude Stein and Alice B. Toklas, and Richard Bruce Nugent are for many fans of queer American modernism today. In See's memorable phrasing, Ford and Tyler fictionalize "modern queers" who "are the age-old 'mythological creatures' that already inhabit the western mythopoeic tradition." The young and evil men and women who walk in and out of the novel are gods and monsters.

These observations about the imaginary created by Ford and Tyler apply not only to the duo's "literary-formal aims" but to See's methodological ventures as well. Just as Ford and Tyler "remake, and retell popular, universal myths" advocated by the likes of Eliot and Joyce, so too does See in 2009 adopt well-worn modes of literary criticism—New Criticism, new historicism, and post-structuralism—to craft his original entry into queer modernist scholarship. In terms of close reading, the essay rivals any formalism. In terms of historicism, his archiving at the Beinecke Rare Book and Manuscript Library and the Harry Ransom Center is comprehensive. In terms of deconstructive technique, the piece erases hierarchies between new/old, tradition/innovation, and what one character calls "the line between the strange and the common." For me, "Making Modernism New" often embodies many of the best aspects of Eve Kosofsky Sedgwick's thinking, herself a queer modernist scholar whose *Epistemology of the Closet* See cites in an endnote.

In keeping with this interpretive tradition of queer deconstruction, See finds Ford and Tyler to be pre-poststructuralists charting an older sexual experimentalism. In his essay's first section he quotes a 1934 letter Tyler wrote to Ezra Pound: "'Antiquity doesn't hold any patents on homosexuality: there is plenty in the modern fauna and flora—so much—that doesn't fit into the greekvase pattern—not to speak of some freshening of myth.'" He later cites another character who observes that "'America is so Greek but doesn't know it'" and glosses that "'Greek' is code for queer." In See's reading, the novel refuses clear-cut oppositionality between Antiquity and modernity, and this insight connects up with complementary readings of Tyler's poetics such as See's piece "The Myth of Nature." Here See interprets Tyler's 1945 poem *The Granite Butterfly: A Poem in Nine Cantos* as a testament to "how queer natures have existed throughout time—from Roman antiquity through American postmodernity." To justify this claim, he quotes Tyler, who "describes the poem as 'a personal revival of myth, not in order to reinforce the Classical form of the Medusa and Oedipus legends' but 'to convert them to my own uses because I identified certain dominant experiences in my life with these two Classical figures.'" See also cites this quote in an endnote to the *ELH* piece, and, as I suggest near the end of these comments, we can better glimpse how his intellectual project anchors itself in modernist literature but widens out to include post-1945 texts.

For now, a closer reading of select moments in *The Young and Evil* confirms See's findings. On the one hand, the novel is hyper-modernist in its knowing citation of all things new. References to psychoanalysis, experimental authors, vanguard print cultures, novel political movements, and urban nightlife proliferate. Reinforcing itself as cutting-edge, the narrator and the novel's characters casually cite Freud, Stein, Eliot, Pound, *The Little Review*, Barnes, Communism, Duke Ellington, elevated subway trains, Harlem drag balls, Wyndham Lewis, cocaine, marijuana, and Sherwood Anderson. Even as they progress through the narrative's linear time, the novel's characters also age into youthfulness by "growing younger over these flowers of concrete."[16] *The Young and Evil* is likewise up-to-the-minute in its sociological accounts of pansy fashion during this time period: "Karel, as he had promised, came by . . . bringing his box of beauty that included eyelash curlers, mascara, various shades of powder, lip and eyebrow pencils, blue and brown eyeshadow and tweezers for the eyebrows" (55).

On the other hand, See observes, Ford and Tyler transform their characters into pre-modern beings and have them do the same to each other. When Karel paints Julian's face, the two engage in a mode of twentieth-century self-fashioning reliant on a new age of beauty cosmetics, as historian Kathy Peiss as well as the Modern Girl around the World Collective have detailed.[17] But the moment Karel and Julian become most modern they also become most ancient: "I'll make you up to the high gods Karel said to the *high* . . ." (55). Engaging in what the narrator terms "artistry" that we could just as much term queer cosmetology, one character mythologizes another (55). Though not announced as such, Karel and Julian together participate in a long-outmoded Grecian and Roman practice of coloring the statues of their gods, or *"graphta andreia."*[18] Queer youth here become ancient divinities when they pansy up via eyebrow pencils—maquillage that one company claims it invented in 1927.[19]

Even the most minor of characters mentioned in the novel get this application of antique modernity. When a made-up Julian, Karel, and their pals attend a Harlem drag ball, Julian witnesses an avant-garde scene of cross-racial intimacies that features comingling African-Americans, Anglo-Americans, and Italian immigrants who were often categorized as white ethnics: "He knew the precise youth of it there and the vulgarity raw enough to be exhilarating" (154). Suddenly, "someone shouted Bessie if you don't believe Heliogabalus died by having his head stuck in a toilet bowl you NEEDN'T COME AROUND any more" (154). Besides their possible allusion to queer blues singer Bessie Smith whom See cites in an essay on Langston Hughes for "engag[ing] in homoerotic behavior," this anonymous reveler also makes campy, anachronistic reference to Heliogabalus/Elagabalus, a young and evil Roman emperor who governed from 218–222 CE.[20] Ill-reputed for his wild same-sex desires, he was assassinated at age eighteen (*contra* the unnamed drag ball participant's screeching his end was not death by water closet). Here Heliogabalus takes his surreal place amidst Harlem-based interracial youth cultures not solely as a namesake but as an ancient young adult mentioned among the reveling many. Ford and Tyler thus revive "an old thing"—a queer Roman teenager—amidst a modernist scene overflowing with other youth (38). This scene recalls both the "primitive drag" that See identified in the poems of Langston Hughes—another essay of his references the literary historical phenomenon of Harlem drag—as it joins up with its ancient counterpart.[21]

In an earlier chapter this sexually charged marbling of ancient/old and modernist/new also functions gerontologically. When Karel prostitutes himself for "an old thing there in evening clothes," the modern elder proves voracious: "To my amazement I was told to go back and send Vincent up and to my utter exhaustion when Vincent came down there was a second request for me . . ." (38). In a subculture where older queer men dreaded "removal from the field of potential sexual partners," we find yet another alternate historical universe embedded in *The Young and Evil*: cross-generational same-sex encounters that complement antiquated Harlem drag balls that blend a bawdy third century with a decadent 1930s.[22] This is the "tradition of queer mythopoeia" that See, Tyler, and Ford concoct as they mix up pansies and gods by introducing Roman emperors alongside experimental bohemians. Manhattan becomes an age- and era-inappropriate temple, Julian's face a fresco, and See's queer modernism a belated classicism.

II

See applies similar interpretive strategies to Eliot, a twice-married modernist giant no stranger to classicism or to queering given his friendship with Jean Verdenal and his intimacies with Pound during *The Waste Land*'s composition.[23] In a talk that See presented on *The Waste Land* while participating on a 2011 MLA session titled "Queer Temporalities of Twentieth-Century Britain," he quotes Eliot's phrase in "*Ulysses*, Order, and Myth" as "manipulating a continuous parallel between contemporaneity and antiquity" (a phrase his *Young and Evil* essay also cites) (this and subsequent quotations and references are to the talk included in the present volume, "The Cruelty of Breeding"). Exploring how *The Waste Land* introduces "a dialectical queer time," See looks at how the poem collages "nonreproductive sexual figures throughout classical and contemporary history and myth." Titling his piece "The Cruelty of Breeding: Queer Time in *The Waste Land*," he finds that Eliot's masterpiece showcases "reproductive time as wasteful"—yet another deconstructive move that enables this scholar to destabilize boundaries between ancient and modern/ist.

This brief piece deepens See's observations made about *The Young and Evil* by turning to *The Waste Land*'s invocation of "classical tragedy, which may be the queerest genre in all of literary history insofar as it ritually emplots the heterosexual nuclear family's destruction." In particular, he homes in on the pivotal figure of Tiresias, whom See considers "a metonym of queer modernity." I want to attend to this last claim. There is little new to stating that Eliot incorporated Antiquity into his poem given that *The Waste Land*'s first section, "The Burial of the Dead," makes reference to the Roman Empire. But See's claim for Tiresias, the disabled ancient Greek clairvoyant, as an "epitome of this poem's queer nonreproductivity" deserves special notice when approached within his overarching investments in aged experimentalism. It's hard to say something original about *The Waste Land* but these twelve unrevised pages do so.

As critics might recall, Tiresias announces himself in the poem's third section:

I Tiresias, though blind, throbbing between two lives,
Old man with wrinkled female breasts, can see
At the violet hour, the evening hour that strives
Homeward, and brings the sailor home from sea, (61)

See identifies Tiresias as "intersex," and this description is apt given that Eliot poem's compresses this oracle's two sex changes into one body.[24] Passing over the narratological details of this Greek myth, Eliot's description subtly alludes to the modern sexological category of "the third sex"—a woman trapped inside a man—as well as modernist queer and trans cultures given Tiresias's self-association with "the violet hour" of twilight. Such intimacy between the senescent and the waning evening light exemplifies the modernist queer time that See diagnoses in the poem. In his *Gay Talk: A Sometimes Outrageous Dictionary of Gay Slang* (1972), lexicographer Bruce Rodgers defines *twilight* as "that hermaphroditic time of day when it is neither night nor day and all the sky is swathed in purple."[25] Rodgers then notes alternate compounds such as *twilight world, twilight crowd, twilight girls,* and *twilight men* and historicizes these colorful terms as *"dated,* '20s–30s."[26] Though outmoded by the time of Gay Liberation, an ancient Tiresias was queerly cutting-edge for the tempo of moderns in 1922. As intersex, "hermaphroditic," or inverted, he typifies queer and trans modernist temporality not in terms of speed—a theme See elsewhere addressed—but in terms of "the evening hour," or when the day grows old and nighttime revelries start in this gloaming. This is, I think, what See means when he states that this most ancient of ancients "is queer modernity" embodied. Speaking an arch gay slang "at the violet hour," Tiresias is a lifetime member in the Ancient Order of Pansies.

Making his claims for this pansy-prophet, See again deconstructs the ancient/modern divide as an old thing from Antiquity becomes the most novel of sexual typologies or, in his own words, "the queerest character." Rendering the antiquity/modernity binary unstable, he relies on the rhetorical device of the *autoantonym* to support his reading. Conducive to deconstruction, these devices—also known as Janus words—refer to terms that "depend upon their antitheses." According to See, Eliot treats concepts such as "order, history, and tradition" as Janus words, but we can add modernity and antiquity to this roster. An "old man with wrinkled female breasts," Tiresias is certainly ancient, but in See's reading he is also as contemporary as participants in Ford and Tyler's drag balls. I realize in drafting this last sentence that the imaginary conjured looks here like the close reading equivalent of an M. C. Escher sketch, but that is precisely See's point.

Curiously, near his presentation's close ancient times sync up not only with twentieth-century modernity but also the twenty-first century. "I suggest that we ourselves become waste lands and practice its ritual methods: we create history as myth," See writes. If we adopt this claim's logic, might we propel *The Waste Land* and its author even further into the "contemporary history" of modern sex in the West? When Tiresias sees the queer future at twilight, he not only foreshadows sailors. He also envisions a female typist who has a rendezvous with a male clerk described as "a youth of twentyone" in the poem's original drafts:

> I Tiresias, old man with wrinkled dugs
> Perceived the scene, and foretold the rest—
> [. . .]
> (And I Tiresias have foresuffered all
> Enacted on this same divan or bed;
> I who have sat by Thebes below the wall
> And walked among the lowest of the dead.) (61, 62)[27]

Unlike his role in the Oedipus cycle, what Tiresias portends is not the downfall of an ancient king but the most mundane and joyless heterosexual hookup in high modernism. The clerk's "vanity requires no response" from the typist, Tiresias observes, "and makes a welcome of indifference" (62). Again, the seer epitomizes a queer modern time in that he prophesizes and sexually enacts—"foresuffered all"—this scene of twentieth-century casual sex as a citizen of ancient Thebes. If we take into consideration See's claim that *The Waste Land*'s modernity is our contemporaneity as "we ourselves become waste lands" in 2011, does Eliot's invert also observe and predict the intensification of hookup culture?

Amplifying See's thesis that Tiresias is "a metonym of queer modernity," the poem foresees swipe left, swipe right encounters. *The Waste Land*'s now-old modernism proves both prescient and present, especially once we accept that "modernism is our antiquity" according to T. J. Clark's memorable epigram.[28] Taking one of the most canonical texts of modernism and rendering it of our moment, See's talk undoes the borderline between older accounts of experimentalism and any new form of modernist aesthetics. After "Making Modernism New" with Ford and Tyler, he does the same for Eliot.

III

In the decades following the publication of these experimental achievements, Tyler, Ford, and Eliot would respectively elaborate on their antiquated modernisms. Eliot released his *Essays Ancient and Modern* (1936) and went on to commend Roman poet Virgil's poetic achievements as unparalleled in his lecture, "What Is a Classic?," which he reproduced in *On Poetry and Poets* (1957). In *Magic and Myth of the Movies* (1947), Tyler would claim that "the actors of Hollywood are an enlarged personnel of the realistically anthropomorphic deities of ancient Greece."[29] Ford would dedicate much of his later life to his Operation Minotaur project in Nepal and then at The Dakota apartment building in New York's Upper West Side with his caretaker Indra Tamang. Along the way he directed the vanguard film *Johnny Minotaur* and published a Surrealist Art collage, "Sleep and Endymion," in the quarterly *Greek Heritage: The American Quarterly of Greek Culture* in 1965. See would have appreciated the final line of Ford's cheeky poem-poster: "This classic blend is still confused."[30]

A book could be written about these modernist writers' meditations on Antiquity during the Cold War and after. For this essay's purposes, one takeaway from my passing mention of their post-1945 productions is that experimental projects of queer Antiquity did not cease even as postmodernist literatures succeeded most modernist endeavors. I find myself intrigued that See's MLA paper notes, "Eliot's poem typifies how queers throughout the twentieth century ranging from Hart Crane to Audre Lorde used mythology to find a time for queerness out of time." Raising the stakes for modernist myth, See widens his thesis to encompass queer writing across the modern/postmodern partition, including Lorde's memoir *Zami: A New Spelling of My Name* (1982). Though he singles out this Afro-Caribbean writer, could we also add twentieth- and twenty-first-century queer theorists to this mix? "*The Waste Land*," See wrote, "has a queer future in the theoretical texts of our immediate present." Read literally, his account situates Eliot as a queer theorist *avant la lettre* who holds his own as a contemporary of José Esteban Muñoz, Heather Love, and others that See lists on queer temporality. To push the logic of his argument a bit more: What David Damrosch terms "ancient modernisms" have queer futures in contemporary North American queer theory.[31] "In this room, in our scholarship, in our classrooms," See writes, "we create a space for queerness . . . by accepting, like Eliot, the inevitability of chrononormativity." "We" contemporary theorists are not historically removed from Eliot but exactly "like"—as in *proximate to*—him.

See's claims for *The Waste Land* prompted me to look into how reliant present-day queer theory may be on antique modernists. Sedgwick first came to mind with her writing on the classicist Nietzsche in *Epistemology of the Closet*. More recent citations can be found in scholarly journals dedicated to pre-twentieth-century American studies, psychoanalytic ruminations on HIV, and the social anthropology of leather. Christopher Nealon, whose thoughts on affect, historiography, and modern American queer literature deeply influenced See, notes that "the left-theoretical stance on fragmentation and modernity in twenty-first-century queer theory . . . has developed a politics of 'queer temporality' that, like many concepts reworked from French poststructuralism, is itself a reworking of avant-garde and modernist practices of collage."[32] I also recall Tim Dean's psychoanalytic account of contemporary gay male barebackers, a twenty-first-century subcultural community that cultivates HIV virus through unprotected sex, or *breeding*: "self-identified barebackers represent themselves as *über*-men—as sexual professionals, experts in eros, and as sexual outlaws, pioneers of the erotic avant-garde."[33] A modernist scholar who has written eloquently on Eliot, Crane, Joyce, and Joseph Conrad, Dean describes these men as both sexual experimentalists and anti-modern modernists. In his account, barebackers carry the negative example of pansified inversion with them: "the persistent *fin-de-siècle* understanding of male homosexuality as gender inversion—a female soul trapped in a male body—has been expunged from bareback subculture, which concedes only degrees of masculinity."[34] As See intuited in his remarks about heteronormative breeding, some of our newest and most insightful forms of queer theory reiterate older modernist idioms that themselves modified ancient idioms. Aspects of its conceptual scaffolding spring from avant-garde waste lands and figures such as Karel, Tiresias, and Heliogabalus.

For a final example of modernist queer temporality in "our immediate present," take urban anthropologist Gayle Rubin, perhaps the most unlikely literary theorist whom See has cited. In a 2003 talk published the same year that See gave his MLA presentation, Rubin made a pitch for writings that queer theory often remainders: "the more I explore these queer knowledges, the more I find out how much we have already forgotten, rediscovered, and promptly forgotten again."[35] Rubin titled this talk "Geologies of Queer Studies: It's Déjà Vu All Over Again," and, "continually shocked," she argued against "the assumption that GLBTQ studies only got started sometime in the 1990s" (354–5). In her account, queer studies began not with post-structuralist theory or the HIV/AIDS crisis but with modernist sexological literatures by the likes of Edward Carpenter and his fellow queer moderns (351–2). Confirming See's observations, she reminds her audience that these authors often relied upon "biographies of famous homosexuals, material gleaned from the Greek and Latin classics" (352). Presenting herself as an intellectual geologist of contemporary queer theory, Rubin makes the same point that See does in his various pieces on mythology and Antiquity.

Her recent book *Deviations* is, in fact, as beholden to antiquated modernity as *The Young and Evil* or *The Waste Land* or See's "Queer Mythologies" project. Like Ford and Tyler, Rubin too dismantles partitions between modernity and antiquity—and had been doing so since at least the 1970s. When studying to become an anthropologist of Bay Area erotic cultures that Dean would also later survey, she thought herself a literary critic of ancient lesbian modernist studies. Included in *Deviations* is her Introduction to British author Renée Vivien's *A Woman Appeared to Me* (1904) that Naiad Press republished in 1976. Noting "Vivien read widely in myth, legend, and ancient literature" (93), Rubin contextualizes this classicist modern novel within Vivien's biography and finds that

> When Renée Vivien and Natalie Barney began their relationship, they each found a comrade in their literary war on behalf of women and lesbianism. Searching for their own roots, they discovered Sappho and Hellenism. They dreamed of establishing a group of women poets dedicated to Sappho, preferably on the island of Mytilene (Lesbos). . . . The two women declared themselves pagans, spiritual descendants of the Greeks. (92)

It seems far-fetched to connect lesbian moderns fantasizing about a colony of Sapphics in the early twentieth-century Aegean Sea with post-Stonewall leather/BDSM subcultures. But take Rubin's word for it in a *Deviations* chapter titled "The Catacombs: A Temple of the Butthole" that ethnographically surveys this sex club: "When I first heard of the Catacombs, the name conjured up images of the underground tombs of ancient Rome" (224). In an analogy paralleling the queer contemporaneity of *The Waste Land*, Rubin deconstructs Roman antiquity and American postmodernity to fashion herself a queer modernist scholar of antiquated kink.

From the 1890s to the 1920s to the 1970s to the 2010s, ancient queer modernism perseveres in Roman callbacks, Greek legends, pseudo-scientific sexology, uptown drag balls, online dating, experimental film, and perhaps the most influential poem of the twentieth century. See saw much of this. Like Rubin, Carpenter, Chauncey, Ford, Tyler, Dean, and Eliot, he performs the perpetual revivification of queer modernist studies that connects up with ancient times. Like Tiresias, he divined modernism—always a strange temporal loop for this scholar—across what may become known as the long twenty-first century. Seventy-six years after *The Young and Evil*, he too told lie after historical lie about queerness in order to make room for pioneering forms of well-established thinking. While recent in its findings, his work should become fabled in our fields.

As should See, a Hermes of making it critically new. So consider this essay an intellectual offering that invites mortal scholars to seek out his prose. May this queer thinker, too, become one of our more ancient—as in *venerable*—theorists. May his work live on in the lore of new modernist studies long after it has grown old. May scholars make good use of his writing and worship—as in *revere*—it as the Greeks did their high gods. May our future endeavors not forget these later "monuments of unaging intellect."[36]

NOTES

1. Katherine Catmull, "The Whole Universe Rocks," *Austin Chronicle*, December 12, 2003, https://www.austinchronicle.com/arts/2003-12-12 /189994/.

2. *"The Old Man and the Sea*: Modernist Literature," Essayworld, accessed July 18, 2017, http://www.essayworld.com/essays/The-Old-Man -Sea-Modernist-Literature/29790.

3. Matei Calinescu, *Five Faces of Modernity: Modernism, Avant-Garde, Decadence, Kitsch, Postmodernism* (Durham, N.C.: Duke University Press, 1987), 35. For a useful reassessment of Calinescu, see Mark Wollaeger, "Modernism under Review: Matei Calinescu's *Five Faces of Modernity:*

Modernism, Avant-Garde, Decadence, Kitsch, Postmodernism (1987)," *Modernist Cultures* 8, no. 2 (2013): 163–78. See also Sean Latham and Gayle Rogers, *Modernism: Evolution of an Idea* (London: Bloomsbury, 2015), 20.

4. Harry Levin, *Memories of the Moderns* (New York: New Directions, 1980), 6, 8.

5. *Oxford English Dictionary*, s.v., "ancient," accessed June 28, 2018, http://www.oed.com.

6. *Oxford English Dictionary*, s.v., "antiquity," accessed June 28, 2018, http://www.oed.com.

7. T. S. Eliot, *The Waste Land*, in *Collected Poems: 1909–1962* (New York: Harcourt, Brace, and World, 1970), 58. Hereafter cited parenthetically in the body of the text.

8. W. B. Yeats, "Sailing to Byzantium," in *The Tower: A Facsimile Edition* (1928; New York: Scribner, 2004), 3.

9. In-depth investigations of this matter include *Byzantium/Modernism: The Byzantine as Method in Modernity*, ed. Roland Betancourt and Maria Taroutina (Leiden, Netherlands: Brill, 2015); Christopher Green and Jens M. Daehner, *Modern Antiquity: Picasso, De Chirico, Léger, Picabia* (Los Angeles: J. Paul Getty Museum, 2011); Dimitrios Yatromanolakis, *Greek Mythologies: Antiquity and Surrealism* (Cambridge: Harvard University Press, 2014); J. Alison Rosenblitt, *E. E. Cummings' Modernism and the Classics: Each Imperishable Stanza* (New York: Oxford University Press, 2016); Leah Culligan Flack, *Modernism and Homer: The Odysseys of H. D., James Joyce, Osip Mandelstam, and Ezra Pound* (Cambridge: Cambridge University Press, 2015); *The Ancient World in Silent Cinema*, ed. Pantelis Michelakis and Maria Wyke (New York: Cambridge University Press, 2013); Ana Carden-Coyne, *Reconstructing the Body: Classicism, Modernism, and the First World War* (New York: Oxford University Press, 2009); *The Classics in Modernist Translation*, ed. Miranda Hickman and Lynn Kozak (London: Bloomsbury, 2019); and Gregory Jusdanis, "Farewell to the Classical: Excavations in Modernism," *Modernism/modernity* 11, no. 1 (2004): 37–53.

10. Michael North, *Novelty: A History of the New* (Chicago: University of Chicago Press, 2013), 205.

11. Richard von Krafft-Ebing, *Psychopathia Sexualis, with Especial Reference to the Antipathic Sexual Instinct: A Medico-Forensic Study*, trans. Franklin S. Klaf (1886; New York: Arcade, 1998), 3.

12. George Chauncey, *Gay New York: Gender, Urban Culture, and the Making of the Gay Male World, 1890–1940* (New York: Basic Books, 1994), 283.

13. Ibid., 284, 285. See cites both texts in an endnote as he further extends Chauncey's claims.

14. The reproduction can be found in *Gay New York*, 53.

15. Steven Watson, Introduction to Charles Henri Ford and Parker Tyler, *The Young and Evil* (1933; New York: Gay Presses of New York, 1988), xxv.

16. Charles Henri Ford and Parker Tyler, *The Young and Evil* (1933; New York: Gay Presses of New York, 1988), 17. Hereafter cited parenthetically in the body of the text.

17. See Kathy Peiss, *Hope in a Jar: The Making of America's Beauty Culture* (New York: Metropolitan, 1998), and *The Modern Girl Around the World: Consumption, Modernity, and Globalization*, ed. The Modern Girl Around the World Research Group (Alys Eve Weinbaum, Lynn M. Thomas, Priti Ramamurthy, Uta G. Poiger, Madeleine Y. Dong, and Tani E. Barlow) (Durham, N.C.: Duke University Press, 2008).

18. Vinzenz Brinkmann, "Research in the Polychromy of Ancient Sculpture: Introduction to the Exhibition," in *Gods in Color: Painted Sculpture of Classical Antiquity*, ed. Vinzenz Brinkmann and Raimund Wünsche (Munich: Stiftung Archäologie Glyptothek Munich, 2007), 21.

19. "The World's First Cosmetic Pencil," Schwan Cosmetics, accessed June 28, 2018, https://www.schwancosmetics.com/en/company/about-us#c9c d6eba3e06e510VgnVCM10000009ie1cacRCRD-6.

20. Sam See, "'Spectacles in Color': The Primitive Drag of Langston Hughes," in the present volume. For more on Bessie Smith's relation to queer Harlem, see Eric Garber, "A Spectacle in Color: The Lesbian and Gay Subculture of Jazz Age Harlem," in *Hidden from History: Reclaiming the Gay and Lesbian Past*, ed. Martin Duberman, Martha Vicinus, and George Chauncey, Jr. (New York: New American Library, 1989), 318–31.

21. Ibid.

22. Chauncey, *Gay New York*, 291.

23. See Tim Dean, "T. S. Eliot, Famous Clairvoyante," in *Gender, Desire, and Sexuality in T. S. Eliot*, ed. Cassandra Laity and Nancy K. Gish (Cambridge: Cambridge University Press, 2004), 43–65, and Wayne Koestenbaum, *Double Talk: The Erotics of Male Literary Collaboration* (New York: Routledge, 1989).

24. For an exhaustive overview of Tiresias's cultural representations, see Ed Madden, *Tiresian Poetics: Modernism, Sexuality, Voice, 1888–2001* (Madison, N.J.: Fairleigh Dickinson University Press, 2008).

25. Bruce Rodgers, *Gay Talk: A (Sometimes Outrageous) Dictionary of Gay Slang* (1972; San Francisco: Paragon, 1979), 202.

26. Ibid.

27. T. S. Eliot, *The Waste Land: A Facsimile and Transcript of the Original Drafts, Including the Annotations of Ezra Pound*, ed. Valerie Eliot (New York: Harvest, 1971). 33. For a keen reading of these lines in relation to modernist impersonality, see Dean, "T. S. Eliot, Famous Clairvoyante," 57–61.

28. T. J. Clark, *Farewell to an Idea: Episodes from a History of Modernism* (New Haven: Yale University Press, 1999), 2.

29. Parker Tyler, *Magic and Myth of the Movies* (New York: Henry Holt, 1947), xxvii. Watson rightly states that "this would be a theme of his film criticism for the next 30 years" (Watson, xix).

30. Charles Henri Ford, "Sleep and Endymion," *Greek Heritage: The American Quarterly of Greek Culture* 2, no. 6 (1965): 41.

31. David Damrosch, "Antiquity," in *A New Vocabulary for Global Modernism*, ed. Eric Hayot and Rebecca L. Walkowitz (New York: Columbia University Press, 2016), 45.

32. Christopher Nealon, "The Matter of Literacy, or, Poetry without Modernity," *J19: The Journal of Nineteenth-Century Americanists* 1, no. 1 (2013): 211.

33. Tim Dean, *Unlimited Intimacy: Reflections on the Subculture of Barebacking* (Chicago: University of Chicago Press, 2009), 39.

34. Ibid., 50.

35. Gayle S. Rubin, *Deviations: A Gayle Rubin Reader* (Durham, N.C.: Duke University Press, 2011), 347. Hereafter cited parenthetically in the body of the text.

36. Yeats, "Sailing to Byzantium," 1.

Contrary/Sexual/Feeling

Heather Love

For had not each
In its own way tried to teach
My will to love you that it cannot be,
As I think, of such consequence to want
What anyone is given, if they want?

—w. h. auden, "A Lesson"

I first met Sam See in 2008 at the Los Angeles Queer Studies conference. I attended his presentation on *Nightwood*, "Djuna Barnes's Concentrated Camp," in which he argued that Barnes "converted a conventionally urbane queer aesthetic into a resource for making politically queer claims on behalf of nature."[1] I was surprised and intrigued by See's claims on behalf of *queer nature*: I couldn't remember having ever heard these words used in the same sentence. I was also impressed by his keen sensitivity to the tonal contradictions of Barnes's novel. We chatted a bit, and I asked him to send me his paper. We wrote back and forth, sharing our fandom for *Nightwood* ("everything is in there and everything is true"), but also testing out some ideas about queer feeling and modernism. There was a kind of urgency to the conversation, and it occurred to me that we were both looking to Barnes's modernist masterpiece for answers to real-time, pressing problems. I identified with See's outsized demands as a reader, and with his attempt to reconcile modernist aesthetics with a full-spectrum experience of queerness—or with a full-spectrum experience of any kind. "Urbane queer aesthetic" and "nature" were See's terms, but I felt it too: a need and, increasingly, a professional obligation, to resolve the tension between high style and low feeling.

Can it be done? Who knows. But *Nightwood* is a good place to turn. T. S. Eliot praised the book for raising "the matter to be communicated . . . to the first intensity" through its "prose rhythm."[2] That is a job of work, since in this case that matter includes cross-dressing, cruising, bestiality, amateur gynecology, epic lesbian stalking, and more. For Eliot, as for many other critics, Barnes's style was understood to save the phenomena, giving a high modernist sheen to activities more closely associated with the gutter, the clinic, and the prison cell. In Los Angeles, See began with a reflection, citing Jane Marcus, about how it is impossible to know whether to laugh or cry at the ending of *Nightwood*. He had a lot to say about the book's final image of a woman "going down" with a dog. "Emotional and physical atavism," he argued, "provide the sympathetic feeling necessary to understand queer difference and queer suffering, none of which *Nightwood*'s denizens comprehends until they 'bow down.'" Many readers would see emotional and physical atavism as precluding an understanding of queer difference and queer suffering, but for See they were the preconditions for sympathetic and political response. Barnes, embracing abjection and willing the reader to do so too ("bow down" is a command), suggested that it was only through identification with all that is low that connection is possible. See writes, "*Nightwood*'s concentrated camp attempts to regenerate the queer community by degrading it. As [Doctor Matthew] O'Connor puts it, 'in the acceptance of depravity the sense of the past is most fully captured [. . .] we do not "climb" to heights, we are eaten away to them, and then conformity, neatness, ceases to entertain us.'"

In collecting and editing See's published and unpublished work, Christopher Looby and Michael North have done a great service to the fields of queer and modernist studies. Page by page, See conducts virtuosic readings across several genres, placing both canonical and non-canonical queer texts in an expansive context of literary and philosophical modernity. These essays are characterized by their formal acuity and historical sensitivity. But beyond the pleasures of the individual readings and essays, one sees the lineaments of major, field-transforming arguments, whose impact, thanks to this collection, is ours to absorb. Through their careful editorial work, Looby and North have allowed the ambition and scope of See's scholarship to become visible. They have presented this material to emphasize two fascinating but unfinished book projects, *Queer Natures: Feeling Degenerate in Literary Modernism* and *Queer*

Mythologies: Community and Memory in Modern Literature. Across these two books, See developed arguments that, if they have an ambiguous status in modernist literature and criticism, are extremely difficult to reconcile with the conceptual and political frameworks of queer studies. Nature and myth point to central but disregarded strands of queer representation, but these are in conflict with the *doxa* of a field that defines itself through its iconoclasm and in its unbending stance against nature.

Queer Natures, Queer Mythologies crystallizes many key issues in recent queer studies, from the concern with affect and sensation to the rethinking of Darwin's legacy to the cultivation of a critical practice defined by reparation and care. At the same time, See's thinking is out ahead of the field, or in opposition to it: In his questioning of the epistemological ground and the political effects of anti-essentialism; in his rethinking of the place of science and of Enlightenment values more broadly; and in his testing of anti-normativity as a framework for politics, See demurs from fundamental principles of queer studies. Throughout, one feels the force of hard-won and deeply personal insights. See's engagements with queer aesthetics and queer history are characterized not only by methodological rigor but also moral seriousness. His ability—in fact, his drive—to follow a question to its end, and to use what Phillip Brian Harper calls "the evidence of felt intuition" to push past agreements in the field, make his work indispensable.[3] The impulse to think against the grain—*à rebours*—is fundamental to queer thought, and See's scholarship is exemplary in its intellectual and political risk-taking. Coming to terms with what is abjected from discourse, even from the discourse of the outcast and the marginalized, is an urgent task, and one that can never be completed. In the wake of Sam See's death and the impossible feelings it occasions, we need his passionate, contrarian thought more than ever.

Queers come by their hatred of nature honestly. From late nineteenth-century aestheticism to the New Queer Cinema, artists proudly took up the mantle of nature's outcasts, choosing to affiliate themselves with artifice, sterility, and perversity instead. Queer criticism, when it emerged in the late 1980s, drew on this tradition as well as popular and activist distrust of medicine and the biological sciences to refuse the discourse of the natural. The energy produced by this refusal of the natural order has been tremendous and has served as a bulwark against the imperatives of health, reproduction, and the optimization of life. As See points out in "Charles Darwin, Queer Theorist," it was not so much nature as "the naturalistic fallacy" that we should be understood as the enemy of queerness: the ideology of nature, or "the association of nature with normativity" (this and subsequent quotations are to the essay in the present volume). By disarticulating nature from the naturalistic fallacy, and by turning his attention away from the dominant discourses of sexology and eugenics, See makes it possible to see the queer energies within nature. This project is at once theoretical and historical. In exploring the potential of Darwinian thought for queer aesthetics and community life, *Queer Natures* has affinities with scholarship in science studies that has centered non-binary and non-reductive traditions of biological thought.[4] But it also anticipates recent work in ontology and ethics that looks to the natural world as a model for the complexity and contingency of queer and feminist modes of life.[5] See's project is not only or even primarily theoretical: It grounds speculative thought in a careful history of late nineteenth- and twentieth-century queer attachments to nature and the natural world. Demonstrating the centrality of the concept of nature in queer modernity— from sexology to radical evolutionary thought to modernist primitivism— See describes aesthetic and philosophical projects that were "natural but not normative." He recalls a powerful but mostly overlooked history of queer feeling: the longing to have a range of sexual practices, dispositions, and gendered forms of being be understood as *natural*—as part of nature's plan rather than a deviation from it. At the same time that queers have embraced artifice and artificiality they have also sought to expand the definition of nature so as to make room for themselves within it.

The claim is striking in its simplicity, and in its sheer descriptive power. See unearths a tradition of queer thought and feeling that is pervasive but sits uneasily within the epistemological and ideological frames of the field. Eve Kosofsky Sedgwick created an opening for this work through her engagement with the mid-century psychologist Silvan Tomkins. In her 1995 essay, co-authored with Adam Frank, "Shame in the Cybernetic Fold," Sedgwick challenged the reflex stance against nature and biology informing critical theory and cultural criticism. The essay begins with a list of a "few things theory knows today," one of which is that "the distance" of "any account of human beings or cultures . . . from a biological basis is assumed to correlate almost precisely with its potential for doing justice to difference (individual, historical, and cross-cultural), to contingency, to performative force, and to the possibility of change."[6] This essay not only brought attention to Tomkins's work but it also was crucial in centering affect in queer studies. See's work can be understood as part of the affective turn in queer studies, but his attention to nature suggests a different genealogy and a different configuration of feeling, the body, the drives, and aesthetics. See not only insists on seeing aesthetics and nature in the same framework; he also grounds this insight in readings of queer history, drawing attention to "an overlooked strain of modernist aesthetics that views nature itself as an aesthetic object, a source of aesthetic and sexual feeling, and literature not just as a representation of nature but as itself a part of nature."

In addition to arguing, contra Kant, for the centrality of desire and sensation in aesthetic judgment, See elaborates a queer modernist tradition of what he calls "evolutionary aesthetics." This tradition includes unexpected figures such as Virginia Woolf, associated with canonical modernism committed to the ironic displacement of necessity and nature. In a reading of Woolf's last novel, *Between the Acts* (1941), See challenges this reception, focusing on the significance of atavism and self-divestiture in her work. Drawing on the image of camp he developed in his account of *Nightwood*, See reads the formal experiment of this novel, which integrates the form of the drama through its staging of a rural pageant, as an attempt to forge the image of a collectivity in conditions of wartime. Again, it is her use of comedy and degradation that, in See's view, allows Woolf to strip down her characters and imagine their relations anew, outside of nationalist allegiance. See contemplates the similarities between Woolf's rhetoric and Hitler's eugenic discourse of degeneration, suggesting that she distinguishes between the ideology of nature and nature itself, and between scientism and science. Recalling Woolf's desire to "take naturalists notes— human naturalists notes," he argues that *Between the Acts* constitutes a parody of appropriations of evolution for eugenic and misogynist ends. Through the representation of this community as "savages," See argues, Woolf "depicts all of humanity under the weight of Darwin's oppressive principle of feminine submission, stripping life of constructed difference to return it to Darwin's infinitely variegated state of nature. Woolf camps sexual selection, in other words, to concentrate natural selection and variation" (see "The Comedy of Nature: Darwinian Feminism in Virginia Woolf's *Between the Acts*" in the present volume).

See draws attention to modernist authors who use laughter to explode the normative conception of nature and to render it queer. The names that See gives to this laughter are defining terms of queer aesthetics, drag, and camp. He thus effects a collapse of nature and culture that has been one of the aims of science studies in the past few decades. But he also expresses faith in the power of queerness to undermine and resist pathologizing taxonomies. In "'Spectacles in Color': The Primitive Drag of Langston Hughes," See considers the coincidence of Hughes's representation of blackness and queerness with stereotypes of degeneracy in his poetry collection *The Weary Blues* (1926). Focusing on Hughes's engagement with "down-low" and "low-down" characters and practices, See discusses how tropes of drag or crossing transmute identity into feeling. For Hughes, as for Barnes and Woolf, there is no escape from the degeneracy that attaches to modernity's outsiders: Instead, he embraces stereotypical qualities such as gender indeterminacy, arrested development, and a taste for spectacle and adornment, and revalues them. As in Woolf's repurposing of terms borrowed from eugenics in the early 1940s, Hughes's engagement with primitivism carried very high stakes during the Harlem Renaissance, when new forms of black social organization and expressive culture flourished alongside anti-black violence, American nativism, and pseudo-scientific discourses of white supremacy. As See shows, by activating the form of the blues, Hughes drew on vernacular aesthetic strategies to "debunk pathologizing taxonomies of blacks and queers even while retaining the nature-based premises of those discursive stereotypes" (see "'Spectacles in Color': The Primitive Drag of Langston Hughes" in the present volume). While some critics might be happy to see those nature-based premises thrown out with the pathologizing taxonomies they underwrote, See insists that the idea of nature is deeply tied to the body, sex, and feeling, and therefore to the material basis for community. To extirpate Hughes's investments in queer nature from the knot of his aesthetic practice is thus to sacrifice too much.

See's second project, *Queer Mythologies*, takes up a term that has—if possible—even less standing in the field of queer literary and cultural studies than nature. Myth is tainted by its association with universalism, cultural tourism, and non-modern forms of thought; nonetheless, as See persuasively shows, myth has been crucial to queer representation and self-understanding across the twentieth century. He writes, "Myth is generically defined as both a falsehood and a foundational tale: it is a factually untrue story that explains inexplicable phenomena in typically supernatural terms; such stories often ground the formation of selves and communities" (this and the subsequent quotation are from "The Myth of Nature" in the present volume). See takes up myth as foundational fiction in order to explore the unexpected paths of community making in the twentieth century. This turn to myth has affinities with the queer desire to "feel historical" described by Christopher Nealon.[7] Given the historical isolation of queers and the burden of pathology, what Nealon calls the "harrowing privacy of the inversion model" (8), twentieth-century queers sought to forge links with a distant past that could authorize them in the present. See cites Parker Tyler's long poem *The Granite Butterfly* (1945), which points to the necessity of myth and its status as fabrication:

> So myth has always been
> A lie, the moment it was uttered
>   just as, the moment it was
> Uttered, it was also a truth:
>   it was a lie to test
> The truth, and a truth to test the
>   lie . . .

Exploring Tyler's engagement with classical myth, See considers the motivations and effects of queer mythmaking, ingeniously linking it to T. S. Eliot's concept of the "mythic method." See counters the view of queer modernism as the minor representation of an isolated community. As he argues, "the queer modernist need to '*feel historical*,' as Nealon says, manifested itself not only as a queer need for personal and ethnic history but as a modernist need for universal history, one accessed in this novel through the conduit of queer desire" (see "Making Modernism New: Queer Mythology in *The Young and Evil*" in the present volume).

See's writing on myth is linked to his writing on nature by a willingness to credit feeling as both evidence and justification. "Feeling natural," or feeling like one is part of nature, should not be judged by the criteria of truth and falsity. It is a state of belief, and its effects are best judged on moral rather than epistemological grounds. See extends this thinking into myth in a reading of the statement "I was born this way." Within the framework of queer critique, this statement appears a naïve and potentially dangerous belief in the power of science to justify homosexuality. According to this line of thought, "born this way" runs the risk of unwitting collaboration with eugenicist thinking and replaces the complexity of queer experience, culture, and politics with a reductive understanding of same-sex desire as programmed in the body and the brain. While making no bones about the falsity of this claim about the etiology of homosexuality, See reframes it as a statement of belief and bodily experience, and urges his readers to respond to it in a different key. In an act of critical and ethical virtuosity, See describes how "born that way" can be understood as "a statement of subjective feeling and belief, outside of politics, that nonetheless offers the grounds for political organization." He continues,

From this view, the feeling (not the etiological content) of "I was born this way" cannot be challenged on scientific grounds—if anything, it can only be supported by them. As a felt belief (rather than a knowledge claim), "I was born this way" is a mythic statement because it is both false and foundational: It is a lie about etiology that tells the truth about sexual feeling. The statement is false because its etiological pronouncement cannot be verified scientifically; and it is foundational insofar as it records the sensational embodiment of queer feeling. [See "The Myth of Nature" in the present volume.]

To foreground feeling in this way—at the expense of truth—is to break with the norms of academic discourse. There are precedents for this kind of deviation in queer studies, however: Since its inception, scholars in the field have made an art of such rule-breaking. Although Sedgwick has given us perhaps the most effective tools to break the spell that "Born this way" has on the popular and political imagination, she also offers a powerful example of a willingness to break with truth as the key criterion of academic writing. Sedgwick's most powerful and explicit argument about the need to loosen the strictures of truth is in her essay "Paranoid Reading and Reparative Reading." The essay opens with a call to attend to the performative effects of knowledge rather than its truth-value: She imagines how we might move from the "rather fixated question" of whether or not a "particular piece of knowledge [is] true" to the question "What does knowledge *do*."[8] Sedgwick, recalling a discussion with Cindy Patton about the origins of HIV, argues for the political and analytical significance of this shift. But in the rest of the essay she goes on to emphasize the affective dimensions, juxtaposing the paranoid epistemology of Freud and the affirmative thought of Proust. Sedgwick describes the Proustian narrator, who "in the last volume" of *Remembrance of Things Past* feels "jostling each other within me a whole host of truths concerning human passions and character and conduct,"—and who recognizes these observations as truths insofar as *"the perception of [them] caused me joy."* Sedgwick continues, "In the paranoid Freudian epistemology, it is implausible enough to suppose that truth could be an even accidental occasion of joy, inconceivable to imagine joy as a guarantor of truth. Indeed, from any point of view it is circular, or something, to suppose that one's pleasure at knowing something could be taken as evidence of the truth of the knowledge" (137–8).

Sedgwick acknowledges that she is treading on strange ground here, because criticism—and academic discourse generally—might be defined by its willingness to play by the rules of truth: to understand truth as a

matter of verifiable reference to an existing state of affairs, rather than as
a tendency to produce joy. Sedgwick does go on to offer a somewhat traditional defense of positive affect theory, suggesting that, if it is "circular,
or something," it is "no more tautological" than the paranoid view (138),
which depends on airless, self-confirming arguments. But suggesting this
equivalence does not solve the problem of the tautological nature of Sedgwick's account of reparative reading. What is so good about reparative
reading: It gives joy, it causes pleasure, it aims to repair rather than to
destroy. Reparative reading is good because it does not traffic in the
scouring, scathing vigilance that characterizes paranoid reading. In
short, reparative reading is good because it is good, because it is grounded
in love and care rather than hate and suspicion. Such claims cannot be
evaluated according to traditional criteria: They break with the protocols
of academic discourse, and they ask us to break with them as well. What
happens in "Paranoid Reading and Reparative Reading," what it performs,
is a defection, necessarily incomplete, from academic criticism.

Throughout his writings, See suggests that such a defection is necessary to attend to the experiments and aspirations of queer authors across
the twentieth century. Mythology was for these authors a supreme fiction,
a falsehood that set queer life in motion. On this point, See cites Parker
Tyler's reflections on the experimental novel that he wrote with Charles
Henri Ford, *The Young and Evil* (1933): "'The main point' of the novel, he
maintained, 'is NOT whether there are any new scientific conclusions but
whether there are any new phenomena'" (see "Making Modernism New:
Queer Mythology in *The Young and Evil*" in the present volume). By refusing the regime of truth and even of reality, early twentieth-century
queers set unheard of desires resonating across the social field and created
the conditions for new forms of community. It is a hallmark of See's
thought, and a sign of his mettle, that he sees the value of these experiments not only in their consequences for community and politics but also
for desire. Setting this claim alongside Sedgwick's suggestion that we judge
the value of forms of thought by their capacity to give joy highlights See's
willingness to break with norms of academic argument and value. Given
that the justification for See is not the (universally) valued positive affect
of joy, but rather desire—and in particular queer, low-down desire—it is
all the more striking that he is willing to make the case. If in writing about
queer nature, See revalues sexual desire by linking it to the aesthetic sense,
in his account of queer myth desire is valued for its own sake.

In a reading of Audre Lorde's biomythography, *Zami: A New Spelling of
My Name* (1982), See considers the narrator's relation to the island of Car-

riacou (*"How Carriacou women love each other is legend in Grenada"*). See
writes, "The source of sexual 'legend,' Carriacou is also for Audre the
source of feeling about the body and sensation . . . Carriacou represents,
then, a 'truly private paradise'; for Audre, where 'private' connotes not only
her selfhood but her body and its feelings, especially the sexual feelings
that connect her to evanescent social networks" (this and the subsequent
quotation are from "The Myth of Nature" in the present volume). Myth
is crucial in conjuring an origin for community, but, as See notes, it is community achieved in and through the body. See focuses on the book's final
sentence—"There it is said that the desire to lie with other women is a drive
from the mother's blood." He writes,

> Though ostensibly an essentialist claim—one that sounds very much
> like I was born this way—this sentence actually propounds a mythic
> claim about the somatic nature of queerness. As she has all along with
> Carriacou lore, Audre acknowledges that this idea is a legend—"there it
> is said"—even as she places this sentence directly after her realization
> that she has "discovered" Carriacou's "latitudes": that she has found a
> way to root her belief in what constitutes "home." What constitutes
> home, for this queer woman, is naturally encoded in "the mother's
> blood": "the desire to lie with other women." "Lie" here functions
> polysemously, as Audre relates how her relationships with women
> often ended on the basis of lies, exemplified by her relationship with
> Muriel. But, just as myths are lies that tell the truth, so too do these
> lies tell the truth of queerness' nature: It is a lie about "the blood" that
> tells the truth about "desire."

For See, myth is a lie that tells the truth, and tells it in the medium of blood.
If arguments against essentialism are effective in disrupting reductive and
pathologizing taxonomies, they produce other forms of damage by failing
to reckon with the "somatic nature of queerness."

See's focus on "lying" here—rather than the more neutral fiction—
suggests how his vision of embodied desire and sexual community are not
pastoral or perfect. Queerness lives in the body, and as a result low feelings, and feeling low, are inseparable from it. In his reading of *The Young
and Evil*, he explores how the process of "turning queer" depends on
"queer turning"—a betrayal of the other and an aestheticized turn toward
"labile and multi-directional desire" (see "Making Modernism New: Queer
Mythology in *The Young and Evil*" in the present volume). In his exploration of "failurism" in Hart Crane's *The Bridge*, See draws on Lee Edelman's
reading of catachresis as "a language whereby Crane might articulate a

desire for which no 'proper' language existed" (this and subsequent quotations are from "American Failurism: Hart Crane's *The Bridge* and Kenneth Burke's Paradox of Purity" in the present volume). See writes, "For Crane, in other words, the failure of linguistic union is analogous to the failure of sexual union, making his broken language assume specifically referential and political significance. Especially for homosexuality, still the love that dare not speak its name in the 1920s, and for unfulfilled, broken erotic unions of any kind, catachresis opens space for poetic expression of unidealized, 'disreputable' desire, or desire that the myth of heterosexual union would efface into namelessness." See reads *The Bridge* as a meditation on the "space of sexual contradiction . . . where failure is success, where the failed attempt at union is tantamount to union," and suggests that Crane uses "unfulfilled, broken erotic unions of any kind" to allegorize the broken unity of the nation. But this brokenness brings with it its own form of paradoxical success: Crane "communize[s] love relations through their brokenness, their failure to signify in absolute ways."

If blood and the body make irrefutable claims on us, it is nonetheless difficult to put those claims into words: This is one of the reasons we turn to literature, which at least makes the enigma of desire central. In a foundational though rarely acknowledged source for queer literary studies, Barbara Johnson writes,

> If human beings were not divided into two biological sexes, there would probably be no need for literature. And if literature could truly say what the relations between the sexes are, we would doubtless not need much of it then, either . . . It is not the life of sexuality that literature cannot capture; it is literature that inhabits the very heart of what makes sexuality problematic for us speaking animals. Literature is not only a thwarted investigator but also an incorrigible perpetrator of the problem of sexuality.[9]

See shows a remarkable sensitivity to this problem, and, as I have suggested, courage in his willingness to wrestle openly with it. See demonstrates an acute awareness of the curtailments of academic discourse, and of how the field of gender and sexuality studies can inadvertently block its objects from view. Nonetheless, he calls on queer critics to engage in a "ritual" and "mythopoeic" criticism, and he leads by example. Across his writing, he engages the body in language, risking exposure and being "wrong." In the late essay, "The Cruelty of Breeding," he describes a queer body that is out of time, inhabited by the waste of history, despoiled. By identifying himself with that waste, by giving himself over to it, See shows us what queer criticism can be: "not only a thwarted investigator but also an incorrigible perpetrator of the problem of sexuality."

NOTES

1. See elaborates this discussion of camp in the book through his reading of Virginia Woolf's *Between the Acts*, not *Nightwood*. See the text that follows for further discussion of his reading of Woolf.

2. T. S. Eliot, Introduction, Djuna Barnes, *Nightwood* (New York: New Directions, 1961), xii.

3. Phillip Brian Harper, "The Evidence of Felt Intuition: Minority Experience, Everyday Life, and Critical Speculative Knowledge" *GLQ: A Journal of Lesbian and Gay Studies* 6, no. 4 (2000): 641–57.

4. See engages especially closely with Elizabeth Grosz's rereading of Darwin, but one might also look to the work of Donna Haraway, Elizabeth Wilson, and Karen Barad.

5. See, for instance, the essays collected in *New Materialisms: Ontology, Agency, and Politics*, ed. Diana Coole and Samantha Frost (Durham, N.C.: Duke University Press, 2010).

6. Eve Kosofsky Sedgwick and Adam Frank, "Shame in the Cybernetic Fold: Reading Silvan Tomkins," *Critical Inquiry* 21 (Winter 1995): 496–522, 496.

7. Christopher Nealon, *Foundlings: Lesbian and Gay Historical Emotion before Stonewall* (Durham, N.C.: Duke University Press, 2001), 8.

8. Sedgwick, "Paranoid Reading and Reparative Reading, or, You're So Paranoid You Probably Think This Essay Is About You," *Touching Feeling: Affect, Pedagogy, Performativity* (Durham, N.C.: Duke University Press, 2002): 123–51, 124 (italics in original).

9. Barbara Johnson, *The Critical Difference: Essays in the Contemporary Rhetoric of Reading* (Baltimore: Johns Hopkins University Press, 1985), 13.

Late Sam See

Wendy Moffat

Knowing When

Late, adj. 9c of the latter part of a creator's career;
10 occurring or taking place toward the end of an event, process, etc.;
that is, far on in the course of proceedings.

—*Oxford English Dictionary*

Late in his life, at a moment when a young scholar might polish his port-folio in a familiar academic ritual, Sam See did something recklessly brave.

Sam had already written a remarkable book discerning Darwin's "comic vision." *Queer Natures* reread both the evolution of literature from Victo-rian to modern and the history of queer theory in oscillating discourse. Sam's clear-eyed interdisciplinary reading found in Darwin's *Origin of Species* the "radical possibility of representing and creating the material mu-tability of the natural world itself" (see "Charles Darwin, Queer Theorist"). In discovering the queer inherent in Darwin's forms, Sam wrested the idea of "the natural" away from the familiar frames of Foucault's archeol-ogy of knowledge and Freud's persistent myth. It was a monumental project to recuperate nature and the natural as an essential category of inquiry for queer theory and modern literature. Sam showed us, to paraphrase Virginia Woolf, how the proper understanding of nature is "a little other than custom would have us believe."[1]

Reclaiming nature as a site of (and for) the queer was not sufficient for Sam. *Queer Natures* accepted Eve Kosofsky Sedgwick's "serpentine claim" that archival examination of the queer past could never distinguish the epistemological dancer from the dance. Sam was aware that the "status of knowledge and the methods by which it's produced, repudiate the category of knowledge" itself.[2] In *Epistemology of the Closet*, Sedgwick argues that

> modern "sexuality" and hence modern homosexuality are so intimately entangled with the historically distinctive contexts and structures that now count as *knowledge* that such "knowledge" can scarcely be a transparent window onto a separate realm of sexuality but, rather, itself constitutes that sexuality.[3]

Sam's critique of Foucault stemmed from two central flaws, both resting on what is afforded the status of evidence in empirical discourse. Foucault, Sam argued, looked away from aesthetic forms; his analysis was limited to "logical discourses" ("Charles Darwin"). And building on this, Sam believed, was an inevitable slippage, which "denaturalized the sexual body," because "science regarded nature as a moral rather than an empirical category" ("Charles Darwin"). Sam sought to rethink the category of the natural to make a space for the "useless," the aesthetic.

But Sam understood that the warp of history—the yearning for a queer past—imposed complex generic and affective constraints of its own. (In Neil Bartlett's *Who Was That Man?: A Present for Mr. Oscar Wilde* and Heather Love's *Feeling Backward: Loss and the Politics of Queer History*, there is an inescapable arc of tragedy in the recuperation of a queer past.) Sam was concerned that queer inquiries themselves have become ritualized claims to knowledge, and that in returning to them time and again we make them into "sacred texts that offer foundational falsehoods about the queerness for which time will never have time."[4] History takes queer inquiry only so far.[5]

And so, Sam sketched out a second, massive project in a different but equally true epistemological register, which he named *Queer Mythologies*. For queers, myth-seeking and mythmaking opened recuperative paths cut off by discourses of logic. For Sam, "queerness lives in myth" and its "dialectical process of union and fracture" across and against time ("The Cruelty of Breeding"). Myth is not only a way to find "a time for queerness out of time"—as queer writers from Hart Crane to E. M. Forster to George

Platt Lynes to Audre Lorde have explored. In *Queer Mythologies*, Sam explored "the appeal of the spiritual" in queer epistemology, the non-logical discourses of desire ("Statement of Plans," 3). He took up Heather Love's statement in *Feeling Backward* that "if queer figures of the past are going to have a future, '*we are that future*'"[6]:

> "we" being the interpreters of artifacts. In ritualizing this claim . . .
> and in allowing ourselves to harbor and enliven the detritus of
> history . . . we ourselves become waste lands and practice its ritual
> methods: We create history as myth, as the utopian space in which
> waste [and degeneration] might reside since it will never, after all,
> reside in time. Queers are too late for time, so we can stop trying to
> catch up with it. History is what creates our waste; it is the impulse of
> mythopoeia, queer time, to find lands, spaces, for that waste. ("Cruelty
> of Breeding")[7]

Myth affords a way to rethink queer identity, untethers desire from the rules of time. Sam argued that

> The myth of nature was one of many myths that allowed queers to
> believe in their own historicity and in the possibility of transhistorical
> and transnational communities that are paradoxically founded on the
> criterion of difference. ("The Myth of Nature")

In Sam's work, the warp of history and the weft of myth open complementary ways of knowing: History, timeful and timebound, anchored in the subjectivity of this moment, looking at the past with fresh eyes, most profoundly, stopping it, writing it, so that it can go forward, and knit the ways of the past to now; Myth, timeless, and allowing time to bend, escape its structure of inevitability, slip off its clothing of the cultural moment, get scrambled, even run backwards. Because he had such profligate intellectual energy, Sam's leavings are impoliticly ambitious. With loving care, Christopher Looby and Michael North have pieced together the brilliant, broken body of Sam's work into an architecture capacious enough to contain all these ways of knowing.

Reading Sam; Sam Reading

Late, adj. 2a. That occurs, comes, or happens after the right, or
expected time;
    9a. Belonging to the latter part of a historical, cultural, or developmental period

I have never met anyone who read as Sam did—voraciously, creatively, capaciously. Just consider the range of the published and unpublished work in this book, written in four short years. Like his mentor Darwin, Sam read by observing, in a "defiance of taxonomy" ("Charles Darwin"). He was deeply serious about *Gray's Anatomy*, Thom Gunn, *Touching Feeling*, and Samuel Beckett—as he was about weeds in his garden or work-in-progress on my Forster biography. Or deeply funny. Both. To talk with Sam was to be simultaneously encouraged and challenged, to veer from sympathy to paralyzing laughter. I always felt that he brought far more to me than I to him. At his memorial service, I discovered that this was a common feeling among his friends. One of his recuperative gifts is to ask us to consider what we *think we know* afresh, to stay open to surprise.

Before he arrived at UCLA, Sam had an unconventional schooling, in high and low culture, interrupted and sped up, autodidactic and deracinated, creative and conscious. He came to literary study without the taxonomies in place. Somehow he suppressed/forgot/missed the idea of *received knowledge* as an *a priori* epistemology so that, relatively late, he could organize his non-canonical knowledge himself. He faced the *episteme* uncontained and, rummaging in his reading with a rapacious eye for patterns, used theoretical tools to see what was in front of him. In all Sam's writing, we sense the freshness of his "sensational responses" ("Charles Darwin"). Sam had the same quality of "concentration" that he admired in Woolf ("The Comedy of Nature"). He could see the whole, but discern within it patterns and forms everywhere. "Seeing steadily," as Forster's Henry Wilcox would have it, was beside the point.

Sam learned his theory quickly, deeply, and well. The weight of this knowledge can make a young critic become a brittle reader. Just as Sam was alert to the danger of romanticizing the archive, so too he was wary of ritualistic readings. In his late work, Sam eschewed the moralistic impulse in what Eve Sedgwick called "paranoid reading," when

> the suspicion resides in the reading eye, not in the read text, but it's a common development, the strange metamorphosis from antiessential to ontological private eye."[8]

To borrow Yeats's dictum, the best paranoid critics become cynical, while the worst police ideological purity. Sam did neither.

Close reading, that old-fashioned tool, saved Sam from this kind of precocious performance. His close readings are a form of scientific inquiry. Late in his life, Sam was concentrating both on *what* he saw and *how* he read the evidence, following Sedgwick's hope for a reparative method:

It would make sense—if one had the choice—not to cultivate the
necessity of a systematic, self-accelerating split between what one is
doing and the reasons one does it.[9]

Sam shattered epistemological certainty by looking at everything. The capaciousness of Sam's vision, his interconnectivity and originality, and the
boldness of his readings seem to come from a different moment in the history of criticism, at some midpoint between Darwin and Derrida. His
historical and mythological scope recall Auerbach, or Frye, or Goffman.

Out of Time

Late, 3b. Of a crop, fruit, flower, etc.: growing, ripening or blossoming
    after the expected or usual time. 11a. Of a person; that was alive not
long ago,
    but is not now; recently deceased.

Of course Samuel Beckett would be the writer to call Sam's bluff. For a
young scholar, especially a young scholar in a white heat of a hurry, the
most reckless decision of all is to pause.

He described his future scholarly plans not quite in the mode of a
confession:

Among the treacherous paradoxes that comprise Samuel Beckett's
Molloy, the clause "to know nothing is nothing" felt the most abyssal
when I taught the novel in my junior seminar on Beckett's work . . . .
Five weeks into the course, my students and I stared at these nothings
knowing that what drew us to the class—to know more about
Beckett—was at odds with our subject ("Statement of Plans," 1).

Sam's final seminar on Beckett opened the door to the wonderland of a rethinking the whole arc of his work on the queer. With his students, Sam
faced the abyss of the failure of the ordinary tools of knowledge production that he had honed in graduate school and his early career. This was
neither a crisis of faith nor a turn to the tragic. Rather, it was a clearing, a
stopped-time, a productive moment of pause. He noted wryly that "to explore every conceivable means of knowing nothing . . . turns out to be a
difficult form of knowledge about which to make knowledge claims"
("Statement of Plans," 1).

What did he know, after all? Sam turned a pitiless eye on his facile
younger self. He was no longer content to "enumerate old themes."[10]

"Unable to decide if I was a historian or a theorist [in graduate school]," Sam wrote, "I was able to argue almost anything but believed next to nothing." It is not a surprise to me that Sam walked "to the lip of the void," and toward the self-discovery that he must "know nothing," and started again from the beginning while he was in the company of his students ("Statement of Plans," 1). He was the bravest teacher I have known.

Sam began to read afresh. We don't know where he would have gone. He stopped. But in his late writing, he eschewed the rituals of academic performance to rethink and reread. Sam's late work on Eliot, "The Cruelty of Breeding," gives a taste of this slow reading. As he had before, he returned to "the rag and bone shop of the heart" to remind himself how he'd "grown wary of knowing nothing, which is what the works I loved were asking me to do" ("Statement of Plans," 1). The echo of Yeats should not be lost on us; nor that these concerns are often an old person's preoccupations.

Sam died too soon to complete the two books and a meditation on postmodern tragedy that he provisionally entitled "Too Late On Time." But as the ground (both spatially and as a kinetic current between his two massive projects), this article was to have looked at "the common interest in knowing the nothing that postmodernism's myths threaten to forget" ("Statement of Plans," 5). "Too Late On Time" takes *knowing nothing* as a reparative space to investigate literature, theory, and history as queer discourses, but not necessarily a recuperative one. Sam asked how to avoid the extinction of the queer in the twinned voids of abstraction—"how queerness can avoid becoming a nothingness so abstract that it becomes a myth that suppresses the historical reality of the life it describes"—or in lack of distinction: "When everything is queer, after all, nothing is. And when nothing is queer or can be queered, queer mythology loses its politics" ("Statement of Plans," 4). In these plans for the future, Sam alloyed his desires to be and to feel and to know—it's his rendering of Blake's "I want! I want!" Sam's late work is risky, human, and vulnerable. Maybe I'm being romantic. I can faintly hear Sam laughing at—or with—me. But I believe that if he had written it fully, we would not be able to think the same way again.

Walking on the razor's edge of affect, belief, event, inquiry, and time, Sam asks us to rethink all kinds of things that are unproductive, and "good for nothing"—queerness and art paramount among them. (Sam would add teaching to this list, raising the ineffable labor of the work that enables our students' insight to become the figure of our purpose. He was all about the value of the non-assessable "waste of time."[11]) Sam's late writing complicates ideas in friendly disagreement with our most powerfully persuasive models of knowing, from Charles Darwin to Sigmund Freud, from Heather Love to Michael Warner, Virginia Woolf to Angela Carter.

Sam did not anticipate this queer afterlife. Nor did I, a biographer, imagine this archival excavation of his thinking through his great preoccupations with queerness, nature, literature, and the myths of desire. This I do know: Just as ontological claims flatten possibilities, so teleological claims distort and foreshorten them. In thinking about Sam, we must resist the siren song of teleology, both as a doctrine of design toward understanding and as the tragic genre of a wasted life. Reading and rereading these shards of Sam's thinking means trying to keep up with him and make him stand still for just a moment. Sam admired Beckett's "provocative relation" to aesthetic categories. The tragicomic vein of Sam's thinking, teaching, and writing embodied, in the end, the task of the writer as Christopher Isherwood defined it: "to follow his experience, to try to understand what it was, and to try not to lie to himself about its meaning."[12] Now that Sam is out of time, we will read him afresh and continue to talk with him.

This piece is dedicated to Janice Carlisle, Sam's great friend.

My thanks to Janice Carlisle and to Langdon Hammer for practical aid in the recuperation of these writings at an early stage, and to Christopher Looby and Michael North for inviting me into this book. The Modernist Studies Association Conference was where I met Sam, and, over the years, it was a psychic home where we did a good deal of thinking together. A version of this writing began in a panel I organized with Scott Herring on Sam See's future, at MSA 17, in 2015.

NOTES

1. Virginia Woolf, "Modern Fiction," in *The Essays of Virginia Woolf, Volume 4: 1925 to 1928*, ed. Andrew McNeillie (London: Hogarth Press, 1984), 161.

2. Sam See, unpublished Statement of Scholarly Plans and Interests (2012), 1. Subsequent citations will appear parenthetically in the text.

3. Eve Kosofsky Sedgwick, *Epistemology of the Closet* (Berkeley: University of California Press, 2008), 44.

4. Sam See, "The Cruelty of Breeding: Queer Time," unpublished MLA Talk, 2011. Subsequent citations will appear parenthetically in the text.

5. See Elizabeth Freeman, *Time Binds: Queer Temporalities, Queer Histories* (Durham, N.C.: Duke University Press, 2010), and Jesse Matz,

"'No Future' vs. 'It Gets Better': Queer Prospects for Narrative Temporality," in *Narrative Theory Unbound: Queer and Feminist Interventions*, ed. Robyn Warhol and Susan S. Lanser (Columbus: Ohio State University Press, 2015) for thoughtful wrestling with the problems of queer temporality in literature. George Chauncey and Jeffrey Weeks have done much to create and complicate the discipline of queer history.

6. Heather Love, *Feeling Backward* (Cambridge: Harvard University Press, 2009), 40.

7. In *Gay and After* (London: Serpent's Tail, 1998), Alan Sinfield claims that Neil Bartlett's *Who Was That Man?* is the first text to apply "we" to a wholly queer audience, marking a seminal moment in the history of queer scholarship (4).

8. Eve Kosofsky Sedgwick, *Touching Feeling: Affect, Performativity, Pedagogy* (Durham, N.C.: Duke University Press, 2003), 110.

9. Sedgwick, *Touching Feeling*, 145.

10. W. B. Yeats, "The Circus Animals' Desertion," in *The Collected Works of W. B. Yeats, Vol. I, The Poems*, ed. Richard J. Finneran (New York: Simon and Schuster, 1989), 355–6.

11. Sam See, unpublished Syllabus for English 342B/THST 381B: *Samuel Beckett*, Spring 2011; "The Cruelty of Breeding: Queer Time."

12. Christopher Isherwood, "Last Lecture," *Isherwood on Writing: The Lectures in California*, ed. James J. Berg (Minneapolis: University of Minnesota Press, 2007), 140.

ACKNOWLEDGMENTS

For various forms of encouragement, support, and assistance, the editors gratefully acknowledge Sunder Ganglani; Ann Sturdivant, Tom See, and the members of Sam See's family; Andrew S. Knott, Esq.; Kate Marshall; Langdon Hammer and Michael Warner; and the anonymous readers for Fordham University Press. This book is published with the assistance of the Frederick W. Hilles Publication Fund of Yale University as well as the UCLA Department of English and the UCLA Friends of English.

Versions of some of these chapters have been previously published and are reprinted here with permission: "The Comedy of Nature: Darwinian Feminism in Virginia Woolf's *Between the Acts*" first appeared in *Modernism/modernity* 17, no. 3 (2010), 639–67; "'Spectacles in Color': The Primitive Drag of Langston Hughes" was originally published in *PMLA* 124, no. 3 (2009): 798–817, and is reprinted by permission of the copyright owner, the Modern Language Association of America; "Fast Books Read Slow: The Shapes of Speed in *Manhattan Transfer* and *The Sun Also Rises*" first appeared in *JNT: Journal of Narrative Theory* 38, no. 3 (2008): 342–77; and "Making Modernism New: Queer Mythology in *The Young and Evil*" was first published in *ELH* 76, no. 4 (2009): 1073–105, copyright © 2009 Johns Hopkins University Press.

CONTRIBUTORS

Scott Herring is the James H. Rudy Professor in the English Department at Indiana University. He is also affiliated with the Kinsey Institute, the Cultural Studies Program, the Department of Gender Studies, and the Department of American Studies. He is the author of three books: *The Hoarders: Material Deviance in Modern American Culture* (University of Chicago Press, 2014), *Another Country: Queer Anti-Urbanism* (New York University Press, 2010), and *Queering the Underworld: Slumming, Literature, and the Undoing of Lesbian and Gay History* (University of Chicago Press, 2007). He received B.A. degrees in both English and History from the University of Alabama at Birmingham and his Ph.D. from the University of Illinois at Urbana-Champaign.

Heather K. Love is an Associate Professor of English at the University of Pennsylvania. She is the author of *Feeling Backward: Loss and the Politics of Queer History* (Harvard University Press, 2007). She has edited and co-edited special issues of *Representations* ("Description Across Disciplines," with Stephen Best and Sharon Marcus, 2016), *GLQ: A Journal of Lesbian and Gay Studies* (on the work of anthropologist Gayle Rubin, 2010), and *New Literary History* ("Is There Life after Identity Politics?," 2000). She received her A.B. in Literature from Harvard University and her M.A. and Ph.D. degrees from the University of Virginia.

Wendy Moffat is Professor of English at Dickinson College, where she holds the Curley Chair in Global Education. She is the author of *A Great Unrecorded History: A New Life of E. M. Forster* (Farrar, Straus and Giroux, 2010), which received the Biographer's Club Prize in 2010 and was runner-up for the PEN Biography Prize in 2011. Her forthcoming book, *Wounded Minds* (Farrar, Straus and Giroux, 2019), recounts the psychic cost of WWI through the stories of two Americans who risked their lives in France: psychiatrist Thomas Salmon, who brought treatment directly to the battlefield, and journalist Elizabeth Shepley Sergeant, who was nearly killed covering the Marne battles for *The New Republic*. She received her Ph.D. in English from Yale University.

Abel, Elizabeth, 64
acceleration. *See* spatial form and
    acceleration
Adorno, Theodor: *Aesthetic Theory*, 34,
    35–36, 85–86n54; on dialectic models,
    231, 250; on Enlightenment aesthetics,
    61, 139–43; on evolutionary aesthetics,
    34, 35–36; on feelings for nature,
    85–86n54, 99; on literature as art's
    "inner life," 19; on modern art's
    definition, 233; and Woolf's *Between
    the Acts*, 73–74, 75
aesthetic feelings: diversity of, 20–28;
    feelings, defined by See, 3; for natural
    beauty vs. artistic beauty, 32–33,
    35–36, 48–49n74; rejection of, 92–95;
    as sexual feelings, 3–4, 14, 29–30,
    47n67; as social experience, 40n27.
    See also evolutionary aesthetics; sexual
    aesthetics; surrealist aesthetics
Aesthetic Theory (Adorno), 34, 35–36,
    85–86n54
African American stereotypes, 108–9,
    118
Ahmed, Sara, 46–47n64
Allen, Grant, 34, 49n83
alliterative fricatives, 169–70
Altieri, Charles, 42n43, 143–4
altruism theory, 24, 143, 155n50
American failurism: long poem paradox
    and, 229–34; long poem modernism
    and, 233, 249–51; pure language
    paradox and, 234–40, 297–98; pure
    sexuality paradox and, 240–9
American Romanticism, 234, 238
ancient/modern opposition: ancient,
    defined, 272; modernism defined by,
    271–2; modernization of classicism,
    272–3; queerness out of time, 281–4;
    See on, 273–4; in *The Waste Land*,

278–81; in *The Young and Evil*,
    274–8
Angel's Wings (Carpenter), 101
"Anon" (Woolf), 68–69
anti-positivism, 207
The Apes of God (Lewis), 211
Aragon, Louis, 211
Aristotle, 80n22
Armstrong, Nancy, 99
atavism: in *Between the Acts*, 52–56, 58,
    292; in biology, 78–79n18; Darwin
    on, 76n11, 78n18; in *Nightwood*, 289;
    sexology and, 144–5
autoantonym, 260, 262, 280
Autobiography of Charles Darwin
    (Darwin), 41–42n40, 43n47
automatism, 213

"Back to Nature with You" (Porter),
    11–12
"A Backward Glance O'er Travel'd
    Roads" (Whitman), 91
Bagemihl, Bruce, 13
Bailey, Nathan W., 36n5
Baker, Houston, 115–16, 119
Barber, Stephen, 73, 85n51
barebackers, 282–3
Barnes, Djuna, 194–5, 288–9
Barthes, Roland, 2–3
Bataille, Georges, 38n16
beauty. *See* aesthetic feelings;
    evolutionary aesthetics; sexual
    aesthetics
Beauty and the Beast (McDowall), 29
Beckett, Samuel, 304
Beer, Gillian, 24
beliefs, 143–6, 294–5, 297
Bell, Michael, 5, 199, 200–1, 210–11, 261
Bender, Bert, 43–44n48
Benston, Kimberly, 126

Bentley, Gladys, 116
Bergson, Henri, 34–35
Berman, Louis, 119
Bernstein, Michael, 230
Bersani, Leo, 58
Between the Acts (Woolf): aesthetic
    concentration of, 50–57, 74–75; camp
    aesthetics of, 56–57, 58, 62–64, 66,
    71–72; as comedy of nature, 55–56,
    70, 73–75, 79n19, 80n24; Darwinian
    feminism in, 57–58, 60–61, 66, 84n49;
    evolutionary aesthetics of, 292;
    homosexuality allusions in, 85n51;
    plays within, 62–64, 66, 70–71, 73–75;
    plot structure, 53–55, 62–64, 66,
    70–73; sexual submission in, 58,
    60–64, 66; as tragedy, 55–56, 73–75,
    79n19, 79–80n22, 80n24
"between the world wars" period,
    159–60, 179
Biological Exuberance (Bagemihl), 13
bio-power, 16
Blackmur, R. P., 230, 240
Blake, David, 91
Blanchot, Maurice, 162
blues drag, 116–17
Bodies that Matter (Butler), 17
Bond, Adrian, 166
Boone, Joseph Allen, 37n11, 194, 195,
    202, 215, 261–2
Boyd, Brian, 23
Breton, André, 211, 213–14
The Bridge (Crane): criticism of, 229–30;
    modernism of long poem and, 5, 233,
    249–51; as paradox of purity, 231–6,
    238–9, 241–2, 244, 249–251; pure
    language paradox of, 234–40; pure
    sexuality paradox of, 233–4, 240–9; as
    splendid failure, 230–4
British war propaganda, 57
Broch, Hermann, 208
Brunner, Edward, 230, 239, 245, 248–9
Bullough, Vern, 145
Burgess, Ernest, 117–18
Burke, Kenneth, 231–3, 235, 253n17
Butler, Judith, 17, 109, 126–7, 128n12

cabaret performances, 81n33
Calinescu, Matei, 271
Calvino, Italo, 163
"camera eye" technique, 164

camp aesthetics: of Ford & Tyler, 218; of
    Hughes, 116–17; of Woolf, 56–57, 58,
    62–64, 66, 71–72
The Cantos (Pound), 194–5, 218, 230,
    250–1
Carpenter, Edward, 2, 98, 100–4, 273
Carroll, Joseph, 23
Carroll, Sean, 22–23
Carter, Angela, 6
Chauncey, George: on censorship,
    219; on gender crossing, 117; on
    mythological allusions, 196; on queer
    communities, 107, 217–18; on urban
    queer modernity, 273
Chomsky, Noam, 2–3
Christianity, 137–9
City of God (Cuadros), 219
Civello, Paul, 137
Comedy and the Woman Writer (Little),
    79n19
communities. *See* queer communities
comrade-love, 91–92
concentration aesthetics, 50–57,
    74–75
concentration camps: ethic of humor in,
    56–57, 82n34; literature on, 78n17,
    81–82n33; Woolf on, 51, 53–54, 57, 74,
    78n17
Consilience (Wilson), 23
constructionism, 37n11
Crane, Hart: on *The Cantos*, 250–1;
    "General Aims and Theories,"
    232, 237, 242; literary relationships
    of, 233, 253n17; on mythic vision of
    America, 245; paradox of, 229, 232–3;
    on *The Waste Land*, 237, 250. See also
    The Bridge
Creative Evolution (Bergson), 34
"The Critic as Artist" (Wilde), 93–94
Critique of Judgment (Kant), 14, 28,
    33–34, 140
"Cross" (Hughes), 111–14
"Cross Road Blues" (Johnson), 111–12,
    113
Cuadros, Gil, 6, 219
The Cultural Politics of Emotion (Ahmed),
    46–47n64
The Culture of Time and Space, 1880–1918
    (Kern), 159–60
Cummings, E. E., 208
Cvetkovich, Ann, 17, 28

Dalziel, Margaret, 207
Damrosch, David, 282
Danson, Lawrence, 93
Darwin, Charles: on aesthetic feelings, 43n47, 46n62; on atavism, 52–53, 55, 76n11, 78–79n18; on beauty, 58–59; descent theory of, 34; Engels on, 99–100; evolutionary aesthetics of, 28–29, 31–34, 36; feminist theory and, 19; Kant comparison to, 27, 31–34, 47n68, 48n72; on limitations of evolutionary theory, 137, 153n11; literature influenced by, 43–44n48; Marx on, 99; on nature as culture, 3; on queer natures, 14–15, 17, 19, 36, 46n62, 86n59; on racial variation, 22, 25, 45n59, 46n62, 80n23; on religion, 138; on sympathy, 76–77n12; on trait variation, 20–28, 44n51, 44–45n52, 55, 59; Wilde on, 93. *See also* evolutionary theory; natural selection; sexual selection
Darwin, Charles, writings of: *Autobiography of Charles Darwin*, 41–42n40, 43n47; *The Descent of Man, and Selection in Relation to Sex*, 21–23, 25–27, 46n62, 58–60, 86n59; *The Expression of the Emotions in Man and Animals*, 21, 27, 45–46n60; *The Origin of Species*, 21–24, 45n59, 86n59, 300; *The Variation of Animals and Plants under Domestication*, 21, 24–27, 41n39, 58, 76n11; *The Voyage of the Beagle*, 20, 42n42, 44n51
Darwin, William, 138
Darwinian feminism, 57–66, 84n49, 84–85n50
"Darwinism—(Then Furthermore)" (Whitman), 91–92
Darwin's Plots (Beer), 24
Däubler, Theodore, 14
Dean, Tim, 282
"The Decay of Lying" (Wilde), 92–93, 94–95
Degeneration (Nordau), 78n18, 208
degeneration theory: defined, 78–79n18; on drag performances, 118–19; Ellis on, 118; eugenics and, 59; illness and, 61, 86n55; as narrative structure, 55; on queer natures, 36–37n6; See on, 4; on sexual identities, 77n14; on women, 58–59

De Profundis (Wilde), 93–95
de Sade, Marquis, 38n16
The Descent of Love (Bender), 44n48
The Descent of Man, and Selection in Relation to Sex (Darwin), 21–23, 25–27, 46n62, 58–60, 86n59
descriptive pauses, 169, 188–9n52
desire, myth of, 6–7
Deviations (Rubin), 283–4
Dialectic of Enlightenment (Horkheimer & Adorno), 139–40
The Diary of Virginia Woolf (Woolf), 51–53, 57, 66, 77n15
Diderot, Denis, 38n16
Dissanayake, Ellen, 24
dollness myth, 208–10, 225–6n48
Dos Passos, John. See *Manhattan Transfer*
down-low, 110–12, 114, 121, 123–6, 293
Dracula (Stoker), 204
drag balls: in *The Weary Blues*, 107–10, 111–14, 116–19, 124, 278; in *The Young and Evil*, 216–17, 277–8
Dutton, Dennis, 23, 43n44, 46n63
dwelling, notion of, 178–80, 182n7

ecopolitics, of queer natures, 38n13
Edelman, Lee, 234–5, 240–2, 258, 263, 297–8
Eliot, T. S.: on artist's progression, 210; critique of, 250–51; *Essays Ancient and Modern*, 281; on mythical method, 139, 195; on *Nightwood*, 289; *On Poetry and Poets*, 281; "Tradition and the Individual Talent," 262–3; on *Ulysses*, 195, 211, 261–2, 278–1. See also *The Waste Land*
elision, 5, 124, 175
Ellis, Havelock, 39n19, 113, 118–19
Ellman, Maud, 261, 263
Endless Forms Most Beautiful (Carroll), 22–23
Engels, Friedrich, 98–100
Enlightenment aesthetics, 61, 139–40
entre deux guerres period, 159–60, 179
epigraphs, 164
Epistemology of the Closet (Sedgwick), 37–38n11, 276, 282, 301
Essays Ancient and Modern (Eliot), 281
essentialism, 37n11
Esty, Jed, 56, 79n19

ethnic communities, 195–7, 215–20
eugenics: Darwin's theories appropriated
    as support for, 16–17, 292–3, 294; of
    Hitler, 53–54, 59–60, 78n17
Evolution (LeConte), 137
Evolution and "the Sex Problem" (Bender),
    44n48
evolutionary aesthetics: cognitive
    approach to, 42n43; degeneration
    discourse of, 292–3; Kant on, 14,
    27, 28–35, 47nn68–69, 47–48n70,
    48nn71–73, 48–49n74; literary
    sexuality and, 11–14; overview, 3–4;
    on queer natures, 11–14, 28–36; See
    on, 292–3; sexual feelings and, 28–36
evolutionary theory: on atavism, 53–54;
    exfoliation theory and, 100–1, 103; on
    feelings, 3–4 (*see also* evolutionary
    aesthetics); fossil evidence for, 137,
    153n11; limitations of, 137; *Maurice*'s
    vision of, 98–99; mythopoeic view of,
    137–8; perversion of, 59; on trait
    variation, 20–28, 41–42n40, 42nn42–
    43; Whitman on, 91–92
Evolution's Rainbow (Roughgarden), 13,
    25–26, 63
exfoliation theory, 100–1, 103
exile literary model, 179–80
*The Expression of the Emotions in Man and
    Animals* (Darwin), 21, 27, 45–46n60

failurism. *See* American failurism
feelings. *See* aesthetic feelings; sexuality
    and sexual feelings; sympathy
felted textures, 118–19, 127
feminist theory: concentration and
    identity of self, 50–57; Darwinian
    feminism, 57–66, 84n49, 84–85n50;
    on public intimacy, 67–72
Féré, Charles Samson, 78n18
Fiedler, Leslie, 204
fin-de-siècle literature, 90–96
Fitzgerald, F. Scott, 198, 274
Five Faces of Modernity (Calinescu), 271
folklore, 195, 197, 200–1, 215–20,
    222–3n13
Ford, Charles Henri, 194–5, 198–9, 217,
    281. See also *The Young and Evil*
Forster, E.M., 2, 98–99, 101–4
Foucault, Michel: on culture as nature,
    2–3; *The History of Sexuality*, 13–14,

15–18, 36; on literary sexuality, 17–18,
    38n16, 39n19; on nature of social
    classes, 39n22; on sexology, 16–17,
    144–5, 265; on sexual aesthetics,
    15–20, 32, 36, 301; on sexuality's
    repressive hypothesis, 13–15; on
    Shakespeare's sexual orientation, 218
Foundlings (Nealon), 196–7
foundling texts, 135, 146–8, 196–7,
    218–19, 293–4
fragmented narrative, 163–5
Frank, Adam, 7, 291
Frank, Joseph, 5, 160, 162, 183n12,
    200–1
Frank, Waldo, 229–30, 245, 249
Frankl, Viktor, 56–57, 82n34
Freeman, Elizabeth, 259, 266
Freud, Sigmund, 14–15, 84, 145, 207–8,
    225n46, 295
Froula, Christine, 57–58, 70
Futurism, 159–61, 182n8

Garber, Eric, 116
Gates, Henry Louis, Jr., 125
"Gay Folklore" (Chauncey), 273
Gay New York (Chauncey), 273
Gay Talk (Rodgers), 279–80
gender performativity, 109, 124–7,
    128n12
gender variation, 25–27, 45n55, 86n59
Genette, Gérard, 164, 169, 188n52
German war propaganda, 57
Gilman, Sander, 36, 78–79n18, 152
The Glands Regulating Personality
    (Berman), 119
Godfrey, Laura, 163
Goodson, A. C., 167–8
Gould, Stephen Jay, 23
The Granite Butterfly (Tyler), 135–7,
    199–200, 253–4n22, 276, 294
Greenwich Village, 194–5, 196, 215–17
Grosz, Elizabeth, 19, 27, 38n13,
    84–85n50, 85n53

Halberstam, Judith Jack, 260
Halperin, David, 17
Hamer, Dean, 143, 144
Haraway, Donna, 19
Harlem Renaissance, 112, 117, 125–7,
    293
Harper, Phillip Brian, 290

Harvey, David, 179
H. D., 6, 261, 272
Heidegger, Martin, 162, 178, 179–80, 181
Hemingway, Ernest. See *The Sun Also Rises*
Hemphill, Essex, 125
Herd, E. W., 200, 208
Herring, Scott, 77n14, 271
Highwater, Jamake, 217
Him (Cummings), 208
historiographies: contemporary, 265–6; erotohistoriographies, 266; *The History of Sexuality*, 13–14, 15–18, 36; literary historiography, 197, 200, 217–18, 220n3, 228n80; modernism and, 196–7, 200, 217–19, 220n3, 228n80, 273–4; mythical method and, 196, 200–1, 261–2
History of England (Trevelyan), 60
The History of Sexuality (Foucault), 13–14, 15–18, 36
Hitler, Adolf: concentration camps of, 51, 53–54, 56–57, 78n17; genocidal campaign of, 51, 53–54, 57, 59, 83n45; *Mein Kampf*, 59; on women, 59, 83n45, 83–84n47; Woolf on, 51, 57, 63
Holcomb, Gary, 116
The Holocaust of Text (Hungerford), 78n17
Homer, 142
homographesis, 233–4, 241–2, 244–9
Horkheimer, Max, 73, 75, 139–43
How the Mind Works (Pinker), 42n43
Hughes, Langston: on blues drag, 116–17; down-low, 110–12, 114, 121, 123–6, 293; drag ball narrative descriptions, 107–8; drag ball poetic descriptions, 107–10, 111–14, 116–19, 124, 278; on Harlem's cultural events, 106–8; low-down, 110–12, 114, 121, 123–6, 130n39, 239; on Negro poetry, 108–9; Nugent on, 125–6; overview, 2, 4; performance readings, 115–19, 124–5; queer-of-color critique of, 125–7; on writing, 110
Hughes, Langston, writings of: "Aunt Sue's Stories," 127; *The Big Sea*, 106–8, 116, 122; "A Black Pierrot," 125; "Cross," 111–14; "Epilogue," 122–3; *Fine Clothes to the Jew*, 118, 130n39;

"Lament," 122–3; "Mother to Son," 122–3; "Negro," 122–3; "Proem," 122–3; *The Weary Blues*, 107–11, 115–16, 119–27, 128n12, 278, 293
Hungerford, Amy, 78n17

imaginative space, 178–81
implicit ellipses, 164
Imre (Prime-Stevenson), 145–6
In Parenthesis (Jones), 66, 259
The Intermediate Sex (Carpenter), 100
Introduction to the Science of Sociology (Park & Burgess), 118
Ioläus (Carpenter), 273
Iser, Wolfgang, 166
Isherwood, Christopher, 306

James, William, 144
Janus words, 280
Johnson, Barbara, 298
Johnson, E. Patrick, 119
Johnson, Robert, 111–12, 113
Jones, David, 66, 259
Jones, Howard Mumford, 115
Jonny Minotaur (film), 281
Joplin, Patricia Klindienst, 52, 76n9
Joyce, James, 195, 210, 211

Kant, Immanuel: aesthetic disinterest principle of, 29–30; *Critique of Judgment*, 14, 28, 33–34, 140; Darwin comparison to, 27, 31–34, 47n68, 48n72; desire theory of, 30; evolutionary aesthetics and, 14, 27, 28–35, 47nn68–69, 47–48n70, 48nn71–73, 48–49n74; on judgment, 48n73; on mythologies, 140; naturalistic fallacy committed by, 31–32; *a priori* principle of, 30–33, 48n73, 48–49n74
Kaplan, Amy, 99
Kern, Stephen, 159–60, 161, 171, 178, 180
Knadler, Stephen, 117
Komunyakaa, Yusef, 116
Krafft-Ebing, Richard von, 39n19, 272

Lamb, Robert, 173
Lancaster, Roger, 38n13
Lawrence, D. H., 38n16
Leaska, Mitchell, 79n19
Leaves of Grass (Whitman), 90, 92

LeConte, Joseph, 137
Lehmann, John, 50–51
leitmotifs, 168–9, 174, 188n51, 204
"Let's Do It" (Porter), 12–15, 16, 28
LeVay, Simon, 145
Levin, Harry, 272
Levine, George, 137–8
Lewis, Wyndham, 72, 211
Lewontin, Richard, 23
Libidinal Currents (Boone), 37n11, 194
Lind, Earl, 107, 127
Lipman, Steve, 56–57, 82n34
literary criticism, 276–7
Literary Darwinism (Carroll), 23
literary historiography, 197, 200, 217–18,
    220n3, 228n80
literary naturalism, 206, 213
literary realism: alternative to, 206,
    213–14; Eliot on, 201 (*see also* mythical
    method); social realism as, 91, 98–100;
    of Whitman, 91; of Wilde, 91, 94
literary sexuality: cognitive approach
    to, 42n43; Darwin's influence on,
    43–44n48; evolutionary aesthetics
    and, 11–14; *fin-de-siècle*, 90–96;
    Foucault on, 17–18, 38n16, 39n19;
    "Let's Do It" as example of, 28;
    problem of, 298–9; queer natures and,
    41n34; Romanticism and, 47n68;
    sexology and, 39n19; sexual aesthetics
    and, 18–20; sexual identities insight at
    fin-de-siècle through, 37–38n11
Literature, Modernism and Myth (Bell), 5,
    199, 261
Little, Judy, 79n19
Locke, Alain, 117, 125
Lombroso, Cesare, 78n18, 144
long poems. See *The Bridge*; *The Cantos*;
    The Granite Butterfly; *The Waste Land*
Looby, Christopher, 216, 273, 289–90
Lorde, Audre, 7, 141, 146–8, 265, 281–2,
    296–7
Love, Heather, 4, 7, 217–18, 264, 288
low-down, 110–12, 114, 121, 123–6,
    130n39, 293
Lukács, Georg, 91, 97–98, 99, 100, 102

Machine-Age Comedy (North), 79–80n22
MacKay, Marina, 74
magical realism, 139, 142–3
Magic and Myth of the Movies (Tyler), 281

Manhattan Transfer (Dos Passos):
    alliterative fricatives in, 169–70;
    character foci in, 166–8; imaginative
    space in, 179–81; leitmotifs in, 174;
    literary writing references in, 176–7;
    overview, 160–2; parataxis in, 171; plot
    structure, 162–5; recursive motion in,
    174–6, 177; syntactic inversion in,
    169–70; timescapes in, 170–1
Manton, G.R., 200
Maquokeeta, 242–4
Marcus, Jane, 63, 289
Marinetti, F. T., 159, 160
Marx, Karl, 99, 100
Marxist socialism, 98–99
Maurice (Forster), 98–99, 101–4
McDowall, Stuart, 28–29, 47n67
McLuhan, Marshall, 164
The Meaning of Contemporary Realism
    (Lukács), 97
Medalie, David, 98
Memories of the Moderns (Levin), 272
Men Without Art (Woolf), 72
Merrill, George, 98
Metamorphoses (Ovid), 142
Mickelson, David, 163, 166–7, 170
Mixed Feelings (Cvetkovich), 17
"Modern Fiction" (Woolf), 69–70
modernism: defined, 271–2; ethnic
    folklore and, 195, 197, 200–1, 215–20,
    222–3n13; failure of (*see* American
    failurism); historiographies and,
    196–7, 200, 217–19, 220n3, 228n80,
    273–4; of long poems, 249–51;
    myth-making and, 199–207; myth-
    questioning and, 207–11; paradox of
    purity and, 231–2; queer mythologies
    and, 194–99; spatial form influenced
    by technology, 161; surrealism and,
    211–15; utopic dystopia of, 263. *See also*
    ancient/modern opposition
modernist realism, 4, 97–105
"Modern Novels" (Woolf), 87n71
Moffat, Wendy, 7, 300
monstrosities, 44–45n52
Morton, Timothy, 38n13, 46n62
Muñoz, José Esteban, 112–13, 263
mysticism, 152
mythical method: Eliot on, 139, 195,
    261–2; magical realism and, 139;
    Nietzsche on, 200–1; See on, 294; in

The Waste Land, 265; in *The Young and Evil*, 195–6, 201, 207, 221–2n8
mythologies. *See* queer mythologies
Mythologies (Barthes), 2–3
mythopoeic literature, 135–43, 199–207, 215, 217–18, 276, 296

narrative method, 201–2
narrative space: acceleration in, 162–77; imaginative space, 178–81
narrative voice fragmentation, 166, 167–8
"The Narrow Bridge of Art" (Woolf), 68
naturalistic fallacy, 16, 31–32, 35–36, 139, 290–1
natural selection: aesthetics of, 33–34; Darwinian feminism and, 58–59; queer theory and, 24–26; sexual selection and, 27; sexual selection as independent from, 3–4; variation of traits and, 20–27, 42n42, 58–60, 80n23; Woolf on, 292
nature. *See* queer natures
Nazi concentration camps, 51, 53–54, 56–57, 78n17
Nealon, Christopher: on *The Bridge*, 231, 233, 236–7; on queer foundling texts, 135, 196–7, 218–19, 293–4; on queer temporality, 282
A New Point of View (Däubler), 14
Newton, Esther, 116–17
Ngai, Sianne, 40n27, 110
Nicholls, Peter, 210, 213
The Nick of Time (Grosz), 84–85n50
Nietzsche, Friedrich, 200–1, 211, 238, 282
Nightwood (Barnes), 194–5, 288–9
No Future (Edelman), 258, 263
Nordau, Max, 34, 49n78, 78–79n18, 103, 152, 208
North, Michael: on ancient/modern opposition, 272; on freedom from oppression, 160; on Hughes's use of blues in poetry, 115; on See's legacy, 273, 289–90; on Woolf's degenerative comedy, 55
Norton, Rictor, 265
Nugent, Richard Bruce, 125–6

Obelisk Press, 219
O'Connor, Matthew, 289
The Odyssey (Homer), 142

Oedipus myth, 208, 264
Oedipus Rex (Sophocles), 208
On Beauty and Being Just (Scarry), 47n67
"On Being Ill" (Woolf), 61, 65–66
On Poetry and Poets (Eliot), 281
On the Origin of Stories (Boyd), 23
"On the Uses and Disadvantages of History for Life" (Nietzsche), 200–1
ontological dwelling, 162
Oranges Are Not the Only Fruit (Winterson), 219
The Origin of Species (Darwin), 21–24, 45n59, 86n59, 300
Our America (Frank), 245
Ovid, 142

Paint It Today (H. D.), 261
pantomime, 124–5
paradox of purity, 231–6, 238–9, 241–2, 244, 249–51, 298
parataxis, 171–4, 189–90n64
Paris Peasant (Aragon), 211
Park, Robert, 117–18
The Particulars of Rapture (Altieri), 42n43
Patton, Cindy, 295
Peiss, Kathy, 277
Perverse Romanticism (Sha), 47n68
Physiological Æsthetics (Allen), 34
The Picture of Dorian Gray (Wilde), 90
Pierrot (pantomime), 124–5
Pinker, Steven, 42n43
place. *See* spatial form and acceleration
Pocahontas, 242–4
poems (long). See *The Bridge; The Cantos; The Granite Butterfly; The Waste Land*
Poetics (Aristotle), 80n22
Ponce, Martin, 113–14, 120
Popper, Karl, 152
Porter, Cole, 12–15, 16, 28, 36–37n6
positive affect theory, 296
positivism, 14, 37–38n11, 42n43, 138–9, 143–4
postexilic eminence, 162, 179–80
Pound, Ezra: *The Cantos*, 194–5, 218, 230, 250–1; literary relationships of, 194–5, 198–9, 202, 276, 278; "tale of the tribe" concept of, 5, 136, 230; "The Three Cantos," 250–1; Tyler on, 218–19; on *The Waste Land*, 261; on *The Young and Evil*, 198–9

Prime-Stevenson, Edward, 145–6
primi, 169–70
primitive drag, 110–11, 114, 116, 124–6, 278
Principles of Psychology (Spencer), 28, 144
Prisms (Adorno), 231, 250
Psychopathia Sexualis (Krafft-Ebing), 272
public intimacy, 67–72

queer communities: communities, defined, 5; as ethnic communities, 195–7, 215–20; folklore of, 195, 197, 200–1, 215–20, 222–3n13, 275; Greenwich Village as, 194–5, 196, 215–17; Harlem Renaissance and, 112, 117, 125–7, 293; identification of, 5–6; lineage of, 135, 146–8, 196–7, 218–19, 293–4; mythologies of, 5–7, 134–7, 146–9, 263, 293; as paradoxical, 197; in Paris, 219; surrealism and, 214–15; "tale of the tribe" concept, 5, 136–7, 230, 232, 234, 250, 258–9
queer criticism, 290–1
queer deconstructionism, 276
"Queer Ecology" (Morton), 38n13
queer feeling, 46–47n64
queer foundling texts, 135, 146–8, 196–7, 218–19, 293–4
Queering the Underworld (Herring), 77n14
queer mythologies: beliefs as, 143–6, 294–5, 297; of Christianity, 137–9; Enlightenment myths, 139–3; ethnic folklore and, 195–7, 200–1, 215–20, 222–3n13; of evolutionary theory, 137–8; false clarity and, 140–1; foundling texts as, 196–7; Kant on, 140; modernism and, 194–9, 263–4; myth, defined, 5, 140, 199, 261, 293, 297; mythopoeia in *The Young and Evil*, 199–207, 275, 296; myth-questioning, 207–11; of queer communities, 5–7, 134–7, 146–9, 263, 293; of queer nature, 145–52; rootedness, as counter-myth, 179; See's approach to, 4–7; sexology's reliance on, 144–5, 265; in *The Waste Land*, 261–5
queer natures: altruism theory of, 24, 143, 155n50; animal studies of, 36n5; Carpenter on, 104; comrade-love by

Whitman, 91–92; culture as nature, 2–3, 13; Darwin on, 14–15, 17, 19, 36, 46n62, 86n59; ecopolitics of, 38n13; evolutionary aesthetics on, 11–14, 28–36; evolutionary theory on, 20–28; feeling as link between art and, 3; Forster on, 2, 98–99, 101–4; of Harlem Renaissance (*see* Hughes, Langston); Kant on, 48n72; of literary sexuality, 41n34; as moral compass, 16–17; naturalistic fallacy and, 16, 31–32, 35–36, 139, 290–1; overview, 2–4; queer feeling and, 46–47n64; See on, 288–92; sexual aesthetics on, 15–20, 38n13; Whitman on, 90–93, 95; Wilde on, 90–91, 92–95
queerness out of time, 281–4
queer stereotypes, 108–9

race of degeneracy, 53–54
racial primitivism, 121
racial variation, 22, 45n59, 80n23
realism, 99, 101. *See also* modernist realism
recursive motion, 5, 174–7, 204–5
reparative reading, 295–6, 301, 303–5
Robertson, Pamela, 58
Rodgers, Bruce, 279–80
Romanticism, 47n68, 234, 238
A Room of One's Own (Woolf), 57, 61, 68, 88nn72–73
Rosario, Vernon, 39n19
Rosenfeld, Natania, 51
Roughgarden, Joan, 13, 24–26, 38n13, 44–45n52, 63
Rubin, Gayle, 6, 283–4

Sacks, Oliver, 170, 189n59
"Sailing to Byzantium" (Yeats), 272
"Same-Sex Sexual Behavior and Evolution" (Bailey & Zuk), 36
Santayana, George, 19
Savage, Derek, 230
Scarry, Elaine, 47n67
Scientific and Esoteric Studies in Sexual Degeneration in Mankind and in Animals (Féré), 78n18
scientific socialism, 100
Sedgwick, Eve Kosofsky: *Epistemology of the Closet*, 37–38n11, 276, 282, 301; Herring on, 276, 282; on paranoid

reading, 295–6, 303; on performative affectivity, 109, 127, 128n12; on queer mythology, 223n16; on queer natures, 18–19, 37–38n11, 38n13, 49n83; on reflexive antibiologism informing queer theory, 7, 37–38n11, 291; on reparative, definition of, 265; on reparative reading, 295–6, 301, 303–4; *Touching Feeling*, 18, 38n11

See, Sam: on ancient/modern opposition, 273–4, 276; on ancient references in *The Waste Land*, 278–81; on ancient references in *The Young and Evil*, 274–8; dissertation republication plans of, 2; education of, 303; on evolutionary aesthetics, 292–3; feeling defined by, 3; legacy of, 2, 4–5, 7, 305–6; on modernism, 4; on modern/postmodern opposition, 281–4; on queer natures, 2–3, 4, 288–92; reparative reading by, 301, 303–5

See, Sam, writings of: "Charles Darwin: Queer Theorist," 2; overview, 300–2; *Queer Mythologies* project, 4–5; *Queer Natures* project, 2; "Statement of Scholarly Interests and Plans" (Yale, third-year review), 6–7; unpublished talk on Carpenter, 97–105; unpublished talk on Forster, 2, 97–105; unpublished talk on modernist realism, 97–105; unpublished talk on Whitman, 2, 90–96; unpublished talk on Wilde, 2, 90–96

Seidel, Michael, 162, 178, 179–80

Seitler, Dana, 55

self, identity of, 50–57

sexology: on degeneration, 118; denaturalization of sex by, 17, 39n19; Foucault's critique of, 16–17, 144–5, 265; history of, 38n17; on sexual identities, 37n11, 39n19; on women, 58–59

sexual aesthetics: Foucault's impact on, 15–20, 32, 36, 301; of Greenwich Village, 217; overview, 3–4; of Porter, 11–14; sexual selection and, 25–28, 43n44, 46n63, 47n67, 58–61; variation of traits and, 20–28

sexual identities: of Antiquity, 272–3; feelings *versus* identity, 39–40n23; modernist literature on, 37–38n11,

77n14; sexology on, 39n19; sexual selection and, 84–85n50

sexuality and sexual feelings: aestheticism and, 3–4, 14, 29–30, 47n67 (*see also* evolutionary aesthetics); aesthetic theory's exclusion of, 49n83; antibiologism on, 7; in *The Bridge*, 240–9; cognitive approach to, 42n43; defined, by Foucault, 15–16; female camp aesthetics and, 58; Foucault on, 15–17; homographesis and, 233–4, 241–2, 244–9; as middle ground between sexual acts and identities, 39–40n23; modernist literature on, 37–38n11; by nature, 3 (*see also* queer natures); nonreproductive sexual figures, 258–61; personal narratives of, 39n19; Porter on, in relation to nature, 11–12; problem of, 298–9; queer feeling, 46–47n64; sexology on, 39n19. *See also* literary sexuality

sexual selection: aesthetics of, 93–94; aesthetic theory misinterpretation of, 47n67; Darwin on, 3–4, 46n63; Darwinian feminism and, 58–61, 63, 292; evolutionary aesthetics and, 29; gender variation and, 25–27, 45n55, 86n59; Hitler on, 59, 60–61; as incomplete theory, 21; reproductive necessity, freedom from, 3–4; sexual aesthetics and, 25–28, 43n44, 46n63, 47n67, 58–61; sexual identities and, 84–85n50; Wilde on, 93

Sha, Richard, 47–48n70, 47n68

Shakespeare, William, 45–46n60, 218

"Shame in the Cybernetic Fold" (Sedgwick & Frank), 291

Shelley, Percy Bysshe, 238

Sherry, Vincent, 4

"A Sketch of the Past" (Woolf), 52, 72

"Sleep and Endymion" (Ford), 281

Smitten, Jeffrey, 183n14

Social Darwinism, 4, 34–35

"Socialism: Utopian and Scientific" (Engels), 99–100

socialist realism, 91, 98–100

"Song of Myself" (Whitman), 92

Sontag, Susan, 56

Sophocles, 208

Spackman, Barbara, 118

Spahr, Juliana, 148–52

spatial form and acceleration:
  deceleration with literary writing
  references, 176–7; dwelling, notion of,
  178–9; historicizing of, 5, 159–62;
  imaginative space, 178–81; overview,
  5, 159–60, 183nn12,14; with parataxis,
  171–4, 189–90n64; spatial acceleration,
  162–77; spatial form, defined, 160,
  183n14; through alliterative fricatives,
  169–70; through character foci, 166–8;
  through descriptive pauses, 169,
  188–9n52; through leitmotifs, 168–9,
  174, 188n51; through narrative voice,
  166; through plot structure, 162–6;
  through recursive motion, 174–7;
  through syntactic inversion, 169–70;
  with timescapes, 170–1, 189n59
Specimen Days (Whitman), 92
speed. *See* spatial form and acceleration
Speed and Politics (Virilio), 159–60
"Speed of Cultural Change" (McLuhan),
  164
Spencer, Herbert, 28, 34
Splendid Failure (Brunner), 230
Stein, Edward, 145, 149, 150
Stein, Gertrude, 188n51, 194–5, 198,
  274
Stevenson, Randall, 98
Stoker, Bram, 204
subjectivization, 166
submission: queer feminist ethic of,
  61, 85n53; sexual submission, 58,
  60–64, 66
The Sun Also Rises (Hemingway):
  descriptive pauses in, 169; imaginative
  space in, 179–81; leitmotifs in, 168–9;
  literary writing references in, 176–7;
  narrative voice in, 166; overview,
  160–2; parataxis in, 171–4; plot
  structure, 162–4, 165–6; recursive
  motion in, 174, 177
surrealist aesthetics, 205, 208, 211–15
surrealist vertigo, 212–13
sympathy, 33, 51–52, 56, 76–77n12
syntactic inversion, 169–70

Talbot, Eugene S., 151–2
"tale of the tribe" concept, 5, 136–7, 230,
  232, 234, 250, 258–9
Tendencies (Sedgwick), 18
"Terminal Note" (Forster), 103

This Side of Paradise (Fitzgerald), 198,
  274
Thornhill, Randy, 47n67
"Thoughts on Peace in an Air Raid"
  (Woolf), 87n66
Thrailkill, Jane, 19
Three Guineas (Woolf), 56, 60, 67
Three Lives (Stein), 194–5
Time and Western Man (Lewis), 211
Time Binds (Freeman), 259
timescapes, 170–1, 189n59
Todorov, Tzvetan, 203
Tomkins, Silvan, 18, 49, 291
Touching Feeling (Sedgwick), 18, 38n11
Trachtenberg, Alan, 249–50
The Transformation (Spahr), 148–52
Transmemberment of Song (Edelman),
  234–5
Trevelyan, George, 60
Trodd, Zoe, 174
tropology, 241
The Trouble with Nature (Lancaster),
  38n13
twilight world, 279–80
Tyler, Parker: on Antiquity and
  homosexuality, 276; *The Granite
  Butterfly*, 135–7, 199–200, 253–4n22,
  276, 294; literary friendships of,
  194–5, 198–9; *Magic and Myth of the
  Movies*, 281; on *The Young and Evil*,
  198–9, 206. See also *The Young and
  Evil*

Ugly Feelings (Ngai), 40n27
Ulysses (Joyce), 195, 210, 211, 261–2,
  278–81
"*Ulysses*, Order, and Myth" (Eliot), 195,
  211, 278–81
Unnatural Formations (Moon, ed.), 15

"The Value of Laughter" (Woolf), 69
Van Vechten, Carl, 120
*The Variation of Animals and Plants under
  Domestication* (Darwin), 21, 24–27,
  41n39, 58, 76n11
The Varieties of Religious Experience
  (James), 144
vertigo, 212–13
Vidan, Ivo, 166
View (magazine), 211
Vincent, John, 247–8

Virilio, Paul: on cult of speed, 159–60,
    162, 178, 180, 182nn7–8; on
    juxtaposition of locality, 164–5
Vivien, Renée, 283–4
The Voyage of the Beagle (Darwin), 20,
    42n42, 44n51

Walkowitz, Rebecca, 58, 66, 83
Warner, Michael, 197, 248
war propaganda, 57
The Waste Land (Eliot): ancient/modern
    opposition in, 278–1; "ancient" slang
    in, 272; Crane's critique of, 237, 250–1;
    overview, 5; queer mythologies in,
    261–6; Rodgers, Bruce, 258–61,
    278–81
"The Watering Place" (Woolf), 64–66
Watson, Steven, 274–5
The Weary Blues (Hughes), 107–11,
    115–16, 119–27, 128n12, 278, 293
Weber, Max, 6, 138, 139
Weeks, Jeffrey, 19, 307
"What I Believe" (Forster), 103–4
whiteness, myth of, 6–7
Whitman, Walt, 2, 4, 90–93, 95, 100,
    249
Wilde, Oscar, 2, 4, 90–91, 92–95
Williams, Raymond, 139
Wilson, David, 24
Wilson, E. O., 23, 24, 143, 155n50
Wilson, Lola, 115
Winters, Yvor, 229–30, 240
Winterson, Jeanette, 219
A Woman Appeared to Me (Vivien),
    283–84
Woolf, Virginia: on atavism, 52–56, 58;
    on Austen, 79, 87–88n72; on the Blitz,
    52, 77n15, 87n66; on comedies, 67–68,
    69–70, 77–78n16, 87n71; on comedy
    of nature, 55–56, 57–58, 70–71; on
    Darwinian feminism, 57–66, 84n49,
    84–85n50; on dramatic tension, 67–69,
    70–72, 74–75; euphemism use by, 62,
    63, 66, 67; evolutionary aesthetics of,
    292; on fascism, 87n66; on Forster,
    98; on Hitler, 51, 57, 63, 78n17; on

masochism, 72; on modernism, 4;
    on natural selection, 292; on public
    intimacy, 67–72; suicide of, 50–51,
    75–76n4, 79n19; on tragedies, 69–70,
    87n71; violence principle of, 52, 54,
    58, 66–67, 72, 76n9, 77–78n16; on war
    propaganda, 57; on World War I and
    II, 52, 53
Woolf, Virginia, writings of: "Anon,"
    68–69; "On Being Ill," 61, 65–66; *The
    Diary of Virginia Woolf*, 51–53, 57, 66,
    77n15; *Men Without Art*, 72; "Modern
    Fiction," 69–70; "Modern Novels,"
    87n71; "The Narrow Bridge of Art,"
    68; *A Room of One's Own*, 57, 61, 68,
    88nn72–73; "A Sketch of the Past," 52,
    72; "Thoughts on Peace in an Air
    Raid," 87n66; *Three Guineas*, 56, 60,
    67; "The Value of Laughter," 69; "The
    Watering Place," 64–66. See also
    Between the Acts
World War I, 52, 135, 160–1, 174, 259
World War II, 50–52, 53, 135

Yeats, W. B., 272
Yingling, Thomas, 234, 242
The Young and Evil (Ford & Tyler):
    ancient references in, 274–8;
    characterizations in, 202–4, 276–7;
    dollness myth in, 208–10, 225–6n48;
    folklore of, 195, 197, 200–1, 215–20;
    leitmotifs in, 204; mythical allusions
    in, 208–11; mythical method applied
    to, 195–6, 207, 221–2n8; as mythopoeic,
    199–207, 215, 217–18, 275, 296; myth-
    questioning in, 207–11; narrative
    method of, 201–2; obscurity of, 194–5;
    plot structure, 195, 204–7, 274–5, 277;
    as queer foundling text, 196–7; queer
    mythology of, 197, 199; spatial narrative
    structure of, 197–8; surrealist imagery
    and thematics of, 197–8, 205, 208,
    211–15

Zami (Lorde), 7, 146–8, 282, 296–7
Zuk, Marlene, 36n5

SAM SEE was a scholar of Modernist literature and sexuality studies and Assistant Professor of English at Yale University.

CHRISTOPHER LOOBY is Professor of English at the University of California, Los Angeles.

MICHAEL NORTH is Professor of English at the University of California, Los Angeles.

www.ingramcontent.com/pod-product-compliance
Lightning Source LLC
Chambersburg PA
CBHW022137020426
42334CB00015B/935